TOLKIEN AND THE GREAT WAR

'To be caught in youth by 1914 was no less hideous an experience than in 1939 . . . by 1918 all but one of my close friends were dead.'

So J. R. R. Tolkien responded to critics who saw *The Lord of the Rings* as a reaction to the Second World War. *Tolkien and the Great War* tells for the first time the full story of how he embarked on the creation of Middle-earth in his youth as the world around him was plunged into catastrophe.

Drawing on Tolkien's personal wartime papers, this major biography reveals the horror and heroism that he experienced as a signals officer in the Battle of the Somme and introduces the circle of close friends who spurred his mythology into life. John Garth argues that the experience of the First World War is key to Middle-earth's enduring power, and that Tolkien used his mythic imagination to reflect the cataclysm of his generation, reshaping a literary tradition that resonates to this day.

John Garth studied English at Oxford University and has since worked as a newspaper journalist in London. A long-standing taste for the works of Tolkien, combined with an interest in the First World War, fuelled the five years of research which have gone into *Tolkien and the Great War*.

'A highly intelligent book exploring Tolkien's personal experience of the First World War . . . Garth displays impressive skills both as a researcher and writer' MAX HASTINGS

'Even if you are not a *Lord of the Rings* fan, I commend this book to you. It is all so interesting in itself, and I have rarely read a book which so intelligently graphed the relation between a writer's inner life and his outward circumstances' A. N. WILSON

'Garth's brilliantly argued study convincingly portrays Tolkien in an entirely different league from other, more familiar writers on war' *Daily Mail*

TOLKIEN AND THE GREAT WAR

The Threshold of Middle-earth

John Garth

HarperCollins*Publishers*

HarperCollins*Publishers*
77–85 Fulham Palace Road,
Hammersmith, London W6 8JB
www.tolkien.co.uk

This paperback edition 2004
1 3 5 7 9 8 6 4 2

First published in Great Britain by
HarperCollins*Publishers* 2003

ISBN 0 00 711953 4

Set in Linotype Minion by
Rowland Phototypesetting Ltd,
Bury St Edmunds, Suffolk

Printed and bound in Great Britain by
Clay Ltd, St Ives plc

In memory of

John Ronald Reuel Tolkien, 1892–1973
Christopher Luke Wiseman, 1893–1987
Robert Quilter Gilson, 1893–1916
Geoffrey Bache Smith, 1894–1916

TCBS

Contents

List of Illustrations

Chronology

Tolkien on the Somme, 1916

6 June	Tolkien arrives in France.
28 June	He joins 11th Lancashire Fusiliers.
1 July	Battle of the Somme begins.
3 July	Tolkien reaches the frontline area.
6–8 July	With G. B. Smith in Bouzincourt.
14–16 July	Tolkien takes part in attack on Ovillers.
17 July	He learns of Rob Gilson's death.
21 July	He becomes battalion signal officer.
24–30 July	Trenches at Auchonvillers.
7–10 August	Trenches east of Colincamps.
16–23 August	Signal officers' course, Acheux.
22 August	Tolkien sees Smith for the last time.
24–26 August	Trenches, Thiepval Wood.
28 August–1 September	Trenches east of Leipzig Salient.
1–5 September	Support trenches near Ovillers.
12–24 September	Training, Franqueville.
27–29 September	Action at Thiepval Wood.
6–12 October	Battalion HQ, Ferme de Mouquet.
13–16 October	Headquarters, Zollern Redoubt.
17–20 October	Ovillers Post and Hessian Trench.
21–22 October	Capture of Regina Trench.
27 October	Tolkien reports sick at Beauval.
28 October	He leaves his service battalion.
29 October–7 November	In hospital, Le Touquet.
8 November	Returns to England on *Asturias*.

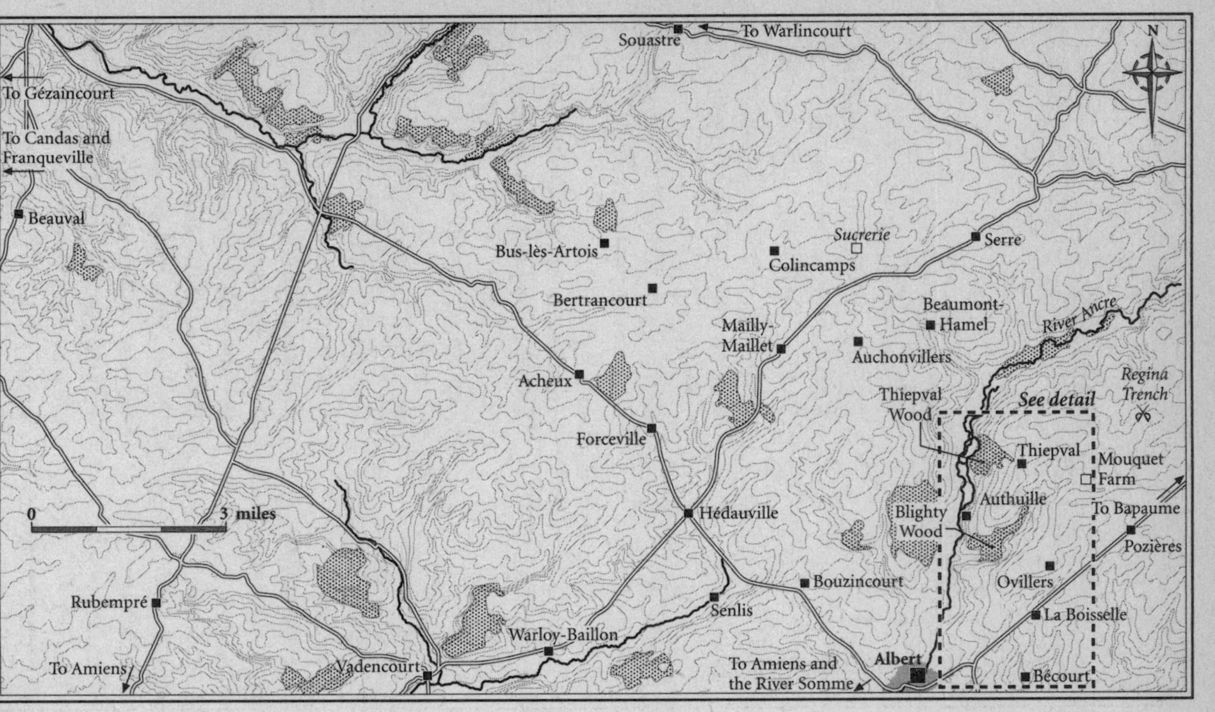

The Somme hinterland

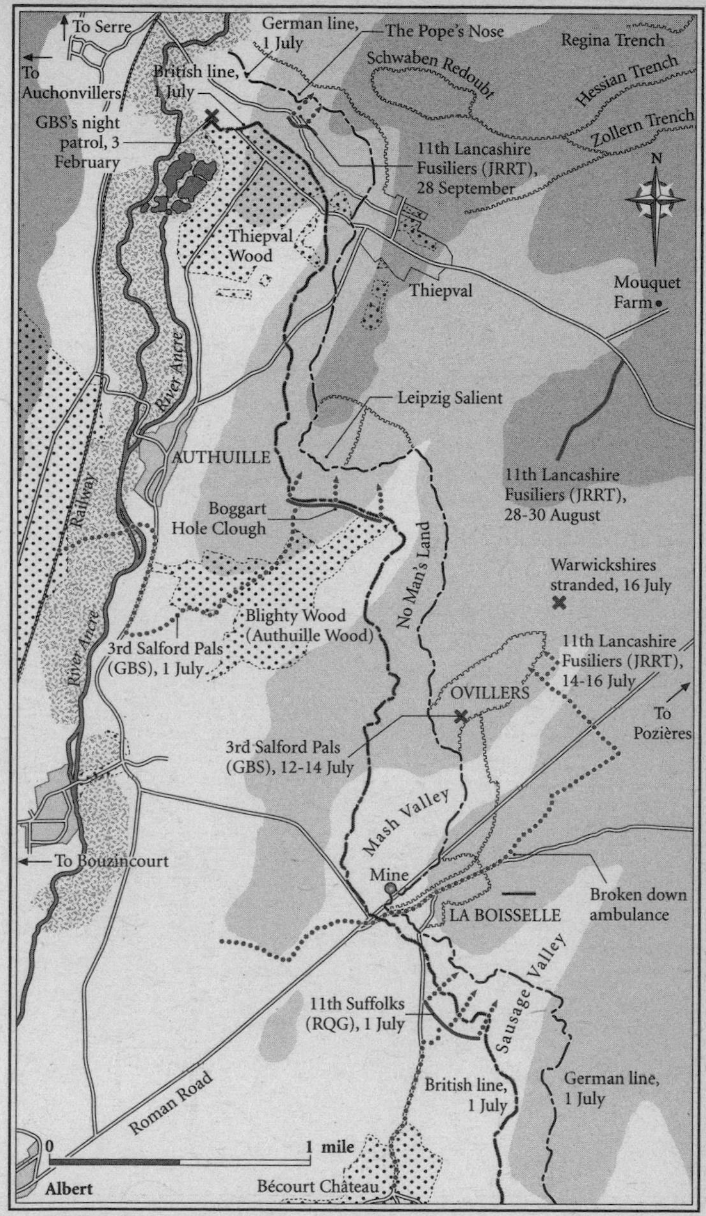

The TCBS on the Somme

Preface

This biographical study arose from a single observation: how strange it is that J. R. R. Tolkien should have embarked upon his monumental mythology in the midst of the First World War, the crisis of disenchantment that shaped the modern era.

It recounts his life and creative endeavours during the years 1914–18, from his initial excursions into his first invented 'Elvish' language as a final-year undergraduate at Oxford, through the opening up of his horizons by arduous army training and then the horror of work as a battalion signal officer on the Somme, to his two years as a chronic invalid standing guard at Britain's seawall and writing the first tales of his legendarium.

Travelling far beyond the military aspects of the war, I have tried to indicate the breadth and depth of Tolkien's interests and inspirations. The growth of his mythology is examined from its first linguistic and poetic seeds to its early bloom in 'The Book of Lost Tales', the forerunner of *The Silmarillion*, envisaged in its beginnings as a compendium of long-forgotten stories of the ancient world as seen through elvish eyes. As well as a critical examination of this first foray into what Tolkien later came to call Middle-earth, I have provided commentaries on many of his early poems, one of which ('The Lonely Isle') appears here in full for the first time since its publication in the 1920s, in a small-press book now long out of print. I hope I have given Tolkien's early poetry and prose the serious consideration they deserve, not as mere juvenilia, but as the vision of a unique writer in the springtime of his powers; a vision already sweeping in its scope and weighty in its themes, yet characteristically rich in detail, insight and life.

One of my aims has been to place Tolkien's creative activities in the context of the international conflict, and the cultural upheavals which accompanied it. I have been greatly assisted, firstly, by the release of the previously restricted service records of the British Army officers of the Great War; secondly, by the kindness of the Tolkien Estate in allowing me to study the wartime papers that Tolkien himself preserved, as well as the extraordinary and moving letters of the TCBS, the circle of former schoolfriends who hoped to achieve greatness but found bitter hardship and grief in the tragedy of their times; thirdly, by the generosity of the family of Tolkien's great friend Rob Gilson in giving me unrestricted access to all of his papers. The intertwined stories of Gilson, Geoffrey Bache Smith, Christopher Wiseman, and Tolkien – their shared or overlapping vision and even their sometimes incendiary disagreements – add greatly, I believe, to an understanding of the latter's motivations as a writer.

Although Tolkien wrote often about his own wartime experiences to his sons Michael and Christopher, when they in their turn served in the Second World War, he left neither autobiography nor memoir. Among his military papers, a brief diary provides little more than an itinerary of his movements during active service in France. However, such is the wealth of published and archival information about the Battle of the Somme that I have been able to provide a detailed picture of Tolkien's months there, down to scenes and events on the very routes he and his battalion followed through the trenches on particular days.

It may be noted here that, although full and detailed surveys of the source material have been published for Smith's and Gilson's battalions (by Michael Stedman and Alfred Peacock, respectively), no similar synthesis has been attempted for Tolkien's for more than fifty years; and none, I believe, that has made use of a similar range of eyewitness reports. This book therefore stands as a unique latter-day account of the experiences of the 11th Lancashire Fusiliers on the Somme. Since my narrative is not primarily concerned with matters of military record, however, I have been at pains not to overburden it with the names of trenches and other lost landmarks (which often have variants in French, official British, and colloquial British), map references, or the details of divisional and brigade dispositions.

If nothing else, the phenomenal worldwide interest in Tolkien is sufficient justification for such a study; but I hope it will prove useful to those who are interested in his depiction of mythological wars from old Beleriand to Rhûn and Harad; and to those who believe, as I do, that the Great War played an essential role in shaping Middle-earth.

In the course of my research, the emergence of this imagined version of our own ancient world from the midst of the First World War has come to seem far from strange, although no less unique for all that. To sum up, I believe that in creating his mythology, Tolkien salvaged from the wreck of history much that it is good still to have; but that he did more than merely preserve the traditions of Faërie: he transformed them and reinvigorated them for the modern age.

So much has the biographical aspect of this book grown, however, that it seemed best, in the end, to restrict my comments on the possible relationship between the life and the writings to a few observations, and to set out my overall case in a 'Postscript'. Having read the story of Tolkien's experiences during the Great War, those who also know *The Hobbit* and *The Lord of the Rings*, or *The Silmarillion* and its antecedents, will be able to draw their own more detailed conclusions, if they wish, about how these stories were shaped by the war.

Perhaps this is the way Tolkien would have wanted it, if indeed he had countenanced any biographical inquiry into his life and work. A few years after the publication of *The Lord of the Rings*, he wrote to an enquirer:

> I object to the contemporary trend in criticism, with its excessive interest in the details of the lives of authors and artists. They only distract attention from an author's works . . . and end, as one now often sees, in becoming the main interest. But only one's Guardian Angel, or indeed God Himself, could unravel the real relationship between personal facts and an author's works. Not the author himself (though he knows more than any investigator), and certainly not so-called 'psychologists' [*Letters*, 288].

I do not claim any divine insight into Tolkien's mind, and I do not pretend to put him on the psychiatrist's couch. I have not gone hunting for shock and scandal, but have focused at all times on matters that seem to me to have played a part in the growth of his legendarium. I hope that this story of the passage of an imaginative genius through the world crisis of his times will cast a little light on the mysteries of its creation.

At all points, matters of opinion, interpretation, and exegesis are my own, and not those of the Tolkien family or the Tolkien Estate. I thank them, however, for permission to reproduce material from private papers and the published writings of J. R. R. Tolkien.

Many other large debts of gratitude have accrued during the writing of this book. First and foremost, I must thank Douglas A. Anderson, David Brawn, and Andrew Palmer for advice and assistance beyond the call of duty or friendship. Without their help, and that of Carl F. Hostetter and Charles Noad, this book would never have seen daylight. I would particularly like to express my gratitude to Christopher Tolkien, for his generosity in sharing with me not only his father's personal papers but also a great deal of his own time; his perceptive comments have rescued me from many pitfalls and have helped to shape *Tolkien and the Great War*. For their great kindness in loaning me letters and photographs of R. Q. Gilson, I would like to thank Julia Margretts and Frances Harper. For hospitably fielding my questions about Christopher Wiseman, and for permission to quote from his letters, I thank his widow Patricia and her daughter, Susan Wood.

David Doughan, Verlyn Flieger, Wayne G. Hammond, John D. Rateliff, Christina Scull, and Tom Shippey have all given me their expertise and insight on multifarious aspects of Tolkien's life and work; the latter's critical study *The Road to Middle-earth* greatly enlarged my understanding of Tolkien's work. But for the help of Christopher Gilson, Arden R. Smith, Bill Welden, and Patrick Wynne, my discussions of linguistic matters would have foundered. Phil Curme, Michael Stedman, Phil Russell, Terry Carter, Tom Morgan, Alfred Peacock, and Paul Reed have all helped me to overcome obstacles to my understanding of Kitchener's army and the Battle of the Somme. Thanks must also go to all those others who have taken the time to answer my endless questions, including Robert Arnott, the Reverend Roger Bellamy, Matt Blessing, Anthony Burnett-Brown, Humphrey Carpenter, Peter Cook, Michael Drout, Cyril Dunn, Paul Hayter, Brian Sibley, Graham Tayar, Timothy Trought, and Catherine Walker.

Of course, none of the above are responsible for any errors of fact or interpretation that may remain.

For help with archival research, I would like to express my gratitude to Lorise Topliffe and Juliet Chadwick at Exeter College, Oxford; Christine Butler at Corpus Christi College, Oxford; Kerry York at King Edward's School, Birmingham; Dr Peter Liddle at the Brotherton Library, the University of Leeds; Tony Sprason at the Lancashire Fusiliers Museum, Bury; as well as the staff of the Public Record Office, Kew, the Departments of Documents, Printed Books, and Photographs at the Imperial War Museum, Lambeth, the Modern Papers Reading Room at the Bodleian Library, Oxford, and Hull Central Library. Archive material and photographs have been reproduced with the permission of the governors of the Schools of King Edward IV and the Rector and Fellows of Exeter College, Oxford. I am grateful to Cynthia Swallow (*née* Ferguson) for permission to make use of material from the papers of Lionel Ferguson; to Mrs T. H. A. Potts and the late Mr T. H. A Potts for permission to quote from the papers of G. A. Potts; and to Mrs S. David for permission to quote from the papers of C. H. David. Every effort has been made to contact the copyright holders for other papers from which I have quoted.

For his meticulous copy-editing, his patience with my stylistic foibles, and his extraordinary fortitude, I must thank Michael Cox. Thanks also go to Clay Harper, Chris Smith, Merryl Futerman, and Ian Pritchard for their help and advice during the course of publication; and to the Evening Standard, for allowing me time off to complete this book.

Throughout, my newspaper colleagues have helped me keep it all in perspective. Ruth Baillie, Iliriana Barileva, Gary Britton, Patrick Curry, Jamie Maclean, Ted Nasmith, Trevor Reynolds, Dee Rudebeck, Claire Struthers, Dan Timmons, Priscilla Tolkien,

A. N. Wilson, Richard Younger, and especially Wendy Hill have all provided much-needed support and encouragement at crucial points. Finally, I would like to thank my family – my parents Jean and Roy Garth, my sisters Lisa and Suzanne, my nephews Simeon and Jackson, and my niece Georgia – and to apologize to them for disappearing behind a pile of papers for two years.

PART ONE

The immortal four

Prologue

It is December 16th, nearly the dead of winter. Chill gusts buffet the flanks and faces of the attackers struggling to advance across a bare hundred yards or so of mud. They are a ramshackle group, some of them mere novices. The minute these young men muster a concerted effort, a few veterans press forward with all their energy and skill. But most of the time there is chaos. Again and again their opponents shrug off the assault and land a fearsome counterblow, so that all the guile, fortitude, and experience of the veterans can barely hold back the assault. Their captain, J. R. R. Tolkien, tries to bring his own experience to bear; but those around him are, in the words of an eyewitness, 'a beaten pack'.

The year is 1913: the Great War is eight months away, and this is just a game. Not yet soldiers, Tolkien and his team-mates are Oxbridge undergraduates back in Birmingham for Christmas, and today, in accordance with annual tradition, they are playing rugby against their old school's First XV.

Just shy of twenty-two, Tolkien is nothing like the professorial figure now familiar from the covers of biographies, all tweed, kindly wrinkles, and ubiquitous pipe. John Ronald (as his old friends call him) cuts a lean, slight figure on the rugby pitch, but in his days as a forward in the King Edward's School First XV he earned a reputation for dash and determination, and now he plays for Exeter College, Oxford.

His mind is a storehouse of images: memories of terrified flight from a venomous spider, of an ogreish miller, of a green valley riven in the mountains, and visions of dragons, of a night-mare wave towering above green fields, and perhaps already of a land of bliss over the sea. The storehouse is not yet a workshop, however, and he is not yet the maker of Middle-earth. But after a mediocre effort in his Classics exams this year he has taken a serendipitous stride towards it. He has said goodbye to Latin and Greek and is now tackling Chaucer and *Beowulf*, scrutinizing the origins and development of the English language. It is the affirmation of an early love for the Northern languages and literatures that will always fire his imagination. The first glimpse of Middle-earth is fast approaching. Far off in the unimagined future a cock crows in the courtyards of a city under siege, and horns answer wildly in the hills.

On the rugby pitch today, however, Tolkien is not at his best. He was meant to open an Old Boys' debate at the school yesterday with the proposition that the world is becoming over-civilized, but he was taken suddenly ill and had to back out.

His other former First XV team-mates on the field have largely given up rugby since leaving school. Christopher Wiseman, tall, leonine, and barrel-chested, used to share the scrum with Tolkien, but at Peterhouse, Cambridge, he has had to stop playing rugby and rowing because of an old heart problem. Today, he is relegated to the less aggressive three-quarter line, near the back of the field and next to another veteran, Sidney Barrowclough. There are others here who were never good enough to play in the First XV against other schools, but all King Edward's boys played a lot of rugby. For internal sports, the school was split into four groups, or 'houses'; and most of those in Tolkien's team on this December day once also belonged to his house. In truth, however, his team's *esprit de corps* comes not from the rugby pitch, but from the old school library.

Tolkien met Christopher Wiseman in 1905. Wiseman, at twelve, was already a talented amateur musician; one of his compositions from about this time ended up in the *Methodist Hymn-Book*. His father, the Reverend Frederick Luke Wiseman, who headed the Wesleyan Methodists' Birmingham Central Mission, had raised him on Handel and his mother Elsie had nurtured in him a love of Brahms and Schumann; his particular delight was in German chorales. But rugby was the start of his friendship with Tolkien. Both played in the red strip of Measures' house (named after the schoolmaster who ran it), and partook in its bitter rivalry with the boys in green from Richards'. Later, they took their place in the scrum in the school's First XV. But they experienced a meeting of minds. Wiseman, a year younger than Tolkien, was his intellectual equal and chased him up the academic ladder at King Edward's. Both lived in the Birmingham suburb of Edgbaston: Christopher in Greenfield Crescent and John Ronald latterly a street away in Highfield Road. They would walk along Broad Street and Harborne Road between home and school immersed in passionate debate: Wiseman was a Liberal in politics, a Wesleyan Methodist by religion, and a musician by taste, while Tolkien was naturally conservative, a Roman Catholic, and (thought Wiseman) tone-deaf. Theirs was an unlikely partnership, but all the richer for it. They discovered that they could argue with an incandescence few friendships could survive, and their disputes only served to seal the intensely strong bond between them. In recognition of this, they called themselves privately the Great Twin Brethren. Even their closest friend on and off the rugby pitch, Vincent Trought, did not share this bond.

When Tolkien's final term at King Edward's arrived he briefly became Librarian. To help him run his little empire he recruited Wiseman, who insisted that Trought must join him as fellow sub-librarian. Tolkien's place at Oxford was by this time assured and he could relax. Soon the library office became unsuitably lively; but the coterie that gathered there could afford to test the Headmaster's patience because his son, Robert Quilter Gilson, was also in the thick of things.

All of Tolkien's friends were capable of intellectual seriousness. They dominated every school debate and play, and they formed the backbone of the Literary Society, to which Tolkien read from the Norse Sagas, Wiseman expounded on historiography, Gilson enthused about the art critic John Ruskin, and Trought delivered a remarkable paper remembered as 'almost the last word' on the Romantics. By dint of their enthusiasm, this artistic little clique wrested school life from the hands of boys who would otherwise have controlled it. In the polarized world of school politics, it was effectively a triumph for Measures' house over Richards' house, the red against the green; but to Tolkien and his friends it constituted a moral victory against cynics who, as Wiseman put it, sneered at everything and lost their temper about nothing.

Much of the time the chief goal of the librarians was much less high-minded, however, and they sought only to incapacitate each other with laughter. In the summer of 1911, the hottest in four decades, Britain boiled in a stew of industrial unrest and (in the words of one historian) 'the sweltering town populations were psychologically not normal'. The library cubby-hole became a hotbed of cultural stratagems, surreal wit, and tomfoolery. While the dead hand of exams laid hold of much of the rest of the school, the librarians brewed clandestine teas on a spirit-stove and established a practice whereby each had to bring in titbits for secretive feasts. Soon the 'Tea Club' was also meeting outside school hours in the tea-room at Barrow's Stores, giving rise to an alternate name, the Barrovian Society.

In December 1913, though Tolkien has been at Oxford for over two years, he remains a member of the Tea Club and Barrovian Society, or 'the TCBS' as it is now known. The clique still meets for 'Barrovians' and is still largely devoted to drollery. Its membership has always fluctuated, but Christopher Wiseman and Rob Gilson remain at its heart, along with a more recent initiate, Geoffrey Bache Smith. On the rugby pitch today, the TCBS is represented by all four, as well as by Wiseman's fellow three-quarter-back, Sidney Barrowclough. But Tolkien is missing an excellent full-back in Vincent Trought. The TCBS's first loss, he died nearly two years ago after a long illness.

The incentive for today's Oxford and Cambridge players is social as much as sporting: what with yesterday's debate, today's match, and tonight's dinner, this is a major reunion of old schoolfriends. It is this, not the rugby itself, that brings the highly sociable Rob Gilson to take his place in the scrum. (He also stood in at the last minute for the ailing Tolkien in the debate.) His passion is for pencil and charcoal rather than mud and sweat. It is hard to say which feature most clearly declares his artistic nature: his sensuous, almost Pre-Raphaelite mouth or his calmly appraising eyes. His chief delight is in the sculptors of the Florentine Renaissance, and he can expound with warmth and clarity on Brunelleschi, Lorenzo Ghiberti, Donatello, and Luca della Robbia. Like John Ronald, Rob is often busy drawing or painting. His avowed object is to record the truth, not merely to satisfy aesthetic appetite (though one visitor has noted sardonically that his rooms at Trinity College, Cambridge, contain only one comfortable seat, the rest being 'artistic'). Since leaving school he has travelled in France and Italy, sketching churches. He is studying Classics but wants to be an architect, and anticipates several years of vocational training after he graduates in 1915.

G. B. Smith, with Gilson in the scrum, considers himself a poet and has voracious and wide-ranging literary tastes, from W. B. Yeats to early English ballads, and from the Georgians to the Welsh *Mabinogion*. Though he used to belong to Richards' house, he gravitated towards the TCBS and he and Tolkien are growing ever closer now that Smith has begun reading history at Corpus Christi College, Oxford, a few minutes' walk from Exeter College. 'GBS' is a witty conversationalist and delights in the fact that he shares his initials with George Bernard Shaw, the greatest debater of the age. Although he comes from a commercial family and agricultural stock, he has his eye on specialist historical research after he finishes his degree. But rugby football has never appealed to him.

Also in the scrum against his own better judgment is T. K. Barnsley, known as 'Tea-Cake', an unflappably light-hearted young man who frequently dominates the TCBS with his brilliant wit. Tea-Cake likes to affect laconic expressions such as 'full marks!' and 'I've got cold feet' and to ride with reckless enthusiasm around Cambridge on a motorbike, never mind that such behaviour hardly befits a future Wesleyan minister. He and Smith have agreed to play on Tolkien's team only if Rob Gilson is there too. Rob calls that 'a left-handed compliment':

in other words, they know his rugby playing is even worse than theirs.

So Tolkien's forwards are fatally compromised by the inexperience of Gilson, Smith, and T. K. Barnsley. The burden of the fight falls to the defensive three-quarter-backs, including the veterans Wiseman and Barrowclough. Barrowclough shakes off a reputation for apathy by charging half the length of the field through the enemy ranks to score first one try, then another. But from early on after the first try, the pressure from their younger opponents is unremitting, and only adroit tackling by Barrowclough and Wiseman keeps the school's lead down. At half-time the score is 11–5 to the school First XV. The teams swap ends, and with the wind in his favour Barrowclough scores his second try and the scrum-half again converts. In the final minutes, though, the school increases its score to 14–10. For all their camaraderie, Tolkien's ragged bunch retires defeated.

But there is dinner with old friends tonight, and the TCBS is not prone to take anything too seriously. These are happy days, and no less happy for being largely taken for granted. On leaving King Edward's in 1911, Tolkien wrote nostalgically in the school *Chronicle*: ''Twas a good road, a little rough, it may be, in places, but they say it is rougher further on . . .'

No one has foreseen just how rough the coming years will be, or to what slaughter this generation is walking. Even now, at the close of 1913, despite growing signs that war impends for this 'over-civilized' world, the time and manner of its unfolding are unforeseeable. Before four years have passed, the conflagration will have left four of Tolkien's fifteen-strong team wounded and four more dead – including T. K. Barnsley, G. B. Smith, and Rob Gilson.

Of every eight men mobilized in Britain during the First World War, one was killed. The losses from Tolkien's team were more than double that, but they bear comparison with the proportion of deaths among King Edward's Old Boys and among former public schoolboys across Great Britain – about one in five. And they match the figures for Oxbridge-educated servicemen of their age, the vast majority of whom became junior officers and had to lead operations and assaults. It has become unfashionable to give credit to Oxford and Cambridge, and to social élites in general; but it remains true that the Great War cut a deeper swathe through Tolkien's peers than among any other social group in Britain. Contemporaries spoke of the Lost Generation. 'By 1918,' Tolkien wrote half a century later in his preface to the second edition of *The Lord of the Rings*, 'all but one of my close friends were dead.'

ONE

Before

If he had been a healthier child, war would have come upon John Ronald Reuel Tolkien before his seventh birthday. He was born on 3 January 1892 in Bloemfontein, the capital of the Orange Free State, one of the two Boer republics that had won independence from British rule in South Africa. There his father managed a branch of the Bank of Africa. But Arthur Tolkien had come from England with his fiancée Mabel Suffield following shortly afterwards, and they had married in Cape Town. To the Dutch Boers in Bloemfontein they were *uitlanders*, foreigners, who enjoyed few rights and paid heavy taxes for the privilege; but the wealth generated by the region's gold and diamond mines drew many to accept the deal. A baby brother, Hilary, was born in 1894 but the elder boy suffered from the torrid climate, and the next year Mabel brought both children back to Birmingham for a break. They never returned. In February 1896, Arthur died from rheumatic fever. So Mabel Tolkien and her sons were spared the harsh shock of the Anglo-Boer war which erupted in late 1898 over *uitlander* rights.

Safe in England, Mabel raised the boys alone, taking them to live in a modest cottage in the village of Sarehole, outside Birmingham. There she taught them at home during a four-year rural idyll, and the climate and character of this older world etched themselves in the young John Ronald's heart: an utter contrast to what he had known until then. 'If your first Christmas tree is a wilting eucalyptus and if you're normally troubled by heat and sun,' he recalled late in life, 'then to have (just at the age when your imagination is opening out) suddenly found yourself in a quiet Warwickshire village . . . engenders a particular love of what you might call central Midland English countryside, based on good water, stones and elm trees and small, quiet rivers and . . . rustic people . . .' But in 1900 John Ronald gained a place at King Edward's and they moved back into industrial Birmingham to be nearer the school. Then, to the anger of Suffields and Tolkiens alike, Mabel embraced Catholicism, and for a while the boys went to a Roman Catholic school under the direction of the priests at the Birmingham Oratory. Tolkien far outstripped his classmates and was back at King Edward's in 1903, but he remained a Catholic all his life. After his mother, who had been ill with diabetes, fell into a coma and died in November 1904, he felt she had martyred herself raising her boys in the faith.

Prior to Mabel's death, the family had lived for a while in rooms at a cottage in Rednal, Worcestershire, outside the city borders. But now their guardian, Father Francis Morgan of the Oratory, found accommodation for the boys in Edgbaston, and in their second set of lodgings, at the age of sixteen, Tolkien met Edith Bratt, a nineteen-year-old who also had a room there. She was pretty, a talented pianist and also an orphan, and by the summer of 1909 the two were in love. But before the year was over, Father Francis got wind of the romance and banned Tolkien from seeing Edith. Stricken but dutiful, he threw himself into his school friendships, the TCBS, and rugby, captaining his house team. He won a place at Oxford (at his second attempt) and £60 a year to fund his undergraduate studies in Classics.

Mabel Tolkien had communicated to her eldest son a taste for drawing. He used his first sketchbook for drawings of starfish and seaweeds. Another seaside holiday, at Whitby in 1910, produced evocative pictures of trees, landscapes, and buildings. Tolkien's artistic response was aesthetic and emotional rather than scientific. His figures and portraits were at best comical or stylized, at worst rudimentary, and he remained modest about his abilities as a visual artist. His greatest strengths lay in decoration and design, exemplified famously by the iconographic covers of *The Hobbit* and *The Lord of the Rings*.

Tolkien had also inherited via Mabel a flair for calligraphy from her father, John Suffield, whose ancestors had been platemakers and engravers. Mabel's own handwriting was highly stylized, with curlicued capitals and descenders, and crossbars slanting expressively upwards. For formal purposes, Tolkien came to favour a script based on the medieval 'foundational hand', but when he wrote letters as a young man he seemed to have a different style of writing for each of his friends, and later when drafting at speed he produced a scrawl resembling nothing so much as an electro-cardiograph image of a frenzied pulse.

Tolkien learned to read by the age of four and absorbed the children's books that were then popular: Robert Browning's 'The Pied Piper of Hamelin', or the stories of Hans Christian Andersen, which irritated him; tales of Red Indians; George MacDonald's *The Princess and the Goblin*, or Andrew Lang's Fairy Books, which stirred a desire for adventure. He particularly yearned for tales of dragons.

But fairy-stories were not the key to his boyhood tastes. 'I was brought up in the Classics,' he wrote later, 'and first discovered the sensation of literary pleasure in Homer.' By the time he was eleven, an Oratory priest told Mabel he had read '*too* much, everything fit for a boy under fifteen, and he doesn't know any single classical thing to recommend him'. It was through the study of classics, and particularly through school exercises translating English verse into Latin or Greek, that Tolkien's taste for poetry was awakened. As a child he had habitually skipped any verse he encountered in the books he read. His King Edward's schoolteacher, R. W. Reynolds, tried largely in vain to spark his interest in the mainstream giants of English poetry, such as Milton and Keats. But the Catholic mystic Francis Thompson won Tolkien's passionate approval for his metrical and verbal accomplishments, his immense imagery, and the visionary faith underpinning his work. Thompson, hugely popular after his early death in 1907, appears to have influenced the content of one of Tolkien's first attempts at poetry, 'Wood-sunshine', written as an eighteen-year-old. Like Thompson's long sequence 'Sister Songs', it dealt with a sylvan vision of fairies:

> Come sing ye light fairy things tripping so gay,
> Like visions, like glinting reflections of joy
> All fashion'd of radiance, careless of grief,
> O'er this green and brown carpet; nor hasten away.
> O! come to me! dance for me! Sprites of the wood,
> O! come to me! Sing to me once ere ye fade!

William Morris's use of verse in his pseudo-medieval romances was also to leave its mark on Tolkien's own early poetry.

Morris was important, too, because of his association with Exeter College, Oxford, where he had formed the self-styled Pre-Raphaelite Brotherhood with fellow student Edward Burne-Jones (himself a former pupil of King Edward's School). Tolkien once likened the TCBS to the Pre-Raphaelites, probably in response to the Brotherhood's preoccupation with restoring medieval values in art. Christopher Wiseman characteristically disagreed, declaring the comparison wide of the mark.

Mabel's attempts to teach her elder son to play the piano foundered. As Humphrey Carpenter writes in his biography of Tolkien, 'It seemed rather as if words took the place of music for him, and that he enjoyed listening to them, reading them, and reciting them, almost regardless of what they meant.' He showed unusual linguistic propensities, in particular a keen sensitivity towards the characteristic sounds of different languages. His mother had started teaching him French and Latin before he went to school, but neither of these languages particularly appealed to him. At eight, however, the strange names on railway coal-trucks had given him a taste for Welsh. He was drawn to a different flavour in some of the names he encountered in history and mythology, writing later: 'The fluidity of Greek, punctuated by hardness, and with its surface glitter, captivated me . . . and I tried to invent a language that would embody the the Greekness of Greek . . .' That was before he even began learning Greek itself, at the age of ten, by which time he was also reading Geoffrey Chaucer. A year later he acquired Chambers' *Etymological Dictionary*, which gave him his first glimpse of the principle of 'sound shift' by which languages evolve.

This opened a new world. Most people never stop to consider the history of the language they speak, just as they never ponder the geology of the ground they stand on; but Tolkien was already contemplating the evidence by reading Chaucer's Middle English. The ancient Romans had recognized that some words in Latin and Greek sounded alike – akin, some thought. Over the centuries, haphazard attention was paid to such similarities in a growing number of languages, and wild claims had been made for the original ancestor of all languages. But in the nineteenth century scientific rigour was finally applied to the subject and the discipline of comparative philology emerged. Its key realization was that languages do not change randomly, but in a regular way. Philologists could codify the phonological 'laws' by which particular sounds had changed at different stages of a language's history. Chambers' dictionary introduced Tolkien to the most famous of all, Grimm's Law, by which Jakob Grimm nearly a century earlier had codified the complex of regular changes that produced (for example) the words *patér* in Greek and *pater* in Latin but *father* in English and *vatar* in Old High German, all from a single unrecorded 'root'. These (though not all) languages were demonstrably related, in ways that were open to rational analysis; furthermore, by comparing them it was possible to reconstruct elements of their ancestral language, Indo-European – a language from before the dawn of history that had left no record whatsoever. This was heady stuff for a young boy, but it would shape his life.

By the time he met Grimm's Law, Tolkien had begun inventing languages of his own. This was partly for the practical fun of making secret codes and partly for sheer aesthetic pleasure. A pot-pourri of mangled classical words called Nevbosh (actually originated by a cousin) was followed in 1907 by the more rigorously constructed Naffarin, influenced by the sounds of Spanish (and so by Father Francis, who was half-Spanish and half-Welsh). For his final four years at King Edward's, Tolkien was in the senior or First Class under the Headmaster, Robert Cary Gilson, who encouraged him to look into the history of Latin and Greek. But soon his wayward tastes led him beyond the Classical world. A former class-teacher, George Brewerton, lent Tolkien an Anglo-Saxon primer, which he studied in his spare time. At school he excelled in German, winning first prize in the subject in July 1910, but by 1908 he had discovered Joseph Wright's *Primer of the Gothic Language*, and this long-dead Germanic tongue on the edges of written history took his linguistic heart 'by storm'.

Others might have kept such recondite interests to themselves, but at school Tolkien was effusive about philology. Rob Gilson described him as 'quite a great authority on etymology – an enthusiast', and indeed Tolkien once lectured the First Class on the origins of Europe's languages. Against the Classicist ethos drummed into King Edward's schoolboys he played the outsider with verve. He combatively told the literary society that the *Volsunga Saga*, the tale of the dragon-slayer Sigurd, displayed 'the highest epic genius struggling out of savagery into complete and conscious humanity'. He even addressed one of the annual Latin debates in Gothic.

The corpus of Gothic is small, and to Tolkien it presented a tantalizing challenge. He would try to imagine what unrecorded Gothic was like. He invented Gothic words; not randomly, but using what he knew about sound-shifts to extrapolate the 'lost' words on the basis of their surviving relatives in other Germanic languages – a linguistic method rather like triangulation, the process by which map-makers record the heights of landmarks they have not visited. This 'private lang.' was an activity he rarely mentioned except to his diary because it often distracted him from 'real' school work, but into the Gothic project he drew as collaborator Christopher Wiseman. The self-deprecating Wiseman later recalled:

> Reading Homer with Cary Gilson sparked off in me what in Tolkien was already well alight, an interest in Philology. In fact John Ronald got to the point where he constructed a language L and another LL representing what L had become after a few centuries. He tried to inculcate me into one of his home-made languages, and wrote me a postcard in it. He said that I replied to it in the same language, but there I think he was wrong.

Philology was the focus of passionate argument between the two, and Wiseman said many decades later that the invention of languages was a cornerstone of their youthful friendship. That may seem a bizarre activity for teenage boys; but Tolkien did not think so, insisting later: 'It's not uncommon, you know. It's mostly done by boys . . . If the main mass of education takes linguistic form, creation will take linguistic form even if it isn't one of their talents.' Language-construction satisfied the urge to create, but it also met the desire for an argot that would 'serve the needs of a secret and persecuted society, or' – in the case of the Great Twin Brethren – 'the queer instinct for pretending you belong to one.'

It is unclear whether Tolkien shared with Wiseman another venture, the invention of an 'unrecorded' Germanic language, Gautisk, and it seems unlikely that the wider TCBS joined in his philological recreations at all.* But Tolkien's motivations in language-building were artistic rather than practical; and even if his friends were not collaborators, at least they would have been a discriminating and appreciative audience. After all, these

* Gautisk might have been an extrapolation from Gothic, but it was probably meant to be the tongue of the Geats of ancient Scandinavia, the language that the monster-slaying hero Beowulf would have spoken before his story was written down in Anglo-Saxon. Although Rob Gilson's grasp of philology was confessedly poor, some of the sobriquets he used in his letters to his friends invite speculation that he was in on his friend's language-invention game. Unfortunately deciphering them is also a matter of guesswork. Tolkien appears to be 'Mr Undarhruiménitupp' and G. B. Smith is 'Haughadel' or 'Hawaughdall'.

were boys who conducted debates in Latin – and took part in King Edward's annual performance of Aristophanes in the original classical Greek. Tolkien himself played an exuberant Hermes in the 1911 production of *The Peace* (his farewell to the school). Wiseman appeared as Socrates and Rob Gilson as Strepsiades in *The Clouds* a year later. Smith alone of the TCBS, being from the school's 'modern' or commercial side, did not study Greek; perhaps this is why he was relegated to the role of the Ass in one of the plays. They were directed by Tolkien's cigar-smoking housemaster, Algy Measures, and the boys feasted on a curious menu of buns, gooseberries, and ginger beer. 'Does nobody else remember these plays?' one Old Edwardian wrote in 1972. 'The grand parade of the chorus, clad in white vestments, down the full length of Big School playing on flageolets? Or Wiseman and Gilson munching gooseberries on stage as they chatted away as though Greek were their normal tongue?'

The TCBS revelled in a degree of outlandishness. Their humour was quickfire and often sophisticated; their interests and talents were many, and they rarely felt the need to draw anyone else into their circle. Another former King Edward's pupil wrote to Tolkien in 1973: 'As a boy you could not imagine how I looked up to you and admired and envied the wit of that select coterie of JRRT, C. L. Wiseman, G.B. Smith, R. Q. Gilson, V. Trought, and Payton. I hovered on the outskirts to gather up the gems. You probably had no idea of this schoolboy worship.' In retrospect Tolkien insisted they had not set out to stand aloof from the ordinary King Edward's pupils but, intentionally or not, they erected barriers.

On the rugby pitch, Wiseman had somehow acquired the title of 'the Prime Minister', and the TCBS elaborated this practice, with Tolkien as the Home Secretary, Vincent Trought as the Chancellor, and the acute and punctilious Wilfrid Hugh Payton (nicknamed also 'Whiffy') as the Whip. G. B. Smith, in tribute to one of his enthusiasms, gloried in the non-governmental title of the Prince of Wales. Furthermore, this was just one set of epithets out of a whole compendium.* In a note from Wiseman just before the TCBS coalesced, Tolkien is addressed as 'My dear Gabriel' and styled apparently the 'Archbishop of Evriu'; the letter is signed 'Beelzebub' (perhaps to make light of the vast gulf between the two friends' religious outlooks) and contains an entirely opaque reference to 'the first Prelate of the Hinter-space, our mutual friend'. An air of playful pomp runs through their correspondence (such as it was before the Great War), so that instead of simply inviting Tolkien to visit, Gilson would write asking whether he would be 'gracing our ancestral hearth' and 'making use of our roof-tree'.

Casting a critical eye on the era in which he too grew up, the author J. B. Priestley saw such wordplay as a sign of shallowness and self-indulgence in the ruling class, who were addicted to 'a daft slang of their own (as they might have called it "a deveen privato slangino"), and . . . the constant use of nick-names'. The TCBS, however, hailed from the middle classes, a broad social spectrum. At the gentrified top was Rob Gilson, with his spacious home, his important father, and his aristocratic acquaintances; at the precarious lower end was Tolkien, an orphan in city lodgings. His 'private lang.' was no mock Italian; and while nicknames and mock-archaisms may have helped keep the Tea Club exclusive, they gently parodied the traditional social hierarchy.

Parody was the mode of Tolkien's first published attempt at epic narrative. It was the natural choice, given that the piece was to appear in the King Edward's School *Chronicle*. 'The Battle

---

* Every participant in the school's annual Latin debates sported a classical tag. By straightforward translation, Wiseman was *Sapientissimo Ingenti* and Barrowclough *Tumulus Vallis*. Cary Gilson was *Carus Helveticus*, in honour of his Alpine enthusiasms, and Rob had been his diminutive, *Carellus Helveticulus*. Wilfrid Payton was *Corcius Pato* and his younger brother Ralph *Corcius Pato Minor*. Vincent Trought was a very fishy *Salmonius Tructa Rufus*; but 'Tea-Cake' Barnsley was *Placenta Horreo*, from the Latin words for 'cake' and 'barn'. Tolkien's tags were all puns on his surname rendered jokily as 'toll keen': *Vectigalius Acer*, *Portorius Acer Germanicus* and, with a nod to his mastery of languages, *Eisphorides Acribus Polyglotteus*.

of the Eastern Field' deals not with war but with rugby, being the tongue-in-cheek account of a match in 1911. Its model was Lord Macaulay's then-popular *Lays of Ancient Rome*, the source of Wiseman and Tolkien's epithet 'the Great Twin Brethren,' and it is at least moderately amusing. In the guise of Roman clans it depicts the rival school houses, Measures' in red and Richards' in green, and it is full of boys charging around in names that are much too big for them. Wiseman surely lurks behind *Sekhet*, a nod to his fair hair and his passion for ancient Egypt. (Tolkien, it seems, did not then realize that Sekhet is a female deity.*)

Sekhet mark'd the slaughter,
And toss'd his flaxen crest
And towards the Green-clad Chieftain
Through the carnage pressed;
Who fiercely flung by Sekhet,
Lay low upon the ground,
Till a thick wall of liegemen
Encompassed him around.
His clients from the battle
Bare him some little space,
And gently rubbed his wounded knee,
And scanned his pallid face.

The archaisms and the illusion of combat give way to a bathetic contemporary cameo. The down-to-earth reality of the rugby pitch gently mocks the heroic pretensions of the literary mode.

The mock-heroism of 'The Battle of the Eastern Field' reflects, consciously or otherwise, a truth about a whole generation's attitudes. The sports field was an arena for feigned combat. In the books most boys read, war was sport continued by other

* He had perhaps only encountered the name in Rider Haggard's *She*, which lists 'Sekhet, the lion-headed' among the Egyptian powers, but does not specify her gender.

means. Honour and glory cast an over-arching glamour over both, as if real combat could be an heroic and essentially decent affair. In his influential 1897 poem 'Vitaï Lampada', Sir Henry Newbolt had imagined a soldier spurring his men through bloody battle by echoing his old school cricket captain's exhortation, 'Play up! Play up! And play the game!' Philip Larkin, a much later poet looking back across the decades, described volunteers queuing to enlist as if outside the Oval cricket ground, and lamented (or exhorted): 'Never such innocence again.' A wiser age had depicted War as one of the Four Horsemen of the Apocalypse, but in the Edwardian era it was as if he were engaged in little worse than a spot of polo.

In the years up to 1914, the prospect of international conflict was often considered. Victorian affluence was ebbing away from Britain, struck by agricultural setbacks and then by the cost of the Boer War. But Germany, unified in 1871, was the braggart youngster among the European powers. Undergoing rapid industrialization, it was manoeuvring for a stronger role in Europe via expansion of its colonial grasp and saw Britain, with its powerful navy, as the prime opponent.

The coming war had cast its shadow on the worldview of Tolkien and his friends when they were still at King Edward's. As early as 1909, W. H. Payton, an excellent shot and a lance-corporal in the school's junior Officer Training Corps, had argued in debate for compulsory military service. 'Our country is now supreme and Germany wishes to be. We should therefore see to it that we are sufficiently protected against the danger of foreign invasion,' he declared. In 1910, Rob Gilson had called for an international court of arbitration to replace war. Tolkien led the opposition. He preferred traditional hierarchies, and for example he once (perhaps not entirely in jest) equated democracy with 'hooliganism and uproar', declaring that it should play no part in foreign policy. An equal distrust of bureaucracy, or internationalism, or vast inhuman enterprises *per se*, lay behind his attack on a 'Court of Arbiters'. With the help of Payton he had successfully dismissed the idea as unworkable. They had insisted that war was both a necessary and a productive aspect of human affairs, though one schoolboy had warned of 'bloodfilled trenches'.

The temperature had risen by October 1911, when the Kaiser's sabre-rattling prompted the debating society motion 'this House demands immediate war with Germany'. But others insisted Germany was primarily a trade rival. G. B. Smith claimed that the growth of democracy in Germany and Russia would curtail any threat of war, assuring the debaters, with his tongue as usual in his cheek, that the only causes for alarm were the bellicose *Daily Mail* 'and the Kaiser's whiskers'. The debating society did not declare war on Germany. Smith wildly overestimated the strength of democracy in both countries, underestimated the influence of the press, and failed to see the real danger posed by Wilhelm II, an autocrat plagued by deep-seated insecurities. Just two days past his seventeenth birthday, and making his maiden speech to the debating chamber, he can be forgiven for naïvety; but in none of these misapprehensions was he alone.

Despite industrial unrest, Home Rule agitation in Ireland, and increasingly militant suffragette activism, to many Britons the era was a time of material comfort and tranquillity stretching into futurity. Only the loss of Captain Robert Scott's Antarctic expedition and of the *Titanic*, both in 1912, raised doubts about the security of such long-term illusions.

King Edward's was a bastion of robust sportsmanship, duty, honour, and vigour, all backed up by a rigorous grounding in Greek and Latin. The school's anthem instructed the pupils:

> Here's no place for fop or idler, they who made our city great
> Feared no hardship, shirked no labour, smiled at death and
> conquered fate;
> They who gave our school its laurels laid on us a sacred trust,
> Forward therefore, live your hardest, die of service, not of rust.

There had been drilling at King Edward's in the Victorian era, though nothing systematic; but in 1907 Cary Gilson obtained military permission to set up an Officer Training Corps as part of national reforms to boost Britain's readiness for military confrontation. The OTC was captained by W. H. Kirkby, Tolkien's first-year master (and a noted shot in the part-time Territorial Army set up in the same reforms). Several of Tolkien's rugby-playing friends became officers in the corps and Tolkien himself was one of 130 cadets. The corps also provided eight members for the school shooting team, with Rob Gilson (an OTC corporal) and W. H. Payton excelling on the ranges. Though Tolkien was also a good shot, he was not on the shooting team, but in the OTC he took part in drills and inspections on the school grounds, competition against the school's other three houses, and field exercises and huge annual camps involving many other schools.

The massed corps was presented to the king and inspected by field marshals Lord Kitchener of Khartoum and Lord Roberts, the liberator of Bloemfontein. The school *Chronicle* concluded: 'It is quite evident that the War Office and the Military Authorities are expecting great things from the OTC.' One midsummer, Tolkien travelled to London with seven other King Edward's cadets to line the route for the coronation of George V. The year was 1911, and gloriously hot; he wrote at the time that it had 'kindled an immovable smile' on his face. But as they camped in the grounds of Lambeth Palace on the eve of the big day, a long dry spell finally broke, and it rained. '*Adfuit omen*', Tolkien later commented: 'It was an omen.'* The contingent stood facing Buckingham Palace watching troops pass up and down under the eye of Kitchener and Roberts. They heard the cheers as the king set out, and finally they got a close-up view as the royal coaches passed right in front of them on their way back to the palace.

For now, these military preparations were an occasion for high spirits. From one Aldershot camp Tolkien brought back

---

* *Adfuit omen* acquires a special force from its contrast with the normal phrase, *Absit omen*, 'Let there not be an omen'. It might be paraphrased, 'It bloody well *was* an omen'.

'harrowing' tales of the devastation wrought among the cadets by punning – inflicted, no doubt, by his own circle. He had returned from another camp, at Tidworth Pennings on Salisbury Plain in 1909, with a real injury, but not one acquired in action. With characteristic impetuousness, he had charged into the bell tent he was sharing with seven others, leapt up and slid down the central pole – to which someone had fixed a candle with a clasp knife. The resulting cut looked as if it would leave him scarred for life.

By the time G. B. Smith was cracking jokes about the Kaiser's moustache, Tolkien was embarking on life at Exeter College, Oxford, where, in step with his generation, he pursued military training. As soon as he arrived he enrolled in King Edward's Horse. This cavalry regiment had been conceived during the Boer War as the King's Colonials, and it recruited men from overseas resident in the British Isles. As such, it enjoyed a dubious status compared to other British military units (and was the only one administered from Whitehall), but royal patronage had helped it grow; it had been renamed after the new king, Edward VII. The large numbers of overseas students at Oxford and Cambridge made the university towns prime targets for recruiting drives, and by 1911 the regiment had a strong following in Exeter College. Tolkien joined it, presumably, because of his South African birth: most new undergraduates enlisted in the university OTC, but those with a 'colonial' background were expected instead to join King Edward's Horse.

Within the regiment, the Oxbridge squadron's members were considered a fractious and independent-minded lot, but they had good mounts borrowed from the local hunts. Tolkien had a strong affinity with horses, which he loved, and became a *de facto* breaker-in. No sooner had he broken one horse in but it was taken away. Another would then be given to him and he had to start the process again. His membership of the regiment was shortlived, however. In July and August of 1912 he spent two weeks with the regiment at its annual camp at Dibgate

Plateau, Shorncliffe, just outside Folkestone on the South Coast. The gales howling up the English Channel from the south-west were so severe that on two nights almost every tent and marquee was levelled. Once, the regiment carried out field manoeuvres after dark and, rather than return to camp, billeted for the night: an uncomfortable foretaste of life during wartime. Tolkien was discharged from the regiment, at his own request, the following January.

In the meantime, academic life at Oxford was relaxed, to say the least: 'In fact we have done nothing; we are content with being,' readers of the school *Chronicle* were told in the annual 'Oxford Letter' reporting on the activities of King Edward's alumni. Tolkien was scarcely committed to the study of Classics. He was already known to old friends for his 'predominant vice of slackness' but now the sub-rector noted next to his name, 'Very lazy'. Actually he was very busy – but not with Æschylus and Sophocles. He joined the college's societies and its rugby team (though because standards were higher here he did not excel, and was regarded as 'a winger pure and simple'). Ultimately far more distracting, however, was his burgeoning fascination with the epic Finnish poem, the *Kalevala*.

Tolkien had encountered this cycle of folk legend at school. He was 'immensely attracted by something in the air' of this verse epic of duelling Northern wizards and lovestruck youths, beer-brewers and shape-changers, then recently published in English in a popular edition. To a young man so drawn to the shadowy border where written historical records give way to the time of half-forgotten oral legends, it was irresistible. The names were quite unlike anything he had encountered in his studies of the Indo-European family of languages from which English sprang: Mielikki the mistress of the forests, Ilmatar the daughter of the air, Lemminkäinen the reckless adventurer. The *Kalevala* so engrossed Tolkien that he had failed to return the school's copy of volume one, as Rob Gilson, his successor as King Edward's librarian, politely pointed out in a letter. Thus equipped with all he needed, or was truly interested in, Tolkien barely used Exeter College's library, and he withdrew only one Classics-related book (Grote's *History of Greece*) in his entire first year. When he did venture in, he strayed outside the Classics shelves and unearthed a treasure: Charles Eliot's pioneering grammar of Finnish. In a letter to W. H. Auden in 1955, he recalled that 'It was like discovering a complete wine-cellar filled with bottles of an amazing wine of a kind and flavour never tasted before.' Ultimately it suffused his language-making with the music and structure of Finnish.

But first he launched into a retelling of part of the *Kalevala*, in the verse-and-prose manner of William Morris. This was the *Story of Kullervo*, about a young fugitive from slavery. It is a strange story to have captured the imagination of a fervent Roman Catholic: Kullervo unwittingly seduces his sister, who kills herself, and then he too commits suicide. But the appeal perhaps lay partly in the brew of maverick heroism, young romance, and despair: Tolkien, after all, was in the midst of his enforced separation from Edith Bratt. The deaths of Kullervo's parents may have struck a chord, too. An overriding attraction, though, was the sounds of the Finnish names, the remote primitivism, and the Northern air.

If Tolkien had merely wanted passionate pessimism he could have found it far closer to home in much of the English literature read avidly by his peers. The four years before the Great War were, in the words of J. B. Priestley, 'hurrying and febrile and strangely fatalistic'. The evocations of doomed youth in A. E. Housman's *A Shropshire Lad* (1896) were immensely popular:

East and west on fields forgotten
Bleach the bones of comrades slain,
Lovely lads and dead and rotten;
None that go return again.

One admirer of Housman was the Great War's first literary celebrity, Rupert Brooke, who wrote that if he died in some corner of a foreign field it would be 'for ever England'. G. B.

Smith's poetry was tinged with something of the same pessimism.

Tolkien, through the loss of his parents, had already known bereavement, and so had several of his friends. Rob Gilson's mother had died in 1907 and Smith's father was dead by the time the young historian got to Oxford. But the lesson of mortality came forcibly home again at the end of Tolkien's first vacation from university.

Back in October 1911 Rob Gilson had written from King Edward's School to lament that 'The passing of certain among the gods seems almost to have robbed the remainder of the light of life.' No one had died: what he meant was that Tolkien was sorely missed, along with W. H. Payton and their waggish friend 'Tea-Cake' Barnsley, both now at Cambridge. 'Alas! for the good days of yore,' Gilson added: 'who knows whether the T. Club will ever meet again?' In fact Birmingham's remaining members continued to gather at 'the old shrine' of Barrow's Stores, and to rule the library office. Now the clique also included Sidney Barrowclough and 'the Baby', Payton's younger brother Ralph. During a mock school strike they demanded that all overdue-book fines be sequestered to pay for tea, cake, and comfortable chairs for themselves. The King Edward's School *Chronicle* sternly admonished Gilson, Tolkien's successor as Librarian, to 'induce the Library to . . . assume a less exhibitionary character'. But the club cultivated its conspiratorial air with sly ostentation. The editors of the *Chronicle*, and the authors of this admonition, were none other than Wiseman and Gilson. It was this issue which distinguished several of the prefects and ex-pupils as 'T.C., B.S., etc.' – initials that were quite inscrutable to most at King Edward's.

Returning to Birmingham for Christmas, Tolkien took part in the annual Old Boys' debate, appearing on midwinter's night as the linguistically incompetent Mrs Malaprop in Rob's extravagant production of Sheridan's *The Rivals* with Christopher Wiseman, Tea-Cake, and G. B. Smith – who was now accorded full TCBS membership.

In effect, Smith was stepping into the void left by Vincent Trought, who had been struck down by a severe illness in the autumn. Trought had now gone down to Cornwall to get away from the city's polluted air and recover his strength. The attempt failed. In the new year, 1912, on the first day of the Oxford term, Wiseman wrote to Tolkien: 'Poor old Vincent passed away at five o'clock yesterday (Saturday) morning. Mrs Trought went down to Cornwall on Monday and thought he was getting better, but he was taken very ill on Friday evening and passed away in the morning. I expect a wreath will be sent from the School, but I am going to try to get one from the TCBS specially.' He added, 'I am in the most miserable of spirits . . . you mustn't expect any TCBSiness in this letter.' Tolkien wanted to attend the funeral, but could not get to Cornwall in time.

Trought's influence on his friends had been quiet but profound. Grimly tenacious on the rugby pitch, he was nervous and retiring in social situations, and prone to slow deliberation where others around him devoted so much energy to repartee. But he epitomized some of the best qualities of the TCBS: not its facetious humour, but its ambitious and creative individualism. For in moments of seriousness the key members of the circle felt that they were a force to be reckoned with: not a grammar school clique, but a republic of individuals with the potential to do something truly significant in the wider world. Vincent's creative strength lay in poetry and, the school *Chronicle* noted after his death, 'some of his verses show great depth of feeling and control of language'. For instruction and inspiration Trought could draw upon the whole lush field of Romanticism. But his tastes were more eclectic than those of his friends, and deeply responsive to beauty in sculpture, painting, and music. He was, his school obituary said, 'a true artist', and would have made an impact had he lived.* In a later year, in the midst of a crisis Trought could not have envisaged, his name would be invoked as an inspiration.

* Vincent Trought was born in Birmingham on 8 April 1893 and died on 20 January 1912 in Gorran Haven, where he is buried.

About the time of Trought's decline and death, Tolkien began a series of twenty or so unusual symbolist designs he called 'Ishnesses', because they illustrated states of mind or being. He had always enjoyed drawing landscapes and medieval buildings, but perhaps such figurative work was now inadequate to his needs. This was a changeful, dark, and reflective period for Tolkien, cut loose from his school and friends and forbidden by Father Francis to contact Edith. He had crossed the threshold of adulthood, and his feelings about it may perhaps be inferred from the contrast between the exuberant *Undertenishness*, with its two trees, and the reluctant *Grownupishness*, with its blind scholarly figure, bearded like the veteran academics of Oxford. More upbeat, bizarrely, was the image of a stick-figure stepping jauntily off *The End of the World* into a swirling celestial void. Much darker were the torchlit rite-of-passage visions, *Before* and *Afterwards*, showing first the approach to a mysterious threshold and then a somnambulist figure passing between torches on the other side of the door. The sense of a fearful transformation is remarkable. Equally apparent is that here was a rich, visionary imagination that had not yet found the medium of its full fluency.

Tolkien's life reached its major personal and academic turning point a year later. Up until 1913 he had lived the mere preliminaries. He had been thwarted in love and it was becoming increasingly clear that in pursuing Classics at Oxford he was heading up a blind alley. Now all that changed. On 3 January 1913 he reached the age of twenty-one, and the guardianship of Father Francis Morgan came to its end. Tolkien immediately contacted Edith Bratt, who had made a new life in Cheltenham. But three years apart had withered her hopes and she was engaged to someone else. Within the week, however, Tolkien was by her side and had persuaded her to marry him instead.

By now, a year had passed in which Tolkien continued to neglect his studies under his Classics tutor, Lewis Farnell. A vigorous, wiry man with a long bespectacled face and drooping whiskers, Farnell was a fastidious scholar who had lately completed a five-volume opus on ancient Greek cults. Twenty years earlier, when Greece was still a remote and relatively untravelled land, he had been something of an adventurer, riding and hiking through bandit country to locate some half-forgotten shrine, or shooting rapids on the upper Danube. Nowadays his archaeological fervour was nourished by the rediscovery of legendary Troy and by excavations at Knossos that annually yielded more secrets of Homeric civilization – and an undeciphered script to tantalize linguists. But neither Farnell nor Sophocles and Aeschylus fired Tolkien's enthusiasm. Most of his time and energies were expended on extra-curricular activities. He socialized with college friends, spoke in debates, trained with his cavalry squadron, and pored over Eliot's *Finnish Grammar*. 'People couldn't make out,' he recalled later, 'why my essays on the Greek drama were getting worse and worse.'

He had one opportunity to follow his heart, in the 'special paper' that gave him the option of studying comparative philology. If he did so, he realized, he would be taught by Joseph Wright, whose Gothic *Primer* had so inspired him as a schoolboy. 'Old Joe', a giant among philologists, who had started out as a millhand but had gone on to compile the massive *English Dialect Dictionary*, gave him a thorough grounding in Greek and Latin philology. But Tolkien's overall failure to apply himself to Classics, together with the dramatic reunion with Edith, took their toll on his mid-course university exams, Honour Moderations. Instead of the first-class result that Cary Gilson thought his former pupil should have achieved, he only just scraped a second, and he would have sunk to a dismal third but for an excellent paper on Greek philology. Luckily Farnell was broad-minded, with an affection for German culture that disposed him favourably towards the field of philological inquiry that truly interested Tolkien. He suggested that Tolkien switch to studying English, and made discreet arrangements so that he would not lose his £60 scholarship money, which had been meant for funding Classical studies. At last Tolkien was in his element, devoting his studies to the languages and literature that had long stirred his imagination.

* * *

Meanwhile, Tolkien's friendship with the TCBS was growing more and more tenuous. He had played no part in a revival of *The Rivals* staged in October 1912 as a farewell to King Edward's by Christopher Wiseman and Rob Gilson, and he had missed the traditional old boys' school debate that Christmas, though he was in Birmingham at the time. At university, Tolkien kept in touch with acquaintances at meetings of the Old Edwardian Society, but very few Birmingham friends had come to Oxford. One, Frederick Scopes, had gone sketching churches in northern France with Gilson during Easter 1912, but Tolkien's own funds were relatively limited, and evaporated in the heat of Oxford life.

At Exeter College, Tolkien had tried to recreate the TCBSian spirit by founding similar clubs, first the Apolausticks and then the Chequers, which substituted lavish dinners for secret snacks and consisted of his new undergraduate friends. He joined the Dialectical Society and the Essay Club, and enjoyed chin-wagging over a pipe. One visitor eyeing the cards on his mantelpiece wryly commented that he appeared to have signed up to every single college association. (Some of these cards were his own work, drawn with characteristic humour and stylish flair: among them an invitation to a 'Smoker', a popular social affair, depicting four students dancing – and falling over – in Turl Street under the disapproving airborne gaze of owls clad in the mortarboards and bowler-hats of the university authorities.) Tolkien was elected 'deputy jester' to the most important of these bodies, the Stapeldon Society, later becoming secretary and finally, at a noisy and anarchic meeting on 1 December 1913, president.

For the TCBS, however, the centre of gravity had shifted from Birmingham to Cambridge, where Wiseman was now at Peterhouse with a maths scholarship and Gilson was studying Classics at Trinity. The group's numbers there were swelled in October 1913 by the arrival of Sidney Barrowclough and Ralph Payton (the Baby).

But at the same time, crucially for Tolkien, G. B. Smith came up to Oxford to study history at Corpus Christi. Wiseman wrote to Tolkien: 'I envy you Smith, for, though we have Barrowclough and Payton, he is the pick of the bunch.' GBS excelled in conversational wit, and he was certainly the most precocious TCBSite, already regarding himself as a poet when he took Vincent Trought's place in the cabal. He also shared some of Tolkien's heartfelt interests, particularly Welsh language and legend; he admired the original stories of King Arthur, and felt that the French troubadours had left these Celtic tales shorn of their native serenity and vigour. Smith's arrival in Oxford was the start of a more meaningful friendship with Tolkien, a friendship that grew apace in isolation from the constant waggishness that afflicted the TCBS *en masse*.

In Cambridge, by contrast, Wiseman found his spirits failing under the relentless *badinage*. Rob Gilson attributed this depression to the health problems that had stopped him playing college rugby, proclaiming ingenuously in a letter to Tolkien: 'We have managed to relieve his boredom at times. On Friday he and I and Tea Cake and the Baby all went for a long walk, and had tea at a pub . . . We were all in the best of spirits – not that Tea Cake's ever fail.' Wiseman found much-needed refreshment when he saw Smith and Tolkien that term, but shortly afterwards wrote to the latter: 'I am very anxious to breathe again the true TCBS spirit fostered by its Oxford branch. Teacake has so fed me lately that I verily believe I shall murder him if he has not altered by next term . . .'

Happily for Wiseman, when most of the old friends were reunited to play their December 1913 rugby match against the King Edward's First XV a few days later, he was well at the back of the field and T. K. Barnsley was in the scrum. But after another two months the ill-assorted pair, both Methodists, had to form a delegation from Cambridge to the Oxford Wesley Society. Rob Gilson came down with them and wrote effusively afterwards: 'We had such a splendid week-end: "Full marks", as Tea-Cake would say . . . I saw lots of [Frederick] Scopes and Tolkien and G. B. Smith, all of whom seem very contented with life . . .'

* * *

Tolkien had reason to feel at ease at the start of 1914. In January, Edith had been received into the Roman Catholic Church in Warwick, where she had now made her home with her cousin, Jennie Grove; soon afterwards Edith and John Ronald were formally betrothed. In preparation for the momentous event Tolkien had finally told his friends about Edith; or rather, he appears to have told Smith, who apparently passed the news on to Gilson and Wiseman. Tolkien feared that his engagement might cut him off from the TCBS. Likewise, their congratulations were tinged with the anxiety that they might lose a friend. Wiseman said as much in a postcard. 'The only fear is that you will rise above the TCBS,' he said, and demanded half-seriously that Tolkien somehow prove 'this most recent folly' was only 'an ebullition of ultra-TCBSianism'. Gilson wrote more frankly: 'Convention bids me congratulate you, and though my feelings are of course a little mixed, I do it with very sincere good wishes for your happiness. And I have no fear at all that such a staunch tcbsite as yourself will ever be anything else.' Would John Ronald reveal the lady's name? he added.

The English course onto which Tolkien had transferred a year ago was a further source of contentment. The Oxford course allowed him to ignore almost completely Shakespeare and other 'modern' writers, in whom he had little interest, and to focus on language and literature up to the end of the fourteenth century, when Geoffrey Chaucer wrote *The Canterbury Tales*. This was the field in which he would work – with the exception of his three unforeseeable years as a soldier – for all his professional life. Meanwhile 'Schools', his final university exams (properly the examinations of the Honour School of English Language and Literature), were a year and a half away, and for now he could afford to explore the subject at his leisure. He studied Germanic origins under the Rawlinsonian Professor of Anglo-Saxon, A. S. Napier. William Craigie, one of the editors of the monumental *Oxford English Dictionary*, taught him in his new special subject, Old Norse, in which he read the Poetic Edda, the collection of heroic and mythological lays that recount, along with much else, the creation and destruction of the world.

Meanwhile, the young Kenneth Sisam tutored him in aspects of historical phonology, as well as in the art of finding cheap second-hand books. Tolkien already knew many of the set texts well, and could devote time to broadening and deepening his knowledge.

He wrote essays on the 'Continental affinities of the English People' and 'Ablaut', constructing intricate tables of the familial words *father*, *mother*, *brother*, and *daughter* in 'Vorgermanisch', 'Urgermanisch', Gothic, Old Norse, and the various Old English dialects, demonstrating the sound shifts that had produced the divergent forms. As well as copious notes on the regular descent of English from Germanic, he also examined the influence of its Celtic neighbours and the linguistic impact of Scandinavian and Norman invasions. He translated the Anglo-Saxon epic *Beowulf* line by line and sampled its various Germanic analogues (among them the story of Frotho, who goes seeking treasure from a 'hoard the hill-haunter holds, a serpent of winding coils'). He speculated on the provenance of the obscure figures of Ing and Finn and King Sheaf in the Germanic literatures. Tolkien was enjoying it so much that he had to share his pleasure. Giving a paper on the Norse sagas to Exeter College's Essay Club, he characteristically thought himself into the part and adopted what a fellow undergraduate described as 'a somewhat unconventional turn of phrase, suiting admirably with his subject'. (We may guess that he used a pseudo-medieval idiom, as William Morris had done in his translations from Icelandic, and as Tolkien would do in many of his own writings.)

A fertile tension is apparent in all this; a tension within philology itself, which stood (unlike modern linguistics) with one foot in science and the other in art, examining the intimate relationship between language and culture. Tolkien was attracted by both the scientific rigour of phonology, morphology, and semantics, and by the imaginative or 'romantic' powers of story, myth, and legend. As yet, he could not entirely reconcile the scientific and romantic sides, but nor could he ignore the thrilling glimpses of the ancient Northern world that kept appearing in the literature with which he was dealing. Furthermore, his hunger for the old world was leading him again beyond the confines of his appointed discipline. When he was awarded the college's Skeat Prize for English in the spring of 1914, to the consternation of his tutors he spent the money not on English set texts, but on books about medieval Welsh, including a new historical *Welsh Grammar*, as well as William Morris's historical romance *The House of the Wolfings*, his epic poem *The Life and Death of Jason*, and his translation of the Icelandic *Volsunga Saga*.

For all his interest in science and scientific stringency, and in keeping with his irrepressibly 'romantic' sensitivities, Tolkien was not satisfied by materialist views of reality. To him, the world resounded to the echoes of the past. In one Stapeldon Society debate he proposed 'That this house believes in ghosts', but his idiosyncratic personal belief, nearer to mysticism than to superstition, is better expressed in a poem published in Exeter College's *Stapeldon Magazine* in December 1913:

From the many-willow'd margin of the immemorial Thames,
  Standing in a vale outcarven in a world-forgotten day,
There is dimly seen uprising through the greenly veilèd stems,
  Many-mansion'd, tower-crownèd in its dreamy robe of grey,
All the city by the fording: agèd in the lives of men,
Proudly wrapt in mystic mem'ry overpassing human ken.

In its rather grandiloquent fashion (with a long line probably inspired by William Morris) this suggests that the enduring character of Oxford predated the arrival of its inhabitants, as if the university were *meant* to emerge in this valley. Here is an early glimpse of the spirit of place that pervades much of Tolkien's work: human variety is partly shaped by geography, the work of a divine hand. Studying the literatures of the old North in Oxford, Tolkien's imaginative faculties began to strain after the forgotten outlines of 'mystic mem'ry' which he believed had made the world what it is.

Tolkien wrote relatively little poetry before the Great War, and certainly did not think of himself as a poet *per se*, unlike

G. B. Smith. In poems such as 'From the many-willow'd margin of the immemorial Thames', though, he took his cue not from the Anglo-Saxons so much as from Francis Thompson and the Romantics (Coleridge's 'Kubla Khan' had inspired a drawing in 1913) and their search for a dimension beyond the mundane. Giving a paper on Thompson to the Essay Club on 4 March 1914, Tolkien depicted a writer who could bridge the divide between rationalism and romanticism, highlighting 'the images drawn from astronomy and geology, and especially those that could be described as Catholic ritual writ large across the universe'.

The fairies of Tolkien's early poem 'Wood-sunshine' may have been nothing more, on one level, than wood-sunshine itself: the imaginative embodiment of light dappling the leaves on tree-branch and forest-floor. Tolkien's Romantic imagination, however, finds them more real than mere photons and chlorophyll. 'Wood-sunshine' may be seen as a plea to these 'glinting reflections of joy / All fashion'd of radiance, careless of grief', a plea from the mundane and suffering world for solace. Lightweight as this imagery may seem, it was linked to substantial themes. By 1914 Tolkien could formulate that link as a precept for readers of Francis Thompson, telling his fellow undergraduates, 'One must begin with the elfin and delicate and progress to the profound: listen first to the violin and the flute, and then learn to hearken to the organ of being's harmony.'

Nothing as momentous as the events of the previous year seemed likely to befall Tolkien in 1914, and the year unfolded much as any other. When the Easter vacation arrived, his term as Stapeldon president expired and he handed over to his friend Colin Cullis, who had been a member of the Apolausticks and had co-founded the later Chequers Club with him. The Stapeldon spent much of the summer term preparing for Exeter College's 600th anniversary: it failed to send out any of its usual insubordinate remonstrances to foreign powers because no 'international affairs of sufficient importance had occurred'. On 4 June the

German Ambassador, Prince Lichnowsky, was the guest of the university's enthusiastic Anglo-German Club, which included Joseph Wright and Lewis Farnell, now the college's Rector, or principal. Mrs Farnell found the prince oddly distracted until she mentioned the activities of the Officer Training Corps, about which he seemed eager to know as much as possible. The dinner, part of the celebrations of Oxford's links with Germany, was just one of a spectacular outcrop of parties at the end of the summer term. Two days later it was Exeter College's sexcentenary dinner, and Tolkien proposed the toast to the college societies (as befitted a member of so many). Then there was the 'Binge' for the Chequers Club, its elegant invitations drawn by Tolkien. Finally, starting on Tuesday 23 June, there were three days of social events marking the college's 600 years, with a summer ball, a gaudy (a reunion for former members of Exeter College, or Old Exonians), a lunch, and a garden party. Some months later Farnell recalled: 'All our festivities were enhanced by charming weather, and our atmosphere was unclouded by any foreboding of the war-storm.'

Term came to an end and so, almost immediately, did the old world. On 28 June, in the Balkan city of Sarajevo, a young Serb nationalist fired a gun at the heir to the Austrian throne, fatally wounding him. International alliances were invoked and states stepped together into a *danse macabre*. Austria-Hungary declared war on Serbia. The Austro-Hungarian empire's friend, Germany, declared war on Serbia's ally, Russia. A day later, fearing encirclement, Germany declared war on France. On 4 August 1914, to circumvent the heavily fortified French–German border, invading troops marched into Belgium. That day Britain declared war on Germany, having pledged to defend Belgian neutrality. Three days later, Lord Kitchener, now Minister of War, called Tolkien's generation to arms.

TWO

A young man with too much imagination

It is an icy day on the uplands of northern France, and to left and right hordes of soldiers advance across No Man's Land in a confusion of smoke, bullets, and bursting shells. In a command dugout giving instructions to runners, or out in the narrow trench trying to grasp the progress of battle, is Second Lieutenant J. R. R. Tolkien, now in charge of signals for a muddy and depleted battalion of four hundred fusiliers. At the end of the carnage, three miles of enemy trench are in British hands. But this is the last combat Tolkien will see. Days later he plunges into a fever, and an odyssey of tents, trains, and ships that will finally bring him back to Birmingham. There, in hospital, he begins to write the dark and complex story of an ancient civilization under siege by nightmare attackers, half-machine and half-monster: 'The Fall of Gondolin'. This is the first leaf of Tolkien's vast tree of tales. Here are 'Gnomes', or Elves; but they are tall, fierce, and grim, far different from the flitting fairies of 'Wood-sunshine'. Here is battle itself: not some rugby match dressed up in mock-heroic garb. Faërie had not entirely captured his heart as a child, Tolkien declared much later: 'A real taste for fairy-stories was wakened by philology on the threshold of manhood, and quickened to full life by war.'

Writing to his son Christopher, serving in the Royal Air Force in the midst of the Second World War, he gave a clear indication of how his own experience of war had influenced his art. 'I sense amongst all your pains (some merely physical) the desire to express your *feeling* about good, evil, fair, foul in some way: to rationalize it, and prevent it just festering,' he said. 'In my case it generated

Morgoth and the History of the Gnomes.' The mythology ultimately published as *The Silmarillion*, depicting a time when Sauron of *The Lord of the Rings* had been merely a servant of the fallen angel Morgoth, arose out of the encounter between an imaginative genius and the war that inaugurated the modern age.

The tree's development would be slow and tortuous. In 1914 Tolkien had barely begun working with the materials that would go into the building of Gondolin and Middle-earth. All he had was a handful of strange visionary pictures, some fragments of lyric poetry, a retelling of a Finnish legend, and a string of experiments in language creation. There was no sign that these things would ever be hammered into the mythic structure that emerged in late 1916, nor is the impact of war immediately apparent in what he wrote following Britain's entry into the European conflict. This was a time of great patriotic outpourings among his contemporaries, epitomized by the elegant poetry of Rupert Brooke. G. B. Smith contributed to the flood with a poem subtitled 'On the Declaration of War', which warned its upstart enemies that England might be old

> But yet a pride is ours that will not brook
> The taunts of fools too saucy grown,
> He that is rash to prove it, let him look
> He kindle not a fire unknown.

Pride and patriotism rarely make good poetry. Tolkien, it seems, kept off the bandwagon. On the face of it, indeed, he appears just as impervious to influence from all things contemporary: not only friends and literary movements, but also current affairs and even personal experience. Some critics have tended to dismiss him as an ostrich with head buried in the past; as a *pasticheur* of medieval or mythological literature desperate to shut out the modern world. But for Tolkien the medieval and the mythological were urgently alive. Their narrative structures and symbolic languages were simply the tools most apt to the hand of this most dissident of twentieth-century writers. Unlike many others shocked by the explosion of 1914–18, he did not discard the old ways of writing, the classicism or medievalism championed by Lord Tennyson and William Morris. In his hands, these traditions were reinvigorated so that they remain powerfully alive for readers today.

A week after Britain's entry into the war, while the German supergun known as Big Bertha pounded the Belgian forts around Liège, Tolkien was in Cornwall sketching the waves and the rocky coast. His letters to Edith reveal a mind already unusually attuned to the landscape, as when he and his companion, Father Vincent Reade of the Oratory, reached Ruan Minor near the end of a long day's hike. 'The light got very "eerie",' he wrote. 'Sometimes we plunged into a belt of trees, and owls and bats made you creep: sometimes a horse with asthma behind a hedge or an old pig with insomnia made your heart jump: or perhaps it was nothing worse than walking into an unexpected stream. The fourteen miles eventually drew to an end – and the last two miles were enlivened by the sweeping flash of the Lizard Lights and the sounds of the sea drawing nearer.' The sea moved him most of all: 'Nothing I could say in a dull old letter would describe it to you. The sun beats down on you and a huge Atlantic swell smashes and spouts over the snags and reefs. The sea has carved weird wind-holes and spouts into the cliffs which blow with trumpety noises or spout foam like a whale, and everywhere you see black and red rock and white foam against violet and transparent seagreen.'

But Tolkien was not eager to embrace the frightening new reality of war. Kitchener wanted 500,000 men to bolster Britain's small standing army. In Birmingham the poor, manual workers or unemployed, were the quickest to step forward. Then British troops were driven with heavy losses from Mons in Belgium – their first battle in mainland Europe since Waterloo in 1815. At the same time, no regular army was left at home to defend against invasion. Now attention turned to the middle classes, and especially to young men such as Tolkien, without dependants. 'Patriotism,' thundered the *Birmingham Daily Post*, 'insists that the unmarried shall offer themselves without thought or hesitation.' At the end of August the city looked to Old Edwardians, in particular, to fill a new battalion. Chivying them along was Tea-Cake's father, Sir John Barnsley, a lieutenant-colonel who had been invited to organize the new unit. T. K. Barnsley tried to persuade Rob Gilson to join him in the 'Birmingham Battalion',* but the most Rob would do was help train the Old Edwardian recruits to shoot. By 5 September, 4,500 men had registered for the unit, enough for a second battalion and more, with Tolkien's brother Hilary joining the rush. The volunteers, whose uniforms would not be ready for some weeks, were issued with badges so they would not be abused in the streets as cowards. Tolkien, who was not among the recruits, recalled later: 'In those days chaps joined up, or were scorned publicly. It was a nasty cleft to be in.' Meanwhile, casualties from Mons were filling the military hospital that had just been set up in Birmingham University, and Belgian refugees were arriving in England with stories of German atrocities.

With the public reproaches came hints from relatives, then outspoken pressure. Tolkien had no parents to tell him what to do, but his aunts and uncles felt that his duty was plain. Late in September, however, when he and Hilary were staying with their widowed aunt, Jane Neave, at Phoenix Farm, in Gedling, Nottinghamshire, John Ronald made it clear that he was considering carrying on at Oxford.

In many ways, Tolkien should have been predisposed to respond promptly to Kitchener's call. He was Catholic, whereas the German invaders of Belgium were reputedly Lutheran zealots who raped nuns and slaughtered priests. He shared the cultural values that were outraged by the German destruction of Louvain, with its churches, university, and its library of 230,000 books that included hundreds of unique medieval manuscripts. And he felt a duty to crown and country.

* Later the 14th, 15th, and 16th Battalions of the Royal Warwickshire Regiment.

But in 1914 J. R. R. Tolkien was being asked to fight soldiers whose home was the land of his own paternal ancestors. There had been Tolkiens in England in the early nineteenth century, but the line (as *Tolkiehn*) went back to Saxony. Ancient Germania had also been the cradle of Anglo-Saxon culture. In one of his notebooks that year, Tolkien painstakingly traced the successive incursions that had brought the Germanic tribes to the island of Britain. At this stage, as he later admitted, he was drawn powerfully to 'the "Germanic" ideal', which Tolkien was to describe even in 1941 (despite its exploitation by Adolf Hitler) as 'that noble northern spirit, a supreme contribution to Europe'. There was also the matter of academic fellowship. Germany was the intellectual fount of the modern science of philology and had hauled Anglo-Saxon into the forefront of English studies. That autumn, his old tutor Farnell relayed tales of German atrocities in Belgium, but Joseph Wright, who was now Tolkien's friend and adviser as well as tutor, was trying to set up a lending library for wounded German soldiers who were being treated in Oxford. Such sympathies and society may not have been entirely forgotten, even under the glaring eye of Lord Kitchener on the recruiting posters. Though many of his countrymen who bore German surnames soon changed them to English ones (among them George V in July 1917), Tolkien did not, noting many years afterwards: 'I have been accustomed . . . to regard my German name with pride, and continued to do so throughout the period of the late regrettable war . . .'

It is possible that his unconventional tastes in Germanic literature gave him a different view of war from that of most contemporaries. Embracing the culture of the ancient European North, Tolkien turned his back enthusiastically on the Classics that had nurtured his generation at school. They had become romantically entangled with Victorian triumphalism; in the words of one commentator, 'As the long prosperous years of the Pax Britannica succeeded one another, the truth about war was forgotten, and in 1914 young officers went into battle with the *Iliad* in their backpacks and the names of Achilles and Hector engraved upon their hearts.' But the names on Tolkien's heart now were Beowulf and Beorhtnoth. Indeed, like the youth Torhthelm in his 1953 verse drama, *The Homecoming of Beorhtnoth Beorhthelm's Son*, Tolkien's head was by now 'full of old lays concerning the heroes of northern antiquity, such as Finn, king of Frisia; Fróda of the Hathobards; Béowulf; and Hengest and Horsa . . .' He had become more entrenched, if anything, in his boyhood view that 'though as a whole the Northern epic has not the charm and delight of the Southern, yet in a certain bare veracity it excels it'. Homer's *Iliad* is in part a catalogue of violent deaths, but it is set in a warm world where seas are sunlit, heroes become demigods, and the rule of the Olympians is unending. The Germanic world was chillier and greyer. It carried a burden of pessimism, and final annihilation awaited *Middangeard* (Middle-earth) and its gods. *Beowulf* was about 'man at war with the hostile world, and his inevitable overthrow in Time', he wrote later in his influential essay, 'Beowulf: The Monsters and the Critics'. 'A young man with too much imagination and little physical courage', as he later described himself, Tolkien could picture war only too well, if not the unprecedented efficiency mechanization would bring to the business of killing.

But the key to Tolkien's decision to defer enlistment lay in his pocket. He was not well off, surviving on his £60 exhibition money and a small annuity. When he had gone to Cheltenham to win Edith back, on turning twenty-one, her protective landlord had warned her guardian, 'I have nothing to say against Tolkien, he is a cultured Gentl[eman], but his prospects are poor in the extreme, and when he will be in a position to marry, I cannot imagine. Had he adopted a Profession it would have been different.' Now that Tolkien and Edith were engaged, he could not consider himself only. Having changed course and finally found his *métier*, though, he hoped to make a living as an academic. But that would be impossible if he did not get his degree. The much wealthier Rob Gilson told his own sweetheart eighteen months later:

> He did not join the Army until later than the rest of us as he finished his schools at Oxford first. It was quite necessary for

> him, as it is his main hope of earning his living and I am glad to say he got his first – in English Literature . . . He has always been desperately poor . . .

So Tolkien told his Aunt Jane that he had resolved to complete his studies. But under the intense pressure he turned to poetry. As a result, the visit to Phoenix Farm proved pivotal in an entirely unexpected way.

Back before war broke out, at the end of the university term, Tolkien had borrowed from the college library Grein and Wülcker's multi-volume *Bibliothek der angelsächsischen Poesie.* This massive work was one of those monuments of German scholarship that had shaped the study of Old English, and it meant Tolkien had the core poetic corpus at hand throughout the long summer vacation. He waded through the *Crist*, by the eighth-century Anglo-Saxon poet Cynewulf, but found it 'a lamentable bore', as he wrote later: 'lamentable, because it is a matter for tears that a man (or men) with talent in word-spinning, who must have heard (or read) so much now lost, should spend their time composing such uninspired stuff'. Boredom could have a paradoxical effect on Tolkien: it set his imagination roaming. Furthermore, the thought of stories lost beyond recall always tantalized him. In the midst of Cynewulf's pious homily, he encountered the words *Eala Earendel! engla beorhtast / ofer middangeard monnum sended*, 'Hail Earendel, brightest of angels, above the middle-earth sent unto men!' The name *Earendel* (or *Éarendel*) struck him in an extraordinary way. Tolkien later expressed his own reaction through Arundel Lowdham, a character in 'The Notion Club Papers', an unfinished story of the 1940s: 'I felt a curious thrill, as if something had stirred in me, half wakened from sleep. There was something very remote and strange and beautiful behind those words, if I could grasp it, far beyond ancient English . . . I don't think it is any irreverence to say that it may derive its curiously moving quality from some older world.' But whose name was *Éarendel*? The question sparked a lifelong answer.

Cynewulf's lines were about an angelic messenger or herald of Christ. The dictionary suggested the word meant a ray of light, or the illumination of dawn. Tolkien felt that it must be a survival from before Anglo-Saxon, even from before Christianity. (Cognate names such as *Aurvandil* and *Orendil* in other ancient records bear this out. According to the rules of comparative philology, they probably descended from a single name before Germanic split into its offspring languages. But the literal and metaphorical meanings of this name are obscure.) Drawing on the dictionary definitions and Cynewulf's reference to Éarendel as being above our world, Tolkien was inspired with the idea that Éarendel could be none other than the steersman of Venus, the planet that presages the dawn. At Phoenix Farm, on 24 September 1914, he began, with startling *éclat*:

> Éarendel sprang up from the Ocean's cup
> In the gloom of the mid-world's rim;
> From the door of Night as a ray of light
> Leapt over the twilight brim,
> And launching his bark like a silver spark
> From the golden-fading sand
> Down the sunlit breath of Day's fiery Death
> He sped from Westerland.

Tolkien embellished 'The Voyage of Éarendel the Evening Star' with a favourite phrase from *Beowulf*, *Ofer ýþa ful*, 'over the cup of the ocean', 'over the ocean's goblet'. A further characteristic of Éarendel may have been suggested to Tolkien by the similarity of his name to the Old English *ēar* 'sea': though his element is the sky, he is a mariner. But these were mere beginnings. He sketched out a character and a cosmology in forty-eight lines of verse that are by turns sublime, vivacious, and sombre. All the heavenly bodies are ships that sail daily through gates at the East and West. The action is simple: Éarendel launches his vessel from the sunset Westerland at the world's rim, skitters past the stars sailing their fixed courses, and escapes the hunting Moon, but dies in the light of the rising Sun.

And Éarendel fled from that Shipman dread
  Beyond the dark earth's pale,
Back under the rim of the Ocean dim,
  And behind the world set sail;
And he heard the mirth of the folk of earth
  And hearkened to their tears,
As the world dropped back in a cloudy wrack
  On its journey down the years.

Then he glimmering passed to the starless vast
  As an isléd lamp at sea,
And beyond the ken of mortal men
  Set his lonely errantry,
Tracking the Sun in his galleon
  And voyaging the skies
Till his splendour was shorn by the birth of Morn
  And he died with the Dawn in his eyes.

It is the kind of myth an ancient people might make to explain celestial phenomena. Tolkien gave the title in Old English too (*Scipfæreld Earendeles Ǽfensteorran*), as if the whole poem were a translation. He was imagining the story Cynewulf might have heard, as if a rival Anglo-Saxon poet had troubled to record it.

As he wrote, German and French armies clashed fiercely at the town of Albert, in the region named for the River Somme, which flows through it. But Éarendel's is a solitary species of daring, driven by an unexplained desire. He is not (as in Cynewulf) *monnum sended*, 'sent unto men' as a messenger or herald; nor is he a warrior. If Éarendel embodies heroism at all, it is the maverick, elemental heroism of individuals such as Sir Ernest Shackleton, who that summer had sailed off on his voyage to traverse the Antarctic continent.

If the shadow of war touches Tolkien's poem at all, it is in a very oblique way. Though he flies from the mundane world, Éarendel listens to its weeping, and while his ship speeds off on its own wayward course, the fixed stars take their appointed places on 'the gathering tide of darkness'. It is impossible to say whether Tolkien meant this to equate in any way to his own situation at the time of writing; but it is interesting that, while he was under intense pressure to fight for King and Country, and while others were burnishing their martial couplets, he eulogized a 'wandering spirit' at odds with the majority course, a fugitive in a lonely pursuit of some elusive ideal.

What is this ideal? Disregarding the later development of his story, we know little more about the Éarendel of this poem than we do about the stick figure stepping into space in Tolkien's drawing *The End of the World*. Still less do we know what Éarendel is thinking, despite his evident daring, eccentricity, and uncontainable curiosity. We might almost conclude that this is truly 'an endless quest' not just without conclusion, but without purpose. If Tolkien had wanted to analyse the heart and mind of his mariner, he might have turned to the great Old English meditations on exile, *The Wanderer* and *The Seafarer*. Instead he turned to Romance, the quest's native mode, in which motivation is either self-evident (love, ambition, greed) or supernatural. Éarendel's motivation is both: after all, he is both a man and a celestial object. Supernaturally, this is an astronomy myth explaining planetary motions, but on a human scale it is also a paean to imagination. 'His heart afire with bright desire', Éarendel is like Francis Thompson (in Tolkien's Stapeldon Society paper), filled with 'a burning enthusiasm for the ethereally fair'. It is tempting to see analogies with Tolkien the writer bursting into creativity. The mariner's quest is that of the Romantic individual who has 'too much imagination', who is not content with the Enlightenment project of examining the known world in ever greater detail. Éarendel overleaps all conventional barriers in a search for self-realization in the face of the natural sublime. In an unspoken religious sense, he seeks to see the face of God.

The week before the start of the Cambridge term found Rob Gilson staying with Christopher Wiseman in Wandsworth, London, where his family had moved following his father's appointment as secretary of the Wesleyan Methodist Home

Mission Department in 1913. It was also the week of the fall of Antwerp. Gilson wrote: 'We are of course very mad and hilarious. Last night we went to see Gerald du Maurier in *Outcast* – such a bad play. I don't know what we are going to do today and shall probably start to do it before we have decided.' At the same time, on 4 October, the last Sunday of the long vacation, Tolkien was back in Birmingham, staying at the Oratory with Father Francis Morgan. T. K. Barnsley, who had now been appointed the first subaltern in the 1st Birmingham Battalion, was leading the new unit in a church parade at the city's central parish church. On the Monday the recruits began training. Saturday's *Daily Post* had carried a list of men accepted to serve in the 3rd Birmingham Battalion. Hilary Tolkien was soon packed off without ceremony to train at a Methodist college in Moseley as a bugler.

Back in Oxford, Tolkien confided in a Catholic professor that the outbreak of war had come as a profound blow to him, 'the collapse of all my world', as he later put it. Tolkien had been prone to fits of profound melancholy, even despair, ever since the death of his mother, though he kept them to himself. The new life he had slowly built up since her death was now in peril. Hearing his complaint, however, the Catholic professor responded that this war was no aberration: on the contrary, for the human race it was merely 'back to normal'.

Yet 'ordinary life', as Tolkien had known it, was an immediate casualty of war, even in Oxford. The university was transformed into a citadel of refugees and war-readiness. The time-honoured flow of undergraduates had haemorrhaged: a committee to process student recruits had dealt with 2,000 by September. Only seventy-five remained at Exeter College, and in the evenings unlit windows loomed over the silent quad. Tolkien was stricken with severe second thoughts about staying and declared: 'It is awful. I really don't think I shall be able to go on: work seems impossible.' The college had become part-barracks, with areas allocated to Oxfordshire Light Infantrymen and batteries of gunners, who came and went in a steady stream. Some of the younger dons had gone off to war, and so had many of the college servants; older men had taken their place. Tolkien was glad to be living for the first time out of college, at 59 St John Street (an address which came to be known as 'the Johnner'), where he shared 'digs' with his last remaining Exeter friend, Colin Cullis, who was not able to join up due to poor health.

The town was largely emptied of its younger men, but it was busier than ever. Women were stepping into men's civilian jobs. Exiled Belgians and Serbs appeared. Convalescent soldiers wandered the streets and the wounded were laid up in the Examination Schools. The troops who were being trained to replace them drilled in the University Parks in their temporary-issue blue uniforms. Quaintly, as it now seems, Farnell the Rector was giving lessons in the épée and the sabre. For the first time since the English Civil War, Oxford had become a military camp.

Urged on by Farnell, Tolkien and his few fellow undergraduates strove to keep the college societies going. The Stapeldon Society, a shadow of its former self under 'lowering clouds of Armageddon', did its trivial best by passing a rousing vote of confidence in all Exonians in the armed forces and sending letters of support to King Albert of Belgium and Winston Churchill (then First Lord of the Admiralty). But the first duty imposed upon Tolkien was to pursue the question of the redecoration of the Junior Common Room, the undergraduates' meeting place. The students were warned that war would mean going short on such luxuries. The sub-rector told Tolkien that student entertainments were unduly wasteful and must be banned. Tolkien turned to humour, poking fun at the first-year intake for not taking baths, 'no doubt,' he said, because they were 'economising with the best of intentions in this time of stress'. The society debated the motion that 'This House disapproves a system of stringent economy in the present crisis.' Tolkien spoke in a debate on 'the Superman and International Law', but his own proposal, that 'This House approves of spelling reform,' suggests an urge to turn aside from the war. It was a necessary appeal to non-martial life, but a puny one as more and more of the globe became entangled in war. At the end of October German forces in Belgium were driven back from the

River Yser by flooding after the Belgians opened the seaward sluices at high tide, but at nearby Ypres British forces were succumbing to exhaustion in the mud, the new enemy. The opposing armies had failed to outflank each other and now began hunkering down in trenches: the Western Front had been established. Meanwhile, a mine sank Britain's super-Dreadnought *Audacious* north of Scotland. Turkey entered the war and became Britain's enemy. Far afield, the Boers of the Orange Free State, whose sympathies were pro-German, were now staging an uprising against British rule.

In lieu of enlisting in Kitchener's army, at the start of term Tolkien had immediately enrolled in the university OTC. There were two courses: one for those hoping for a commission imminently, the other for those who wished to delay enlistment. Tolkien was one of twenty-five Exeter College men on the latter, which meant about six and a half hours' drill and one military lecture per week. 'We had a drill all afternoon and got soaked several times and our rifles got all filthy and took ages to clean afterwards,' Tolkien wrote to Edith at the end of his first week. For those of a more sensitive nature, any military training could be sufficiently unpleasant: Rob Gilson, who loathed militarism, had taken *Paradise Lost* to read at the OTC summer camp at Aldershot the year before, and found that a like-minded friend (Frederick Scopes) had brought Dante's *Inferno*. For Tolkien, though, years of playing rugby meant that the physical discomforts, at least, held no horror. The university corps were remote from real soldiering, with no field days or route marches, and rifles were soon taken away for the real war, but the active physical life banished the notorious 'Oxford "sleepies"' and brought fresh energy. 'Drill is a godsend,' he told Edith.

Reinvigorated, he worked on his *Story of Kullervo*, a dark tale for dark times, and enthused about the Finnish *Kalevala* to T. W. Earp, a member of the Exeter College literati. This epic poem was the work of Elias Lönnrot, collated from folk songs passed down orally by generations of 'rune singers' in the

Karelian region of Finland. Fragmentary and lyrical though these songs were, many referred tantalizingly to an apparently pre-Christian cast of heroic or divine figures headed by the sage Väinamöinen, the smith Ilmarinen, and the boastful rogue Lemminkäinen. Lönnrot had seen his chance to create a Finnish equivalent of what contemporary Iceland and Greece had inherited, a mythological literature; and he did so at a time when the Finns were struggling to find a voice. Finland, ruled by Sweden since the twelfth century but entirely distinct in language, culture, and ethnic history, had become a personal grand duchy of the Tsar of Russia in 1809. Just then the notion that ancient literature expressed the ancestral voice of a people was sweeping through Europe's academies and salons. When the *Kalevala* arrived in 1835, it had been embraced by Finnish nationalists, whose goal of independence was still unachieved in 1914.

Tolkien spoke in defence of nationalism at a college debate that November, even as the pride of nations was plunging Europe into catastrophe. Nationalism has carried even sourer connotations since the 1930s, but Tolkien's version had nothing to do with vaunting one nation above others. To him the nation's greatest goal was cultural self-realisation, not power over others; but essential to this were patriotism and a community of belief. 'I don't defend "Deutschland über alles" but certainly do in Norwegian "Alt for Norge" [All for Norway],' he told Wiseman on the eve of the debate. By his own admission, therefore, Tolkien was both an English patriot and a supporter of Home Rule for the Irish. He could appreciate the Romantic notion of language as an ancestral voice, but he went further: he felt he had actually inherited from his maternal ancestors a taste and an aptitude for the Middle English of the West Midlands, a dialect he was studying for his English course in the religious text *Ancrene Riwle*. Writing about his life and influences much later, he declared:

> I am indeed in English terms a West-midlander at home only in the counties upon the Welsh Marches; and it is, I believe, as much due to descent as to opportunity that Anglo-Saxon and

> Western Middle English and alliterative verse have been both a childhood attraction and my main professional sphere.

Like Lönnrot, Tolkien felt that his true culture had been crushed and forgotten; but, characteristically, he saw things on a vast timescale, with the Norman Conquest as the turning point. William the Conqueror's invasion in 1066 had brought the curtain down on the use of English in courtly language and in literature for centuries, and ultimately left English laced with non-Germanic words. The voice of a people, effectively, had been silenced for generations, and the continuity of the record had been severed. Tolkien had launched an ingenious counterattack at school, deploring the Norman Conquest 'in a speech attempting to return to something of Saxon purity of diction', as the school *Chronicle* reported – or as Tolkien himself put it, 'right English goodliness of speechcraft': a language purged of Latin and French derivatives (though before the end of his speech he forgot, in his excitement, not to use 'such outlandish horrors as "famous" and "barbarous"'). Old English, though only written down by Christian Anglo-Saxons, had preserved glimpses of the older traditions that fascinated Tolkien in its literature and in the very fabric of its language; and undoubtedly much more had been swept away by the Norman Conquest.

In contrast, the *Kalevala* had preserved the Finns' old traditions. Addressing Corpus Christi College's Sundial Society, at G. B. Smith's invitation, on 22 November 1914, he declared: 'These mythological ballads are full of that very primitive undergrowth that the literature of Europe has on the whole been steadily cutting and reducing for many centuries with different and earlier completeness among different people.' He told the Sundial Society: 'I would that we had more of it left – something of the same sort that belonged to the English.' This, in effect, was the young J. R. R. Tolkien's creative manifesto.

Tolkien had read 'The Voyage of Éarendel' aloud on 27 November 1914 to Exeter College's Essay Club, at a poorly attended meeting which he called 'an informal kind of last gasp' as war emptied Oxford of its undergraduates. G. B. Smith also read the poem and asked his friend what it was really about. Tolkien's reply speaks volumes about his creative method, even at this early stage. 'I don't know,' he said. 'I'll try to find out.' He had already emulated Lönnrot by working back through the Old English *Crist* into the 'undergrowth' of Germanic tradition, where a mariner called Éarendel might have sailed the skies. The celestial heroes of myth always have earthbound origins, but Tolkien had so far 'discovered' nothing about Éarendel's. Around now he scribbled down some ideas:

> Earendel's boat goes through North. Iceland. Greenland, and the wild islands: a mighty wind and crest of great wave carry him to hotter climes, to back of West Wind. Land of strange men, land of magic. The home of Night. The Spider. He escapes from the meshes of Night with a few comrades, sees a great mountain island and a golden city – wind blows him southward. Tree-men, Sun-dwellers, spices, fire-mountains, red sea: Mediterranean (loses his boat (travels afoot through wilds of Europe?)) or Atlantic . . .'

The notes then bring the seafarer to the point in 'The Voyage of Éarendel' where he sails over the rim of the world in pursuit of the Sun. The scale of Tolkien's imaginative ambitions is at once astonishingly clear. This is an *Odyssey* in embryo, but one in which the classical milieu of the Mediterranean appears only as an afterthought and whose heart lies in the bitter northern seas around Tolkien's island home. But startling, too, is the way this elliptical note already foreshadows fundamental moments from *The Silmarillion*, from the Atlantis-story of Númenor, and even from *The Lord of the Rings*. Here, perhaps for the first time, these blurred images found their way onto paper. Many of them may have existed in some form already for a long time. But Cynewulf, the *Kalevala*, G. B. Smith's probing questions, and arguably even Tolkien's anxieties over enlistment, all conspired to bring them pouring out now.

THREE

The Council of London

It had been agreed that the Oxford contingent of the TCBS would go up to Cambridge for a weekend in the middle of term, on Saturday 31 October 1914, but in the event only G. B. Smith turned up. 'Tolkien was to come too, but hasn't, as was to be expected,' wrote Rob Gilson disappointedly. 'No one knows why he couldn't come, least of all Smith, who was with him on Friday night.' The pair lunched with Christopher Wiseman, attended a Sunday service at King's College chapel, and strolled around Cambridge. Smith was voluble about what he liked in the rival university town, and deployed his dazzling wit against what he disliked. Gilson wrote: 'I always value his judgment though I often disagree with it, and am pleased to find that he is immensely enthusiastic about my rooms, and has never seen ones that he preferred – even in Oxford. I had a breakfast party this morning and they looked their best. A sunny morning with shadows across the Bowling Green and just enough mist to make the background of trees a perfect thing – blue and orange . . . I am having quite a perfect week-end.' Smith clearly enjoyed it too, for he came back for more the following weekend. There was talk of a further get-together in Oxford.

In fact Tolkien had simply stopped attending TCBS reunions. What seemed perfect to the impressionable Gilson was, to Tolkien, now tainted by a mood antithetical to the original spirit of the club. Humour had always been essential to the group, but originally each member had brought his own brand. Tolkien's was occasionally boisterous, but he shared with Gilson a gentle delight in the lesser human follies, and he often indulged in wordplay. G. B. Smith had 'a gift for rapping out preposterous paradoxes' and for stylistic parody: 'I played Rugger yesterday, and am one of the three stiffest mortals in Europe in consequence,' is GBS parodying the superlative triads of the Welsh *Mabinogion*. Wiseman enjoyed impromptu farce and abstruse mathematical wit. Sidney Barrowclough, on the other hand, affected a cold cynicism, robing his sarcasm in verbal elegance, and T. K. Barnsley and W. H. Payton favoured Barrowclough's brand of repartee. Tolkien no longer cared to spend his time with a TCBS under their shadow.

He was not alone. After enduring an evening of inane banter, with which he could not and would not compete, Wiseman had decided to sever his links with the TCBS. He wrote to Tolkien to say that he would not come to the Oxford meeting, declaring, 'I should only go there, talk a little bilge for the space of a couple of days and go down again. I am getting very bored with the TCBS; none of them seem to have any mortal thing about which they can get angry; they merely make light and clever remarks (GBS is a perfect genius at it, I admit) about nothing at all.' According to Wiseman, Barnsley and Barrowclough had demolished his own self-confidence, and Gilson's. Now, before it was too late, he appealed to his oldest friend 'by all the memories of VT [Vincent Trought], of Gothic, of binges in Highfield Road, of quarrels about philology' to come to a crisis meeting after term with Gilson, Smith, and himself.

Such was his disenchantment that he scarcely expected a reply. Instead, he found that for once he and Tolkien were in total agreement. 'I tell you, when I had finished your letter I felt I could hug you,' Wiseman wrote back. Neither Oxford nor Cambridge had 'destroyed what made you and me the Twin Brethren in the good old school days before there was a TCBS apart from us and VT', he said.

Tolkien defended G. B. Smith, saying his superficiality was just a mask adopted in response to the 'alien spirit' now dominating their conclaves; but he agreed that Gilson had gradually lost interest in matters of moral weight and was now simply an aesthete. Tolkien thought Smith fell broadly into the same category, but he suspected that both men were still simply a trifle callow, rather than intrinsically shallow. Certainly he had no thought of excluding them. About one thing Tolkien was adamant: 'the TCBS is four and four only'; the 'hangers-on' must be ejected.

Despite his strictures, Tolkien maintained that the society was 'a great idea which has never become quite articulate'. Its two poles, the moral and the aesthetic, could be complementary if kept in balance, yet its members did not actually know each other well enough. While the Great Twin Brethren had discussed the fundamentals of existence, neither of them had done so with Gilson or Smith. As a result, Tolkien declared, the potential these four '*amazing*' individuals contained in combination remained unbroached. So it was that the moral wing of the TCBS determined that the four should meet in Wandsworth two weeks before Christmas. 'TCBS über alles,' Wiseman signed off, wryly, at the end of a frantic few days' correspondence.

It was touch-and-go whether G. B. Smith and Rob Gilson would be able to get to the 'Council of London', as the crisis summit was dubbed. Wiseman, like Tolkien, had early on decided to complete his degree before enlisting, on the basis that Kaiser Wilhelm had declared his soldiers would be back home by the time the leaves had fallen from the trees. Smith and Gilson, however, both now joined Kitchener's army.

Gilson had found Cambridge as sad and dark in wartime as Tolkien found Oxford, and since the start of term had been pondering cutting short his final year. His father, the Headmaster of King Edward's, had advised him to get his degree before enlisting, and told him (with some sophistry but more foresight) that he had no right to desert Cambridge now, when the university corps needed every man it could get in order to ensure a future supply of officers as the war went on. The turning point seems to have come for Gilson in early November, when a shy and difficult undergraduate whom he had just befriended,

F. L. Lucas, reluctantly joined up. 'He is not at all the sort of person who rushes into it without thinking what it means,' wrote Gilson. 'He is really rather a hero . . .'* Military lectures had impressed upon the sensitive Gilson 'what a fearful responsibility it is to be entrusted with so many men's lives'. On the other hand, he felt guilty for not volunteering, and was surprised to find himself enjoying even the most gruelling field exercises. Others of the broader TCBS had now joined up. Sidney Barrowclough had been accepted in the Royal Field Artillery, and Ralph Payton had become a private in the 1st Birmingham Battalion, T. K. Barnsley's unit; though W. H. Payton had found an honourable alternative to combat by signing up for the Indian Civil Service in August. Desperate to put an end to months of doubt and guilt, Gilson waited until his twenty-first birthday was past, and on 28 November he joined the Cambridgeshire Battalion as a second lieutenant.

It was a relief, for although Gilson was strictly too sensitive for military life, he was sociable and found it easy to get on with his fellow officers. G. B. Smith, however, who was also sensitive but considerably less tolerant and naturally undisciplined, felt 'much more a fish out of water' after he followed suit on 1 December. Cary Gilson provided a character reference, and Oxford's home regiment, the Oxfordshire and Buckinghamshire Light Infantry, took the young poet on. It meant Smith would be training in Oxford and billeted at Magdalen College, where he would be on hand to see Tolkien's burgeoning efforts at writing. One of Smith's own poems, 'Ave Atque Vale' ('hail and farewell'), had just appeared in the *Oxford Magazine*: a paean to his university town (but also to life itself) announcing 'we may not linger here. A little while, and we are gone . . .'

In the event, the two new subalterns both managed to arrange leave so that they could come to London on Saturday, 12

---

* The classicist F. L. Lucas survived the war to become a fellow of King's College, Cambridge, and a critic, poet, and dramatist.

December. Gilson had moved the day before into officers' huts at his battalion's newly built camp at Cherry Hinton, just outside Cambridge. Under the auspices of Wiseman, in normal circumstances the visit would have been hilarious and carefree, with impromptu outings, missed trains, and countless telephone calls as he tried to keep his mother informed of his schedule. What with the family talent for chaos, and his father's unpredictable hours, formality had given up the ghost at 33 Routh Road, Wandsworth. But now the four friends had urgent matters to discuss. They closeted themselves in Wiseman's upstairs room and talked late into the night.

They dubbed the reunion 'the Council of London' as if it were a council of war; in fact it was a council of life. War did not intrude, despite the enlistment of Smith and Gilson: in Rob's words, the four of them were 'absolutely undistracted by the outside world'. They had made a timely decision, though, to combine and consider the matter in hand: the greatness of the TCBS. That the TCBS was somehow great was a long-standing conviction based on mutual admiration. Gilson now doubted the truth of it, but Wiseman thought that together they each seemed 'four times the intellectual size', as if each one absorbed the capabilities of all. Tolkien felt the same way about 'the inspiration that even a few hours with the four always brought to all of us'; but the inanity that had overtaken the wider group in recent years had left Tolkien and Wiseman convinced that it must now plant its feet firmly in the bedrock of fundamental principles: in other words, all four must open up about their deepest convictions, as the Great Twin Brethren had done long ago. Tolkien put religion, human love, patriotic duty, and nationalism on the agenda. It was not necessary that they all agree, but it was important that they discover the 'allowable distance apart', as he put it: in other words, how much internal dissent the club could accommodate.

The Council surpassed all their hopes. 'I *never* spent happier hours,' Rob wrote to John Ronald afterwards. For Tolkien, the weekend was a revelation, and he came to regard it as a turning point in his creative life. It was, he said eighteen months later, the moment when he first became conscious of 'the hope and ambitions (inchoate and cloudy I know)' that had driven him ever since, and were to drive him for the rest of his life.

Tolkien had long harboured creative ambitions, but they had found their outlet in his invented languages, at one extreme, or in drawings. Now all that changed. It may well be that, under the oppressive weight of war, he felt an answering pressure from within that could find no outlet in the old creative habits. He had experimented with prose in his *Story of Kullervo*. Now, however, he was going to take his cue from the *Kalevala* itself, from the verse into which *Kullervo* had fallen with increasing frequency, and from G. B. Smith. He would become a poet.

In fact he had started already, a week before the Council, by writing an ambitious poem in a percussive version of the long line he had used in 'From the many-willow'd margin of the immemorial Thames'. In its earliest published form, 'The Tides' begins:

I sat on the ruined margin of the deep voiced echoing sea
Whose roaring foaming music crashed in endless cadency
On the land besieged for ever in an aeon of assaults
And torn in towers and pinnacles and caverned in great vaults:
And its arches shook with thunder and its feet were piled with
shapes
Riven in old sea-warfare from those crags and sable capes
By ancient battailous tempest and primeval mighty tide . . .

Subtitled 'On the Cornish Coast', this was the poetic expression of the sea-awe that Tolkien had described in his letters and drawings in Cornwall that summer of 1914. While the martial imagery might have been coloured by the fact that this was written at a moment of war, and amid widespread fear of invasion, he was concerned with processes on a geological time-scale. The poet's presence is almost incidental: he is there merely to witness the action of primal oceanic forces, inhuman and sublime. The piece gives a very early glimpse of Tolkien's intense awareness of the vast histories inscribed within a landscape – an awareness that gives his mythological world the texture of reality.

Very soon he was adding more poems to his corpus, in a rush of creativity that for him was unprecedented. 'That Council,' Tolkien told G. B. Smith, 'was . . . followed in my own case with my finding a voice for all kinds of pent up things and a tremendous opening up of everything.' A painting made two days after Christmas captures this strange mood of uplift in the midst of dark times: *The Land of Pohja*, depicting a scene from the *Kalevala* in which the Sun and Moon, drawn by the beauty of the wizard Väinämöinen's harp-playing, settle in the branches of two trees, filling the icebound wastes with light.

Tolkien was also absorbed once more in the Finnish language itself, and it played the most productive role in a creative breakthrough. When he had borrowed a college library copy of Chaucer to continue studying for his English course during the Christmas vacation, he had also taken Eliot's *Finnish Grammar* out again. He immersed himself in the book, but not in order to read more Finnish; rather, he was allowing Finnish to shape the language he now hoped to devise. The language of the *Kalevala* had long been supplanting the earlier primacy of Gothic in his philological heart. At some point as 1915 came in, Tolkien took an exercise book, in which he had apparently been outlining aspects of Gautisk, and struck out his old notes, ready to make a fresh beginning. He tried out several names for the new language, eventually settling on *Qenya*.

To Tolkien, working in the familiar fields of English and its Indo-European relatives, Finnish was remote, mysterious, and peculiarly beautiful. Its culture was pre-industrial, with ancient roots. By tapping into it, Tolkien was following, in his idiosyncratic way, the contemporary vogue for primitivism that had attracted Picasso to African masks. In the *Kalevala*, the natural and the supernatural were intimate and intermingled: the language, as Tolkien said, revealed 'an entirely different mythological world'.

The small, stark array of consonants and the chiming inflexional word-endings of Finnish produce a distinctive musicality that Tolkien adapted for Qenya; but he wanted a language with its own past, so he detailed how Qenya had evolved from an ancestral tongue that he soon named Primitive Eldarin. As in any real-world language, the process was a combination of sound shifts (phonology), the deployment of word-building elements (morphology) like the *-s* or *-es* that commonly pluralize an English noun, and developments in meaning (semantics).* A further fascination of this linguistic alchemy was that, as in the real world, an alternative set of sound-changes and morphological elements would produce elsewhere a quite different language from the same ancestral stock – an option Tolkien also began to explore before long.

Tolkien's sound-shift 'laws' fill many dry pages of his early Qenya notebook, but they were as essential to Qenya as the changes codified in Grimm's Law are to German or English. He often wrote as if, like Jakob Grimm, he too were merely an observer looking back at the unrecorded but nonetheless real past of a living language. Even in these phonological notes, Tolkien was already entering into his world as a fiction writer does. From this 'internal' viewpoint, the sound shifts were unalterable facts of observed history.

---

* A single illustration may serve. Tolkien decided that a primitive 'root' LIŘI had survived almost unchanged in Qenya as *liri-*, the stem of a verb meaning 'to sing'. By adding various noun-forming suffixes, it also produced *liritta*, 'poem, lay, written poem', and *lirilla*, 'lay, song'. However, the past tense was *lindë*, apparently formed by inserting an 'infix', *-n-* (a morphological change), which combined with the original *-ř-* shifted to *-nd-* (a phonological change). But *lindë* acted as a stem in its own right, adding a suffix to produce *lindelë*, 'song, music', or losing its unaccented final syllable for *lin*, 'musical voice, air, melody, tune'. It also appears in compounds with other Qenya words as *lindōrëa*, 'singing at dawn' (applied especially to birds), and *lindeloktë*, 'singing cluster', the name for the laburnum (where we see the semantic process of metaphor at work). All these transformation-types have their equivalents in real-world languages.

In practice, though, Tolkien also played God (or sub-creator emulating the Creator, as he would later have put it). He did not just observe history; he made it. Instead of working back from recorded evidence to reconstruct the lost ancestral 'roots' of words, as Grimm had done to arrive at a picture of ancient Germanic, he could invent Primitive Eldarin roots and move forward, adding affixes and applying sound shifts to arrive at Qenya. Furthermore, Tolkien could change a sound-shift law, and he sometimes did. Because each law should apply across the language, this might entail alterations to any number of words and their individual histories. Revision on that scale was a painstaking process, but it gave Tolkien a perfectionist's pleasure. There was scope here for a lifetime's tinkering, and he used it.

If these austere sound-shift laws were the 'scientific' formulae by which Tolkien generated his 'romantic' language – as essential to its personal character as DNA is to our own – inventing Qenya was also an exercise in taste as heartfelt as any art. Tolkien's sound-pictures were always acute: the bassy *kalongalan*, 'ringing or jangling of (large) bells', and its alto counterpart *kilinkelë*, 'jingling of (small) bells'; the elegant alternations of *vassivaswë* for 'beating or rushing of wings'; or the tongue-twisting *pataktata-pakta*, 'rat-a-tat'. Qenya is more than onomatopoeic, though: *nang-*, 'I have a cold', and *miqë*, 'a kiss' (pronounced more or less as 'mee-kweh'), mimic what the speech organs do when your nose is blocked or your mouth is amorously engaged. Of course, most concepts have no intrinsic connection with any particular sound or mouth-movement. Tolkien tried to match sound and sense much as an expressionist painter might use colour, form, and shade to evoke a mood. Derivation aside, only taste dictated that *fūmelot* means 'poppy', *eressëa* means 'lonely', or *morwen*, 'daughter of the dark', signifies the glimmering planet Jupiter.

Crucially, Tolkien used Qenya to create a world like our own, yet unlike. Its trees are ours but their names make them sound as if they are on the verge of communication: the laburnum is *lindeloktë*, 'singing cluster', while *siqilissë*, 'weeping willow', also means 'lamentation' itself. This is a world of *austa* and *yelin*, 'summer' and 'winter'; of *lisēlë*, *piqēlë*, and *piqissë*, 'sweetness', 'bitterness', and 'grief'. But enchantment courses through Qenya: from *kuru* 'magic, wizardry' to *Kampo* the Leaper, a name for Eärendel, and to a whole host of other names for peoples and places that emerged during a couple of years' work on the lexicon. For Tolkien, to a greater extent even than Charles Dickens, a name was the first principle of story-making. His Qenya lexicon was a writer's notebook.

At the start of March, Rob Gilson wrote inviting Tolkien to join Wiseman and himself in Cambridge. Smith was going too, and Gilson was eager to repeat the experience of the 'Council of London'. Ever since that weekend he had been enduring the unaccustomed hardships of military training, living in a hut in an often flooded field, sometimes ill from inoculations, and suffering a growing sense of pessimism. 'I have quite lost now any conviction that the war is likely to end within the next six months,' Gilson wrote home. 'If anyone with a gift of prophecy were to tell me that the war would last ten years, I shouldn't feel the least surprise.' He told Tolkien, 'My whole endurance of the present is founded on the remembrance that I am a TCBSite . . . But another conclave would be the most perfect bliss imaginable.' If Tolkien could not come to Cambridge the following weekend, Gilson would be '*bitterly* disappointed'.

Nevertheless, he did not turn up. On the Saturday the three wired an ultimatum calling on him to appear, or resign from the TCBS. It was not, of course, entirely serious. 'When we sent the telegram,' Wiseman wrote to Tolkien the following week, 'we were groping for the thousand and first time in the dark for a John Ronald of whom there appeared no sound or sight or rumour in any direction . . . It always seems to us odd that you should so consistently be the only one left out of the TCBS.'

'Schools' were fast approaching, and Tolkien had to prepare for ten papers. Most of them covered areas in which he was an enthusiast: Gothic and Germanic philology, Old Icelandic, Old and Middle English language and literature. *Volsunga Saga*, *The Seafarer*, *Havelock the Dane*, *Troilus and Criseyde*: these he should have no trouble with. He had been familiar with some of this material for several years prior to joining the English course at Oxford, and ever since switching from Classics he had been breezily confident about doing well. But a week after the missed Cambridge meeting (as a three-day British offensive failed at Neuve-Chapelle) he headed off for the Easter vacation armed with set texts, and at Edith's in Warwick he worked through the Middle English poem *The Owl and the Nightingale* line by line, making thorough notes on vocabulary (such as *attercoppe*, 'poisonheads', which he later gave to Bilbo Baggins as a taunt against the spiders of Mirkwood).

His other work, poetry, occupied him too. At the end of term Tolkien had again found an audience for his poetry at Exeter College's Essay Club (the club had in fact survived well beyond its November 'last gasp'), which listened to him read 'The Tides', or as he had named his revision of the poem, 'Sea Chant of an Elder Day'. G. B. Smith had seen at least 'The Voyage of Éarendel' in manuscript, but now Tolkien wanted to submit a whole set of poems to the TCBS for criticism. He had typescripts made of various Eärendel 'fragments' and other poems and sent them to Smith at his Magdalen College billets.

Smith was perplexed. As a conservative and a lover of classical form, he found Tolkien's wayward romanticism problematic. He also favoured the new simplicity of *Georgian Poetry*, an influential 1913 anthology edited by Edward Marsh, which included poems by Rupert Brooke, Lascelles Abercrombie, G. K. Chesterton, W. H. Davies, and Walter de la Mare. Accordingly Smith urged Tolkien to simplify the syntax of 'Sea Chant' and others. He advised him to read and learn from 'good authors'; although his idea of a 'good' author was not exactly congruent with Tolkien's. However, he thought the poems 'amazingly good' and showed them to Henry Theodore Wade-Gery, a former Oxford Classics don who was a captain in Smith's battalion and himself an accomplished poet.* Wade-Gery agreed

* Wade-Gery took over as commanding officer of the 3rd Salford Pals from April 1917 to May 1918 and was awarded the Military Cross. He was

that the syntax was occasionally too difficult, but like Smith he strongly approved of this love-poem:

> Lo! young we are and yet have stood
> like planted hearts in the great Sun
> of Love so long (as two fair trees
> in woodland or in open dale
> stand utterly entwined, and breathe
> the airs, and suck the very light
> together) that we have become
> as one, deep-rooted in the soil
> of Life, and tangled in sweet growth.

The parenthetical aside introduces an eloquent delay, as if to suggest the duration of the lovers' growth together before the final clause reveals the result of that long entanglement.

Light as a tangible substance (often a liquid) was to become a recurrent feature of Tolkien's mythology. It is tempting to locate its origin here. It is noteworthy, too, that the Two Trees of Valinor, which were to illumine his created world, had their progenitors here in a poem celebrating his relationship with Edith and in his symbolic drawing *Undertenishness*.

Both Smith and Wade-Gery also favoured a poem written in March called 'Why the Man in the Moon came down too soon', in which Tolkien took a well-known nursery rhyme and retold it at length. The original version is nonsensical:

> The man in the moon
> came down too soon,
> And asked the way to Norwich;
> He went by the south
> And burned his mouth
> With supping cold plum porridge.

---

later Wykeham Professor of Ancient History at Oxford and a fellow of Merton College near the end of Tolkien's professorship there. He published several books on ancient Greek history and literature.

Tolkien's retelling makes sense of the story (thankfully, without sacrificing any of its absurdity). The Man in the Moon acquires both personality and motive, leaving his chill and colourless lunar kingdom because he craves the exuberance of the Earth. In counterpoint to the 'viands hot, and wine' the Man in the Moon desires, his accustomed diet of 'pearly cakes of light snowflakes' and 'thin moonshine' sounds royally unsatisfying. Grandiose latinisms embellish the Man in the Moon's vain imaginings until he is brought down to earth with a bump – or rather a splash. With the help of some deliciously pithy images ('his round heart nearly broke'), the blunter Germanic words help to win him some sympathy.

> He twinkled his feet as he thought of the meat,
>   Of the punch and the peppery stew,
> Till he tripped unaware on his slanting stair,
>   And fell like meteors do;
> As the whickering sparks in splashing arcs
>   Of stars blown down like rain
> From his laddery path took a foaming bath
>   In the Ocean of Almain.

Tolkien is seen at play in the English language. To *twinkle* is to move with a flutter (the *Oxford English Dictionary* cites a dance, the twinkle-step, in 1920), but appropriately it is also to glimmer like stars; *whickering* is the sound of something hurtling through air, but aptly enough it is also sniggering laughter. Of course, the Man in the Moon's adventure ends ignominiously. He is fished out by trawlermen who take him to Norwich, where, instead of a royal welcome, in exchange for his jewels and 'faerie cloak' he gets merely a bowl of gruel.

The poem is a fine example of Tolkien's lightness of touch and as a piece of comic verse marks a great step from the merely parodic 'The Battle of the Eastern Field'. At first it was not connected with the mythological world then being sketched out in the Qenya lexicon; but (as Tom Shippey has pointed out) the extraction of a whole story from six lines of nursery nonsense shows the same fascination with reconstructing the true tales behind garbled survivals that powered Tolkien's myth-making.

Smith welcomed the arrival of another poet in the TCBS and had sent the poems on to Gilson by the end of March. To both John Ronald and Rob he also despatched copies of his own work, a long Arthurian piece called 'Glastonbury' he had written for Oxford University's annual Newdigate Prize and described as 'the most TCBSian mosaic of styles and seasons'.*

There was another abortive attempt to arrange a TCBS meeting, this time in Oxford, where Tolkien would play host at St John Street. It seemed, perhaps, the only way to guarantee his involvement, but just ahead of the appointed date G. B. Smith wrote to say that the 'Council of Oxford' was off: he was at home on sick leave and caught up in a whirlwind attempt to leave the Oxfordshire and Buckinghamshire Light Infantry so that he and Tolkien could be soldiers together.

The battalion had taken him on as a 'supernumerary' in December 1914 because its officer quota was full. It would certainly have no vacancy for Tolkien when he finished Schools. Accordingly, Smith had decided to transfer with Wade-Gery, his favourite among the officers, into another battalion. 'I suppose I have your approval?' he wrote to Tolkien on Easter Monday. An acquaintance at the War Office arranged the transfer to the 19th Lancashire Fusiliers, which was training at Penmaenmawr on Conwy Bay in North Wales. When all was fixed, Smith had to face another week with his existing battalion during which, he said, he would 'think often of the TCBS, possibly to the strains of a Court-Martial'.

He warned, though, that there could be no guarantees of a commission in his new battalion for Tolkien, but advised him, 'You can be sure of getting somewhere in the Army I think,

* The title 'Glastonbury' was prescribed in the rebus for the Newdigate competition, worth about £300 to the winner. (Among the other aspiring Oxford poets who wrote a 'Glastonbury' entry was Aldous Huxley.)

unless things have collapsed by June.' If the war was still under way, Smith said, he could recommend battalions in which his life would not be at great risk and Tolkien could save up to £50 a year for his fiancée. 'I can't help thinking that your prospects afterwards would be improved,' he added, 'unless you could snap up a good thing [a civilian job] at once in June, in which case I should advise you to take it, and let the old country go hang. You can always join a volunteer defence corps, to make your mind easy.'

Smith and Wade-Gery were among a set of 'other literary Oxford lights' who, as Rob Gilson put it, 'had gone in a body to officer the Lancashire Fusiliers'. The move perhaps reflected the mood of 'mucking in together' by people from all walks of life, very different from the rancour and industrial class-strife that had preceded the war. For the battalion Smith was joining was known informally as the 3rd Salford Pals and had just been formed in an industrial suburb of Manchester.* Its rank and file were drawn from towns of the East Lancashire coalfield. The Oxford University men duly took their place as officers beside the bankers and businessmen of Eccles, Swinton, and Salford. The 'Pals' battalions, such as those in Birmingham which Hilary Tolkien, T. K. Barnsley, and Ralph Payton had joined, emerged from the parochial pride and close-knit friendships within English towns and villages, especially in the North: recruits would be largely drummed up en masse from a single place, and groups of friends would be encouraged to join together. It could be a haphazard process: the 3rd Salford Pals consisted of men who had been meant for another Salford unit but had missed the train.

The Lancashire Fusiliers had a fine reputation dating back to the landing of William of Orange in England in 1688, and in the Seven Years War its infantry had shattered the charge of the supposedly invincible French cavalry at Minden. After the

* The 19th Battalion of the Lancashire Fusiliers is usually referred to here as the '3rd Salford Pals' to distinguish it from the three other battalions of the Lancashire Fusiliers that come into this story.

Napoleonic Wars, the Duke of Wellington described it as 'the best and most distinguished' of British regiments. Most recently, during the Boer War, the Lancashire Fusiliers had suffered the heaviest casualties in the disastrous attack on Spion Kop, but had gone on to the relief of Ladysmith.

When G. B. Smith joined the 19th Battalion, the regiment had just etched its name bloodily and tragically in the history books again. As the Oxford term began, on Sunday 25 April 1915, the British-Anzac assault was launched at Gallipoli against the Turkish allies of Germany and Austria-Hungary. The day was a foretaste of thirty-seven weeks to come: a disastrously unequal fight, with British and Anzac troops wading ashore under cruel cliffs surmounted by wire and machine-gun posts. Nevertheless, the worn word 'hero' was being reforged in galvanizing fires. In the forefront of the assault, the Lancashire Fusiliers rowed into a hail of bullets at 'W Beach' on Cape Helles. As they leapt from their boats, seventy pounds of equipment dragged many of the injured to death by drowning. On reaching the shore, others foundered on the barbed wire, which a preceding naval bombardment had failed to break. The beach was secured that day but 260 of the 950 attacking Fusiliers were killed and 283 wounded. In the eyes of many at home, however, the regiment covered itself in glory, and eventually it reaped a historic six Victoria Crosses for that morning on the beach.

Tolkien soon decided he would indeed try to follow Smith into the 19th Lancashire Fusiliers. His reasons are not recorded, but if he succeeded he would be going to war with his closest friend. He would also be surrounded by Oxford men who shared a literary outlook, and (a factor that should not be underestimated) training would take place in Wales, a land whose native tongue was rapidly joining Finnish as an inspiration for his language invention and legend-making.

On the day of the Gallipoli landings, Wiseman wrote to Tolkien to say that he had now read his poems, which Gilson had sent on to him a couple of weeks before. G. B. Smith had commended the verses, but until he saw them for himself Wiseman was far from convinced that his old friend from the Great Twin Brethren had now become a poet. 'I can't think where you get all your amazing words from,' he wrote. 'The Man in the Moon' he called 'magnificently gaudy' and thought that 'Two Trees' was quite the best poem he had read in ages. Wiseman had even gone so far as to start composing an accompaniment to 'Wood-sunshine' for two violins, cello, and bassoon. Plucking a simile from the world at war, he described the ending of another poem, 'Copernicus and Ptolemy', as being 'rather like a systematic and well thought out bombardment with asphyxiating bombs'. Tolkien's poems had astonished him, he said. 'They burst on me like a bolt from the blue.'

FOUR

The shores of Faërie

April 1915, bringing the Great War's first spring, could have been 'the cruellest month' T. S. Eliot had in mind when he wrote *The Waste Land*: halcyon weather, everywhere the stirrings of life, and enervating horror as news and rumour told of thousands of young men dying on all fronts. Closer to home, Zeppelins struck the Essex coast just where the Anglo-Saxon earl Beorhtnoth and his household troop had been defeated by Viking raiders almost ten centuries before. Tolkien, who was now studying that earlier clash between the continental Teutons and their island cousins in the Old English poem *The Battle of Maldon*, was already familiar with the lines uttered by one of Beorhtnoth's retainers as fortune turned against the English:

> Hige sceal þe heardra, heorte þe cenre,
> mod sceal þe mare þe ure maegen lytlað.

As Tolkien later translated it: 'Will shall be the sterner, heart the bolder, spirit the greater as our strength lessens.' Ancient it might be, but this summation of the old Northern heroic code answered eloquently to the needs of Tolkien's day. It contains the awareness that death may come, but it focuses doggedly on achieving the most with what strength remains: it had more to commend it, in terms of personal and strategic morale, than the self-sacrificial and quasi-mystical tone of Rupert Brooke's already-famous *The Soldier*, which implied that a soldier's worth to his nation was greater in death than life:

If I should die, think only this of me:
That there's some corner of a foreign field
That is for ever England.

G.B. Smith admired Brooke's poetry and thought Tolkien should read it, but the poems Tolkien wrote when he settled back in at 59 St John Street at the end of the month could hardly have been more different. On Tuesday 27 April he set to work on two 'fairy' pieces, finishing them the next day. One of these, 'You and Me and the Cottage of Lost Play', is a 65-line love poem to Edith. Hauntingly, it suggests that when they first met they had already known each other in dreams:

You and me – we know that land
  And often have been there
In the long old days, old nursery days,
  A dark child and a fair.
Was it down the paths of firelight dreams
  In winter cold and white,
Or in the blue-spun twilit hours
Of little early tucked-up beds
  In drowsy summer night,
That You and I got lost in Sleep
  And met each other there –
Your dark hair on your white nightgown,
  And mine was tangled fair?

The poem recalls the two dreamers arriving at a strange and mystical cottage whose windows look towards the sea. Of course, this is quite unlike the urban setting in which he and Edith had actually come to know each other. It was an expression of tastes that had responded so strongly to Sarehole, Rednal, and holidays on the coast, or that had been shaped by those places. But already Tolkien was being pulled in opposite directions, towards nostalgic, rustic beauty and also towards unknown, untamed sublimity. Curiously, the activities of the other dreaming children at the Cottage of Lost Play hint at Tolkien's world-building urges, for while some dance and sing and play, others lay 'plans / To build them houses, fairy towns, / Or dwellings in the trees'.

A debt is surely owed to *Peter Pan*'s Neverland. Tolkien had seen J. M. Barrie's masterpiece at the theatre as an eighteen-year-old in 1910, writing afterwards: 'Indescribable but shall never forget it as long as I live.' This was a play aimed squarely at an orphan's heart, featuring a cast of children severed from their mothers by distance or death. A chiaroscuro by turns sentimental and cynical, playful and deadly serious, *Peter Pan* took a rapier to mortality itself – its hero a boy who refuses to grow up and who declares that 'To die will be an awfully big adventure.'

But Tolkien's idyll, for all its carefree joy, is lost in the past. Time has reasserted itself, to the grief and bewilderment of the dreamers.

> And why it was Tomorrow came
>   And with his grey hand led us back;
> And why we never found the same
>   Old cottage, or the magic track
> That leads between a silver sea
>   And those old shores and gardens fair
> Where all things are, that ever were –
>   We know not, You and Me.

The companion piece Tolkien wrote at the same time, 'Goblin Feet', finds us on a similar magic track surrounded by a twilight hum of bats and beetles and sighing leaves. A procession of fairy-folk approaches and the poem slips into an ecstatic sequence of exclamations.

> O! the lights: O! the gleams: O! the little tinkly sounds:
>   O! the rustle of their noiseless little robes:
> O! the echo of their feet – of their little happy feet:
>   O! their swinging lamps in little starlit globes.

Yet 'Goblin Feet' turns in an instant from rising joy to loss and sadness, capturing once again a very Tolkienian yearning. The mortal onlooker wants to pursue the happy band, or rather he feels compelled to do so; but no sooner is the thought formed than the troop disappears around a bend.

> I must follow in their train
> Down the crooked fairy lane
> Where the coney-rabbits long ago have gone,
> And where silverly they sing
> In a moving moonlit ring
> All a-twinkle with the jewels they have on.
> They are fading round the turn
> Where the glow-worms palely burn
> And the echo of their padding feet is dying!
> O! it's knocking at my heart –
> Let me go! O! let me start!
> For the little magic hours are all a-flying.
>
> O! the warmth! O! the hum! O! the colours in the dark!
> O! the gauzy wings of golden honey-flies!
> O! the music of their feet – of their dancing goblin feet!
> O! the magic! O! the sorrow when it dies.

Enchantment, as we know from fairy-tale tradition, tends to slip away from envious eyes and possessive fingers – though there is no moral judgement implied in 'Goblin Feet'. Faërie and the mortal yearning it evokes seem two sides of a single coin, a fact of life.

In a third, slighter, piece that followed on 29 and 30 April, Tolkien pushed the idea of faëry exclusiveness further. 'Tinfang Warble' is a short carol, barely more than a sound-experiment, perhaps written to be set to music, with its echo ('O the hoot! O the hoot!') of the exclamatory chorus of 'Goblin Feet'. In part, the figure of Tinfang Warble is descended in literary tradition from Pan, the piper-god of nature; in part, he comes from a long line of shepherds in pastoral verse, except he has no flock. Now the faëry performance lacks even the communal impulse of the earlier poem's marching band. It is either put on for the benefit of a single glimmering star, or it is entirely solipsistic.

Dancing all alone,
Hopping on a stone,
Flitting like a faun,
In the twilight on the lawn,
And his name is Tinfang Warble!

The first star has shown
And its lamp is blown
To a flame of flickering blue.
He pipes not to me,
He pipes not to thee,
He whistles for none of you.

Tinfang Warble is a wisp of a figure, barely glimpsed. Meanwhile everything about the rather sugar-spun and Victorianesque marching figures of 'Goblin Feet' is miniature; the word 'little' becomes a tinkling refrain. Tolkien was clearly tailoring these poems for Edith, whom he would habitually address as 'little one' and whose home he called a 'little house'. Late in life he declared of 'Goblin Feet' – with perhaps a hint of self-parody – 'I wish the unhappy little thing, representing all that I came (so soon after) to fervently dislike, could be buried for ever.' Nevertheless, although these 1915 'leprechauns' have almost nothing in common with the Eldar of Tolkien's mature work, they represent (with the distant exception of 1910's 'Wood-sunshine') the first irruption of Faërie into Tolkien's writings. In fact the idea that 'fairies' or Elves were physically slight persisted for some years in his mythology, which never shed the idea that they fade into evanescence as the dominion of mortals grows stronger.

Tolkien's April 1915 poems were not especially innovatory in their use of fantasy landscapes and figures; indeed they drew on the imagery and ideas of the fairy tradition in English literature. Since the Reformation, Faërie had undergone major revolutions in the hands of Spenser, Shakespeare, the Puritans, the Victorians, and most recently J. M. Barrie. Its denizens had been noble, mischievous, helpful, devilish; tiny, tall; grossly physical or ethereal and beautiful; sylvan, subterranean, or sea-dwelling; utterly remote or constantly intruding in human affairs; allies of the aristocracy or friends of the labouring poor. This long tradition had left the words *elf*, *gnome*, and *fay/fairy* with diverse and sometimes contradictory associations. Small wonder that Christopher Wiseman was confused by 'Wood-sunshine' and (as he confessed to Tolkien) 'mistook elves for gnomes, with bigger heads than bodies'.

In 'Goblin Feet', goblins and gnomes are interchangeable, as they were in the 'Curdie' books of George MacDonald, which Tolkien had loved as a child ('a strange race of beings, called by some gnomes, by some kobolds, by some goblins'). Initially, Tolkien's Qenya lexicon conflated them as well and related them to the elvish word for 'mole', evidently because Tolkien was thinking of Paracelsus' *gnomus*, an elemental creature that moves through earth as a fish swims in water. Very soon, however, he assigned the terms *goblin* and *gnome* to members of distinct races at daggers drawn. He used *gnome* (Greek *gnōmē*, 'thought, intelligence') for a member of an Elf-kindred who embody a profound scientific and artistic understanding of the natural world from gemcraft to phonology: its Qenya equivalent was *noldo*, related to the word for 'to know'. Thanks to the later British fad for ornamental garden gnomes (not so named until 1938), *gnome* is now liable to raise a smirk, and Tolkien eventually abandoned it.

Yet even in 1915 *fairy* was a problematic term: too generic, and with increasingly diverse connotations. Tolkien's old King Edward's schoolteacher, R. W. Reynolds, soon warned him that the title he proposed for his volume of verse, *The Trumpets of Faërie* (after a poem written in the summer), was 'a little precious': the word *faërie* had become 'rather spoiled of late'. Reynolds was thinking, perhaps, not of recent trends in fairy writing, but of the use of *fairy* to mean 'homosexual', which dated from the mid-1890s.

For now, though, the fate of the word was not yet sealed, and Tolkien stuck pugnaciously to it. He was not alone: Robert Graves entitled his 1917 collection *Fairies and Fusiliers*, with no pun apparently intended. Great War soldiers were weaned on Andrew Lang's fairy-tale anthologies and original stories such as George MacDonald's *The Princess and the Goblin*, and Faërie's stock had surged with the success of *Peter Pan*, a story of adventure and eternal youth that now had additional relevance for boys on the threshold of manhood facing battle. Tinfang Warble had a contemporary visual counterpart in a painting that found a mass-market in Kitchener's Army. Eleanor Canziani's *Piper of Dreams*, which proved to be the belated swansong of the Victorian fairy-painting tradition, depicts a boy sitting alone in a springtime wood playing to a half-seen flight of fairies. Reproduced by the Medici Society in 1915, it sold an unprecedented 250,000 copies before the year was out. In the trenches, *The Piper of Dreams* became, in one appraisal, 'a sort of talisman'.

A more cynical view is that 'the war called up the fairies. Like other idle consumers, they were forced into essential war-work.' A 1917 stage play had 'Fairy voices calling, *Britain needs your aid*'. Occasionally, soldiers' taste for the supernatural might be used to perk up an otherwise dull and arduous training exercise, as Rob Gilson discovered on one bitterly cold battalion field day: 'There was a fantastic "scheme" involving a Witch-Doctor who was supposed to be performing incantations in Madingley Church. C and D Companies represented a flying column sent from a force to the West to capture the wizard.' On the whole, however, the fairies were spared from the recruitment drive and wizards were relieved from military manoeuvres. Faërie still entered the lives of soldiers, but it was left to work on the imagination in a more traditional and indefinable way. Though George MacDonald had urged against attempts to pin down the meaning of fairy-tale, declaring 'I should as soon think of describing the abstract human face, or stating what must go to constitute a human being', Tolkien made the attempt twenty-four years later in his paper 'On Fairy-stories', in which he maintained that Faërie provided the means of recovery, escape, and consolation. The rubric may be illustrated by applying it to the Great War, when Faërie allowed the soldier to recover a sense of beauty and wonder, escape mentally from the ills confining him, and find consolation for the losses afflicting him – even for the loss of a paradise he has never known except in the imagination.

To brighten up trench dugouts, one philanthropist sent specially illustrated posters of Robert Louis Stevenson's poem 'The Land of Nod', with its half-haunting, half-alluring version of fairyland. To raise money for orphans of the war at sea, a *Navy Book of Fairy Tales* was published in which Admiral Sir John Jellicoe noted that 'Unhappily a great many of our sailors and marines (unlike the more fortunate fairies) do get killed in the process of killing the giant.' Faërie as a version of Olde England could evoke home or childhood and inspire patriotism, while Faërie as the land of the dead or the ever-young could suggest an afterlife less austere and remote than the Judaeo-Christian heaven.

Tolkien's new poems, read as the imaginings of a young man on the brink of wartime military service, seem poignantly wistful. He was facing the relinquishment of long-cherished hopes. His undergraduate education was coming to its end in a matter of weeks, but the ever-lengthening war had taken away any immediate chance of settling down with Edith. Hopes of an academic career must be put on hold. As rumour filtered back from the front line, it was growing increasingly clear too that (to paraphrase the famous subtitle of *The Hobbit*) he could not go there and be sure of coming back again.

The rush of creativity was not over, but finally Tolkien adopted a quite different register for 'Kôr', a sonnet of sublimity and grandeur. Kôr was the name of a city in Henry Rider Haggard's *She* (1887), the tale of Ayesha, a woman blessed and cursed with apparently eternal youth. Haggard had been a favourite in the King Edward's library; during the mock school strike of 1911 the sub-librarians called for a ban on 'Henty, Haggard, School Tales, etc . . . that can be read out in one breath'. (The following year

Tolkien had presented the school library with another Haggard-esque 'lost race' yarn, *The Lost Explorers* by Alexander Macdonald.) Tolkien's 30 April poem was subtitled 'In a City Lost and Dead', and indeed Haggard's Kôr is also deserted, the enduring memorial to a great civilization that flourished six thousand years before modern adventurers stumble upon it, but now is utterly lost to memory:

> I know not how I am to describe what we saw, magnificent as it was even in its ruin, almost beyond the power of realisation. Court upon dim court, row upon row of mighty pillars – some of them (especially at the gateways) sculptured from pedestal to capital – space upon space of empty chambers that spoke more eloquently to the imagination than any crowded streets. And over all, the dead silence of the dead, the sense of utter loneliness, and the brooding spirit of the Past! How beautiful it was, and yet how drear! We did not dare to speak aloud.

Both men's versions of Kôr are inhabited only by shadows and stone; but whereas Haggard's is seen, with overt symbolism, under the changeful Moon, Tolkien's city basks under the steadily blazing Sun.

> A sable hill, gigantic, rampart-crowned
> Stands gazing out across an azure sea
> Under an azure sky, on whose dark ground
> Impearled as 'gainst a floor of porphyry
> Gleam marble temples white, and dazzling halls;
> And tawny shadows fingered long are made
> In fretted bars upon their ivory walls
> By massy trees rock-rooted in the shade
> Like stony chiselled pillars of the vault
> With shaft and capital of black basalt.
> There slow forgotten days for ever reap
> The silent shadows counting out rich hours;
> And no voice stirs; and all the marble towers
> White, hot and soundless, ever burn and sleep.

The shift is significant. Haggard's narrator sees the city as a symbol of transience, a *memento mori*, a mockery of its builders' hubristic ambition: Tolkien holds the grandeur and the emptiness of his Kôr in a fine balance. Even empty, his city stands as an enduring tribute to its unnamed inhabitants – a mood that anticipates Moria in *The Lord of the Rings*. Life, though now absent from Kôr, retains its significance. Nihilism is replaced by a consolatory vision.

Tolkien's Kôr differs from Haggard's in other, more tangible ways. It is embattled and built atop a vast black hill, and it stands by the sea, recalling a painting he had made earlier in 1915: the mysteriously named *Tanaqui*. It is clear that Tolkien already had his own vision of a city quite distinct from Haggard's; but his use of the name 'Kôr' now, instead of 'Tanaqui', may be seen as a direct challenge to Haggard's despairing view of mortality, memory, and meaning.

The city of Kôr appears in the Qenya lexicon too, again situated on a shoreland height. Here, though, a more important feature cuts it well and truly adrift from Haggard. Tolkien's Kôr is located not in Africa but in Faërie: it is 'the ancient town built above the rocks of Eldamar, whence the fairies marched into the world'. Other early entries give the words *inwë* for 'fairy' and *elda* for 'beach-fay or *Solosimpë* (shore-piper)'. *Eldamar*, Tolkien wrote, is 'the rocky beach in Western Inwinóre (Faëry), whence the Solosimpeli have danced along the beaches of the world. Upon this rock was the white town built called Kor, whence the fairies came to teach men song and holiness.' In other words, Eldamar is the 'fairy sand' of 'You and Me and the Cottage of Lost Play'. The 'rampart-crowned' city, superhuman in scale, cannot, however, be the work of fairies like J. M. Barrie's Tinkerbell. Barrie and his Victorian predecessors were no more than a starting point for Tolkien, as Haggard had been. These are fairies prone to dancing on beaches, yet not only capable of building enduring monuments but also laden with a spiritual mission. They span the great divide between innocence and responsibility.

But why is Kôr 'a City Lost and Dead' in the poem? The answer appears in notes Tolkien added to his little prose outline about Éarendel's Atlantic voyagings, an outline that clearly preceded

Tolkien's great Adamic works of name-giving. It had referred to a 'golden city' somewhere at the back of the West Wind. Now he added: 'The golden city was Kôr and [Eärendel] had caught the music of the Solosimpë, and returns to find it, only to find that the fairies have departed from Eldamar.' Kôr, in other words, was left empty by the Elves when they 'marched into the world'.

It is a melancholy glimmer of story that, some years later, would form a climactic part of Tolkien's mythological epic. Perhaps the idea owed something to the fact that, in 1915, his familiar haunts were virtually emptied of his peers, who were heading across the sea to fight. If so, Tolkien's vision encapsulated mythological reconstructions and contemporary observation in one multi-faceted symbol.

If these April poems were a sudden spring bloom, then the Qenya Lexicon was root, stock, and bough. It is impossible, and perhaps meaningless, to give exact dates of composition for the lexicon, which was a work in progress during much of 1915 and accrued new words in no discernible order. It was a painstaking and time-consuming labour, and must have been set aside as Schools drew near. On 10 May, though, Tolkien was still musing on his mythology and painted a picture entitled *The Shores of Faëry* showing the white town of Kôr on its black rock, framed by trees from which the Moon and Sun hang like fruit.

From this, Tolkien had to turn to less enticing work: the much-neglected preparation for the two Schools papers he would rather not have had to sit at all. There was Shakespeare's *Hamlet, Antony and Cleopatra*, *Love's Labour's Lost*, and *Henry IV*; and other 'modern' literature such as the works of Christopher Marlowe, John Dryden, and Samuel Johnson, none of which suited his maverick taste.* His preparation for these papers was perfunctory

* In his biography of Tolkien, Humphrey Carpenter overplays Tolkien's dislike of Shakespeare on the evidence of a bombastic piece of school debate polemic. Tolkien disliked *reading* Shakespeare but could enjoy watching *Hamlet* and, as Tom Shippey has argued, his own work was influenced by *Macbeth*. He came to blame Shakespeare for bastardizing the 'fairy' tradition with *A Midsummer Night's Dream*, but 'Goblin Feet' shows that, in 1915, Tolkien had not yet rebelled fully against the Shakespearean approach.

and saw the future Oxford professor of English borrowing introductions to Dryden and Keats from the library, as well as primers in Shakespeare and poetry, as late as the eve of his first paper.

Anxiety about his examinations was dwarfed by the fear of what lay beyond. Writing from Penmaenmawr at the start of June, G. B. Smith reassured him that the war would be over in a matter of months now that Italy had thrown its weight behind Britain and France. Smith, who shared his friend's interest in the language and myth of Wales and had requested he send out a Welsh grammar, added: 'Don't worry about Schools, and don't worry yourself about coming here.' Four weeks would be quite enough time to sort out a place for Tolkien in the same battalion.

On Thursday 10 June, Tolkien started his exams. Just eight men and seventeen women in the whole university were left to endure the anticlimactic flurry of summing up three years' work on English language and literature (or slightly less in Tolkien's case) in ten sittings. In the middle of the ordeal, Smith wrote saying that Colonel Stainforth, his commanding officer (or 'CO'), seemed certain to find space in the 19th Lancashire Fusiliers for Tolkien if he would write requesting a place. Schools finished the next week and Tolkien's undergraduate life was behind him. Now for enlistment, training, and war.

Smith had sent a note on 'matters Martian' – advice on what kit to buy together with a facetious lexicon explaining the application procedure. The most important entry in *Smith's Concise Military Dictionary* ran: '*Worry*: The thing to be avoided. Keep perfectly calm, and everything will settle itself.' The policy worked for GBS, who was now a lieutenant. From Brough Hall, near Catterick Bridge in Yorkshire, where the Salford Pals had moved on midsummer's day, Smith sent the reassuring suggestion, 'Do not be afraid to bring a book or two, and a few paints, but let them be portable.' Smith was now only a few miles to the north of Rob Gilson and the Cambridgeshires, who had marched out of their home town to Lindrick Camp near

Fountains Abbey on 19 June. Gilson's letters had dried up, however, and he was probably unaware of their proximity.

Tolkien was at last catching up with his friends and getting into step with this world in motion, yielding to the pressures he had resisted for almost a year. Unsurprisingly, he wasted no time and, in his own words, 'bolted' into the army. On 28 June he applied at the Oxford recruiting office for a temporary officer's commission 'for the duration of the war'. Captain Whatley of the university OTC sponsored his application and a Royal Army Medical Corps officer pronounced him fit. The form pointed out that there were no guarantees of appointment to any particular unit, but noting Tolkien's preference a military pen-pusher scrawled '19/Lancs Fusiliers' in the top corner.

Tolkien packed up the 'Johnner', his digs in St John Street, and bade farewell to Oxford, perhaps forever. When the English School results were issued, on Friday 2 July, he knew that his commitment to philology had been vindicated and that if he survived the war he would be able to pursue his academic ambitions. Alongside two women and an American Yale scholar, he had achieved First Class Honours. On Saturday the results were published in *The Times* and the next day Smith sent congratulations on 'one of the highest distinctions an Englishman can obtain'. He again urged Tolkien to write to Colonel Stainforth.

After some time with Edith in Warwick, Tolkien went to Birmingham, where he spent part of the next three weeks with his maternal aunt, May Incledon, and her husband Walter, in Barnt Green, just beyond the southern limits of Birmingham – a house he associated with childhood security and early language games with his cousins Marjorie and Mary. Travelling on foot and riding the bus between Edgbaston and Moseley, he was consumed one day in thoughts of his mythology and, in his *Book of Ishness*, he wrote out a poem on 8–9 July entitled 'The Shores of Faëry' opposite his May painting of the same name. It describes the setting of Kôr. Eärendel makes an appearance and, for the first time outside the Qenya lexicon, essential and permanent features of the legendarium are named: the Two Trees, the mountain of Taniquetil, and the land of Valinor.

East of the Moon
West of the Sun
There stands a lonely hill
Its feet are in the pale green Sea
Its towers are white & still
Beyond Taniquetil in Valinor
No stars come there but one alone
That hunted with the Moon
For there the Two Trees naked grow
That bear Night's silver bloom;
That bear the globed fruit of Noon
In Valinor.
There are the Shores of Faery
With their moonlit pebbled Strand
Whose foam is silver music
On the opalescent floor
Beyond the great sea-shadows
On the margent of the Sand
That stretches on for ever
From the golden feet of Kôr
Beyond Taniquetil
In Valinor.
O West of the Sun, East of the Moon
Lies the Haven of the Star
The white tower of the Wanderer,
And the rock of Eglamar,
Where Vingelot is harboured
While Earendel looks afar
On the magic and the wonder
'Tween here and Eglamar
Out, out beyond Taniquetil
In Valinor – afar.

'The Shores of Faëry' is pivotal. Tolkien intended to make it the first part of a 'Lay of Eärendel' that would fully integrate the mariner into his embryonic invented world. He noted on a later copy that this was the 'first poem of my mythology'. The key step forward was that here Tolkien finally fused language and mythology in literary art: the fusion that was to become the wellspring and hallmark of his creative life.

'It was just as the 1914 War burst on me,' Tolkien wrote later, 'that I made the discovery that "legends" depend on the language to which they belong; but a living language depends equally on the "legends" which it conveys by tradition.' The discovery offered a new life for his creation: 'So though being a philologist by nature and trade (yet one always primarily interested in the aesthetic rather than the functional aspects of language) I began with language, I found myself involved in inventing "legends" of the same "taste".'

He had for years been unable to reconcile the scientific rigour he applied in the strictly linguistic aspects of philology with his taste for the otherworldly, the dragon-inhabited, and the sublime that appeared in ancient literatures. It was as an undergraduate, he later said, that 'thought and experience revealed to me that these were not divergent interests – opposite poles of science and romance – but integrally related.'

The *Kalevala* had shown that myth-making could play a part in the revival of a language and a national culture, but it may be that there was a more immediate catalyst. During the Great War, a similar process took place on a vast scale, quite impromptu. For the first time in history, most soldiers were literate, but more than ever before they were kept in the dark. They made up for this with opinion and rumour, ranging from the prosaic to the fantastical: stories about a German corpse-rendering works, a crucified Canadian soldier, and the troglodytic wild men of No Man's Land who, the story went, were deserters from both sides. First World War history is often concerned with assessing the truth and impact of the seemingly more plausible 'myths' that have arisen from it: the 'lions led by donkeys', or the 'rape of Belgium'. From the outset there were also myths of supernatural intercession. Exhausted British troops in retreat from Mons had apparently seen an angel astride a white horse brandishing a flaming sword; or a troop of heavenly archers; or three angels in the sky. The 'Angels of Mons' had forbidden the German advance, it was said. The incident had originated as a piece of fiction, 'The Bowmen' by Arthur Machen, in which the English archers of Agincourt return to fight the advancing Germans of 1914; but it had quickly assumed the authority of fact. At the same time that the war produced myths, the vast outpouring of Great War letters, diaries, and poetry enriched the languages of Europe with new words, phrases, and even registers, subtly altering and defining the perceptions of national character that were so important to the patriotic effort. All this was a living example of the interrelationship between language and myth.

If the early conception of an undying land owes something to *Peter Pan*, as the child's dream-world of 'You and Me and the Cottage of Lost Play' seems to have done, Tolkien's Valinor was less haphazard than Neverland, a version of Faërie that Barrie had filched audaciously from every popular children's bedtime genre, with pirates and mermaids, Red Indians, crocodiles, and pixies. Yet Valinor was broader still in its embrace. Here the Elves lived side by side with the gods, and here mortal souls went after death to be judged and apportioned torment, twilit wandering, or Elysian joy.

The Qenya lexicon translates *Valinor* as 'Asgard', the 'home of the gods' where the Norsemen feasted after they had been slain in battle. Tolkien was undoubtedly developing the conceit that the Germanic Vikings modelled their mythical Asgard on the 'true' myth of Valinor. In place of the Norse Æsir, or gods, are the *Valar*.

In the same spirit, 'The Shores of Faëry' purports to show a glimpse of the truth behind a Germanic tradition as fragmentary and enigmatic as Éarendel's. The mariner's ship in 'The Shores of Faëry' is called *Vingelot* (or *Wingelot*, *Wingilot*), which the lexicon explains is the Qenya for 'foamflower'. But Tolkien chose the name 'to resemble and "explain" the name of Wade's boat Guingelot', as he later wrote. Wade, like Éarendel, crops up all over Germanic legend, as a hero associated with the sea, as the son of a king and a merwoman, and as the father of the hero Wayland or Völund. The name of his vessel would have been lost to history but for an annotation that a sixteenth-century antiquarian had made in his edition of Chaucer: 'Concerning Wade and his boat *Guingelot*, as also his strange exploits in the same, because the matter is long and fabulous, I passe it over.' Tolkien, having read the tantalizing note, now aimed to recreate the 'long and fabulous' story. The great German linguist and folklorist Jakob Grimm (mentioning Wade in almost the same breath as Éarendel) had argued that Guingelot ought to be ascribed instead to Völund, who 'timbered a boat out of the trunk of a tree, and sailed over seas', and who 'forged for himself a winged garment, and took his flight through the air'. Out of this tangle of names and associations, Tolkien had begun to construct a story of singular clarity.

On Sunday 11 July Christopher Wiseman wrote to Tolkien announcing that he was going to sea. In June he had seen a Royal Navy recruiting advertisement saying that mathematicians were wanted as instructors; now he would soon be off to Greenwich to learn basic navigation 'and the meaning of those mysterious words *port*, and *starboard*'. Wiseman proclaimed himself thoroughly jealous of Tolkien's First – he himself had only achieved the grade of *senior optime*, the equivalent of a second-class: 'I am now the only one to have disgraced the TCBS,' he said. 'I have written begging for mercy . . .'

Behind the glib tone, Wiseman was seriously missing his friends. He wished they could get together for a whole fortnight for once. It was manifestly impossible. Smith had written to him repeatedly about an unwelcome sense of growing up. 'I don't know whether it is only the additional weight of his moustache, but I presume there must be something in it,' Wiseman commented. He too felt that they were all being pitched into maturity, Gilson and Tolkien even faster than Smith and himself. 'It seems to proceed by a realization of one's minuteness and impotence,' he mused disconsolately. 'One begins to fail for the first time, and to see the driving power necessary to force one's stamp on the world.'

When Wiseman's letter came, Tolkien was freshly and painfully alive to this process of diminution. On Friday 9 July the War Office had written to tell him he was a second lieutenant with effect from the following Thursday. Kitchener's latest recruit also received a printed calligraphic letter addressed 'To our trusty and well-beloved J.R.R. Tolkien[,] Greeting,' and signed by King George, confirming the appointment and outlining his duties of command and service. But Tolkien's plans had gone awry. 'You have been posted to the 13th Service Battalion Lancashire Fusiliers,' the War Office letter announced.

When Smith heard, four days later, he wrote from Yorkshire, 'I am simply bowled over by your horrible news.' He blamed himself for not slowing Tolkien down in his headlong rush to enlist. Somewhat unconvincingly, he said the appointment might be a mistake, or short-term; but as things turned out he was right to guess that Tolkien would be in less danger in the 13th Lancashire Fusiliers than in the 19th.

Tolkien was not going to rendezvous with the 13th straight away. First he had to take an officers' course in Bedford. He received the regulation £50 allowance for uniform and other kit. Smith had outlined his needs in his discourse on 'matters Martian': a canvas bed, pillow, sleeping-bag and blankets; a bath- and wash-stand, a steel shaving mirror and a soap-box; tent-pole hooks and perhaps a ground-sheet. All this would have to fit in a large canvas kit-bag. In addition he should equip himself with two or three pairs of boots and a pair of shoes; a decent watch; a Sam Browne belt, mackintosh, light haversack and waterbottle; and, most expensive of all, binoculars and prismatic compasses. 'All else seems to me unnecessary,' Smith had said. 'My table and chairs I intend to be soap-boxes bought on the spot, also I mean to buy an honest tin bucket.' Creature comforts, it was clear, were going to be few and far between.

FIVE

Benighted wanderers

Second Lieutenant J. R. R. Tolkien reported to a Colonel Tobin in Bedford's leafy De Parys Avenue on Monday 19 July 1915. The short course was his first taste of 24-hour military life since that windblown camp with King Edward's Horse in 1912. He was in comfortable quarters, sharing a house with six other officers, attending military lectures, and learning how to drill a platoon.

Despite the shock of his appointment, Tolkien held on to the hope of joining the 'Oxford literary lights'. In fact, as Smith noted, he was 'philosophick' about his posting to the 13th Lancashire Fusiliers. It turned out that Colonel Stainforth would be happy to take him on in the Salford Pals. Tolkien must take up his appointed position before he could apply formally for a transfer, wrote Smith, urging '*tact*, *tact*, *tact*'. All depended on the 13th Battalion commander and whether he had enough officers. 'If one keeps one's cool one is always alright,' Smith said. 'After all what does this stupid army matter to a member of the TCBS who has got a first at Oxford?'

The very first weekend of the Bedford course, Tolkien took leave and went back to Barnt Green. Here, on Saturday 24 July, he wrote the decidedly unhappy 'Happy Mariners', in which a figure imprisoned in a tower of pearl listens achingly to the voices of men who sail by into the mystical West. The poem reads like an opening-up of Keats's evocative lines in his 'Ode to a Nightingale' about 'magic casements, opening on the foam / Of perilous seas, in faery lands forlorn'. But the faëry lands lie quite beyond reach, and the magic merely tantalizes. Indeed, the poem follows an arc remarkably similar to that of 'Goblin Feet', with the sea taking the place of the magic road and the mariners passing by like the fairy troop whom the observer is unable to follow. Now, though, Tolkien eschewed all Victorian dainties and wrote about the lure of enchantment using imagery that is both original and haunting.

I know a window in a western tower
That opens on celestial seas,
And wind that has been blowing through the stars
Comes to nestle in its tossing draperies.
It is a white tower builded in the Twilit Isles
Where Evening sits for ever in the shade;
It glimmers like a spike of lonely pearl
That mirrors beams forlorn and lights that fade;
And sea goes washing round the dark rock where it stands,
And fairy boats go by to gloaming lands
All piled and twinkling in the gloom
With hoarded sparks of orient fire
That divers won in waters of the unknown sun:
And, maybe, 'tis a throbbing silver lyre
Or voices of grey sailors echo up,
Afloat among the shadows of the world
In oarless shallop and with canvas furled,
For often seems there ring of feet, or song,
Or twilit twinkle of a trembling gong.—

O! happy mariners upon a journey long
To those great portals on the Western shores
Where, far away, constellate fountains leap,
And dashed against Night's dragon-headed doors
In foam of stars fall sparkling in the deep.
While I, alone, look out behind the moon
From in my white and windy tower,
Ye bide no moment and await no hour,
But chanting snatches of a secret tune
Go through the shadows and the dangerous seas

Past sunless lands to fairy leas,
Where stars upon the jacinth wall of space
Do tangle, burst, and interlace.
Ye follow Eärendel through the West –
The Shining Mariner – to islands blest,
While only from beyond that sombre rim
A wind returns to stir these crystal panes,
And murmur magically of golden rains
That fall for ever in those spaces dim.

These last lines, in which a hint of paradise is borne on the air through intervening rains, read almost like a premonition of Elvenhome as it is seen at the end of *The Lord of the Rings*:

> And the ship went out into the High Sea and passed on into the West, until at last on a night of rain Frodo smelled a sweet fragrance on the air and heard the sound of singing that came over the water. And then it seemed to him that . . . the grey rain-curtain turned all to silver glass and was rolled back, and he beheld white shores and beyond them a far green country under a swift sunrise.

It is remarkable to see such a moment of vision, or partial vision, established decades before Tolkien's epic romance was written.

On the other hand, in the context of what he had put in writing by July 1915, 'The Happy Mariners' contains many apparent enigmas. Some of these are only explicable with the help of the first fully-fledged prose form of Tolkien's mythology, 'The Book of Lost Tales'. Its introductory narrative, written in the winter of 1916–17, mentions 'the Sleeper in the Tower of Pearl that stands far out to west in the Twilit Isles', who was awoken when one of Eärendel's companions in the voyage to Kôr sounded a great gong. Further details resurface in a passage written during the two years after the Great War. Then, the world would be visualized as a flat disc surrounded by the deep blue 'Wall of Things'. The Moon and Sun would pass this wall in their diurnal courses through the basalt Door of Night, carved with great dragon-shapes. The 'sparks of orient fire' won by divers 'in waters of the unknown sun' would be explained as the ancient sunlight scattered during attempts to pilot the new-born Sun beneath the roots of the world at night. As Christopher Tolkien notes, 'The Happy Mariners' was apparently the song of the Sleeper in the Tower of Pearl mentioned in the same passage.

But the story of the Sleeper was never developed, and at this early stage it is not at all clear that Tolkien himself knew exactly what place his images might take within his mythology, any more than he had known exactly who Eärendel was when he first wrote about him. It is possible that in 'The Happy Mariners' these details are seen at the time of their first emergence into his consciousness and that he then set about 'discovering' their significance.

Eärendel's poetic function here is quite different to what it was in 'The Voyage of Éarendel the Evening Star', written ten months earlier. Then, Tolkien had celebrated the star-mariner's daring twilight flight, and the poem had followed him across the night sky. But the speaker in 'The Happy Mariners' is apparently confined in this tower and cannot sail in Eärendel's wake; the twilight is a paralysing veil. Perhaps these differences of viewpoint reflect the change in Tolkien's own situation and mood between defying the rush to arms in 1914 and committing himself now, in 1915, as a soldier. Read this way, the statement that the enviable mariners 'bide no moment and await no hour' looks less opaque, implying that Tolkien, as he began training for war, voiced some of his own anxiety about the future through the figure in the tower of pearl.

The war had now been raging for a year, claiming up to 131,000 British and five million European lives; and there was stalemate on the Western Front, where Germany had just added the flame-thrower to the arsenal of new technologies. Parallels between Tolkien's life and his art are debatable, but the war certainly had a practical impact on him as a writer. Newly bound to military duty, and with the prospect of battle growing suddenly more real, he took action to bring his poetry to light.

He and Smith were set to appear in an annual anthology of

Oxford poetry being co-edited by T. W. Earp, whom Tolkien had known at Exeter College. Each had submitted several poems; 'Goblin Feet' had been chosen for inclusion along with two of Smith's. Tolkien had also sent copies of his work to his old schoolmaster, R. W. Reynolds. 'Dickie' Reynolds had been in the background throughout the public development of the TCBS at school, as chairman of the literary and debating societies as well as the library committee. A mild man of whimsical humour but broad experience, before becoming a teacher he had tried for the Bar and been secretary of the Fabian Society. But in the 1890s he had been part of W. E. Henley's team of literary critics on the prestigious *National Observer*, which had published work by writers of stature including W. B. Yeats, H. G. Wells, Kenneth Grahame, Rudyard Kipling, and J. M. Barrie. Tolkien did not entirely trust Dickie Reynolds' opinions, but he respected the fact that the teacher had once been a literary critic on a London journal, and during the Bedford course Tolkien turned to him for advice on getting a whole collection published. Normally a poet could expect to make his reputation by publishing a poem here and there in magazines and newspapers, but the war had changed all that, Reynolds said. Tolkien should indeed try to get his volume published.*

Tolkien eagerly embraced further opportunities for weekend leave and visits to Edith, riding the fifty miles from Bedford to Warwick on a motorcycle he had bought with a fellow officer. When the course ended in August, he travelled to Staffordshire and joined his 2,000-strong battalion encamped with the four other units of the 3rd Reserve Brigade on Whittington Heath, just outside Lichfield. Apart from the OTC trips of his youth,

* It appears that Tolkien had a running order for the poems he planned to include. Intriguingly, Reynolds told Tolkien, 'On the whole I think I should advise you to accept your friend's offer. Though it is hardly necessary to warn you that you must be prepared for the book to fall very flat.' There is no indication of what this publication offer was.

this was his first experience of a full-scale military camp under canvas. Formed at Hull the previous December, the 13th Battalion of the Lancashire Fusiliers was a 'draft-finding unit', created to drum up fresh soldiers to replace those lost in the front line by other battalions; as such, it would not be the unit in which Tolkien fought. He was one of fifty or so officers with the battalion when he arrived, but he spent most of his time with the handful in the platoon to which he was assigned. Unlike G. B. Smith and Rob Gilson, who were lucky to be with commanding officers they genuinely liked, Tolkien did not find the higher-ranking officers congenial. 'Gentlemen are non-existent among the superiors, and even human beings rare indeed,' he wrote to Edith.

The platoon comprised some sixty men of all ranks. It was the subaltern's duty to pass on what he had learned to the 'other ranks' and prepare them for battle. At this stage the training was basic, and physical. 'All the hot days of summer we doubled about at full speed and perspiration,' Tolkien wrote with chagrin when winter came and these exertions were replaced by chilly open-air lectures. Such was military life in the early twentieth century, and it sharpened Tolkien's dislike of bureaucracy. 'What makes it so exasperating,' he said later of life in camp, 'is the fact that all its worst features are unnecessary, and due to human stupidity which (as "planners" refuse to see) is always magnified indefinitely by "organization".' Elsewhere he was comically precise, declaring that 'war multiplies the stupidity by 3 and its power by itself: so one's precious days are ruled by $(3x)^2$ when x = normal human crassitude'. The diligent, meticulous, and imaginative thinker felt like a 'toad under the harrow' and would vent his feelings in letters, particularly to Father Vincent Reade, a priest at the Birmingham Oratory. Yet in retrospect, as Tolkien told his son Christopher in 1944, this was the time when he made the acquaintance of 'men and things'. Although Kitchener's army enshrined old social boundaries, it also chipped away at the class divide by throwing men from all walks of life into a desperate situation together. Tolkien wrote that the experience taught him 'a deep sympathy and feeling for the "tommy", especially the plain soldier from the agricultural counties'. He remained profoundly grateful for the lesson. For a long time he had been sitting in a tower not of pearl, but of ivory.

Army life could not challenge Tolkien intellectually. His mind would inevitably roam beyond the job at hand – if there was one: 'It isn't the tough stuff one minds so much,' he commented, but 'the waste of time and militarism of the army'. Rob Gilson found time amid his duties to work on embroidery designs for furnishings at Marston Green, his family home near Birmingham; G. B. Smith worked on his poetry, especially his long 'Burial of Sophocles'. Tolkien read Icelandic and continued to focus on his creative ambitions. He later recalled that most of the 'early work' on the legendarium had been carried out in the training camps (and in hospitals, later in the war) 'when time allowed'.

Life in camp appears to have helped Tolkien extend the bounds of his imagined world in a quite direct way. Hitherto, Tolkien's mythological poetry had gazed across the western ocean to Valinor. Now he began to name and describe the mortal lands on this side of the Great Sea, starting with a poem that described an encampment of men 'In the vales of Aryador / By the wooded inland shore'. 'A Song of Aryador', written at Lichfield on 12 September, inhabits the twilight hours that Tolkien already favoured as a time when the enchanted world is most keenly perceived. But now the gulf between fairies and humankind seems vaster than ever. No goblin troop pads happily by, and no piper-fay is glimpsed making ecstatic music. Only, after the sun has gone down, 'the upland slowly fills / With the shadow-folk that murmur in the fern'.

Despite the mountains, the scene perhaps owes something to Tolkien's situation, and even (with poetic exaggerations) to the topography of Whittington Heath, in the Tame valley, with a wood and a lake, and the distant heights of Cannock Chase to the west and the Pennines to the north. This was once the heartland of Mercia, the Anglo-Saxon kingdom that encompassed both Birmingham and Oxford, and with which Tolkien felt a special affinity. Lichfield was the seat of its bishopric and Tamworth, a few miles away, the seat of the Mercian kings.

With its Anglo-Saxon subtitle, *Án léoþ Éargedores*, 'A Song of Aryador' might describe the founding fathers of ancient Mercia.

Tolkien's imagination flew way back before the Mercians, however, and further afield. He looked to the dim era of their ancestors in the wilds of Europe, for this was where his imaginary history dovetailed with the legendary time of the Germanic peoples: the vanishing point where names of half-forgotten significance such as *Éarendel* glimmered like distant beacons.

Aryador is not quite one of those historically attested names that tantalized Tolkien; but it almost is. The Qenya lexicon says that it is the 'name of a mountainous district, the abode of the Shadow Folk', which adds nothing to the enigmatic phrases of the Whittington Heath poem. One of the first bits of Elvish most readers of *The Lord of the Rings* learn is the element *-dor*, 'land', seen in the names *Gondor* and *Mordor*. Strip that away from *Aryador* and we are left with *Arya-*. The Qenya lexicon provides a complex etymology deriving this element from a Primitive Eldarin root; but at the same time it is impossible to miss the resemblance to a real-world name: *Aryan*. Long before it was misapplied by Hitler as an expression of Nordic racial superiority, *Aryan* was the nineteenth-century philological term for proto-Indo-European, the ancestral language of many European and Asian tongues. Linguistic consensus is that the real-world word *Aryan* applies properly only to the Indo-Iranians; but some have found traces of the word in the names of other Indo-European peoples, such as *Eriu*, 'Ireland'. The word is supposed to derive (via Sanskrit) from the prehistoric name of a nation – a name of unknown meaning that puts it in the same tantalizing category as *Éarendel*. A year earlier, Tolkien had 'rediscovered' the star-mariner behind that name, and since then he had invented a language in which the name had a meaning. Now, likewise, he implied that a place-name in Elvish was the ultimate source for Sanskrit *Aryan*. In the process, he 'rediscovered' the inhabitants of *Aryador*, who are presumably to be seen as the speakers of the Indo-European ancestral language.

Many years later, when *The Lord of the Rings* had made him famous, Tolkien expressed his puzzlement and irritation at the many 'guesses at the "sources" of the nomenclature, and theories or fancies concerning hidden meanings' proffered by enthusiastic readers. 'These seem to me no more than private amusements,' he said, dismissing them as 'valueless for the elucidation or interpretation of my fiction'. The true sources of his names, he wished to emphasize, were his own invented languages, the on-going products of decades of painstaking craft. His statements were undoubtedly true in 1967, and reflected his creative practice over the previous two, three, or four decades. They also reflect the fact that chance resemblances will inevitably occur between a large invented vocabulary and words in real languages. But evidence suggests that in 1915, at least, Tolkien did create a small but significant proportion of his Qenya words specifically to show kinship with ancient recorded or reconstructed words. The names of Eärendel and his boat Wingelot have already been cited; Tolkien also stated that he originally derived the name of the 'nectar' of the gods, *miruvōrë*, from Gothic **midu*, 'mead' (the asterisk indicates that this is an unrecorded form deduced by philologists), and *woþeis*, 'sweet'. Other possible examples may be adduced from the Qenya lexicon. The stem *ulband-*, 'monster, giant', must literally mean 'unlovely one', and it descends according to the regular sound-shift laws from a Primitive Eldarin negative UL- /and a derivative of VANA-, the root for words for 'beauty'. But in form, Qenya *ulband-* closely resembles Gothic *ulbandus*, 'camel'. Philologists do not know where *ulbandus* came from, except that English *elephant* came from the same lost word. In Tolkien's fictional linguistic world, the common ancestors of the Goths and Anglo-Saxons had borrowed the word from Qenya. The skein of designations – ugly creature, giant, monster, camel, elephant – implies a whole history of travellers' tales and mistransmission. Tolkien would later write about this in a comic poem, 'Iumbo, or ye Kinde of ye Oliphaunt':

> The Indic oliphaunt's a burly lump,
> A moving mountain, a majestic mammal
> (But those that fancy that he wears a hump
> Confuse him incorrectly with the camel).

Elsewhere in the lexicon, to take a more mundane example, the stem OWO, whence Qenya *oa*, 'wool', suggests the reconstructed Indo-European word **owis*, whence Latin *ovis*, 'sheep', and English *ewe*.

These do not seem to be coincidences; Tolkien was certainly not short of imagination, and produced plenty of Qenya words with no near real-world homonyms. He had a reason to scatter such words throughout his Elvish language. As with *Arya-*, the real-world words he dropped in were frequently ones whose original meaning is now lost. Jakob Grimm had been much exercised by the Irminsûl, a mysterious Germanic totem. In his capacity as a professional philologist, Tolkien later surmised that the old Germanic element *irmin* was a mythological term imported by the migrant Anglo-Saxons and applied to the 'works of the giants' they found in Britain, hence the Roman road name Ermine Street. But the Qenya lexicon entries for *irmin*, 'the inhabited world', and *sūlë*, 'pillar, column', suggest that Tolkien was working towards a fictional explanation for *Irminsûl*. Philologists have derived the Greek and Sanskrit words for 'axe', *pelekus* and *parasu*, from a lost non-Indo-European source; but Tolkien 'rediscovered' that source in the Qenya word *pelekko*. Tolkien also seeded his invented language with words the Indo-Europeans did not borrow, such as *ond*, 'stone', which, he had read as a child, was virtually the only word reconstructed from the lost language of pre-Celtic Britain.

Tolkien meant Qenya to be a language that the illiterate peoples of pre-Christian Europe had heard, and had borrowed from, when they were singing their unrecorded epics. Elves and gods had walked in those epics, and so had dwarves, dragons, and goblins; but only fragments of their stories were written down when literacy and Christianity arrived. Tolkien, with his lexicon of a fictional, forgotten civilization in hand, was now disinterring the fragments and restoring them to life.

The most striking feature of 'A Song of Aryador' is that these tribespeople seem profoundly ill at ease in this *Aryador*, the land from which implicitly they were to derive their name. They are not native at all, but pioneers; intruders at odds with their natural surroundings; benighted wanderers despite their attempts to make a home of the place. In fact, as the Qenya lexicon explains, this is not really their home at all, but 'the abode of the Shadow Folk'. The mortals by the lake shore in the poem seem oblivious to this faint faëry presence, but 'A Song of Aryador' looks to an epoch older still, when humans had not arrived.

  Men are kindling tiny gleams
  Far below by mountain-streams
Where they dwell among the beechwoods near the shore,
  But the great woods on the height
  Watch the waning western light
And whisper to the wind of things of yore,

  When the valley was unknown,
  And the waters roared alone,
And the shadow-folk danced downward all the night,
  When the Sun had fared abroad
  Through great forests unexplored
And the woods were full of wandering beams of light.

  Then were voices on the fells
  And a sound of ghostly bells
And a march of shadow-people o'er the height.
  In the mountains by the shore
  In forgotten Aryador
  There was dancing and was ringing;
  There were shadow-people singing
Ancient songs of olden gods in Aryador.

Clearly, these shadow-people are Elves, perhaps hymning the Valar, the 'olden gods' of Valinor over the western ocean, but they seem to have since been driven into hiding by the intrusion of Men.* Similarly, in Irish myth, the faëry Tuatha Dé Danann retreated underground when the Celts invaded. Tolkien's 'shadow-people' embody the spirit of the natural world. The human interlopers in Aryador are aliens here, blind to its wonders or just plain scared of them.

'I am really angry with myself for the way I have treated all along your invitation to criticize,' Rob Gilson wrote out of the blue in September, breaking months of silence. 'Because I do feel that it is one of the best things the TCBS can possibly do at present. Some day I want to submit a book of designs in like manner.' Gilson had received Tolkien's first batch of poems from G. B. Smith in the spring but had passed them on to Christopher Wiseman a fortnight later without comment. Probably it was neither laziness nor reticence that stopped him, but distraction. At the time, Gilson had been on the brink of one of the defining acts of his short life. In recent years he had spent long holidays with the family of a retired American consul, Wilson King, who was a Birmingham friend of the Headmaster's. The Kings had taken him into their hearts as a dear friend, but Gilson had long ago developed a secret passion for Estelle, Wilson King's English daughter. In April 1915 he had finally revealed his feelings and asked her to marry him. However, she had recoiled in surprise and confusion and her father warned Gilson that he would not countenance her betrothal to a lowly subaltern with no immediate prospects and a war to fight.

Tolkien, it seems certain, knew none of this: the TCBS did not share such confidences. He had only told the others about Edith Bratt when they were at last betrothed over four years after they had fallen in love. He had told Wiseman once that he could not bear 'a compartmented life' in which the TCBS and Edith were unaware of each other. He made efforts to introduce his friends to his fiancée, and they made a fuss of her.

* Tolkien gave further information about the Shadow-folk in 'The Book of Lost Tales' a few years later; see p. 259 below.

(Wiseman once even wrote to Tolkien that the TCBS 'of course includes your missis'.) But in reality romantic love posed a threat to the tight-knit circle. Since his failed declaration to Estelle, Rob Gilson had cut off communication with her; but his letters to the TCBS had apparently ceased too, and Tolkien had appealed in vain for a response to his letters when he wrote to Gilson with news of his commission back in July 1915.

Now, after a long hard summer debating whether to renew his suit to Estelle, Gilson was laid up in hospital in industrial Sunderland, on the north-east coast, recovering from the 'flu and profoundly miserable. He had come with his battalion for a musketry course but now the Cambridgeshires had left for the south of England. In Birmingham his stepmother had heard from Dickie Reynolds about *Oxford Poetry 1915*. Gilson was eager for news of his old friends and wrote, 'I confess that I have often felt that the TCBS seemed very remote. That way lies despair.' He asked Tolkien to send more of his verse, adding, 'I have oceans of time on my hands.'

Tolkien now sent him a second sheaf of his poems and Gilson, feeling revivified by the TCBSian spirit, promised to criticize them. Abruptly, he had learned he was about to be released from hospital, and was going on leave to Marston Green. He determined to visit Tolkien at Lichfield and sent telegrams summoning Smith and Wiseman as well. 'At times like this when I am alive to it, it is so obvious that the TCBS is one of the deepest things in my life,' he told Tolkien, 'and I can hardly understand how I can be content to let slip so many opportunities.' Wiseman came up from Greenwich, where he had begun his navigation course, and Smith travelled from Salisbury Plain, where the Salford Pals were now encamped. Arriving first, Smith and Gilson – now cutting a much thinner figure than in school and college days – visited the cathedral and the birthplace of Dr Johnson. Tolkien joined them, and finally so did Wiseman, and the four stayed at the George Hotel for an evening of 'that delightful and valued conversation which ever illumines a council of the TCBS', as Smith put it. The four were assembled for the last time. It was Saturday 25 September 1915. In northern France, in a foretaste of the battle that lay in store for three of the TCBS, the British army at Loos (including the first Kitchener volunteers) launched an assault so disastrous that, as the attackers turned to retreat, the German machine gunners who had mowed down eight thousand men ceased firing, finally overcome with pity.

On Sunday afternoon the friends repaired to Marston Green and then went their separate ways. By a quirk of military organization, when Gilson rejoined his battalion on Salisbury Plain a week later, disorientated and unhappy, he found his unit on the point of moving to the village of Sutton Veny, a mere five miles up the Wylye Valley from Codford St Mary, where Smith was. A rainy weekend together shopping and eating cheered him immensely. They went to Salisbury and then to the pretty village of Westbury, which, to their great pleasure, was 'almost without soldiers'. Gilson wrote home:

> The rain stopped just as we got there and the evening was beautiful. We walked up on to the top of the bastions of the Plain, and sat down with a wonderful view all around us – greys and dull blues and greens, with wet trees down in the valley all blurred and misty. I drew a little picture of a copse – a thin line of blue trees with a black group of buildings behind it, and the thin straight trunks making a lovely pattern against the sky in the darkening light. G. B. Smith wrote a poem about it some time ago, the one thing I believe of his which is being printed in *Oxford Poetry 1915*, so I gave him the drawing. He read Herrick to me while I drew, and we got miles away from the war.

Smith's poem about the copse was 'Songs on the Downs', a reflection on the Roman road crossing the Plain upon which 'The years have fallen like dead leaves, / Unwept, uncounted, and unstayed . . .' Smith's mood was febrile and fretful, and, reflecting on his imminent coming of age, he wrote darkly to Tolkien: 'The steps I have taken in the direction of growing up have been simply steps farther away from my blessèd days at school, and towards the absolutely unknown, whether it be a business career or a shattered skull.'

He and Gilson laid plans for a TCBS meeting in Bath, a short train ride from the Salisbury Plain camps. They reconnoitred the town as Smith intoned comments in long 'Gibbonian periods', revelling in its eighteenth-century heritage and anticipating the pleasures of a gathering there of the four. Smith, for one, lurched feverishly towards such oases. 'I feel that we shall inevitably enact scenes from *The Rivals* at every street-corner,' he declared. Meanwhile he wanted Tolkien to send copies of his recent poems to show Captain Wade-Gery, the former classics don now in the Salford Pals. Gilson and Smith plotted Tolkien's literary future and urged him to get his poetry off to a publisher such as Hodder & Stoughton or Sidgwick & Jackson.

Tolkien's life was far removed from this kind of companionship, and around the middle of October his battalion moved again, leaving Lichfield for the broad, windswept upland of Cannock Chase, north of Birmingham. The Earl of Lichfield had granted the army use of the Chase, which he owned, at the outbreak of war. In those days, before it was furred over with forestry plantations, it was almost treeless, with a raw, desolate beauty. But a vast, unbeautiful military complex had been grafted on to the face of the heath where the Sher Brook ran off it northwards. On the shallow banks of the stream the army had established Rugeley Camp and its neighbour Brocton Camp, together big enough to process 40,000 men at a time. Grim barrack huts were arranged in straight parallel lines around a complex of parade grounds, above which loomed a square water-tower and a power station whose four chimneys pumped smoke into the sky. German prisoners were held behind wire, watched from guard towers. Hogsbacks of gravel lounged on the surrounding heath, the stop-ends of rifle ranges. Construction work was still in progress when Tolkien's battalion arrived, and it went on until February.

The battalions of the 3rd Reserve Brigade trained here in musketry, scouting, physical training, gas warfare, and other disciplines, including signalling. Concerts and gatherings in cramped YMCA huts provided some social life for the rank-and-file soldiers, but escape was sought as often as possible in the pubs of villages around the Chase; boredom and drink, however, proved an inevitably fractious brew, and discipline was enforced with extra drills and fatigues, or confinement to the guardroom. The winter barracks were bitter with coke fumes and tobacco smoke, mingling oppressively with the smell of boot polish, sweat, beer, rifle-oil, and wet floors.

As a subaltern with the brigade Officers' Company, Tolkien was much better off. In Penkridge Camp, he shared a small officers' hut heated by a stove. Off duty, he could try to close his ears to the sound of marching boots, barked orders, bugles, rifle-fire, and the constant wind in order to work on his expanding Qenya lexicon or his ever more ambitious writings. But during the day there was no escape from the cold, wet weather of the Chase. This was a dark period for Tolkien. 'These grey days wasted in wearily going over, over and over again, the dreary topics, the dull backwaters of the art of killing, are not enjoyable,' he wrote. A typical day was physically unpleasant and mentally enervating:

> The usual kind of morning standing about freezing and then trotting to get warmer so as to freeze again. We ended up by an hour's bomb-throwing with dummies. Lunch and a freezing afternoon . . . we stand in icy groups in the open being talked at! Tea and another scramble – I fought for a place at the stove and made a piece of toast on the end of a knife: what days!

Meanwhile Tolkien had evidently failed to achieve a transfer to Smith's battalion, or had given up trying. Edith was unwell and in Warwick. The war filled him with fear for his friends and for England itself.

The Council of Bath did not take place. On impulse, Smith and Gilson took the train to see Wiseman in London because Tolkien could not make it. Gilson wrote: 'I never before felt quite so keenly the four-squareness of the TCBS. Take one away and it is like cutting a quarter of the canvas from the Granduca

Madonna.' They watched Pinero's *The Big Drum* enjoyably, though only Wiseman actually *liked* it. 'I laughed a little, generally at the right places,' he wrote, 'while Rob and GBS laughed at the wrong places, being of superior dramatic insight.'

Smith and Gilson had sat up late with Wiseman at his Wandsworth home, bemoaning the state of modern theatre. London was full of libidinous soldiers home from the Western Front looking for a 'bit of fun' and leaving 'war babies' in their wake. The Routh Road conclave blamed George Bernard Shaw and Henrik Ibsen for doing away with Victorian prudery but putting nothing in its place to prevent moral freefall. Gilson proposed that feminism would help by banishing the view that 'woman was just an apparatus for man's pleasure'. But they pinned their real reformist hopes on the TCBS itself.

Smith declared that, through art, the four would have to leave the world better than they had found it. Their role would be 'to drive from life, letters, the stage and society that dabbling in and hankering after the unpleasant sides and incidents in life and nature which have captured the larger and worser tastes in Oxford, London and the world . . . to re-establish sanity, cleanliness, and the love of real and true beauty in everyone's breast.' Smith wrote to Tolkien the next day: 'It struck me last night that you might write a fearfully good romantic drama, with as much of the "supernatural" as you cared to introduce. Have you ever thought of it?'

None of these young idealists seems to have baulked at the vast evangelizing task they were setting themselves. Gilson told Tolkien that, sitting in Routh Road, where the inspiration of last year's Council of London hung over them, 'I suddenly saw the TCBS in a blaze of light as a great moral reformer . . . England purified of its loathsome insidious disease by the TCBS spirit. It is an enormous task and we shall not see it accomplished in our lifetime.' Wiseman, who was very modest about his own artistic abilities, was slightly more reserved. 'You and GBS have been given your weapon early and are sharpening it,' he wrote. 'I don't know what mine is, but you shall see it one day. I am not going to be content with a Civil Commission in the TCBS.'

Meanwhile there was the real war to face. If Germany conquered, Wiseman declared, drawing on old school memories for a burst of boyish pluck, 'The TCBS stays in old England and fights the fight as begun in the Richards' matches.'

Despite the crusading language, the TCBSian cultural and moral manifesto did not involve telling people what to do. This is clear from what both Smith and Tolkien were writing. Smith's poetry had always displayed a misanthropic hunger for solitudes of wind and sea; now it occasionally exulted in war as a purgative to wash away the old and stale, revealing a new, better world. Its most biting criticism was aimed at the confident, golf-playing 'sons of culture' and their 'polite laughter', a class-diatribe against the likes of T. K. Barnsley and Sidney Barrowclough, perhaps. Fundamentally, however, what Smith expressed in his poetry was a desire to escape from society, rather than to change it. Tolkien's poems were even less didactic and morally charged, yet Smith was full of praise for the batch he received just before the Routh Road meeting. 'I have never read anything in the least like them,' he wrote back, 'and certainly nothing better than the best. "The Happy Mariners" is a magnificent effort.' If this was the glint of weaponry in the war on decadence, then the TCBSian strategy was indirect, to say the least: inspirational, rather than confrontational.

The Great War was a time of enormous upheaval, when old orders were indeed thrust aside; the desire for a newer, better world was everywhere and took many forms. For the revolutionaries now plotting the downfall of Tsarist Russia, new meant new. For Tolkien, Smith, and Gilson (none of whom shared much of Wiseman's progressive, scientific liberalism), new meant a variety of old. Each had his personal, nostalgic Parnassus: the Anglo-Saxon period, the eighteenth century, the Italian Renaissance. None of these eras had been utopian, but distance lent them a glittering clarity. The twentieth century seemed a fogbound wilderness in comparison, and now civilization truly seemed to have lost its way. It may be that Tolkien was expressing this sentiment in 'The Happy Mariners', which yearns towards a different time and place, the immortal West.

But this was not the escapist urge it appears at first glance. The West of Tolkien's imagination was the heartland of a revolution of sorts: a cultural and spiritual revolution. Like so many of his major ideas, this thought seems to have appeared first in his early lexicon of Qenya. There he had written that it was from Kôr, west over the ocean, that 'the fairies came to teach men song and holiness'. Song and holiness: the fairies had the same method and mission as the TCBS.

'Kortirion among the Trees', a long November 1915 poem and Tolkien's most ambitious work so far, laments the fairies' decline. The Qenya lexicon calls *Kortirion* 'the new capital of the Fairies after their retreat from the hostile world to the Tol Eressëa': to the 'Lonely Isle', implicitly the island of Britain. Aryador might have borrowed from Whittington Heath a few topographical features, but Kortirion *is* Warwick, in a mythic prehistory: 'the city of the Land of Elms, / Alalminórë in the Faery Realms', and Alalminórë is glossed 'Warwickshire' in the Qenya lexicon. However, the lexicon tells us that Kortirion was named after Kôr, the city from which the Elves came over the western sea on their mission into 'the hostile world'. So Tolkien's Elvish history presents a double decline, first from Kôr across the sea to Kortirion, then from Kortirion down the years to Warwick.

This provided an elegant 'explanation' for the presence in fairy-tale tradition of two apparently contradictory versions of Faërie. *The Canterbury Tales* mentions both. Chaucer's Merchant depicts Pluto and Proserpine as the king and queen of fairyland, which is therefore a land of the dead; and here Chaucer was tapping into a tradition in which Faërie is an Otherworld like the Arthurian Avalon, the Welsh Annwn, or the Irish land of eternal youth, Tir-na-Nog. However, the Wife of Bath recalls that, in King Arthur's day, all Britain was 'fulfild of fayerye' and the elf-queen danced in many a meadow; yet now, she says, 'kan no man se none elves mo'; so now Chaucer was drawing on the rival tradition, of a fairyland that once flourished openly in our own mortal world but had since faded from general view. Tolkien's idea was that each of the two traditions could represent a different stage in Elvish history. When Elves dwelt openly here in mortal lands they (or some of them at least) were exiles from an Otherworld Faërie cut off by perilous enchanted seas.

The double decline in Tolkien's Elvish history is matched by two levels of nostalgia. Of Kôr the original and splendid, now empty, Kortirion was merely a consolatory memorial built in defeat. Of Kortirion, modern Warwick knows next to nothing:

> O fading town upon a little hill,
> Old memory is waning in thine ancient gates,
> Thy robe gone gray, thine old heart almost still;
> The castle only, frowning, ever waits
> And ponders how among the towering elms
> The Gliding Water leaves these inland realms
> And slips between long meadows to the western sea –
> Still bearing downward over murmurous falls
> One year and then another to the sea;
> And slowly thither have a many gone
> Since first the fairies built Kortirion.

The lengthy 'Kortirion' gave Tolkien room to make the most of his imagery. Trees yield some extraordinary extended metaphors: trunks and foliage are seen as masts and canvas on ships sailing off to other shores, and the wind-loosed leaves of autumn are likened to bird wings:

> Then their hour is done,
> And wanly borne on wings of amber pale
> They beat the wide airs of the fading vale
> And fly like birds across the misty meres.

The image anticipates Galadriel's song of farewell in *The Lord of the Rings*: 'Ah! like gold fall the leaves in the wind, long years numberless as the wings of trees!' The Ents of Fangorn Forest are a long way off, but already in 'Kortirion' tree and leaf are far more than objects of beauty: they count the seasons, they sail or soar away, they entangle the stars.

In this 1915 poem, Tolkien struck the first note of the mood that underpins his entire legendarium: a wistful nostalgia for a world slipping away. The spring and summer represent the lost past when Elves walked England openly. Winter is the harbinger of mortality:

> Strange sad October robes her dewy furze
> In netted sheen of gold-shot gossamers,
> And then the wide-umbraged elm begins to fail;
> Her mourning multitudes of leaves go pale
>   Seeing afar the icy shears
>   Of Winter, and his blue-tipped spears
> Marching unconquerable upon the sun
> Of bright All-Hallows.

More immediate concerns, perhaps, also register in Tolkien's poem. The summer to which 'Kortirion' looks back may be seen as a symbol of both childhood and the pre-war past, and winter, with his on-coming army, as the uniquely lethal future allotted to Tolkien's generation.

However that may be, the poem confesses that autumn/winter 'is the season dearest to my heart, / Most fitting to the little faded town'. This seems a paradox, but 'fitness', the accord of symbol and meaning, was essential to Tolkien's aesthetics, as can be seen from the careful matching of sound to sense in his invented languages. Another young soldier-poet, Robert Graves, said during the Great War that he could not write about 'England in June attire' when 'Cherries are out of season, / Ice grips at branch and root'. But 'Kortirion' actually discovers beauty in the way the autumn embodies the evanescence of youth or elfinesse.

The overriding metaphor of the seasons also provides a note of consolation, suggesting not only loss and death but also renewal and rebirth. To similar effect, the fairies of faded Kortirion sing a 'wistful song of things that were, and could be yet'. Thus it is not sadness that finally prevails in 'Kortirion' but an acceptance approaching contentment.

The mood is most apparent in the poem's sense of rootedness. In contrast to Éarendel or the envious figure in 'The Happy Mariners', the voice hymning Kortirion concludes that it has no desire for adventure:

> I need not know the desert or red palaces
> Where dwells the sun, the great seas or the magic isles,
> The pinewoods piled on mountain-terraces . . .

The sentiment is central to Tolkien's character. Later, when he had put the years of enforced wandering behind him, he rarely travelled far except in his imagination. It was landscape and climate more than political statehood that fired his idea of nationalism. The spirit of place, so potent in Tolkien's mythology, seems to have emerged fully fledged just as the subaltern poet was swept into a life outdoors and on the move: his eye was sharpened, but so was his longing for home, which Warwick had come to embody. Stray workings for this latest poem (relating to the army of winter) suggest that he may have begun the poem shortly after arriving at Penkridge Camp, with its grey waste, its boredom and its grind. But Tolkien created the Elf-haunted town of Kortirion from life when, following army inoculations, he spent a week of frost and clear skies with Edith in Warwick. On his return to camp, he sent her a copy of the poem and then wrote out another, despatching it at the end of November to Rob Gilson for circulation among the TCBS.

'I am now 21 years of age, and cannot help doubting whether I shall ever be 22,' G. B. Smith had written from Salisbury Plain in mid-October. 'Our departure for France is almost within sight. The King is going to inspect us shortly. I hope he will be duly impressed by this member of the TCBS.' The Salford Pals were waiting to move out along with eleven other battalions, including Ralph Payton's and Hilary Tolkien's, all of which belonged to a single vast army division encamped around Codford St Mary. In November, Smith worked hard to finish a long poem of his own, 'The Burial of Sophocles', before embarkation. He rushed home to West Bromwich to say goodbye to his widowed mother and dined at Codford for the last time with Gilson, who wrote: 'It is impossible for us to tell him all the hopes and wishes and prayers that the first TCBSite to set forth carries with him . . . I feel that this is a memorable day in TCBSian history.'

The day had already come for some of those who had belonged to the TCBS before the Council of London. Sidney Barrowclough had sailed with the Royal Field Artillery in September for Salonica, the staging-post for British troops fighting in the Balkans. T. K. Barnsley, who had switched his ambitions from the Methodist ministry to professional soldiering, was now in the trenches with the élite Coldstream Guards, having transferred from the Warwickshires in August. Smith, waiting to go as the first of the 'foursquare' TCBS, wrote to Tolkien:

> We are now so pledged to see the matter through, that no reasoning or thinking about it will do anything except waste time and undermine resolution. I often thought that we should be put to the fiery trial: the time is almost upon us. If we emerge, we emerge victorious, if not, I hope I shall be proud to die for my country and the TCBS. But who knows what is hidden in the black darkness between now and the spring? It is the most anxious hour of my life.

On 21 November 1915, in rain and biting wind, Lieutenant G. B. Smith paraded at the head of his platoon on the Wiltshire downs and then took the train to Southampton. After a night crossing to Le Havre, shadowed by a British destroyer, Smith and the Salford Pals marched off the blacked-out troop ship *Princess Caroline* onto beleaguered French soil.

On 2 December, following a week of route marches, GBS wrote from the front to say that he had visited the trenches 'to the peril of neither body or soul'. He was cheerful, if somewhat overworked. Far more distressing to him than the trenches was the fact that somewhere on the journey he had lost his great poem, 'The Burial of Sophocles'. Military censorship prevented him from pinpointing his position, but in fact he was in Albert, near the River Somme, an area that would become darkly familiar to Tolkien and notorious in history.

Ever since joining the army in July, Tolkien had turned his attention away from Kôr and the Otherworld over the sea and had focused on Kortirion and mortal lands, where the elves are a fading, elusive 'shadow-people'. But Tolkien's wartime poem 'Habbanan beneath the Stars' was peopled by the figures of men and was set neither in England nor in Aryador. He later recalled that it was written either at Brocton Camp in December 1915, or the following June in the massive transit camp at Étaples on the French coast. Either way, it seems apt that the poem should depict an encampment of men.

> There is a sound of faint guitars
> And distant echoes of a song,
> For there men gather into rings
> Round their red fires while one voice sings –
> And all about is night.

The Qenya lexicon describes Habbanan simply as 'a region on the borders of Valinor', and prior to the post-war 'Lost Tales' there is no further elucidation of its significance.

But there is a spiritual and religious dimension to Tolkien's world, never absent though rarely blatant, that was notably pronounced in his original conceptions. Side by side with terms for different Elvish tribes in the lexicon are words for 'saint', 'monastery', and 'crucifixion', 'nun', 'gospel', and 'Christian missionary'. There is even a Qenya aphorism, *perilmë metto aimaktur perperienta*, 'We indeed endure things but the martyrs endured and to the end' – an interesting perspective from a member of the Great War generation. The Valar who rule

Valinor, or 'Asgard', are only gods in pagan eyes: in reality they are angels under 'God Almighty, the creator who dwells without the world'. Although Tolkien later refined this religious element, and in *The Lord of the Rings* made it all but invisible to the inattentive eye, he never removed it from his conception of Middle-earth.

The religious dimension helps to explain how the elves could come to 'teach men song and holiness'. Tolkien's conviction at this time appears not to have been far different from the view he propounded later in his essay 'On Fairy-stories': that although myths and fairy-tales contradicted the Christian story, they were not lies. Because they were the work of human beings 'sub-creating' in emulation of their own Creator, he felt that they must contain seeds of the truth. The idea was not entirely new, and had been expressed the other way round by G. K. Chesterton in his 1908 essay 'The Ethics of Elfland': 'I had always felt life first as a story: and if there is a story there is a story-teller.' Before Christ, in Tolkien's benighted Aryador, myth and Faërie would have been as close to that truth as the wandering peoples of Europe could attain. The Elvish religious mission, then, can be seen as a metaphor for the enlightening impact of fairy-stories.

In literal terms, however, the Elves come from Kôr, which abuts the land of the Valar: they have lived alongside the angels. Tolkien's synthesis of human supernatural beliefs is staggeringly ambitious. Habbanan, which also borders Valinor, is the place 'where all roads end however long' this side of Heaven itself. It is a vision, perhaps, to console those facing death: the Christian purgatory seen through a faëry glass.

> There on a sudden did my heart perceive
> That they who sang about the Eve,
> Who answered the bright-shining stars
> With gleaming music of their strange guitars,
> These were His wandering happy sons
> Encamped upon those aëry leas
> Where God's unsullied garment runs
> In glory down His mighty knees.

SIX

Too long in slumber

Tolkien had always been fascinated by codes and alphabets, and in his teens had made many of his own – the beginning of a lifelong passion. Once in the army, he decided to specialize in signals, in which cryptography played a small part. Training would be more interesting and he would be playing to his strengths, putting his unusual aptitudes at the army's disposal. Consciously or otherwise, he was also boosting his chances of surviving the war, which would be poor indeed at the head of a routine patrol or an attacking platoon in No Man's Land. It is a strange thought that, without such decisions, children might never have heard of Bilbo Baggins, or Winnie-the-Pooh either, for that matter: elsewhere in the army, a subaltern called A. A. Milne also opted to be a signaller quite consciously to save his skin. But Milne also called signalling 'much the most interesting work in the infantry, with the great advantage that one is the only officer in the Battalion who knows anything about it, and is consequently one's own master – a great thing to a civilian in the Army'.

By late December 1915, when the 13th Lancashire Fusiliers had shifted from Penkridge Camp to the neighbouring Brocton Camp, Tolkien was engrossed in cryptanalytic exercises and scribbling his workings on the backs of envelopes. But of course signalling was not just about making and breaking codes. The more mechanical aspect of the job dealt with ways of transmitting the coded message, and so Tolkien learned how to signal to an observer with semaphore flags, or with Morse 'dots' and 'dashes' flashed out with a lamp by night or with a heliograph by day. For longer-distance work, or for times when flashing a light was inadequate or dangerous, he had to master the use and maintenance of a field telephone. The other two items in his armoury were rather less sophisticated: rockets and carrier pigeons. He also learned map-reading and took part in the usual military manoeuvres on Cannock Chase. It was a bitter place to call home in the middle of winter, and he was miserable.

Rob Gilson's fears of being sent to France or Flanders had been banished before Christmas by rumours that they were off to Egypt and by the issuing of desert kit. 'Imagine the general rejoicing at the awakening from our long nightmare of the cold, wet, muddy, and worst of all, the ragtime, trenches,' he wrote to Tolkien on Boxing Day. But that day the Cambridgeshires had been ordered to relinquish their sun-helmets, and their hopes. 'The whole world looks gray again. It is worse than ever for the sunny dream that has intervened.'

Gilson soon rallied. His long anguish over Estelle King had come to an end. His stepmother Donna, learning that Estelle wished to see him before he left, had brought them face to face for the first time since his disastrous April proposal. At the end of November, Gilson had renewed his petition and she had returned his love. Proud and head-over-heels, he desperately wanted to tell his friends but refrained at the request of Estelle, whose parents still forbade any formal engagement. However, she heard all about the TCBS, and when 'Kortirion among the Trees' reached Gilson on Salisbury Plain he promised he would one day show her Tolkien's poetry. As 1916 came in he told her: 'What a wonderful year! I expected nothing but wretchedness and I have found —! I wish I were a poet and then I might be able to express myself.'

The same day Christopher Wiseman, now a naval officer with two gold stripes on his arm, reported for duty in Scotland, where he joined the HMS *Superb* at Invergordon on 2 January. 'Then I plunge myself into the middle of 870 other mortals, about whom I know nothing, and who know and care nothing about me,' he had written to Tolkien. His arrival was more alarming than he feared. The battleship was berthed with its squadron in Cromarty Firth, where a mysterious explosion had just sunk an armoured cruiser, killing more than three hundred seamen. Amid suspicions that a German submarine was hunting in the Firth, the big ships were ringed by their torpedo nets, which hung suspended forty feet out from the vessels' flanks. To board the *Superb*, Wiseman had to climb up a rope ladder and along the boom straddling the shielded gap.

Gilson was promoted to lieutenant and sailed for France on 8 January 1916 – the same day, coincidentally, that Estelle King took ship for Holland as a volunteer nurse. He wrote to her: 'I wish I could describe or draw for you the lovely sunrise we watched this morning from the train – like one of the Bellinis in the National Gallery, with Salisbury Plain standing up against the sky, bounded by a lovely velvety black line . . . It is a long time since I have felt the sheer beauty of things so strongly. It really seems for the moment more like a holiday.' He promised that, when the war was over, they would travel to his beloved Italy together. He carried with him a New Testament and the *Odyssey*, both in Greek.

Tolkien had just turned twenty-four. In the space of seven weeks, all three of his dearest friends had gone to war. In the midst of it all, *Oxford Poetry 1915* had been published, containing his poem 'Goblin Feet'. A thousand copies were printed, and it marked the first time a piece of his writing had reached a wider audience than school or college.

A critic in the *Oxford Magazine* reflected that no Pope or Tennyson held sway now: 'The idols have fallen . . . The pedestal stands empty.' Some of the poets were exploring new modes of expression, such as *vers libre*, and new subjects, such as motor-bikes and (in the case of T. W. Earp of Exeter College) mechanical cranes, the anonymous reviewer noted approvingly; and he was pleased to see that the old conventions of love poetry, the language of 'christal eyes and cherrie lippes', had been exhausted.

From France, G. B. Smith opined vigorously that the reviewer ought to be shot. 'The truth is,' he told Tolkien, 'that everything which is prosaic and noisy passes nowadays as being clever.' He assured Tolkien that 'Goblin Feet' read splendidly, though he added that it was far from being his best work. More than two weeks later, on 12 January, Smith was still cursing that 'terrible fellow' Earp. By that time Gilson had forwarded 'Kortirion' to him. Smith was living in a trench dugout and had been attached to a battalion of professional soldiers for instruction;* he was feeling lost and incompetent, he said, but was uplifted by Tolkien's 'great and noble poem'. He wrote:

> I carry your last verses . . . about with me like a treasure . . . You know as well as I do, my dear John Ronald, that I don't care a damn if the Bosch drops half-a-dozen high explosives all round and on top of this dugout I am writing in, so long as people go on making verses about 'Kortirion among the Trees' and such other topics – that indeed is why I am here, to keep them and preserve them . . .

After eighteen months' anticipation, Rob Gilson had his first taste of the trenches on 2 February a few miles south of Armentières, in the lowland of canals and poplars near the Belgian border. 'It is a strange and dreary looking place – wasteland and shattered trees and houses,' he told Estelle. 'What most impresses me at first is the appalling expenditure of human labour on merely hiding each other from each other's devilishness. I had never grasped it with my imagination. It is one of the very saddest sights I have ever seen.' At one point Gilson had an absurd vision of his younger self – the cultured and fastidious undergraduate who had thought 'the real business of life' was touring Normandy churches with a sketchbook – seeing the soldier he had now become crawling on his belly in a French

* The unit to which Smith was attached temporarily in Thiepval Wood on the Somme was the 2nd Manchesters, in which the war poet Wilfred Owen later served and died.

field on a wet winter's night. Out in the middle of No Man's Land, he had to suppress a guffaw.

The same week, and fifty miles away, Smith (now back with his own battalion) faced patrol with the benefit of neither comedy nor novelty. He had spent half the ten weeks since reaching France either in the trenches or close behind them, but this was the worst stretch of line the Salford Pals had experienced. A hundred yards of the frontline trench, together with all the protecting barbed wire, had been blown in during heavy bombardment just before they arrived. They had to post men in shell holes to guard the line while going out again and again under cover of darkness to put up new wire. Enemy patrols were on the prowl every night and there had been clashes: an officer who was leading a British scouting party on 2 February had attacked with grenades and gunfire but had been wounded. The next day the battalion's bombing officer led another group out and did not come back.

'A good friend of mine has been wounded on patrol and captured by the Germans. God knows if he is still living,' Smith wrote as he prepared to set out into No Man's Land that night. Face to face with death, he urged Tolkien,

> My dear John Ronald, publish by all means. I am a wild and whole-hearted admirer, and my chief consolation is, that if I am scuppered to-night – I am off on duty in a few minutes – there will still be left a member of the great TCBS to voice what I dreamed and what we all agreed upon. For the death of one of its members cannot, I am determined, dissolve the TCBS. Death is so close to me now that I feel – and I am sure you feel, and all the three other heroes feel, how impuissant it is. Death can make us loathsome and helpless as individuals, but it cannot put an end to the immortal four! . . .
>
> Yes, publish – write to Sidgwick and Jackson or who you will. You I am sure are chosen, like Saul among the Children of Israel. Make haste, before you come out to this orgy of death and cruelty . . .
>
> May God bless you, my dear John Ronald, and may you say

> the things I have tried to say long after I am not there to say them, if such be my lot.

Patrols went out with blackened faces, armed like thieves with clubs and knives, and would crawl along at a rate of perhaps forty yards an hour until they had covered their allotted stretch of No Man's Land. Smith returned safely with all three of his men that night, having seen and heard nothing of the enemy, and lived to lead further patrols. Later, a Turkish flag was hoisted above the enemy trench: clearly the Germans had learned from their captive that they faced the Lancashire Fusiliers and aimed to discomfort them with a reminder of their fruitless losses at Gallipoli. But Smith's captured friend, a nineteen-year-old called Arthur Dixon, was never seen again; he died the next day of wounds sustained during the encounter in No Man's Land and was buried behind German lines.

Within a week Tolkien wrote to Smith announcing that he had submitted his collection of poems, *The Trumpets of Faërie*, to Sidgwick & Jackson. Smith cautioned him not to raise his hopes, and when he realized that 'Kortirion' had not been submitted pressed him to send it off. 'I remember how your first verses perplexed me,' Smith wrote. 'I am glad to say I see now that my criticism of them was just.'

'Kortirion' was taken to heart by all the TCBS. Ever the most hesitant, Rob Gilson suggested it had 'too many precious stones' but said the poem had frequently cheered him up during hours of dull routine. But Christopher Wiseman wholeheartedly shared Smith's view. 'I am immensely braced with it,' he wrote in February from the *Superb*, now with the Grand Fleet at Scapa Flow. 'You seem to have got out of underground caverns full of stalactites lit up with magnesium wire . . . I used to be afraid you would never write anything but freak poetry, however clever it might be, and however beautiful the effect . . . But Kortirion seems to me to be as "John Ronaldian" as ever, but less "freakish".'

Prior to this breakthrough, in other words, Tolkien had been labouring, with too much artifice, after the strange and the unfamiliar. Wiseman was right about the breakthrough. There are qualitative differences between 'Kortirion among the Trees' and – to take a quartet of 1915 poems that mark four points on the Tolkienian compass – the formal 'Why the Man in the Moon came down too soon'; the faery 'Goblin Feet'; the heraldic 'Shores of Faëry'; and the psychological 'Happy Mariners'. The first of the four is a virtuoso metrical and verbal performance built around a slight joke: an accomplished piece of light entertainment. The second is a generic faëry piece, standing self-consciously apart from the mainstream: it looks like an act of defiance against the stylistic experimentation and quotidian subject-matter that dominated *Oxford Poetry 1915*. The third is startling, to be sure, but less like a piece of literature than a symbolist painting (which is how it started), with stark emblems and strange names unmediated by commentary or characterization. The fourth, paralysed, fearful, and introspective, suggests a deeply troubled state of mind. Each of these poems might be described as 'freakish' in its way.

'Kortirion' follows each of these four directions to some extent, but largely avoids their pitfalls. Like the earlier 'Man in the Moon' it is technically brilliant, but it is not the case that 'there was more form than content about it', as R. W. Reynolds said of the later poem: its expansive structure allows its symbolic core to be explored from all angles, and gives breathing-space for meditation and the modulation of feeling. 'Kortirion' is a generic piece of faëry writing like 'Goblin Feet', but it also embraces the broader tradition of English landscape writing. Like 'The Shores of Faëry', it depicts mysterious peoples and places, but the brush-strokes are intimate and naturalistic, the invitation to explore is more enticing, and the location is real. Finally, like 'The Happy Mariners', 'Kortirion' may be seen as a window onto a psychological state, but now the claustrophobia is banished, the mind expands, and the mood moves towards reconciliation with reality, 'a haunting ever-near content' with the fading year.

Understandably, Tolkien was hurt to hear his best friend apparently dismiss the bulk of his work as 'freakish'. He accused Wiseman of a lack of sympathy with his primary inspirations: the glory of the night, the twilight and stars. Wiseman returned that Tolkien failed to appreciate 'the grandeur of the glare of the noon'. They were talking in metaphors: Tolkien's imagination was fired by vast mysteries and remote beauty, but Wiseman was enthralled by the human endeavour unravelling the riddles of the universe. The argument drew a dividing line between the medievalist, mystical, Catholic Tolkien and the rationalist, humanist, Methodist Wiseman. But Wiseman relished the fight. 'Old days, Harborne Road and Broad Street again,' he wrote. 'A grand old quarrel! . . . Such openness in speech is what has kept the TCBS together for so long.' He now confessed to long-suppressed reservations about Tolkien's entire project:

> You are fascinated by little, delicate, beautiful creatures; and when I am with you, I am too. So I do sympathize with you. But I feel more thrilled by enormous, slow moving, omnipotent things, and if I had greater artistic gifts I would make you feel the thrill too. And having been led by the hand of God into the borderland of the fringe of science that man has conquered, I can see that there are such enormous numbers of wonderful and beautiful things that really exist, that in my ordinary frame of mind I feel no need to search after things that man has used before these could fill a certain place in the sum of his desires.

Tolkien was far from pacified. He responded that his own work expressed his love of God's creation: the winds, trees, and flowers. His Elves were a way of expressing it, too, primarily because they were *creatures*, things created. They caught a mystical truth about the natural world that eluded science, he said, insisting that 'the Eldar, the Solosimpë, the Noldoli are better, warmer, fairer to the heart than the mathematics of the tide or the vortices that are the winds.' Wiseman countered:

> I say they are not. Neither are good warm or fair. What is good, warm and fair, is your creating one and the scientist creating the other. The completed work is vanity; the process of the working is everlasting. Why these creatures live to you is because you are still creating them. When you have finished creating them they will be as dead to you as the atoms that make our living food, and they will only live when you or I go through your process of creation once more. How I hate you when you begin to talk of the 'conquests of science'! Then you become just like the inartistic boor in the street. The 'conquests' vanish when they are made; they are only vital in the making. Just as the fugue is nothing on the page; it is only vital as it works its way out.

But he drew a line under the altercation, writing: 'I am very sorry indeed if I have hurt you. The precise form of abnormality which your work took seemed to me to be a fault, which, as far as I could see, you were gradually and consciously eliminating. And now I have said far too much. Indeed we all have.'

Christopher Wiseman was not alone in doubting the value of Faërie. Whatever the TCBSian creed was, it was not founded on a fascination with the supernatural. Rob Gilson confided to Estelle King that he was 'lacking in the strings that ought to vibrate to faint fantastic fairy music'. He thought such music strayed from the real theme on which the best art elaborated: 'I like to say and to hear it said and to feel boldly that the glory of beauty and order and joyful contentment in the universe is the presence of God . . . I love best the men who are so certain of it that they can stand up and proclaim it to the world. That is why I love Browning so dearly . . . Heaven knows I have not that great certainty myself.'

G. B. Smith was closely attentive to Tolkien's vision, and in some measure shared it (despite his avowed antipathy to romanticism), just as he shared a delight in Arthur and the Welsh cycle of legends, the *Mabinogion*. Smith saw no demarcation between holiness and Faërie. One of his own poems,

'Legend', has a monk returning from a morning's stroll during which he listened, transfixed, as a bird sang 'diviner music / Than the greatest harpers made',

> Sang of blessed shores and golden
>   Where the old, dim heroes be,
> Distant isles of sunset glory,
>   Set beyond the western sea.
>
> Sang of Christ and Mary Mother
>   Hearkening unto angels seven
> Playing on their golden harp-strings
>   In the far courts of high Heaven.

Back at the monastery, none of the other monks recognizes him. After he has retreated to a cell they discover that he has crumbled to dust: he had set off on his stroll a hundred years previously and strayed into a timeless Otherworld. But the bird's song is Tolkien's, too: the shores of Faërie may not be Heaven, but they are illuminated by it.

Wiseman was mistaken to think that Tolkien was at heart an anti-rationalist. There was a strain of scientific curiosity and discipline in his work, in the development of Qenya on rigorous phonological principles. Although this took place behind the scenes in the pages of a lexicon, it was the reason why Tolkien wanted to make myths: to give life to his language. Wiseman was wrong, too, in supposing that Tolkien's gaze was turned away from humankind. In pursuing the link between language and mythology, Tolkien was acting upon his revelation, kindled by the *Kalevala* and perhaps by war, that human language and human beliefs were intimately bound up together.

The mythology surrounding Tolkien's poems had not yet coalesced; no wonder they seemed strange and disconnected from one another, like inconclusive forays into an unfathomably vast subterranean complex. None of the many TCBS letters discussing his work mentions an 'epic' or 'mythology' until 1917.

Yet Wiseman knew enough from Tolkien by now not to baulk at invented clan-denominations of Faërie such as 'the Eldar, the Solosimpë, the Noldoli'. Taken together, the poems hinted at the bigger picture, if you squinted; but in conversation Tolkien could reveal still more of the mythology he had sketched out in his lexicon.

Every language draws its vital force from the culture it expresses, and English received an enormous jolt of electricity from the new technologies and experiences of the Great War. Old words received new meanings; new words were coined; foreign phrases were bastardized. *Air raids* were deterred by captive balloons or *blimps*, a portmanteau-word (Tolkien opined) formed from *blister* and *lump* in which 'the vowel *i* not *u* was chosen because of its diminutive significance – typical of war humour'. Servicemen, who had a nickname for everyone and everything, utilized this changed language in its most concentrated form. Smith casually used *Bosch* (French *Boche*) for 'German'; but Gilson relished his role as upholder of inflexible English, proclaiming from his *cushy* spot in the *front line*: 'I fully intended to eschew trench slang when I came out here – it is particularly obnoxious – but I never hoped to persuade a whole mess to do the same. If anyone here refers to "Huns" or "Bosches" or "strafing" . . . he is severely sat upon.' Britain was *Blighty* (from Hindi), and a *blighty* was a wound serious enough to bring you home. The flares used for observation and signals, Very lights, were inevitably dubbed *Fairy lights*. Tolkien was surrounded by wordsmiths. But soldiers' slang, which spanned death, drink, food, women, weapons, the battlefield, and the warring nations, grew out of irony and contempt for what was intolerable; it was as crude and unlovely as camp life itself.

Qenya thrived in the same soil, but not in the same mood. Nothing could be further removed from the unbeautiful inflexible practicalities Tolkien was being taught than the invention of a language for the joy of its sounds. It was a solitary and shy pleasure, but in fact he discovered he was not the only member of Kitchener's army engaged in the 'secret vice'. One day, sitting through a military lecture 'in a dirty wet marquee filled with trestle tables smelling of stale mutton fat, crowded with (mostly) depressed and wet creatures' (as he recalled in a talk on inventing languages), he was exploring the further reaches of boredom when a man nearby muttered, as if in reverie, 'Yes, I think I shall express the accusative case by a prefix!' Tolkien tried to prise from the soldier more about this private grammar, but he proved 'as close as an oyster'.

Tolkien, too, usually kept his hobby to himself, or else made light of it; so he would write to Edith: 'I have been reading up old military lecture-notes again:– and getting bored with them after an hour and a half. I have done some touches to my nonsense fairy language . . .' But Qenya was a serious matter to him, and the 'touches' he made to it in March meant he could write poetry in it: the crowning achievement. He had attempted to do so back in November, but he had produced no more than a quatrain paraphrasing the lines in 'Kortirion among the Trees' in which falling leaves are likened to bird-wings. Now he expanded it to a full twenty lines.

Having brought Qenya to this stage of sophistication, and having submitted his poetry to the publishers, Tolkien had brought his mythological project to a watershed. Undoubtedly he pondered his next move, but he knew embarkation could not be far off and personal matters required his attention before he left England. This may therefore be an appropriate point to survey, albeit tentatively, the state of the mythology at the time that Tolkien went to war.

Enu, whom men refer to as *Ilūvatar*, the Heavenly Father, created the world and dwells outside it. But within the world dwell the 'pagan gods' or *ainur*, who, with their attendants, here are called the *Valar* or 'happy folk' (in the original sense of 'blessed with good fortune'). Few of them are named: notably *Makar* the god of battle (also known as *Ramandor*, the shouter); and the *Sūlimi* of the winds; *Ui*, who is queen of the *Oaritsi*, the mermaids; and *Niëliqi*, a little girl whose laughter brings forth daffodils and whose tears are snowdrops. The home of the Valar is *Valinor* or 'Asgard', which lies at the feet of lofty, snow-capped *Taniqetil* at the western rim of the flat earth.

Beside Valinor is the rocky beach of *Eldamar*, once home of the Elvish *Eldar* or *Solosimpë*, the beach-fays or shoreland-pipers. The royal house of the fairies, the *Inweli*, was headed by their ancient king, *Inwë*, and their capital was the white town of *Kôr* on the rocks of Eldamar. Now it is deserted: Inwë led the fairies dancing out into the world to teach song and holiness to mortal men. But the mission failed and the Elves who remained in *Aryador* (Europe?) are reduced to a furtive 'shadow-people'.

The *Noldoli* or Gnomes, wisest of the faëry tribes, were led from their land of *Noldomar* to the Lonely Isle of *Tol Eressëa* (England) by the god *Lirillo*. The other fairies retreated from the hostile world to the island, which is now called *Ingilnōrë* after Inwë's son *Ingil* (or *Ingilmo*). In *Alalminórë* (Warwickshire), the land of elms at the heart of the island, they built a new capital, *Kortirion* (Warwick). Here the goddess *Erinti* lives in a circle of elms, and she has a tower which the fairies guard. She came from Valinor with Lirillo and his brother *Amillo* to dwell on the isle among the Elvish tribes in exile. Now the fairy pipers haunt the beaches and weedy sea-caves of the island; but one, *Timpinen* or *Tinfang Warble*, pipes in the woods.

The name *Inwinórë*, Faërie, was used by Tolkien for both Eldamar and Tol Eressëa. The Elves are immortal and they drink a liquid called *limpë* (whereas the Valar drink *miruvōrë*). They are generally diminutive, some especially so: a mushroom is known as a 'fairy canopy', *Nardi* is a flower fairy, and likewise *Tetillë*, who lives in a poppy. Are such beings as these, or the sea-nymphs, akin to the 'fairies' who built Kôr? It is impossible to judge from the evidence of Qenya at this stage. *Qenya* is only one of several elvish languages; the lexicon also lists dozens of words in another, *Gnomish*.

Sky-myths figure prominently side-by-side with the saga of the Elvish exile to the Lonely Isle/England. Valinor is (or was?) lit by *the Two Trees* that bore the fruit of Sun and Moon. The Sun herself, *Ur*, issues from her white gates to sail in the sky, but this is the hunting ground of *Silmo*, the Moon, from whom the Sun once fled by diving into the sea and wandering through the caverns of the mermaids. Also hunted by the Moon is *Eärendel*, steersman of the morning or evening star. He was once a great mariner who sailed the oceans of the world in his ship *Wingelot*, or Foamflower. On his final voyage he passed the Twilit Isles, with their tower of pearl, to reach Kôr, whence he sailed off the edge of the world into the skies; his earthly wife *Voronwë* is now *Morwen* (Jupiter), 'daughter of the dark'. Other stars in *Ilu*, the slender airs beyond the earth, include the blue bee *Nierninwa* (Sirius), and here too are constellations such as *Telimektar* (Orion), the Swordsman of Heaven. The Moon is also thought of as the crystalline palace of the Moon King *Uolë·mi·Kūmë*, who once traded his riches for a bowl of cold Norwich pudding after falling to earth.

Besides wonders, there are monsters in these pages too: *Tevildo* the hateful, prince of cats, and *Ungwë·Tuita*, the Spider of Night, whose webs in dark *Ruamōrë* Earendel once narrowly escaped. *Fentor*, lord of dragons, was slain by *Ingilmo* or by the hero *Turambar*, who had a mighty sword called *Sangahyando*, or 'cleaver of throngs' (and who is compared to Sigurðr of Norse myth). But there are other perilous creatures: *Angaino* ('tormentor') is the name of a giant, while *ork* means 'monster, ogre, demon'. *Raukë* also means 'demon' and *fandor* 'monster'.

The fairies know of Christian tradition with its saints, martyrs, monks, and nuns; they have words for 'grace' and 'blessed', and mystic names for the Trinity. The spirits of mortal men wander outside Valinor in the region of *Habbanan*, which in the abstract is perhaps *manimuinë*, Purgatory. But there are various names for hell (*Mandos*, *Eremandos*, and *Angamandos*) and also *Utumna*, the lower regions of darkness. The souls of the blessed dwell in *iluindo* beyond the stars.

It is curious – especially in contrast to his later, famous writings – that Tolkien's own life is directly mythologized in these early conceptions. He left his discreet signature on his art, and at times the lexicon is a *roman à clef*. The Lonely Isle's only named locations are those important to him when he began work on it: Warwick, Warwickshire, Exeter (*Estirin*), after which his college was named, and Oxford itself (*Taruktarna*). Possibly we see John Ronald and Edith in Eärendel and Voronwë, but Edith is also certainly represented by Erinti, the goddess who presides aptly over 'love, music, beauty and purity' and lives in Warwick, while Amillo equates to Hilary Tolkien. John Ronald was perhaps declaring his own literary ambitions as Lirillo, god of song, also called *Noldorin* because he brought the Noldoli back to Tol Eressëa.* Tolkien's writings, he may have been hinting, would signal a renaissance for Faërie.

War also intrudes. Makar the battle god seems to have been one of the first named Valar. As well as describing the natural world, Qenya furnishes a vocabulary for wartime. Almost all of this accords with the sense that the mythology takes place in the ancient world (*kasien*, 'helm'; *makil*, 'sword'); but some of it smells distinctly twentieth-century. One could easily enumerate features of the trenches: *londa-*, 'to boom, bang'; *qolimo*, 'an invalid'; *qonda*, 'choking smoke, fog'; *enya*, 'device, machine, engine'; *pusulpë*, 'gas-bag, balloon'. Entirely anachronistic is *tompo-tompo*, 'noise of drums (or guns)': an onomatopoeia, surely, for the deep repercussive boom and recoil of heavy artillery, but not, one would think, a word Tolkien could use in his faëry mythology.

Particularly striking is how Qenya at this stage equates Germans with barbarity. *Kalimban* is '"Barbary", Germany'; *kalimbarië* is 'barbarity', *kalimbo* is 'a savage, uncivilized man, barbarian. – giant, monster, troll', and *kalimbardi* is glossed 'the Germans'. There is a strong sense of disillusionment in these definitions, so devoid of the attraction Tolkien had felt towards 'the "Germanic" ideal' as an undergraduate. He lived in a country wracked with fear, grief, and hatred, and by now people he knew had been killed by Germans.

---

* February, the month of Hilary Tolkien's birth, is named *Amillion* after Amillo; but Tolkien had to split January in two so he could name the second half, *Erintion*, in honour of Edith's birthday (21 January) and the first half, *Lirillion*, in honour of his own (3 January).

The concept of the devilish Germans was popular, not least among some military minds. For many, it was increasingly difficult to remain high-minded, especially when in 1916 Germany adopted the slaughter of enemy soldiers as a key strategy in a new 'war of attrition'. On 21 February a furious assault was unleashed against Verdun, a fortress that held special symbolic significance in the French national consciousness because it barred the road to Paris from the east. It did not matter whether or not Verdun was captured, the Kaiser had been advised: in trying to defend it France would pour in its troops and 'bleed to death'. Thousands upon thousands on either side were now dying in the pitiless siege.

Knowing he could be called to fight overseas any time now, Tolkien could wait no longer to be married to Edith: he found the situation 'intolerable'. The prospects for both of them were grim. As he summed it up later, 'I was a young fellow, with a moderate degree, and apt to write verse, a few dwindling pounds p.a. (£20–40), and no prospects, a Second Lieut. on 7/6 a day in the infantry where the chances of survival were against you heavily (as a subaltern).'* He sold his share in the motorbike he jointly owned with a fellow officer and went to see Father Francis Morgan in Birmingham to make further financial arrangements. When it came to telling him that he was to marry Edith, the subject of his guardian's ban six years previously, his nerve failed. He delayed until two weeks before the event, and Father Francis's conciliatory offer of an Oratory wedding came too late. He was also worried about how his friends would react. But G. B. Smith, writing back to wish them both the best, reassured him: 'My goodness, John Ronald, nothing could ever cut you off from the TCBS!' Wiseman gently chided him for imagining that the three would disapprove and declared that, 'on the contrary, the TCBS heartily approves, in the full belief that you are not likely to be "foolish" in these matters'. Gilson

* In real terms today, up to £1,480 a year and about £14 a day.

was taken aback when he heard, and wrote home, 'The imminence of the date is a complete surprise to me, as all his movements nearly always are.' But he was genuinely pleased for his friend: 'I rejoice many times for your sake that you are thus able to raise yourself out of this mire of existence.'

To Estelle King, Gilson confided his sympathy for Tolkien's lot, explaining that his friend had lost both parents and had 'always had something of a wanderer's life'. Tolkien was contemplating that same fact when he returned to Oxford for his long-delayed degree ceremony on Thursday 16 March 1916. That day he started a long new poem, continuing it when he returned to Warwick: 'The Wanderer's Allegiance'. Correspondence aside, it is the most overtly personal of Tolkien's published writings. The mythology was in abeyance. It is perhaps no coincidence that Tolkien experimented in this more conventional direction in the midst of his argument with Wiseman about the 'freakishness' of his other poetry.

A prelude depicts an unidentified landscape of orchard, mead, and grassland settled by 'my father's sires'; which, if Wiseman read it right, is to be taken literally as a description of Tolkien's paternal ancestors in ancient Germania.

> There daffodils among the ordered trees
> Did nod in spring, and men laughed deep and long
> Singing as they laboured happy lays
> And lighting even with a drinking-song.
> There sleep came easy for the drone of bees
> Thronging about cottage gardens heaped with flowers;
> In love of sunlit goodliness of days
> There richly flowed their lives in settled hours . . .

But Tolkien's roots in Saxony lie in the remote past, and he is an 'unsettled wanderer' in Britain, where the scene shifts to Warwick and Oxford.

In Warwick's fourteenth-century keep, the Norman earls lie as if in a blissful reverie, silently rebuked by the passing seasons.

No watchfulness disturbs their splendid dream,
Though laughing radiance dance down the stream;
And be they clad in snow or lashed by windy rains,
Or may March whirl the dust about the winding lanes,
The Elm robe and disrobe her of a million leaves
Like moments clustered in a crowded year,
Still their old heart unmoved nor weeps nor grieves,
Uncomprehending of this evil tide,
Today's great sadness, or Tomorrow's fear:
Faint echoes fade within their drowsy halls
Like ghosts; the daylight creeps across their walls.

'Tomorrow' here is not just age, as it had been in 'You and Me and the Cottage of Lost Play', but the dreadful prospect of battle that Tolkien and his peers faced. Against this terrible upheaval, the 'old lords too long in slumber lain' represent a deceptive continuity, an inertia that rolls unheeding through the changing years. They are complacent, unadaptable, and incapable of vigilance. We may catch a hint of the anger shared by many of Tolkien's generation, whose world seemed to have been consigned to disaster by the negligence of their elders.

But if so, Tolkien was conscious that he too had been dreaming. 'The Wanderer's Allegiance' takes a distinctly different view from 'Kortirion among the Trees', in which he had proclaimed his sense of 'ever-near content' in Warwick. For in his new poem he wrote:

Here many days once gently past me crept
In this dear town of old forgetfulness;
Here all entwined in dreams once long I slept
And heard no echo of the world's distress.

Now he had grasped the urgency of the moment, as his official graduation, his attempt at publication and his marriage all demonstrate. After the wedding Edith was going to stay as close as possible to him, and would be leaving Warwick: 'The Wanderer's Allegiance' bids the town and its dreams goodbye.

Tolkien was no mere nostalgist. The passing of time was the subject of a constant internal debate: part of him mourned what was gone and part of him knew change was necessary. In the Oxford of this poem, the past achieves an ideal status, not embalmed and half-forgotten, but vitally alive and full of significance for today.

> Thy thousand pinnacles and fretted spires
> Are lit with echoes and the lambent fires
> Of many companies of bells that ring
> Rousing pale visions of majestic days
> The windy years have strewn down distant ways;
> And in thy halls still doth thy spirit sing
> Songs of old memory amid thy present tears,
> Or hope of days to come half-sad with many fears.

In contrast to Warwick's inertia, Oxford shows true continuity, based on academic erudition and the perpetual renewal of its membership.

On a personal level, memories of undergraduate life crowd in. Tolkien, whose stays in Warwick were private, domestic, and circumscribed, had been the most sociable of Oxonians: understandably he used the university to symbolize lost fellowship and the tragedy of the war. The past is unnervingly present, so that in a visionary moment the intervening years or months are swept aside:

> O agéd city of an all too brief sojourn,
> I see thy clustered windows each one burn
> With lamps and candles of departed men.
> The misty stars thy crown, the night thy dress,
> Most peerless-magical thou dost possess
> My heart, and old days come to life again . . .

Despite its elegant use of autobiographical material for symbolic purposes, 'The Wanderer's Allegiance' is not altogether successful. Wiseman told Tolkien it was not 'quite up to your usual standard' and said the Oxford passage was unworthy of 'the greatest city but London in the Empire of England'. A more serious flaw is that its attempt to locate consolation and hope in the university city seems merely wishful when its Belgian counterpart, Louvain, had been all but destroyed. The final optimistic assertion sounds a trifle shrill:

> Lo! though along thy paths no laughter runns
> While war untimely takes thy many sons,
> No tide of evil can thy glory drown
> Robed in sad majesty, the stars thy crown.

The wanderer pledges allegiance to learning, living memory, and alertness, but (understandably) invests them with an unrealistic impregnability.

Wiseman felt there was an 'apparent lack of connection' between the sections of the poem and said, 'I am left hung up at the end between the Tolkienian ancestors taking root in Germany, and the Norman feudalists of the Castle while the author is still, as I know to my cost, an unsettled wanderer.' But Oxford and Warwick seem to symbolize two responses to temporal change – responses that now appear to be mutually incompatible but which had co-existed blissfully in ancient Saxony. Without booklore, Tolkien's remote Saxon ancestors had sung the 'Songs of old memory' now remembered in Oxford (at least in the English department); simultaneously they had listened to the pulse of the seasons without drifting into a static slumber like the Warwick nobles. The poem describes a fall into division of being.

What goes unmentioned is Saxony's situation in the Great War, the fate of Tolkien's relatives there, or how his ancestry affected Tolkien's patriotic allegiance to England (with its Norman aristocracy). The poem never sets out to deal with these subjects, but inevitably they hover around it.

* * *

Tolkien remained in Warwick after completing the poem. On Wednesday 22 March 1916 he and Edith were married at the Roman Catholic church of St Mary Immaculate, near Warwick Castle. It was Lent: accordingly, they could only take part in the Marriage Service, and not the Nuptial Mass that would otherwise have followed. They spent a week's honeymoon in the windswept village of Clevedon on the Severn Estuary during which they visited the caves at Cheddar. When they returned to Warwick, Tolkien found a letter from Sidgwick & Jackson informing him that they had decided not to publish *The Trumpets of Faërie*. He now faced the possibility that he might be killed with all his extraordinary words unheard.

Meanwhile, Edith had little chance to see her new husband. Within a month of their wedding he was in Yorkshire taking a course at a signals school run by the army's Northern Command at Farnley Park, Otley, and was away for several weeks of training and tests. On practical matters his performance was mediocre: using a lamp he could signal at six words per minute, but the average speed was between seven and ten words. He did well in the written test and on map reading, however, and on 13 May he was issued with a provisional certificate permitting him to instruct army signallers. Tolkien left the same day for Warwick, having been given just two of the four days' leave he had requested.

Edith was now leaving the town for good. Tolkien's battalion duties meant that they could not live together, but they had decided that Edith would take rooms as near as possible to his camp. Accordingly, she moved with her cousin Jennie Grove into the home of a Mrs Kendrick in Great Haywood, an attractive village on a beautiful stretch of the River Trent just below the northern shoulders of Cannock Chase. Across the Trent lay the manorial elegance of Shugborough Park, the seat of the Earls of Lichfield. An old and narrow packhorse bridge with fourteen arches spanned the stream here where it took in the waters of the River Sow. At Great Haywood the newlyweds received a nuptial blessing at the Roman Catholic church of St John the Baptist, in front of a Sunday congregation who (amid the national atmosphere of moral turpitude the TCBS so detested) seemed convinced that they had so far been living in sin.

On the Somme, the squirming misery of the winter mud had given way to an incongruous renascence of anemones, poppies, bluebells, and cowslips. In some snatched moment of tranquillity, G. B. Smith had written:

> Now spring has come upon the hills in France,
> And all the trees are delicately fair,
> As heeding not the great guns' voice, by chance
> Brought down the valley on a wandering air ...

Smith had sent home for a copy of the *Odyssey*, and the compartmentalized life continued in his letters to Tolkien, which dwelt almost exclusively on the poetry for which he fought, not on trench life itself – though he had mentioned a narrow escape on April Fool's Day when an aeroplane deposited two bombs nearby. Censorship was not the reason: usually only details of troop movements were suppressed. Smith simply preferred (like many soldiers) to keep the horror and exhaustion out of his letters. But he longed for the company of his old friends: 'I wish another council were possible ... All the TCBS is ever in my thoughts, it is for them I carry on, and in the hope of a reunion refuse to be broken in spirit,' he had written some time ago. A council of the four remained impossible, but now the opportunity came for a reunion with Tolkien.

The week after Tolkien's signals course ended, a telegram announced that Smith was back at home. The two quickly arranged to meet and, on the last Saturday of May 1916, a train carrying Smith pulled into Stafford station. Eight months had passed since the friends last met at Lichfield. Smith stayed overnight at Great Haywood, and for most of the Sunday too, eking out the splendid reunion as long as he could. 'Nothing could have been more reassuring or more encouraging and inspiring than to see once again a TCBSite in the flesh and realise that he had changed not at all,' Smith wrote on returning to his battalion in France. 'Me I have no doubt you found different: more tired and less vigorous: but neither, I firmly believe, have I changed in any one vital particular. The TCBS has not shirked its plain duty: it will never shirk it: I am beyond words thankful for that.'

The plain duty of the TCBS entailed the relinquishment of pleasure, and perhaps life itself, as Smith wrote in his spring poem:

> There be still some, whose glad heart suffereth
> All hate can bring from her misbegotten stores,
> Telling themselves, so England's self draw breath,
> That's all the happiness on this side death.

This was a fellowship founded on laughter, schoolboy pranks, and youthful enthusiasms. At times, happiness seemed to live in the past, in the tea room at Barrow's Stores, in the library cubby-hole at King Edward's, or even in the Governor's Room, sitting exams as the master paced silently up and down behind their backs and the smell of tar drifted in from New Street. 'The real days', a dejected Wiseman called them, 'when one felt oneself to be somebody, and had something to substantiate the feeling, when it was possible to get something done, such as win a match or act a play or pass an exam, the most important things that ever can be done . . .' Doubtless Tolkien, busily creative and newly married, felt rather differently about the value of his life since leaving school. Nevertheless, he saw the TCBS as an 'oasis' in an inhospitable world.

Yet the Tea Club was now much more than a refuge. As well as hilarity and good conversation, TCBSianism had come to mean fortitude and courage and alliance. Smith, displaying his weakness for bombast, had once likened the four to the Russian army battling vastly superior German and Austro-Hungarian forces ('the most magnificent spectacle Europe has seen for generations', as he called it). But the TCBS had absorbed patriotic duty into its constitution not simply because its members were all patriots. The war mattered because it was being fought 'so England's self draw breath': so that the inspirations of 'the real days' of peace might survive.

One facet of their duty was not so plain. Somewhere along the line the TCBS had decided it could change the world. The view had been born on the rugby pitch in the spirited exploits of Wiseman and Tolkien, the Great Twin Brethren. It had grown during the battle to wrest control of school life from boorishness and cynicism – a prolonged struggle from which the TCBS had emerged victorious. The ejection of 'Tea-Cake' Barnsley and the vapid, irony-obsessed members of the TCBS had left the Council of London free to reaffirm the society's sense of mission. Tolkien had told them that they had a 'world-shaking power', and (with the occasional exception of the more cautious Gilson) they all believed it.

Now they felt that, for them, the war was only the preparation for the task that lay in store. It was a 'travail underground' from which they would emerge enriched, Gilson said. 'I have faith,' he ventured, 'that the TCBS may for itself – never for the world – thank God for this war some day.' Smith observed that 'Providence insists on making each TCBSian fight his first battles alone', and Wiseman underlined the fortifying virtue of the divine scheme. 'Really you three, especially Rob, are heroes,' he wrote. 'Fortunately we are not entirely masters of our fate, so that what we do now will make us the better for uniting in the great work that is to come, whatever it may be.'

All this might sound like so much hot air, were it not for two considerations. These young men were gifted members of a gifted generation; and they included in their 'republic' of equals a genius whose work has since reached an audience of millions. When orders arrived on Friday 2 June instructing him to travel to Folkestone for embarkation overseas, Tolkien already believed that the terrors to come might serve him in the visionary work of his life – if he survived.

* * *

There was no fanfare when he left Cannock Chase. In contrast to his friends, who had marched out of their training camps with their entire divisions of more than 10,000 men, Tolkien went alone: his training battalion stayed at home and sent men out as and when the fighting battalions of the Lancashire Fusiliers needed reinforcements.

Tolkien was given forty-eight hours for his 'last leave'. He and Edith went back to Birmingham, where on Saturday they spent a final night together at the Plough and Harrow Hotel in Edgbaston, just down the road from the Oratory and Father Francis. The house in Duchess Road where he and Edith had met as lodgers was minutes away. Visible across the street was the Highfield Road house where he had lived with Hilary after contact with Edith was banned.

Late on Sunday 4 June, 1916, Tolkien set off for the war. He did not expect to survive. 'Junior officers were being killed off, a dozen a minute,' he later recalled. 'Parting from my wife then . . . it was like a death.'

PART TWO

Tears unnumbered

SEVEN

Larkspur and Canterbury-bells

It was the darkest hour of the war so far for Tolkien. So it was for the Allies too. France had been bleeding at Verdun for fifteen pitiless weeks. Ireland, meanwhile, was simmering after the failed Easter Rising against British rule. But on Saturday 3 June 1916, newspapers proclaimed the biggest blow so far to British self-confidence. The Grand Fleet had finally met the German navy in battle and, it seemed at first, had got the worst of it.

Guiltily, Christopher Wiseman had come to enjoy life aboard his vast 'Dreadnought' warship, much of it spent at anchor in Scapa Flow. The Navy breed were contemptuous of landlubbers like himself; he was teetotal, whereas many of the officers seemed to live for drink; and they spoke without moving their lips. But there were occasional trips to the town of Kirkwall on Orkney or, weather permitting, rounds of golf on the tiny island of Flotta. Once, indulging his passion for archaeology, Wiseman led an expedition to explore the prehistoric barrow of Maes Howe. Teaching was also becoming something of a hobby, even though the trainee midshipmen in his care, colourfully known as 'snotties', proved intractable. He taught them mathematics, mechanics, and navigation, but like a true TCBSian he also tried to plug the gap in their literary education. 'The Snotty,' he told Tolkien, 'is the stupidest boy in existence, and withal the most conceited. However, I like them all very much . . .' Occasionally the *Superb* would sweep the North Sea up to Norway, but the Germans were never to be seen: the naval blockade was working, and the sole danger seemed to be boredom.

But on 31 May 1916, the 101st day of the Battle of Verdun, Germany's High Seas Fleet ventured out of port and Britain's Grand Fleet took the bait, racing out from Scapa Flow to meet them off the coast of Denmark. Wiseman was set to oversee the *Superb*'s range-finding table. Early in the evening the *Superb* fired off several salvoes at a light cruiser over 10,000 yards away and flames were seen to burst out amidships. Surely this was a palpable hit, and the German vessel had been sunk. But no, it was afterwards seen, still in one piece, by ships astern. Again an hour later the *Superb* opened fire and struck home on the third and fourth salvoes; the enemy ship turned away, burning. The gunnery commander, who could see the battle with his own eyes, doubted many of Wiseman's calculations; but the mist and the smoke of confrontation meant the fleets were fighting half-blind, and mathematics came into its own.

If the *Superb* had been hit, the decks, which had no airtight compartments, would have swiftly flooded from prow to stern, as Wiseman was only too conscious: 'No one below decks would get away in the case of a torpedo,' he said. So it was fortunate for him and his 732 crewmates that she was in the centre of the fleet and never came under enemy fire, though between its two bursts of action the *Superb* passed close to the wreckage of the flagship *Invincible*, one of three British battle cruisers lost at Jutland. Men were in the chill water, clinging to flotsam and waving and cheering at the oncoming vessels. But the ships were ploughing ahead at full speed in a vast manoeuvre involving the whole Grand Fleet, and the men were swept under, or left bobbing in the wake. By the time the German fleet disengaged after nightfall, with the loss of just one of its own battle cruisers, over six thousand British seamen had been killed. All this overturned deeply held convictions that Britannia ruled the waves, even though it had kept its lead in the naval arms race against German rivalry during the run-up to the war. The news from Jutland, on the eve of Tolkien's departure for France, was a profound blow to morale.

* * *

When his train from London's Charing Cross Station pulled in to Folkestone at one o'clock the following Monday, Tolkien found a town transformed from the quiet port he had seen in 1912 on camp with King Edward's Horse. Now it was humming with activity, its hotels full of soldiers. He spent Monday night there and the next day, 6 June, boarded a troop ship that steamed across the Channel under escort by a destroyer. He watched the sea-birds wheeling over the grey waters and England recede, the Lonely Isle of his mythology.

Somewhere inland from the French shores ahead, Rob Gilson was making a thumbnail sketch that day of his battalion as they snatched a rest at the side of a long tree-lined road, with the yellow sun westering behind them. The Cambridgeshires had moved south from the lowlands of Flanders into rolling Picardy, the ancient region through which the Somme wound; G. B. Smith was close by. Christopher Wiseman, now back at Scapa Flow, was having a rather chillier time as he led a party of snotties that day onto Hoy, the tallest of the Orkney islands. Disaster had befallen the British High Command. Lord Kitchener, the man whose rallying cry had propelled their generation into military service, had sailed the same day for Russia, and his ship had struck a mine shortly after sailing from Scapa Flow. Wiseman's men were supposed to be searching for confidential documents that might have been washed ashore, but they found none; the snotties were more interested in hunting out puffins' eggs: to his great consternation, they were quite unperturbed by Hoy's 200-foot cliffs.

At Calais the soldiers returning from leave were sent straight off to their battalions, but those arriving for the first time were sent to Étaples, the British Expeditionary Force's base depot. 'Eat-apples', as it was known to the insular Tommy, was a veritable prison, notorious for its vindictive regime. Fenced in among the shoreland sands and pines, it consisted of a sprawl of warehouses and the tented camps run by each army division, British, Canadian, South African, Australian or New Zealand. Now, transferred out of his training battalion, Tolkien bedded down that first night with other men bound for the 32nd Division, to which G. B. Smith's 19th Lancashire Fusiliers belonged. But it proved a false start. The next day he was assigned to the 25th Division and the *11th* Lancashire Fusiliers, which had seen heavy, and costly, fighting at Vimy Ridge in May. Possibly the posting was connected with the fact that the 11th Battalion's signals officer, Lieutenant W. H. Reynolds, had been noticed for his exceptional work at Vimy and was about to be promoted above battalion level, thus creating a vacancy. But for Tolkien this was a blow to long-cherished hopes. To compound his bad luck, the kit he had bought at such expense on Smith's advice had disappeared in transit, forcing him to cobble together a whole new set of equipment, including camp-bed and sleeping bag, for nights under canvas in the chill of what turned out to be a most wintry June.

A message was sent off to tell the 11th Lancashire Fusiliers that he was there awaiting orders. The sense of edgy excitement evaporated, and Tolkien sank into boredom. Now he slept on the dusty hilltop where the 25th Division recruits were encamped, writing letters. To circumvent the censor, Tolkien adopted a code of dots by which Edith could locate him, and while he was in France she traced his movements on a large map pinned to the wall at Great Haywood. He was issued with a gas helmet (a chemically treated flannel bag with glass eyepieces and a valve for the mouth), the newly compulsory tin hat, and a rifle for drill. Every day he would march out in a column of over 50,000 men to the vast sandy bowl known as the Bull Ring, where he was mercilessly put through his paces along with hundreds of other officers. On days when it was not pelting with rain, the troops came back white with dust. The road to the Bull Ring passed the lines of many hospitals, and a huge military cemetery. Tolkien later recalled that his vision of a purgatorial encampment, the poem 'Habbanan beneath the Stars', might have originated here.

Out of acute homesickness a new poem emerged, 'The Lonely Isle', describing his sea-crossing from England, to which the verse is dedicated.

O glimmering island set sea-girdled and alone —
A gleam of white rock through a sunny haze;
O all ye hoary caverns ringing with the moan
Of long green waters in the southern bays;
Ye murmurous never-ceasing voices of the tide;
Ye plumèd foams wherein the shoreland spirits ride;
Ye white birds flying from the whispering coast
And wailing conclaves of the silver shore,
Sea-voiced, sea-wingèd, lamentable host
Who cry about unharboured beaches evermore,
Who sadly whistling skim these waters grey
And wheel about my lonely outward way –

For me for ever thy forbidden marge appears
A gleam of white rock over sundering seas,
And thou art crowned in glory through a mist of tears,
Thy shores all full of music, and thy lands of ease —
Old haunts of many children robed in flowers,
Until the sun pace down his arch of hours,
When in the silence fairies with a wistful heart
Dance to soft airs their harps and viols weave.
Down the great wastes and in a gloom apart
I long for thee and thy fair citadel,
Where echoing through the lighted elms at eve
In a high inland tower there peals a bell:
  O lonely, sparkling isle, farewell!

G. B. Smith sent condolences that the hoped-for summer with Edith at Great Haywood had been cut short and that Tolkien would not be coming to join him in the Salford Pals. 'I do pray for you at all times and in all places,' he added, 'and may you survive, and we survive the fiery trial of these events without loss of our powers or our determination. So shall all things be for good. Meanwhile trust God and keep your powder dry, and be assured that to three other men you are more than their own selves.'

By the middle of June it was clear that something major was

afoot in the counsels of the chiefs of staff. Rumours of spies abounded, but what was planned seemed public knowledge: a 'show' was to be launched somewhere near the Somme town of Albert at the end of the month. The ominous signs were apparent in a letter from Gilson thanking Tolkien for a note that had arrived as he came in from a trench working party on mid-summer's night. A friend and fellow officer had been struck by shell fragments while on a working party, and was thought to be near death. Gilson had travelled far since his school debating days, when he had once asserted that 'war was not now of the first importance, and . . . was a scientific contest of calculation rather than of personal prowess' – making it all sound rather bloodless. Now he wrote to Tolkien: 'I have never felt more forcibly than in the last few weeks, the truth of your words about the oasis of TCBSianism. Life just now is a veritable desert: a fiery one. The TCBS never despised the ordeal and I don't think they underrated it, mine has of late increased in intensity. None the less I am cheerful enough and more grateful than I can say for the breaths of cool fresh air which the various members of the TCBS have given me from time to time.'

Gilson had been in and out of the trenches near Albert for weeks. Now that the news of Jutland had been recast in a more favourable light, and with Russia making sweeping gains on the Eastern Front, he was beginning to sense 'the war at last moving – towards the end'. He found time to marvel at the broad cloud-strewn skies or at the gothic genius behind Amiens cathedral, where he had managed to snatch several happy hours. But he had seen nothing of Smith, though he knew him to be tantalizingly near. The leave he had been hoping for since March had been postponed indefinitely, and he was exhausted. Wiseman had confided in Tolkien that he feared for Rob's sanity. His real lifeline had been his correspondence not with the TCBS, but with Estelle King in Holland, yet twice now he had been disciplined by the censor for revealing too much about the military situation. 'I feel now as if I hardly know what I might write of except the weather,' he told her. Often in his almost daily letters he bemoaned the callousness war had instilled in him, but it was clearly a fragile veneer. 'When it comes down to single human beings,' he wrote, 'I can hardly bear the horror of this war. Men you have known and lived and worked with for eighteen months carried away on stretchers, bleeding. It makes me feel like "peace at any price" . . . It is all cold-blooded and horrible.'

Gilson told his father on 25 June that he could at least quash one bit of tittle-tattle with some confidence: that peace was being declared on the 26th. The incommunicable reality was rather different. On 24 June the massed British artillery had unleashed an unprecedented bombardment against seventeen miles of German trenches north of the River Somme. It went on steadily throughout the day, halving in force through the night but redoubling for ninety minutes the following morning. And so it was to continue every day: the prelude to the biggest battle the world had yet seen.

'I often think,' Gilson told his father, 'of the extraordinary walk that might be made all along the line between the two systems of trenches, that narrow strip of "No Man's Land" stretching from the Alps to the sea . . .' But out of the whole line it was just here, around the River Somme, that the Allies were aiming their might. The German invaders had marched over the region in 1914, but when their bid to encircle Paris failed they had fallen back to the low hills to the east of Albert, cutting an unyielding double line of trenches deep into the chalk. The French had dug a similar, though less extravagant, set of trenches opposite, but now they had retired to concentrate their forces south of the river, and Kitchener's armies had stepped in to the breach. The volunteers were not ready for battle, but Sir Douglas Haig, the British commander-in-chief, had agreed to commit these half-soldiers to a decisive attack before the French army could be wiped out at Verdun. Where the British and French lines met on the Somme, the hammerblow would fall.

At last the orders came from the 11th Lancashire Fusiliers summoning their new subaltern, and Tolkien left sand-blown Étaples on Tuesday 27 June 1916, two days before the planned offensive. The unseasonal chill had given way to a summer heat interspersed with thundery showers. He slept on the train near Abbeville, but when it finally rolled in to Amiens the attack planned for Thursday had been postponed because of the weather. Tolkien ate a meal doled out at a field kitchen in the square, turned his back on the great cathedral, and marched up the road northward into the undulating cornfields and orchard-lands of Picardy, where cornflowers and poppies still bloomed blue and red, and feverfew and camomile and wormwood grew. But the skies opened, the road turned into a river, and he was drenched by the time he met up with his battalion.

The eight hundred or so men of the 11th Lancashire Fusiliers were lodged in barns at Rubempré, a cluster of old but sturdy farms north-east of Amiens and thirteen miles from the front. It was just about the cleanest and most comfortable spot in the British army area behind the Somme front line, but Tolkien had to set up his new camp bed on a farmhouse floor. Late in the evening, another battalion of the same brigade marched in, tired and muddy, only to be sent on elsewhere because there was no room left. Flashes of artillery fire lit up expanses of sky all through the night, accompanied only by an incessant dull thudding.

At seven o'clock the next morning, Thursday 29 June, to the accompaniment of intensive artillery fire away to the east, the men were outside for a last-ditch attempt to shape them up for combat. First they had an hour-long physical workout, then an hour of bayonet practice, drill, and marching 'on the double'. About a quarter of the men were almost as new to the 11th Lancashire Fusiliers as Tolkien, and four other officers had only arrived a day earlier. The commanding officer, Lieutenant-Colonel Laurence Godfrey Bird, had stepped in less than two weeks previously. Most of the rest had been in France for nine months now, miners or weavers from the close-knit Lancashire towns of Burnley, Oldham, Bolton, Wigan, Preston, and Blackburn. North Lancashire miners also dominated a second battalion in the four-strong brigade, while a further battalion had been recruited largely from white-collar workers in the Wirral,

Cheshire. This was a migrant community exiled from home, without women or children or old people, and the vast majority had joined up in the first two months of the war, many of them in their mill clogs. They had embarked from England on the day of the Loos offensive, and tradition held that they had been meant for the battle there but had got lost in transit.

Tolkien felt an affinity with these working-class men. He had, after all, spent significant portions of his childhood either in run-down urban areas of Birmingham or among labouring folk in the villages on the outskirts of the city. But military protocol did not permit him to make friends among the 'other ranks'. He had to take charge of them, discipline them, train them, and probably censor their letters – the kind of job that would be done by any officer available, whether a platoon commander or not. If possible, he was supposed to inspire their love and loyalty.

As before, however, he shared billets and meals and a social life with the thirty or so other officers, particularly those in the company to which he was assigned, 'A' Company, who included several subalterns as platoon leaders under a captain. The brigade – the 74th – had been 'stiffened' by the addition of a regular army battalion from the Royal Irish Rifles, and a handful of the officers in the 11th Lancashire Fusiliers had also been career soldiers before the war. The older officers 'were in many cases professional soldiers dug out of retirement', notes Humphrey Carpenter in his biography of Tolkien, 'men with narrow minds and endless stories of India or the Boer War'. Such old campaigners Tolkien did not find so congenial: they treated him like an inferior schoolboy, he said. None of the officers he had got to know at Lichfield and Cannock Chase had been posted to the 11th Battalion, and he found he had little in common with many of the younger subalterns here. It became Tolkien's confirmed opinion that 'the most improper job of any man . . . is bossing other men' and, he complained, 'Not one in a million is fit for it, and least of all those who seek the opportunity.'

The battalion was on short notice to move in case of a sudden change of plan, but the clouds lowered, the winds gusted, and no attack took place. The men were given no chance to sit and brood on what lay in store for them in the coming days, and specialist officers gave instruction in machine-gunnery or bombing or (in Tolkien's case) signals. The following day, 30 June, there was more of the same. Several officers and men were handed awards for acts of bravery back at Vimy Ridge. The brigade broke camp and, under cover of darkness, made a three-and-a-half-hour march towards the flickering eastern horizon, halting at one o'clock in the morning in a larger village, Warloy-Baillon, seven miles from the front line. During the afternoon strong winds had dispersed the rain clouds and the word had gone out that the great assault was now set for the next morning. Tolkien's battalion was being saved for follow-up attacks. It was clear, however, that G. B. Smith's was not.

'My dear John Ronald,' he had written five days earlier, in a letter that found Tolkien with his new battalion, 'the very best of luck in all that may happen to you within the next few months, and may we live beyond them to see a better time. For although I do not set much store upon my own powers, I set great store upon the combined work of the TCBS. And because we have been friends God bless you and preserve you to return to England and your wife.

'After which the Deluge. If ever there was an hour in which that old priceless humour of the TCBS had an opportunity of surmounting all obstacles thrown in its way, it now is upon us . . . I would have written more but have had no time. And you must expect none in the future . . . Goodbye in the TCBS.'

The same day, Rob Gilson had written to his father and to Estelle King describing a deserted and overgrown garden he had seen, 'Larkspur and Canterbury-bells and cornflowers and poppies of every shade and kind growing in a tangled mass.'*

* Gilson was referring, perhaps, to Bécourt château near La Boisselle, where his battalion spent much time in the run-up to the Somme. The garden there is described in similar terms in C. C. R Murphy's *History of the Suffolk Regiment*.

It was, he commented, 'One of the few really lovely things that the devastation of war produces. There are many grand and awe-inspiring sights. Guns firing at night are beautiful – if they were not so terrible. They have the grandeur of thunderstorms. But how one clutches at the glimpses of peaceful scenes. It would be wonderful to be a hundred miles from the firing line once again.' Gilson wrote no valedictions. Pacing among the tents behind the ruins of Albert on one of those wet and muddy nights, he told a friend: 'It is no use harrowing people with farewell letters; it is not as if we were prodigal sons. Those who survive can write all that is necessary.'

EIGHT

A bitter winnowing

The first of July 1916 dawned with a light mist but with all the signs of a glorious summer's day. Hope ran high. Behind the front line, a great cavalry stood like something out of the old picture books, ready to ride through the breach the infantry would make. The army poised to fight had grown hugely since its losses at Loos last year. Three times larger than any army Britain had ever fielded, this was Kitchener's army, brought there by optimism and enthusiasm. New arrivals at Warloy, where Tolkien slept, were startled awake by the astonishing crash of artillery – 'drum-fire', they called it – as the guns in the east launched into their morning cannonade. It went on for over an hour, towards the end somehow redoubling in fury. A Royal Flying Corps observer high above the Somme front said it was 'as if Wotan, in some paroxysm of rage, were using the hollow world as a drum and under his beat the crust of it was shaking'.

A thousand yards from the German line, Rob Gilson and his battalion spent the night in and around the small château in trench-riddled Bécourt Wood, where his captain friend had been hit by shell-burst two weeks previously. Even here, despite the unrelenting British bombardment, war seemed remote. Cuckoos called, nightingales sang, dogs barked at the guns; wild and garden flowers grew in profusion. A light rain pattered through the leaves for soldiers to catch in their hats to drink. 'Jerry' could scarcely have survived the merciless week-long bombardment and tomorrow would be a walkover. At breakfast in the yard, spirits rose further still with the help of a dose of treacly army rum in the soldiers' tea. Rob's batman, Bradnam, packed his master's things and at five Gilson marched his platoon out of the wood along the trenches. Dressed not as an officer but as one of the men, so he would not be instantly shot down, Gilson, like everyone else, carried sixty-six pounds of gear. The Cambridgeshires arrayed themselves in trenches to the rear of another unit, from Grimsby. Gilson's platoon, composed largely of men from the Isle of Ely, was in his battalion's fourth and final 'wave'.

At 7.20 a.m., ten minutes to 'zero hour', every gun in the artillery accelerated to its maximum rate of fire in a hurricane bombardment. The air was brown with the chalk dust of disrupted fields and red with the pulverized brick of village and farmstead. Then, with two minutes to go, the ground reeled. Lieutenant Gilson and his men had been warned to expect this; they had been kept back to protect them from concussion. Across No Man's Land, and a little to Gilson's left, the earth erupted thousands of feet into the smoky blue air as twenty-four tons of explosive ammonal (ammonium nitrate mixed with aluminium) were detonated under the enemy trenches where they formed a strongly protected salient. Clods of soil and chunks of chalk rained down, as big as wheelbarrows.

For the first time in a week all the guns stopped. In No Man's Land, long ranks of men rose from where they had been crouching on the ground. The skirl of bagpipes started up nearby. The British artillery lengthened its aim so the infantry could safely enter the German front line. Then it resumed its bombardment. The shriek and roar pressed in from all around.

Gilson waited for the Cambridgeshires' third wave to leave. He checked his watch and, at two and a half minutes after zero hour, blew his whistle and waved his platoon forward some four hundred yards up to the front line.

Something was amiss. Now the space above his trench was alive with bullets, and shells the size of two-gallon oildrums sailed through the air, spinning with a sinister *wouf, wouf, wouf.* Nervous men, astonished that the pulverized enemy was firing back, looked at each other; but they were ashamed to show their fear. Gilson spread the soldiers of his 'dear, stupid, agricultural platoon' along a hundred-yard stretch of trench, checked his watch, and waved them up the ladders.

The German trench mortar shells, or 'sausages', now somersaulting overhead had given their name to Sausage Valley, the shallow depression up which Rob Gilson and the Cambridgeshires were supposed to advance. Away to the left, beyond the rise on which stood the smashed enemy-held village of La Boisselle, it was paralleled by a further depression, Mash Valley. Beyond that, another entrenched spur ran out from the German-held high ground, and then there was the long dell containing Blighty Wood, so called because of the numbers of wounded who regularly left there bound for home. Here G. B. Smith and the Salford Pals were due to head across No Man's Land, two miles along the line to Gilson's left. Crammed into the trenches between the two TCBSites were eighteen whole battalions: men in their thousands from Tyneside and Devon, from Yorkshire, Scotland, Nottingham, and elsewhere. In the knotted trenches and the press of bodies, amid the killing cloud of artillery and the secrecy and confusion of the assault, those two miles might have been a million.

The Cambridgeshires were in extremis. Within an hour and a half, Rob Gilson's platoon was supposed to advance nearly two miles up Sausage Valley to an enemy strongpoint; in the plan, it had their regimental name on it: Suffolk Redoubt. The strongpoint lay just beyond a wood on the skyline, but as Gilson hauled himself out of the trench it is doubtful that he could see beyond the curtain of British shell explosions behind the German front line. That curtain – the barrage – would move in stages just in front of the advancing soldiers. It was in the plans. The bodies already strewn on the sweep of wasteland in front, up to the white lip of the newly blasted crater, were not. Nor was the machine-gun fire cutting the air from La Boisselle. The artillery had failed to destroy or drive out the German defenders there.

Rob Gilson had half-predicted the problem. 'I am astonished by the small material damage which a single shell, say a 4.2", does,' he had written home. 'If it explodes in the open it makes quite a shallow and small hole and throws the earth about a bit . . . But it does not look as if it had a radius of much more than 2 yards and one may burst just in front of, or even on, the parapet . . . without doing the smallest damage . . . On the other hand if a shell happens to explode right in a trench the damage it does to men is worse than I imagined.'

As soon as the barrage lifted from their front line, the Germans rushed from the dugouts in which they had crouched fearfully all week and took to their guns. No Man's Land was up to six hundred yards wide here, but soldiers from the foremost three waves of Cambridgeshires had begun to fall within the first hundred. They went down 'just like corn in front of the farmer's reaper', one of Gilson's men remembered. Bullets spun men around and dropped them in strangely awkward postures; it felt like being hit by half a house. The enemy's shells dealt with those the bullets missed. But the advance went on, somehow: men with heads bowed as if walking into a gale. By the time Gilson led his platoon out, the machine-gunners had found their range and were working with improved efficiency.

Rob Gilson had described No Man's Land as 'the most absolute barrier that can be constructed between men'. The details of what happened inside it seem almost an indeterminable mystery. Yet a captain friend, injured by a bullet ten minutes in, said he watched Gilson leading his soldiers forward 'perfectly calmly and confidently'. For Rob's batman Bradnam, time and distance stretched out: as he remembered it, Gilson was still moving forward at about nine o'clock and had advanced several hundred yards (which would have taken him beyond the German front line) when Bradnam himself was hit and cried out; but the orders were cruelly clear: nothing must stop the advance. Then Gilson's beloved old Major Morton was knocked out of action. His company was leaderless, and the Major passed on a message to Gilson in the middle of No Man's Land to take over. He did so, and was moving forward again, as if on parade, when he and his sergeant-major, Brooks, were killed by a shellburst. A soldier crawling back told the injured Bradnam that his lieutenant was dead. Another said later that he found Gilson back in the front trench, as if he had been dragged or had dragged himself all the way back there; but there was no sign of life.

Far away, Rob Gilson's father, the Headmaster, was preparing to officiate at the King Edward's annual Sports Day. Rob's sister Molly was going to serve tea to the schoolboys' parents. His stepmother Donna, who usually handed out prizes, was giving it a miss this year and was going to 'revel in a quiet and lovely afternoon' at home instead.

'I hope I may never find myself in command of the company when we are in the trenches,' Gilson had once said. Such responsibility did not sit easily on him, but in his final minutes he had to lead the men he loved, and who loved him in return, into virtual annihilation. Many times he had told his fellow officers that he would rather die 'in a big affair and not by a shell or chance bullet in the trenches'. But he was a gentle aesthete in the midst of absolute horror. His friend Andrew Wright, a fellow officer in the Cambridgeshires, told Gilson's father: 'It was the final but not the first triumph of determination over his sensitive nature – He alone is brave who goes to face everything with a full knowledge of [his own] cowardice.'

Gilson did not live to see the full scale of the disaster that day. More than five hundred of the Cambridgeshires were wounded or killed. Of the sixteen officers the battalion had fielded, Gilson and three others died, two more were never found, and only one, Wright, emerged unhurt. No Man's Land was dotted everywhere with bodies. A dozen of the Cambridgeshires made it across to the edge of one of the enemy redoubts but were caught in the blast of a flamethrower and died horribly. Others made it behind the German lines but were hopelessly cut off. Later in the day the German machine gunners strafed

No Man's Land methodically, in zigzags, to finish off the wounded and stranded volunteers of Kitchener's armies.

On Sunday 2 July 1916, Tolkien attended Mass in front of a portable altar in a field at Warloy. The battalion's padre, Mervyn Evers, was a Church of England man, chirpy but averse to Roman Catholics. The brigade's Catholics, such as Tolkien, were ministered to by the chaplain with the Royal Irish Rifles. The British were rumoured to have taken the entire German frontline system, but no official news had come. All through Saturday the main road had carried an endless procession of troops and laden trucks heading for the front. There was also traffic in the other direction, including a few German prisoners, but it seemed that everything with wheels was being used to bring wounded men in to the temporary hospital at Warloy. The exodus continued unabated on Sunday, the second day of the battle. It was often tranquil apart from the humming of aeroplanes (two fought an inconclusive dogfight above the village), but every now and then the distant artillery would burst into deafening fusilades. In the afternoon the first official word came on progress so far: said to be 'rather obscure'.

Through these days Tolkien and the Lancashire Fusiliers were held in a state of battle-readiness. A rumour arose that they were going into trenches near the German-held hamlet of Thiepval, but when the brigade left Warloy on Monday 3 July it was for Bouzincourt, a village three miles behind the front. In the dusk, as they set out, an exhausted Highland Division straggled past, broken by battle, its unshaven and mud-plastered men clutching each other for support.

Three miles was not far enough. Just before dawn, as Tolkien lay in a hut, a German field gun bombarded Bouzincourt. He was now on the Western Front, and it was his first time under fire. The tiny French farming village was not hit – fortunately, for soldiers filled its every house, cellar, barn, and orchard. When a thunderstorm broke out, the men of Tolkien's battalion were drenched where they lay out in a field. It rained still harder throughout the next day, 4 July, which was spent largely cooped up because no one was allowed out from under the shelter of the village's trees for fear of enemy observation. But a ridge nearby offered a grandstand view of the battle line, on the hillside eastward across the wooded valley of the River Ancre, where shells could be seen bursting among the German trenches. The sky was no friendlier. At the front, Tolkien said, 'German captive-balloons . . . hung swollen and menacing on many a horizon.' Men were arriving in their hundreds to have wounds dressed, but some were horribly mutilated. Rob Gilson's division had lost most heavily of all on the first day of the Battle of the Somme, but along the British front there had been 57,000 casualties: out of the 100,000 who entered No Man's Land, 20,000 had been killed and twice as many wounded. On the second day there were 30,000 more casualties.

In between training and instruction, Tolkien's battalion provided working parties to dig graves in the suddenly expanding cemetery. Units from his division had taken over the line from Gilson's last night; but what had become of him, and where was G. B. Smith? Tolkien looked over their letters: Smith's prayer that they might all survive 'the fiery trial'; Gilson's terse hints about his own harrowing ordeal; and Smith's 25 June warning about correspondence, 'You must expect none in the future.'

On Wednesday afternoon, 5 July, orders came at last: the four battalions of Tolkien's brigade were needed to help another division that had suffered heavily in fighting at La Boisselle. That village had at last been taken, but fresh troops were needed to push further into enemy territory. They set out under Lieutenant-Colonel Bird at lunchtime on 6 July, but all ranks not required for combat were left behind. The 11th Lancashire Fusiliers' signal officer, W. H. Reynolds, went to run communications at their trench headquarters, but Tolkien did not go with him. Instead he stayed put at Bouzincourt, along with the signal office running communications for the whole 25th Division. So he was still there when G. B. Smith arrived on 6 July.

* * *

Smith had received his orders for the Big Push a week after his return from his May leave in England, and on the eve of Tolkien's crossing. Since then, he had hardly been out of the trenches. On the day Tolkien left Étaples, Smith's men had set out from Warloy for their battle station, singing. Orders were that they would wait until after the initial assault before emerging to consolidate the British gains, taking their picks and shovels so they could dig in. But after twenty-four hours crammed into sodden dugouts in the wood west of the Ancre, they had been told the attack was off and had retired to billets to wait.

The night before the rescheduled attack they moved into dugouts further forward, near a pontoon bridge across the rivermeads at Authuille, for four hours' fitful sleep, and were up at five o'clock. At six the bombardment began again, deafening in its intensity, shaking the ground. They crossed the bridge just after 'zero hour'. Now they struck uphill, passing brigades of artillerymen stripped to the waist as they slaved to feed the huge guns, and reached the trenches that ran into the southern edge of Blighty Wood.

Several hundred yards beyond the small, much-battered wood, up a steady slope, was the British front line, a stretch known as Boggart Hole Clough. On the far side of No Man's Land, where Smith had patrolled it one night in May, was the heavily fortified Leipzig Salient, at the toe of Thiepval Ridge. By now it should have been overrun and left far behind by the advance. The Salford Pals would simply walk across the open country from the wood and climb down into the Salient with their picks and shovels. Later they would move on nearly two more miles to refortify another conquered enemy strongpoint.

But no sooner was Smith under the trees than walking wounded and stretcher cases began to stream past. Further in, the wood was full of corpses. Now the battalion in front started to bunch up, and the labourers and businessmen of Salford, and the Oxford University men, paused. Their eyes streamed from tear gas; their ears were filled with the *ping* of bullets and the crack of falling branches. Smith, now the battalion intelligence officer, attempted to take in the situation from a trench at the far edge of the wood. Across the blasted desolation through which the British communication trenches ran up to Boggart Hole Clough, enemy machine guns were rattling away from the high ground to the east.

The idea of an orderly march forward was rejected at last but, three hours into the battle, the Pals' advance resumed. The first company was sent out of the wood in rushes, but platoon by platoon they withered into the ground. The next group went out under a smokescreen, dashing from shellhole to shellhole, but no news came back out of the chaos. Orders came down to advance along the crowded trenches instead. This was done by men including Smith's old platoon, collierymen mostly, but they sent word back that their front line was choked with the dead and the wounded, and was impassable. Furthermore, the German artillery had now turned its attention on Boggart Hole Clough. The Pals were ordered back to the confines of Blighty Wood, which came under a rain of shells for the rest of the day.

Remarkably, a few Salford Pals had already defied the odds to reach Leipzig Salient, parts of which were by now in British hands. There they were trapped all day with pockets of men from other battalions, desperately fighting off German troops with bombs and bayonets. They could not be pulled back until night fell, when the survivors of Smith's battalion withdrew from Salient and wood. Heading back the way they had come that morning, they found the whole area now littered with discarded guns, grenades, and ammunition. Everywhere, men sat brokenly, or lay silent in the darkness. After a second day under shellfire in the trenches around Authuille, Smith's platoon and others were sent back to man Boggart Hole Clough for a further twenty-four hours under intermittent but intense bombardment.

Only half the battalion had returned to its village billets in the small hours of 4 July. G. B. Smith was fortunate that he no longer commanded a platoon: four of the Pals' officers had been killed and seven wounded. Thirty-six of the 'ordinary' soldiers were dead or missing and more than two hundred and thirty had suffered wounds. Most had fallen on the first morning before they even reached their own front line.

* * *

For Tolkien, the relief of seeing his friend safe and sound on Thursday 6 July was overwhelming. GBS arrived alone ahead of the Salford Pals, who followed early the next morning. These were fraught days. The divisional signal office at Bouzincourt was hit by shells on Friday night and its cabling wrecked. Meanwhile, Smith, recovering from his sixty-hour ordeal under fire, was involved in the hasty reorganization of his depleted battalion into just two companies; but between their chores in this garrisoned Picardy village smelling of death, the two Oxford TCBSites spent as much time together as they could. Waiting for news of Rob Gilson, they talked about the war, strolled in an unspoilt field of poppies, or took shelter, on Friday, from the heavy rain that fell all day; and in true TCBSian fashion they discussed poetry and the future. But on Saturday the Salford Pals left for the trenches due east across the Ancre, where they were going to back up the continuing British assault on Ovillers, the German strongpoint overlooking the valleys of Sausage and Mash and Blighty Wood. After seeing his old friend once more, Smith departed.

The 11th Lancashire Fusiliers limped back into Bouzincourt on the morning of Monday 10 July 1916 and collapsed into their billets. After a few hours' sleep, the men were roused and the battalion moved to Senlis, another crowded hamlet a mile further from the front, to rest in more comfortable billets and to take stock. They had found La Boisselle thick with the bodies of the dead, hundreds of them wherever the eye looked, and far more in British khaki than German field-grey. In several assaults on the German lines to the south of Ovillers they had added to the carnage fifty-six of their own men, killed or missing; twice that number were wounded. Even counting those who had remained at Bouzincourt, only a dozen soldiers of 'C' Company were left.

Though the full-scale assault had now given way to many smaller skirmishes, the chance of injury was still high, and the chance of being killed considerable. If you were an officer, it was clear, the odds were stacked against you. One subaltern was dead, one had been left to succumb to his wounds in a German dugout, and one (who had simply been carrying supplies) had been shot in the knee. Frederick Dunn, the 23-year-old captain of 'A' Company, had been shot through the head. Such were the facts before Tolkien as he headed for the first time into the trenches of the Western Front.

The orders to move came on 14 July, after a night interrupted by sudden, thunderous noise. With its French ally in mind, the British High Command had planned a decisive stroke for Bastille Day: as dawn reached Tolkien at Senlis, 22,000 soldiers were sweeping across the German second line from the southern British positions on the Somme. The 11th Lancashire Fusiliers marched off at mid-morning through Bouzincourt and down into the Ancre valley. The road was flanked by resting soldiers and bustling with men, wagons, horses, and mules in motion. Old and new flowed together: for every motorized vehicle, there were roughly two horse-drawn wagons or carts and three riding horses. 'That road was like a pageant,' wrote Charles Carrington, a subaltern of the Royal Warwickshires whose experiences over the next few days closely relate to Tolkien's. 'The quieter men lay down, but the younger ones, officers and men, ran about like children to see the sights.' Further down towards Albert, big pieces of artillery boomed away in hollow or copse or ruinous house. On top of the town's war-damaged basilica glimmered a golden statue of the Virgin Mary, half-toppled, with the infant Christ in her outstretched arms. Superstition held that when she fell the war would end.

Tolkien's brigade skirted the northern edge of the town, crossed the river, and bivouacked by an embankment, where the stream ran out of a wood at the foot of the long chalk down that rose to the German heights. Around the Roman road running north-east from Albert was a panorama of tentless bivouacs where soldiers brewed tea around stacks of rifles, or hurried on errands, or aimlessly foraged for souvenirs among the strewn detritus of armies. Some even managed to sleep, though the ground here was shelled intermittently. The land now was scarred, and the rural backdrop of the hinterland torn away.

As the afternoon waned, Tolkien's battalion and the Royal Irish regulars were told that they were to take part in a 'show', as soldierly euphemism had it. They left the rest of the 74th Brigade by the embankment and headed up the busy road lined by scorched, stunted trees, turning left in the lee of a ridge to find the entrenched headquarters of their two divisional sister brigades. Beyond the grey ridge lay No Man's Land. Bodies lay out there still from 1 July. To the right glimmered a vast white crater, where Rob Gilson had watched the enormous mine explode at the start of the battle. To the left, the height of Ovillers thrust forward like a finger from the chalk uplands behind it.

'Something in the make of this hill, in its shape, or in the way it catches the light, gives it a strangeness which other parts of the battlefield have not,' wrote John Masefield in his 1917 survey of the area, *The Old Front Line*. The height does not seem especially prominent, yet from here the German invaders could survey the battlefield from Bécourt, where the Cambridgeshires had launched their attack, to Leipzig Salient, where so many Salford Pals died. Trying to take the hill of Ovillers on the day of the Big Push, five thousand men had been wounded or killed. Two days later, the tally had risen by half as many again. While Tolkien was meeting with G. B. Smith at Bouzincourt, the 11th Lancashire Fusiliers had joined a third assault, which petered out in costly and inconclusive manoeuvres. In recent days, with La Boisselle in British hands, Smith had seen battle inside the strongpoint on the hilltop itself.

Ovillers remained a powerful obstacle, fiercely defended. In the southern face of the hill, just below its crest and amid the rubble of a French hamlet with its burnt-down church, a labyrinth of trenches had been cut, guarded by hidden machine guns. At dawn that Bastille Day the garrison at Ovillers had fought off battalions advancing from north-west, south, and south-east. Though the attack was no more than a diversion from the main assault further along the front line, Ovillers had appeared (as *The Times* said) 'like a volcano in violent eruption'. Now the 7th Brigade, part of Tolkien's division, was renewing its assault on the south-eastern defences, but it was battle-weary and depleted. The 11th Lancashire Fusiliers and the Royal Irish were being sent up to lend a hand.

As dusk fell on 14 July, Tolkien tramped with his companions up into La Boisselle. Sewn into his uniform was the regulation first-aid packet, containing a sterile field dressing in case he was wounded. Underfoot the ground was clay, stiff yet sodden from the rains and torn by traffic. Nightfall inevitably brought movement in the other direction: the wounded being evacuated from the battlefield. The moon was brilliant, and the sky full of starburst shells and flares. Many small wooden crosses could be glimpsed as the old British front line fell behind. It was, wrote Carrington, 'a new country . . . a desert of broken chalk – ditches, holes, craters, mounds and ridges, dry and thinly overgrown with weeds, and all interlaced with rusty strands of barbed wire'. The village of La Boisselle itself had been erased, yet still shells fell on it with a rising shriek, a roar and a crash. Then suddenly the trenchworks changed: the churned muck underfoot was replaced by straight duckboards and the walls now soared fifteen feet up, each fire-bay equipped with its own ladder. This was a monument of German engineering, and it showed scant sign of damage after the great bombardment.

The Lancashire Fusiliers passed into the maze and on uphill by German trenches to the right of the Roman way. The road was now raised on an embankment, but no longer lined by trees: they had been blasted out of existence. Going was slow, and single-file. Part way along they passed through an open area containing a broken-down ambulance wagon. This was land newly taken from the Germans, and at high cost. So it was on the approach to Ovillers that Tolkien first encountered the lost of the Somme: heralded by their stench, darkly hunched or prone, or hanging on the wire until a stab of brightness revealed them, the bloated and putrescent dead.

With the old front line a mile behind them, they turned left into a trench that cut across the road, dipped into Mash Valley, and climbed again directly towards Ovillers, a low silhouette of hedges and ruins against the black sky. The trench was soon crammed with anxious soldiers, jostling with a digging party of Royal Engineers.

The hill ahead erupted in light and noise shortly before midnight on 14 July 1916 as the 7th Brigade attacked. The Lancashire Fusiliers watched, waiting in reserve and ready to move into the captured ground to hold it against any counterattacks. But the brigade was beaten back. Abruptly, the order came for the reserve troops to join in a second attack at two o'clock. There was barely time for the Fusiliers to line up to the right of the survivors of the previous charge before they were launched, bayonets fixed, into the assault.

The first objective, the trench guarding Ovillers' south-eastern perimeter, lay 120 yards uphill, opposite a parallel trench tenuously held by the British. But the two were actually linked at their eastern ends by a third, perpendicular trench, where German soldiers lurked around the corner. Thus the attackers would have to traverse an open square held on two sides by the enemy and swept by up to six machine guns.

The Lancashire Fusiliers, however, never entered the fatal square. First they had to negotiate an obstacle course. Farmers had cut the slope into terraces, the Germans had sown it with barbed wire, and the British had ploughed it up again with enormous shellholes. The Fusiliers walked into a storm of bullets and a chaos of wire entanglements, and they scarcely reached their own forward trench.

One subaltern, a 30-year-old Lancastrian, died leading his platoon in the charge that night. Five officers were wounded. Tolkien, it seems, was there to wrestle with the muddled and inadequate communications system: a safer job, but certainly not peripheral. In this war of men and machines, the infantry counted little, the artillery rather more, and the word most of all: without fast and accurate communications, no one could hope to have the upper hand. A vast buried cable system had been installed prior to the Battle of the Somme, but of course it extended no further than the front line. Beyond its reach soldiers worked in a zone of mystery, in which thousands of them simply disappeared. The job of the signaller was to shed some light on the mystery by helping to set up a battlefield communications system and using it.

In practice this was an almost hopeless task, as Tolkien learned at Ovillers. There were now surface lines running back to La Boisselle, and field telephones. The battalion's signallers carried coils of wire ready to set up new phone stations in captured territory. The surface lines, however, were easily tapped and Morse buzzers could be heard within three hundred yards as the signal leaked into the chalky ground. The phone was meant as a last resort, to be used with 'station call signs' that Tolkien had to memorize ('AE' for the Fusiliers, 'CB' for the brigade, and so on). Flags, lamps, and flares simply drew fire from the enemy ramparts. Most messages were sent by runner, but runners were reluctant to run headlong across danger areas under fire. Orders from the generals at corps HQ took at least eight hours to reach the attacking troops.

The three battalions fell back; there would be no more attacks that night. Saturday 15 July broke grey and misty over the slope up to Ovillers, strewn with fallen figures. The Fusiliers left one company to hold the forward trench and drew back to a safer distance. In the afternoon they returned to La Boisselle to provide carrying parties for their own brigade, which now took over the siege.

Daylight only reinforced the sense of horror brooding over the desolation. The artist Gerald Brenan, likening it to 'a treacherous, chaotic region recently abandoned by the tide', recalled that the ground between the two villages was 'torn up by shells and littered with dead bodies, some of which had been lying around for three weeks . . . In the first attack on 1 July it had been impossible to rescue the wounded and one could see how they had crowded into shell-holes, drawn their waterproof sheets over them and died like that. Some of them – they were north-country lads – had taken out their Bibles.' The forest of barbed wire towards

Ovillers was thick with bodies, their faces purple-black. 'The flies were buzzing obscenely over the damp earth,' Charles Carrington recalled; 'morbid scarlet poppies grew scantily along the white chalk mounds; the air was thick and heavy with rank pungent explosives and the sickly stench of corruption.'

But there were rumours of a great cavalry breakthrough at High Wood to the east, and at least the enemy artillery was no longer shelling La Boisselle. The German dugouts were also quite secure, barring a direct hit on the entrance. 'Ours compared very unfavourably . . . a hole dug out of the side of the trench with a bit of corrugated iron for its use, whereas theirs led down by steps some fifty feet or so and were even lit by electric light,' the Fusiliers' padre, Evers, wrote later. 'When one compares their arrangements with ours one wonders how in all conscience we managed to win the war!' Here a garrison had laid low under the great bombardment: a rank smell of sweat, wet paper, and unfamiliar foods pervaded the subterranean halls, and they were filthy. Tolkien found a space in one of these dugouts and bedded down.

His battalion was called out again that evening to line up in reserve in the trenches to the right of the Roman road. Now the Royal Irish regulars were up ahead holding the British forward trench. The attack was set for ten o'clock, but then postponed for three hours. The was a hint of drizzle in the air. The German resistance seemed undented, and the charge proved a virtual re-run of the night before. This time, though, the Fusiliers watched the *Sturm und Drang* from the rear. Among the orders that Tolkien passed was one for fifty men from 'A' Company to go to the ammunition dump near La Boisselle to collect bombs for the fighting line. But signals problems recurred and it was an hour or more before news reached the division back at Bouzincourt that the attack had failed. None of its objectives had been gained, and its sole success – distracting the Germans so that a British battalion could cut them off from behind – almost proved disastrous.

A battalion to the right, the Warwickshires, had reached unopposed a trench running north-east from Ovillers – the Germans' final link with reinforcements and rations; but when the bleared sun rose on 16 July, the Warwickshires were stranded. 'To look for help we must turn back across the 1,000 yards of rough grass, impassable by day, which we had rushed across at night,' wrote Charles Carrington, who was one of the officers in the stranded battalion, in a memoir. Prussian Guardsmen were now sniping and throwing bombs at them in a bid to relieve the embattled garrison.

Through the muggy day, Tolkien's brigade tried to reach the Warwickshires from their position in front of Ovillers. There could be no daylight charge across open ground, so the Lancashire Fusiliers brought up bombs, which the Royal Irish hurled around the guarded angle of their trench at the German defenders. But the enemy had roofs and deep dugouts, and retaliatory bombs wore the Royal Irish down.

Tolkien's battalion finally broke the deadlock as the day ran out, sending in fresh men with a rain of rifle- and hand-grenades. Just before sunset a white flag appeared, followed by a soldier in field-grey. So the garrison of Ovillers surrendered: 2 officers and 124 soldiers, all unwounded. The Fusiliers pushed on until they reached the stranded Warwickshires and came back out of Ovillers with trophies: machine guns and other *matériel*.

By the time the last pockets of resistance were driven out the next day, Monday 17 July, Tolkien was asleep. He had been relieved an hour after midnight and reached Bouzincourt at six o'clock, after some fifty hours in battle.

In the midst of his own trials at Ovillers, five days earlier, G. B. Smith had sent him a field postcard – the official kind printed with various routine messages to be deleted as appropriate – declaring simply 'I am quite well'. Arriving at Bouzincourt Tolkien found a letter from him. Smith had returned from Ovillers just as Tolkien was going in, and on Saturday he had seen in the newspaper Rob's name among the lists of dead. 'I am safe but what does that matter?' he said. 'Do please stick to me, you and Christopher. I am very tired and most frightfully depressed at this worst of news. Now one realises in despair what the TCBS really was. O my dear John Ronald what ever are we going to do?'

NINE

'Something has gone crack'

The Somme offensive had been a secret so widely shared that the name 'Albert' was on everyone's lips back in England well before 1 July 1916. News of the attack broke the afternoon of that terrible Saturday, but there was no indication of casualties or intimation of disaster. The following Thursday Cary Gilson arrived back with his wife from a trip to London to find a multiple-choice field postcard from his son stating, 'I am quite well. Letter follows at first opportunity.' That evening the Headmaster wrote a teasing reply mentioning a family friend who 'never sends anything but cards, and never crosses out anything, so that each missive announces his perfect health, the fact that he is wounded and has been conveyed to a base hospital, etc.' Reflecting the general view that 1 July had been a turning point, he added: 'The Germans have the wolf at their door.' But by now family after family had heard of the loss or injury of a son. The Gilsons knew Rob had been around Albert. On Friday 6 July, Rob's stepmother Donna could hardly bear to go home because she felt sure a War Office telegram would be awaiting her. On the Saturday a letter arrived that dashed all hopes. Arthur Seddon, one of Rob's best friends among the Cambridgeshire Battalion officers, sent condolences on his death.

Cary Gilson mastered or masked his grief with expressions of glorious sacrifice, and busied himself making further inquiries and writing an obituary. Rob's sister Molly threw herself into her war work, dressing wounds at the hospital set up in Birmingham University. But Rob's half-brothers, six-year-old Hugh and John, not quite four, wept bitterly when they learned their beloved 'Roddie' was gone. Donna was crushed by the loss of her 'greatest friend'. She prayed that Estelle King, who happened to be on her way back from Holland, had not seen the newspapers.

Seddon's letter said that Rob 'was loved by all those with whom he came into contact'. The loyal Bradnam declared that he had been 'loved by all the men in the platoon and, I may say, company, as he was a very good officer and a good leader.' Old Major Morton said Gilson had been like a son to him, adding: 'I am almost glad to be incapable of going back to my company, I feel I should miss him so at every turn.'* Wright, the subaltern who had shared huts and billets with Gilson for eighteen months, wrote that their friendship had been 'everything to me in a life I cannot love' and said, 'I looked forward to a time when it should grow to immeasurable maturity in days of Peace.'

For Tolkien, as for Gilson's friends in the Cambridgeshires, personal loss was piled on top of the horror and exhaustion of battle. There was no counselling for bereavement or post-traumatic stress in this army; it was business as usual. But by chance Tolkien was given a brief respite after his arrival back in Bouzincourt from the attack on Ovillers. That night, Monday 17 July 1916, he bivouacked at Forceville, on the road to the elegant country town of Beauval, where the 25th Division moved for a rest fifteen miles from the front. After an inspection by the divisional commander on 19 July, Tolkien sat down to dinner with the other officers of 'A' Company – those that were left. The man who commanded the company when Tolkien had joined it was already dead. Two subalterns had been packed off

* The Gilsons sent the batman £50 that Rob had left him (the equivalent of nearly £2,000 today); but Bradnam had not mentioned the severity of his condition, and he was dead by the end of the first week in August following two amputations of parts of his leg. Major Philip Morton died in Rouen a few days later, an old soldier of fifty-two.

wounded four nights ago from Ovillers (Waite, a Lincolns Inn lawyer, having taken a couple of bullets in his abdomen and hip). That left Fawcett-Barry, an army careerist earmarked as the new company commander; Altham, the intelligence officer, from battalion headquarters; Captain Edwards, the machine-gun officer, also from headquarters and just nineteen years old; plus the recent arrivals – Tolkien, Loseby, and Atkins. Tolkien appears to have been mess officer that day. Dinner and whiskey were served by the batmen, Harrison, Arden, and Kershaw.

The batman performed domestic chores for an officer: making his bed, tidying and polishing, and furnishing his table with the best. This was a practical arrangement, not just a luxury. Officers undoubtedly led a cushier life than the other ranks, but they had little time to spare from training, directing working parties, and, on 'days off', censoring the men's inevitable letters home (a deeply divisive and unpopular duty). A resourceful batman could win a great deal of gratitude and respect. Tolkien, who found it hard to warm to his fellow officers, developed a profound admiration for the batmen he knew. However, the batman was not primarily a servant but a private soldier who acted as a runner for officers in action. As such he had to be both fit and intelligent so that he did not garble the orders or reports. Like any other private, he also fought in the field. One of the 'A' Company batmen, Thomas Gaskin, a working-class Manchester man, was among the thirty-six Fusiliers killed or missing at Ovillers. Tolkien preserved a poignant letter from Gaskin's mother asking about her son.

The 11th Lancashire Fusiliers had suffered 267 casualties in a fortnight. At that rate, without fresh drafts and a lengthy break from combat, the unit would have ceased to exist in another month; but the battalion had to be reorganized at Beauval because of its losses.

At the same time, Tolkien was appointed battalion signal officer (and probably acting lieutenant). His predecessor left to work for the brigade and Tolkien was put in charge of all the unit's communications, with a team of non-commissioned officers and privates to work for him as runners, wirers, and telephone operators and to help him set up signal stations wherever the battalion moved. It was a heavy responsibility at a difficult time. He needed to know the locations and station calls of all coordinating units; to be *au fait* with the plans and intentions of Lieutenant-Colonel Bird, the CO; and to keep the brigade informed about any unit movements or signals problems. But all this information had to be kept a close secret. The first soldiers to penetrate Ovillers had made an unpleasant discovery among the enemy papers: a verbatim transcript of the British order to attack the village on 1 July. Signalling was the focus of fresh paranoia, and was under severe scrutiny from above. There were lectures for officers and tickings-off for battalion commanders about the ineffective use of signals on the Somme.

Tolkien stepped up to his new role on Friday 21 July 1916, just in time to make even more of a challenge of his first experience of that staple of life on the Western Front, trench duty. That Sunday, the next phase of the Somme offensive was launched, a furious and tragically costly attack on Pozières, up the Roman road from Albert, by Australian volunteers fighting for King and motherland. On 24 July, Tolkien's unit was called instead to trenches at the north of the Somme front. Here near Auchonvillers – inevitably dubbed by the troops 'Ocean Villas' – another great mine had been exploded at the start of the Big Push, but no ground had been gained. Tolkien was on the old front line facing Beaumont-Hamel, a German position nestled in a deep gash. To the south-east the land dipped steeply to the Ancre, and beyond it, two miles away, the Schwaben Redoubt hunched above the battlefield, at the high head of Thiepval Ridge. The Fusiliers were welcomed by shellfire as they were settling in. In the dugout of battalion headquarters Tolkien worked alongside Bird, his adjutant Kempson, Altham the intelligence officer, and John Metcalfe, who had become one of the army's youngest captains after running away from home to enlist and was now acting as second-in-command to Bird. Over the next five days Tolkien ran communications to the brigade command post in a village a mile and a half off, and the Royal Engineers came to lay a new cable. The Fusiliers were busy, especially after dark, digging deep dugouts and widening the trenches for use in a later attack. The working parties were spotted one night and shells cascaded about them.

The 11th Lancashire Fusiliers were withdrawn from 'Ocean Villas' on the morning of 30 July and went into divisional reserve in a wood near the village of Mailly-Maillet. Regimental battle honours were celebrated on Minden Day, 1 August, the anniversary of the Battle of Minden of 1759 in which the Lancashire Fusiliers had helped defeat the French. There was a rose for every soldier – and blindfold boxing, an apt though unintentional parody of the Somme. After a hot and busy week (the soldiers were repairing trenches by night) they were pulled out of reserve on Saturday 5 August to a camp another few miles back, and the next day Tolkien was able to attend Mass in the Roman Catholic church at the village of Bertrancourt.

On Monday morning Tolkien was ordered to go with one other subaltern, Second Lieutenant Potts, and five sergeant-majors to set up battalion headquarters in trenches yet further north, near the ruined *sucrerie* or sugar beet refinery and the new mass grave between Colincamps and the German trenches at Serre. They found the front line itself badly blown-in and impassable by daylight, having been virtually obliterated at the start of the Somme. Nevertheless the battalion had to follow Tolkien's advance party in and set to work with pick and shovel amid intermittent bombardments that killed four men. But on 10 August, a day of rain, the Fusiliers marched back to Bus-lès-Artois, where they had stayed *en route* from Beauval to their first stint of trench-duty. From this vantage point, war seemed far away; cornfields rolled into the distance, and gardens and orchards concealed the surrounding villages. As before, they were lodged in huts in a wood on the northern edge of the village. For two nights, however, Tolkien sat out under the wet trees, deep in thought.

A note from G. B. Smith had reached him some two weeks earlier, voluble in its brevity. He had been re-reading a poem by Tolkien about England (probably 'The Lonely Isle'): one of the best, he said. But Smith's note carried no reference to Gilson's death, nor any indication of what Tolkien had written in response to the news. The impression is of thoughts inexpressible or shut away, and vitality sapped.

Since then he had forwarded a brief letter from Christopher Wiseman regarding Rob's death. The two were in agreement: weighed in the scales of life, Gilson for all his flaws was as gold compared to the drossy mass of people. In Smith's words, 'such a life, even though its accomplishment was nothing, even though it passed almost unseen, even though no guiding principle ruled it and marked it out, even though doubt and misgiving, storm and stress raged always in his developing mind, is in the sight of God and all men worthy of the name of a value inconceivably higher than those of the idle chatterers who fill the world with noise, and leave it no emptier for their loss. Because the nobility of character and action once sent into the world does not return again empty.'

Tolkien had replied in a similar vein. Regarding, presumably, those same 'idle chatterers', the journalists and their readers whom Smith execrated, he wrote that 'No filter of true sentiment, no ray of real feeling for beauty, women, history or their country shall ever reach them again.' Evidently all three were in the grip of the anger that comes with grief. Their choice of target was entirely in keeping with TCBSian precepts. After all, the TCBS had vied against the boorish and empty-headed set at school, and the Council of London had cast out T. K. Barnsley and his fellow ironists. This is the spirit in which Smith wrote,

Save that poetic fire
  Burns in the hidden heart,
Save that the full-voiced choir
  Sings in a place apart,

Man that's of woman born,
  With all his imaginings,
Were less than the dew of morn,
  Less than the least of things.

At the same time, war-propaganda and its consumers were regularly demonized by soldiers of the Great War. The feeling arose from a combination of factors: knowledge that the propaganda was false, suspicion that those at home would never comprehend the reality of the trenches, and bitterness that friends and heroes died while the profiteers and their dupes sat in comfort and safety. The mood finds its most famous expression in Siegfried Sassoon's 'Blighters', a mortal curse upon music-hall jingoists ('I'd love to see a tank come down the stalls, / Lurching to ragtime tunes . . .'). Smith expressed an apocalyptic variant in 'To the Cultured':

> What are we, what am I?
> Poor rough creatures, whose life
> Is 'depressing' and 'grey',
> Is a heart-breaking strife
> With death and with shame
> And your polite laughter,
> Till – the world pass away
> In smoke and in flame,
> And some of us die,
> And some live on after
> To build it anew.

A glance across the Channel to these 'cultured' rich and those 'idle chatterers' was enough to confirm that, although Rob Gilson was dead, his worth outlived him.

Wiseman found further consolation in one of Gilson's sentiments, that 'the entirety of the TCBS was its whole value to itself': in other words, its point was simply the best kind of fellowship. It is indeed hard to escape the impression that constant reference to the impersonal initials 'TCBS' in the correspondence between the four was a way of concealing the mutual affection these young men felt towards each other. Yet Gilson's sentiment ran counter to the vision they had also shared of 'the great work' they would ultimately do together. It was truly the sentiment of a 'doubting Thomas', as Smith described Gilson, and it implied that what the TCBS achieved in life mattered not a jot.

Tolkien had posted Wiseman's letter back to Smith, adding his own underlinings and annotations. With these he now found that he disagreed. He could scarcely express much of what had gone through his mind since then. He felt hungry, lonely, and powerless, and oppressed by 'the universal weariness of all this war'. Despite rumour, he had no more idea of the battalion's next move than of Smith's whereabouts; but following his vigil in the wood, Tolkien wrote a long letter amid the noise of several meals in the company mess. 'I have lots of jobs on,' he said before he signed off. 'The Bde. Sig. Offr. is after me for a confabulation, and I have two rows to have with the QM and a detestable 6.30 parade – 6.30pm of a sunny Sabbath.'* His declaration to Smith was austere. 'I have sat solemnly down and tried to tell you drily just what I think,' he admitted. 'I have made it sound very cold and distant.'

Gilson had achieved the greatness of sacrifice but not, Tolkien wrote, greatness of the particular sort the TCBS had envisioned. 'The death of any of its members is but a bitter winnowing of those who were not meant to be great – at least directly,' he said. As for the fellowship that had shared those dreams, Tolkien's conclusion was no less stark.

> So far my chief impression is that something has gone crack. I feel just the same to both of you – nearer if anything and very much in need of you . . . but I don't feel a member of a little complete body now. I honestly feel that the TCBS has ended . . . I feel a mere individual . . .

Wiseman indeed had placed such faith in God's plan for the four that he had denied any might die before its fruition. If it

* The brigade signal officer was Tolkien's predecessor at battalion level, Lieutenant W. H. Reynolds. The quartermaster (killed in 1917) was Lieutenant Joseph Bowyer, a professional soldier twice Tolkien's age and the grandson of a Lancashire Fusilier from the Peninsular War.

was God's purpose that the TCBS should do some work as a unity, he had written back in March, 'and I can't help thinking it is, then He will hear our prayer and we shall all be kept safe and united until it is His pleasure to stop this eruption of Hell.' Wiseman's worst apprehensions had indeed been focused on Gilson, but they had been of an entirely different nature. 'He will come out of this an enormous man . . . if he can keep his senses,' he had added. 'Insanity is what I fear most.' The expression *shell shock* had now entered the English language. In fact Gilson's foresight had been the clearer: the TCBS faced an enormous task, he had said; 'we shall not see it accomplished in our lifetime'. But Tolkien's declaration at Bus-lès-Artois flew in the face of G. B. Smith's most solemn convictions. Facing the horror of a night patrol back in February, Smith had stated expressly that 'the death of one of its members cannot, I am determined, dissolve the TCBS . . . Death can make us loathsome and helpless as individuals, but it cannot put an end to the immortal four!'

G. B. Smith had learned of Rob's death at the end of an ordeal at Ovillers probably more hellish than Tolkien's. The Salford Pals, half the battalion they had been at the start of the Somme offensive, had succeeded in seizing the south-west corner of the German stronghold during three days and nights of bayonet-fighting and bomb-throwing in smashed trenches. Enemy snipers had been ceaselessly active, claiming many victims. Smith, as intelligence officer, had questioned a group of German soldiers who were caught as they tried to flee. The interrogation was not harsh. 'They were lost, nearly surrounded, and hungry and thirsty,' he wrote in his report. But other duties were nightmarish: he had to collect letters and papers from the wounded and dead Prussian Guards (some killed up to two weeks previously in the great bombardment), and examine identity discs for information about the enemy's deployments. And trenches the Pals took were choked with corpses.

'I am truly afraid we can't possibly meet,' Smith had written in his taciturn note about 'The Lonely Isle'. He had then been thirty miles away from the Somme, and on the verge of moving elsewhere again for a while. Immediately after Ovillers, the Salford Pals had marched north, but at the end of July they had left their brigade and moved on to retrain under the Royal Engineers as a 'pioneer' battalion. Tough men, largely recruited from the coalfields, they had long been marked down for this: pioneers carried out an infantry division's heavy labour. Smith (though Tolkien did not know it) was now back, based in Hédauville not far from Bouzincourt. Half the Pals were running a supplies railway in the wood west of the Ancre, near where they had spent the night before the Big Push. The other half were excavating new trenches on the other side of the river and out to the eastern tip of Blighty Wood, where hundreds of their friends and comrades had been shot down on the first day of the great battle. The men worked under sporadic shellfire.

Now Smith desperately wanted to see Tolkien. 'Tonight I cannot sleep for memories of Rob and the last time I saw him,' he wrote on 15 August. 'I wish I could find you – I search for you everywhere.' Three days later he received Tolkien's obituary on the TCBS. He disagreed with it at almost every point.

As chance would have it, that day Tolkien's division moved its headquarters to Hédauville. Its battalions were going to take over a two-mile stretch of the front line from the fighting units of Smith's division. Accordingly, the following afternoon, Saturday 19 August, the 11th Lancashire Fusiliers marched into Hédauville and set up their tents south of the village, *en route* to the trenches. Smith went looking for Tolkien, but was told that he was away on a course.

The 25th Division had recalled all its battalion signal officers that Wednesday for a week of instruction, during which they were taught the error of their ways: their messages were too wordy, their phone calls too long, their battlefield stations too conspicuous; they relied too heavily on their runners and too little on their pigeons. But there was good news for Tolkien and the other battalion signal officers. Amid the enormous losses on the Somme, some of them had been made to fill in for fallen company commanders, but as part of the ongoing shake-up in communications this was now stopped.

Failing to find his friend, Smith decided forthwith to communicate his righteous anger by mail. 'I want you to regard this rather violent letter as a sort of triumphal ode to the glorious memories and undiminished activity of RQG who although gone from among us is still altogether with us,' he wrote. He was returning Tolkien's long letter – with the addition of some 'rather curt and perhaps rude' annotations. 'We are sure to meet presently, to which I enormously look forward. I am not quite sure whether I shall shake you by the hand or take you by the throat . . .'

The chance to find out arose that day. Tolkien was at Acheux, less than three miles away, and in the event the two finally caught up with each other. Signal instruction detained Tolkien when his battalion moved into the trenches, and from Saturday until the course ended he was able to see Smith every day.

Three issues were at stake: the 'greatness' of Rob Gilson, the purpose of the TCBS, and whether the club had survived his death. Smith was furious that Tolkien had concluded their friend was 'not meant to be great' and had responded with the question: 'Who knows whether Rob has not already spread an essence as widely as we ever shall . . . ?' (The frankly stricken letters from Rob's fellow Cambridgeshires to Cary Gilson suggest that this was not mere sentimentality: the Headmaster's son clearly affected many friends deeply.) 'He certainly was a doubting Thomas,' Smith added, 'but . . . I never expect to look upon his like again.'

He had missed Tolkien's point. Death had prevented their friend from taking his 'holiness and nobility' and his inspirational qualities to the wider world. 'His greatness is in other words now a personal matter with us,' Tolkien said, 'but only touches the TCBS on that precise side which perhaps . . . was the only one that Rob really felt – "Friendship to the Nth power".'

The essence of TCBSianism was more than friendship, he reminded Smith. 'What I meant, and thought Chris meant, and am almost sure you meant, was that the TCBS had been granted some spark of fire – certainly as a body if not singly – that was destined to kindle a new light, or, what is the same thing, rekindle an old light in the world; that the TCBS was destined to testify for God and Truth in a more direct way even than by laying down its several lives in this war . . .'

Both he and Smith had already begun, through their literary efforts, to strive for this goal. Smith too believed in the 'poetic fire'; but Tolkien was simply determined that it should not remain 'in the hidden heart', as it did in Smith's poem.

So soon after Gilson's death, quite understandably, dreams of future achievement scarcely mattered to Smith. 'As to the winnowing of the TCBS,' he said, 'I really do not care two straws. It only refers to its executive capacity . . .' The group was spiritual in character, 'an influence on the state of being', and as such it transcended mortality; it was 'as permanently inseparable as Thor and his hammer'. The influence, he said, was 'a tradition, which forty years from now will still be as strong to us (if we are alive, and if we are not) as it is today . . .'

In truth this is perhaps what Tolkien wanted to hear. His letter from Bus-lès-Artois is not the cold-eyed assessment of harsh realities it sets out to be. Rather, it is the letter of a devout man trying hard to find a divine pattern behind an ostensibly senseless and cruel waste. But its logic appears flawed: after all, if Rob Gilson was not meant to be great, why should his death end the TCBSian dream of achieving greatness as a unity? Furthermore, the letter undergoes a dramatic volte-face. Immediately after declaring 'I honestly feel that the TCBS has ended', Tolkien had added a caveat: 'but I am not at all sure that it is not an unreliable feeling that will vanish – like magic perhaps when we come together again . . .' Furthermore, he had conceded, 'the TCBS may have been all we dreamt – and its work in the end be done by three or two or one survivor . . . To this I now pin my hopes . . .' The indications are that what Tolkien wanted, in his isolation and grief and doubt, was not agreement that the TCBS had ended, but reassurance that it still lived.

For Smith, at least, the argument had put an end to doubt: his mind was made up about Rob's value and the role of the TCBS, and of these things he was glad. Yet although he claimed to care so little for the 'executive' aspects of the TCBS, he had in fact been doing some writing since he and Tolkien last met. Among his poems are two brief elegies to Gilson: reflexes of grief, but also responses to the inspiration that had fired Tolkien, too, since the Council of London. One piece declares a stark view of divine providence: Gilson's death is 'a sacrifice of blood outpoured' to a God whose purposes are utterly inscrutable and who 'only canst be glorified / By man's own passion and the supreme pain'. The other betrays Smith's urgent nostalgia:

> Let us tell quiet stories of kind eyes
>   And placid brows where peace and learning sate:
> Of misty gardens under evening skies
>   Where four would walk of old, with steps sedate.
>
> Let's have no word of all the sweat and blood,
>   Of all the noise and strife and dust and smoke
> (We who have seen Death surging like a flood,
>   Wave upon wave, that leaped and raced and broke).
>
> Or let's sit quietly, we three together,
>   Around a wide hearth-fire that's glowing red,
> Giving no thought to all the stormy weather
>   That flies above the roof-tree overhead.
>
> And he, the fourth, that lies all silently
>   In some far-distant and untended grave,
> Under the shadow of a shattered tree,
>   Shall leave the company of the hapless brave,

And draw nigh unto us for memory's sake,
  Because a look, a word, a deed, a friend,
Are bound with cords that never a man may break,
  Unto his heart for ever, until the end.

So 'the fourth' could return even now to be present at the conclaves of 'we three together' and, in Smith's view, the TCBS could remain whole. Is there some consolatory glimpse here, too, of a gathering of the spirits of dead men, as Tolkien visualized in 'Habbanan beneath the Stars'? If so, the impression is confounded with one much more bleak: that 'the company of the hapless brave' resides not in Heaven, Hell, or Purgatory, but here on Earth, in the battlefield graves of the Somme. Such a reading suggests that in Smith, as in many of his contemporaries, there lurked by now the seeds of a rationalist despair. In the meantime, the old beliefs were intact. With Gilson's silent blessing, the TCBS could go on to tell their stories, not of war, but of peace and the good old days.

Those days were growing increasingly remote. Rob's father had replied to a letter of condolence from Tolkien with the news that Ralph Payton had also died. W. H. Payton, the elder brother and the TCBS's old 'Whip', was safely in Burma working for the Indian Civil Service, but 'the Baby' had been killed on 22 July. The 1st Birmingham Battalion,* also home to several other Old Edwardians, had been positioned south-east along the Somme line from La Boisselle. Like Tolkien, they had not taken part in the 1 July attack but had been sent into action in the wake of the Bastille Day offensive. Ralph, now a lieutenant in charge of the battalion machine gunners, had been in a night assault on high ground between High Wood and Delville Wood, amid the carcasses of horses killed in the Somme's only cavalry charge.

* Officially renamed the 14th Battalion of the Royal Warwickshire Regiment, it had been part of Smith's division, the 32nd, during training but their paths diverged on arrival in France when the unit (with Hilary Tolkien's 16th Royal Warwickshires) transferred to another division.

The 1st Birmingham Battalion had been all but destroyed in what was now a familiar story. The attack had been hastily prepared, and the artillery had failed to destroy the German defences. Almost two hundred of the battalion were slaughtered; Payton was never found. A rather shy and nervous humorist, he had taken on the burden of running the King Edward's debating society after the death of Vincent Trought in 1912. At Birmingham gatherings of the larger TCBS at Barrow's Stores, before the Council of London, he had been, in Wiseman's words, 'the Barrovian-par-excellence'.

'Heaven grant that enough of you may be left to carry on the national life,' said Cary Gilson, who had led a minute's silence at the school's annual Speech Day at the end of July 1916 to the memory of the forty-two Old Edwardians who had been killed in the previous twelve months. 'Would to God that we men "past military age" could go and do this business instead of you young fellows. We have had a good innings: there would be little difficulty in "declaring".' The Headmaster thanked Tolkien heartily for his sympathy, and said that Rob had left him several books and drawings.

Christopher Wiseman wrote to Smith expressing envy over his 'frequent meetings with JR'. His letter appears to have been the last word in the debate over whether the TCBS lived or died, and deserves to be quoted at length. Gilson's death had left Wiseman reflecting on the clique's history:

> At first nebulous and intensely witty, it then revolts against Tea-cake and Barrowclough and crystallizes it into a still intensely witty but less vapid TCBS. Finally the war. Now I think the TCBS is probably greatest in the third phase, but felt greatest in the first. We none of us had in those old days this horrible feeling of how puny, ineffectual and impossible we were. I don't know how far JR has been in this pot, but the revelation seems to have come most unpleasantly home to you and me, and if we don't look out we shall think of nothing else. On the other hand we

> did very little except live in a state of acute tension, act the Rivals, clothe a Roman remain in trousers, run Latin debates, and have tea in the Library, which enormous works as they were compared to our present occupation were possessed of highly 'factitious' greatness. In those days we stood on our heads; but one can't stand on one's head for ever. But I do believe we still have this advantage over other people, that when we want we can stand on our heads.

Wiseman was baffled by Tolkien's assertion that he no longer felt part of a 'little complete body', and went on:

> Speaking for myself I know that I belong to a coterie of three. Inside that coterie I find a real and absolutely unique inspiration . . . Now this coterie is for me quite sufficient. It is the TCBS. I don't see that there can yet be anything complete about the TCBS. We may have got rid of a lot of deliberate self-delusions, but I as yet see no reason to doubt that there is an achievement for our striving and a prize for our winning provided we are willing to pay the price. I cannot see that the TCBS is altered. Who is to say that we are less complete than we were? Or even if we are not, how does completeness, whatever it may be, affect the greatness of the TCBS? In the old days we could sit tight together and hug ourselves over the fire in the thought of what we were going to do. Now we stand with our backs to the wall, and yet we haver and question as to whether we had better not all put our backs against separate walls. Rob has shewn the temper of the steel we hold. Because he had got his prize so soon, is that a sign that the steel is less proof?
>
> Don't imagine that Rob means nothing to me. He probably means more to me than to either of you. In the dark days of Teacakianism he was the only link I had with the TCBS. He used to see the TCBS more nearly as it was than any of us, I think. I cannot estimate how much I learned from Rob. I feel to have learned something from both you and JR, as how could I help doing. But Rob and I, and chiefly Rob, built up whole systems of thought which I find now part and parcel of my attitude to

nearly every question . . . And I totally and vehemently deny that, as you once said, in a recent letter, he never understood the TCBS so well as you or I or JR. He understood it better; for he understood JR better. And, if you report JR correctly, I begin to think he understood it less, confusing it with Pre-Raphaelite brotherhoods and associations of Old Edwardians under William Morris, which he originally introduced merely by way of comparison, and which I always thought and said were indifferent at that.

However all this may be, I know I am a TCBSite; I intend achieving greatness, and, if the Lord will, public notability in my country; thirdly, in any greatness I achieve you and JR will be indissolubly bound up, because I don't believe I could get on without you. I believe we are not now getting on without Rob; we are getting on with Rob. It is by no means nonsense, though we have no reason to suppose, that Rob is still of the TCBS. But I believe there is something in what the Church calls the Communion of Saints.

Receiving Wiseman's letter a fortnight or so later, Smith forwarded it to Tolkien with the words, 'On the constitution of the TCBS I have nothing to add to what Chris says here, and what I have already said to you. My belief in it is undiminished.' The corollary to this is that when they parted some, at least, of Tolkien's doubts remained.

Smith and Tolkien ate a last meal together at Bouzincourt with Wade-Gery, the Oxford don-turned-captain, who (probably on this occasion) presented Tolkien with a volume of William Morris's *The Earthly Paradise*. But war was inescapable, and the omens poor, and even as they ate they came under enemy fire.

TEN

In a hole in the ground

It is often said that Tolkien wrote the first stories of his mythology in the trenches. 'That's all spoof,' he cautioned fifty years after the event. 'You might scribble something on the back of an envelope and shove it in your back pocket, but that's all. You couldn't write . . . You'd be crouching down among flies and filth.' After rejoining his battalion, he made revisions to 'Kortirion among the Trees' during two days in a dugout in the Thiepval Wood front line; but none of the 'Lost Tales' that form the basis for the much later 'Silmarillion' can be dated from Tolkien's time in France, let alone from the trenches themselves. The first problem was finding the requisite concentration; then there was the strong risk of losing anything you had actually written. Rob Gilson had declared from the trenches: 'Some people talk of reading books here, but I don't understand how they can manage it.' The voracious G. B. Smith managed to consume a great many books while in France, but after the loss of his long poem 'The Burial of Sophocles' *en route* from England he was constantly concerned to send home anything he wrote. When he received Tolkien's 'The Lonely Isle', he had made a copy of that too and sent it back to West Bromwich for safekeeping. Composing a sustained narrative was impossible amid the strain and interruptions of trench life. Picturing the elms of Warwick must have been challenge enough, for Thiepval Wood was far from tranquil. Edmund Blunden spoke of its 'ghastly gallows-trees', while Charles Douie wrote in his war memoir,

The Weary Road, 'The wood was never silent, for shell and rifle fire echoed endlessly through the trees, in testimony of the unceasing vigil of the opposing lines. At night the flares, as they rose and fell, threw the wood into deeper shadow and made it yet more dark and menacing.'

Elsewhere Tolkien did recall writing some of the mythology 'down in dugouts under shell fire', but it can have been little more than jotted ideas, outlines, or names. The anxieties of war, however, stoked the creative fires. His mind wandered through the world that had started to evolve at Oxford and in the training camps, in his lexicon, and in his poems. As he later reflected, 'I think a lot of this kind of work goes on at other (to say lower, deeper, or higher introduces a false gradation) levels, when one is saying how-do-you-do, or even "sleeping".' He was conscious, in retrospect at least, that such activity constituted a minor dereliction of duty, and confessed guiltily, 'It did not make for efficiency and present-mindedness, of course, and I was not a good officer . . .'

On the Western Front the present, for all its urgent terror, could not obscure the lamentable wreckage of the past all around, and even the recent past might seem bizarrely ancient. 'The Old British Line,' Edmund Blunden observed, 'was already venerable. It shared the past with the defences of Troy. The skulls which spades disturbed about it were in a manner coeval with those of the most distant wars; there is an obstinate remoteness about a skull.' Tolkien never merely observed the past. He recreated it in his own wayward imagination, focusing not on Troy but on Kortirion and, by now perhaps, on the great city of Gondolin too.

Some of those old bones protruding from the trench walls on the northern edge of Thiepval Wood were the relics, it may be, of men known to G. B. Smith when he first carried 'Kortirion' around these same trenches 'like a treasure' and headed off on night patrol exhorting Tolkien to publish. The line here had scarcely moved since Smith's winter vigil, but as Tolkien arrived the day after his signalling course ended, Thursday 24 August 1916, a mile away the Germans finally relinquished most of the Leipzig Salient, the fortification that had defeated the Salford Pals on 1 July. The 11th Lancashire Fusiliers let off smoke barrages in support of the attack (by battalions of Tolkien's division), drawing artillery fire from the Germans. The next two days poured with rain.

Relief on Friday took nearly five hours: not until the incoming battalion had filed in with all its gear and settled down could the Fusiliers squeeze past and stumble out into the dark trees. The process was 'always long and a trial to the temper', Gilson had written, but 'the joy of getting out of the trenches is quite indescribable ... The removal of the strain of responsibility, though it be only partial, is like a great load off the mind.' They reached Bouzincourt at 1.30 in the morning on Sunday 27 August – only to be sent back to the front line after less than twenty-eight hours' respite, as Tolkien noted punctiliously, at the crack of dawn on Monday.

But now he was on the other side of the old No Man's Land, east of the Leipzig Salient in trenches that had been seized just hours before. His new home was strewn with the bodies of dead German soldiers. In the dugouts were prisoners, many of them wounded. It was, in the words of the chaplain, Evers, 'an appalling bit of line ... no better than a hen-run, with precious little protection'. They were under shellfire, and to make a thoroughly miserable situation worse, the rain returned with a vengeance, turning the ground underfoot to a grey glue on the Tuesday. 'I feel that if I survive this war the only classification of weather that will ever matter to me will be into dry and muddy,' Rob Gilson had written in March. 'I could almost cry sometimes at the universal mud and the utter impossibility of escaping from it ...' As the summer passed away, the Somme began to revert to that primeval ooze. The men, though, had at their command an 'extraordinary cheeriness', as Evers said: 'If one got at all down the cure was to go and visit the men in a dug-out; the worse the conditions the cheerier they were and one came away cheered up oneself.'

On Friday 1 September, Tolkien moved back to relief trenches around the charnel-house of Ovillers, and he did not reach his bivouac at Bouzincourt until the following Tuesday night.

Aside from its wine, which he liked, France can have given Tolkien small compensation for the miseries of war. He disliked the native language and detested French cooking. On his sole previous visit, in the summer of 1913 as tutor to two Mexican boys, his warm impressions of Paris had been marred by 'the vulgarity and the jabber and the spitting and the indecency' of the Frenchmen in the streets, and he had been glad to leave for Celtic Brittany; but the trip had ended with one of the boys' aunts being run over by a car and fatally injured before Tolkien's eyes. If history had placed him in Saxony, defending the Weser against marauding Frenchmen, as the Lancashire Fusiliers had done in 1759, doubtless he would have been happier.

Yet Humphrey Carpenter, describing this attitude as 'Gallophobia', surely pays too much attention to mischievous hyperbole (as he does regarding Tolkien's views on Shakespeare and Wagner). Later, Tolkien's knowledge of French extended to the niceties of dialectal Eastern Walloon pronunciation, according to his protégé and friend, Simonne d'Ardenne. Certainly, he felt a lingering attachment towards the region of France in which he served. In 1945 he wrote, 'I can see clearly now in my mind's eye the old trenches and the squalid houses and the long roads of Artois, and I would visit them again if I could.'* It is a nostalgia not for remembered happiness but for a lost intimacy, even with horror, drudgery, and ugliness.

For five mostly dry days in the second week of September 1916, the 25th Division clogged the long roads with its dusty columns of troops and horses and its lumbering lines of support vehicles as it hauled its serpentine bulk west. Tolkien was at last granted a respite after two months of fighting and trench-duty.

---

* 'Artois' is an odd error for *Picardy*, perhaps prompted by Tolkien's acquaintance with Bus-lès-Artois.

Many officers made such journeys on horseback; but, as it turned out, when he was in France he walked everywhere: 'endless marching, always on foot,' as his children recalled him saying, 'sometimes carrying the men's equipment as well as his own to encourage them to keep going'.

At Franqueville, midway between the Western Front and the Atlantic, the division rested and trained from 12 September. By the end of the fortnight Tolkien had at his disposal six men freshly trained in visual signals. More importantly, he had been reunited with an old friend from Cannock Chase.

This was Leslie Risdon Huxtable. Raised in Tiverton, Devon, and nearly three years younger than Tolkien, he had thrown in his undergraduate studies at Cambridge to enlist, with his heart set on a rifle regiment. Instead he had been posted, within two weeks of the similarly disappointed Tolkien, for training with the 13th Lancashire Fusiliers. From Cannock Chase, Second Lieutenant Huxtable had made two trips to Otley in Yorkshire for signals training, and now (as it seems) he had been summoned to act as Tolkien's understudy, ready to take over as battalion signals officer should Tolkien be put out of action. He arrived at the right time: Tolkien had been at the sharp end of a disagreement with a superior. ('I am intensely sorry to hear of your frictions with others,' Smith wrote. 'I know how one officer can make a beast of himself to his junior, if he is swine enough to do so.' The battalion was temporarily in the hands of the twenty-year-old Captain Metcalfe, Bird having gone on leave for ten days.) 'Hux', as Tolkien called him, joined him in 'A' Company, and when the Fusiliers arrived back at Hédauville near the Somme front, on 26 September, the two shared a tent. During their time at rest, momentous and fateful events had transpired on the battlefield.

In 1945, Tolkien described the Second World War as 'the first War of the Machines', noting that its close left 'everyone the poorer, many bereaved or maimed and millions dead, and only one thing triumphant: the Machines'. By contrast, the conflict of 1914–18 was a war of manpower against machines, of the old world against the new. By September 1916, the battle of the Somme had become, like the siege of Verdun, a ghastly and almost fruitless exercise in attrition. A major breakthrough by infantry advancing against the entrenched machine guns now seemed inconceivable, so instead the primary goal was to kill as many Germans as possible. Such vast squandering of young lives left an indelible mark on Tolkien's generation, who refused to commit their own sons to similar static bloodbaths in the next war. More often they put the machines in charge – the Flying Fortress, the doodlebug, the aircraft carrier, the A-bomb – pitting them against each other, or against civilians. But the tide of history turned at the Somme, with the advent of the tank.

Rumour was dominated by this new wire-crushing, trench-bridging, bullet-proof monster. It had been deployed by surprise on 15 September, and the third 'big push' of the Somme offensive had swept the Germans back until the line ran for five miles due eastward from Thiepval. Over this ruinous shambles, once a pretty red-tiled village, the Fusiliers returning from the west could see the artillery blaze day and night. When they arrived back in Thiepval Wood, on Wednesday 27 September, the village had all but fallen. Some of its garrison had fought to the death; others had surrendered when a tank lumbered into view.

The wood had suffered in the attack: since Tolkien's last visit it had become a wilderness of toppled trunks and black stumps, hung with rags of bark. Battalion headquarters was now in a frontline trench north of the trees, so that Bird, the commanding officer, could see what was going on: here Tolkien had eight runners. The trench gave a vivid view on Thursday afternoon as waves of troops swept on from Thiepval in the first major attack on the Schwaben Redoubt.*

Late in the day the assault force sent a warning that Germans were making a getaway down the trenches opposite, which ran west to the Ancre. Ordered to head them off, three groups of

* The Fusiliers were in the same trenches they had held from 28 to 31 August: new 'parallels' at the head of Elgin and Inniskilling Avenues.

Fusiliers made to dash across No Man's Land and through a weak point in the wire. A machine gun started up, cutting down several men before the rest were told to hang back, but the first patrol was in the enemy trench and forcing a passage with grenades. They killed the machine gunners and the raid captured the Pope's Nose, a jocularly named but lethal salient in the enemy line. Throughout the night one of Tolkien's lance-corporals, thrown on his wits after a shell shattered his lamp, flashed his messages back across No Man's Land using a salvaged German torch. More than thirty prisoners had been taken; Tolkien, speaking German, offered a drink of water to a wounded captive officer, who corrected him on his pronunciation. Ironically, some of the captives belonged to a Saxon regiment that had fought side-by-side with the Lancashire Fusiliers at the Battle of Minden. But they were lucky to be alive: the Fusiliers had been told only days before that when 'cleaning up' a captured trench, 'If guards [are] insufficient, prisoners are often treacherous – so at times prisoners cannot be made.'

The captain who had led the Fusiliers' raid fell with a sniper's bullet through his head the next morning as he was returning to his own trench after delivering several more prisoners. Rain, mist, and smoke obscured visual signals all that day. Tolkien had a miraculous addition to his equipment, a new portable Morse telegraph set that could be used freely, unlike the conventional field telephone, because it did not leak its signal via the earth for all to hear. The 'Fullerphone', though, was a rather complicated array,* and in any case the line back through the wood was cut repeatedly by heavy shellfire.

The shells, of course, also found more grievous targets. Before

* It remained essential, and a bafflement to its users, in the Second World War: 'What is my greatest joy in life, / More precious even than my wife, / So comforting 'midst all this strife? / My Fullerphone. / How well I love your merry tricks; / Even when your buzzer sticks; / Delighting me with faint key clicks; / Oh Fullerphone . . . / Potentiometer, it's true / I'm not sure what to do with you. / Yet even you add beauty to / My Fullerphone.' – from R. Mellor, 'Ode to a Fullerphone'.

the raid, 'A' Company had been threading its way through the trenches in the wood towards the front line when the leading subaltern, Rowson, stopped for a chat with the commanding officer, Lieutenant-Colonel Bird (now back from leave). Huxtable, bringing up the rear, heard their voices, but shortly afterwards a message came down from the head of the column saying it was leaderless. A private who had been with Rowson described how they had just left the CO when a shell had burst between them: 'I was blown up in the air without a wound in me . . . Directly I recovered myself from being covered with dirt I looked for the officer, he was no where to be seen.' The shell had simply annihilated Rowson.

About the same time, Tolkien was passed a letter from the wife of a signaller, Private Sydney Sumner. 'I have not heard from him for this long time but we have had news from the army chaplain that he has been missing since July the 9th,' she wrote. 'Dear Sir I would not care if I only knew how he went. I know they cannot all be saved to come home . . .' Replying to such pitiable letters (Sumner had left a one-year-old daughter too) was one of the hardest tasks a sensitive officer faced; Tolkien preserved several of them.

Not far from the lines that Tolkien's battalion held late in September 1916 stands the Thiepval Memorial, inscribed with more than seventy thousand names. Many of these belong to unidentified bodies buried under the simple white stones in 242 cemeteries dotting the rural landscape of the Somme; the others belong to soldiers who, like Rowson, vanished without trace.*

After six days' rest, mostly at Bouzincourt, where he again shared a tent with Huxtable, Tolkien was sent back into the line with the Fusiliers, and from now on he lived almost constantly in a dugout. The tanks had not, after all, brought the sweeping

* The Gilsons remained in some uncertainty over the exact location of Rob's grave for three months until inquiries by his father and sister confirmed that he had been buried in Bécourt Cemetery.

breakthrough planned for September, and the grapple for ever more desolate yards of mud went on as winter drew near. Now his battalion was sent in to the upland behind Thiepval, a mile or more from the old British front line: a wilderness that, though relatively unscarred by shellfire, was arduous to negotiate and remote from established supply lines. The signallers synchronized the battalion's watches, and the Fusiliers were off, marching up the hill to Ovillers, past what had once been its church, and slogging onward into a maze of narrow trenches. Tolkien settled in on 6 October at battalion headquarters in front of the Ferme de Mouquet, unaffectionately known as Mucky Farm, a warren of fortified cellars that had finally been taken a week ago. (Its roofs could be seen sparkling from Blighty Wood when G. B. Smith and the Salford Pals had prepared to attack on 1 July; they had been given a map of the farm on the supposition that they would arrive there with their picks and shovels an hour and forty minutes after leaving the wood.)

The Fusiliers moved into a sequence of three trenches, with Huxtable and 'A' Company in the frontline Hessian Trench. Opposite lay the long Regina Trench, held by German Marines. To the right, and eastward, Regina Trench was under attack by Canadian troops. To the left, the endless rattle of gunfire and the *crump* of explosions marked the ongoing struggle for the Schwaben Redoubt. Ration parties leading mules repeatedly came under shellfire on the exposed brow of the land, where the trenches were barely worth the name. Ten men on a working party were killed this way returning from the front line, and the officer in charge succumbed to wounds the next day.

Now, less than a month after it began, Huxtable's stay on the Somme came to a sudden close. A shell burst on the parados or rear wall of his trench on 10 October, bringing it down on top of him. He was freed, but splinters of shrapnel had shot through his leg and one shard remained embedded in the bone of his calf. Huxtable was packed off to the casualty clearing station and thence to England. He had gained what many soldiers craved, a Blighty wound; but Tolkien had lost a deputy and a companionable friend.

The same day 'A' Company and the others were pulled back to the reserve trenches between Mouquet Farm and the front line and set to work digging, as ever, to deepen, widen, and strengthen the trenches. They vacated Hessian Trench in the nick of time, for on Thursday 12 October the Germans counter-attacked all along the line. The next day Tolkien and battalion headquarters moved forward to the Zollern Redoubt, five hundred yards to the rear of Hessian Trench. They were greeted that evening and through the night by tear gas shells, but on Saturday there was encouraging news: the Schwaben Redoubt had fallen. Two days later instructions came down from the generals that they now wanted Regina Trench.

The weather had held out well, apart from a single day's downpour, but a white frost ushered in Monday 16 October. There was not much time before winter locked the infantry down. Possession of Regina Trench would afford the British a panoramic view across German-held roads, fields, and towns to the north. Prisoners had been interrogated, planes had flown reconnaissance missions. For the first time, Tolkien had been issued with a fresh set of coded unit designations to confuse German intelligence. On Tuesday the Fusiliers, now numbering less than four hundred, descended from the plateau to rehearse for the attack in a safe area at Ovillers Post, just behind the old British front line west of Ovillers village. The four-mile trudge up the trenches to the front line began after dark on Wednesday 18 October 1916.

It was G. B. Smith's twenty-second birthday. He had outlived his worst apprehensions, but a darkening of mood was apparent in his letters. After the August reunion he had spoken of the pleasure of re-reading the *Mabinogion* and warned Tolkien that his title of 'Raconteur of the TCBS' was under threat from Christopher Wiseman (who had sent tales of 'his discovery of Brazilian Beetle Bangles in the wilds of Cumberland'). But soon Smith was mourning his own lost capacity for lunacy; he felt burdened with regrets and responsibilities. 'Perhaps this note of regret would be drowned did I feel that I was now doing things that are in any way worth doing,' he wrote. 'Yes, I think it is sheer vacancy which is destroying me.' His letters dwindled to little more than notes pleading for some word from his friend, or craving escape. 'Thoughts of leave are already beginning to play about my leaden brows. Roll on! as they say in Lancashire. Twice I have dreamed of it: surely after the third time it will come to pass.' For Tolkien, too, leave was always tantalizingly just around the corner, but his ordeal was now more acute than Smith's. If August had been 'universal weariness', October must have been near exhaustion. 'There were times when the constant deprivation of sleep drove men almost out of their mind,' recalled Charles Douie. With mud and slush everywhere and winds blowing ever chillier, others were 'astonished that flesh and blood can stand this sort of thing'.

Zero hour for the attack by Tolkien's battalion on the German-held Regina Trench was set for just after midday on Thursday, 19 October 1916; but, having at last deposited themselves in Hessian Trench with their load of bombs and sandbags at four o'clock in the morning, the Fusiliers had to turn around and go back to Ovillers Post. Heavy rain on Wednesday, and torrents still falling through Thursday morning, had made a morass of the upland. No Man's Land would be an impassable slough. Telegraph lines had gone down and the foul weather precluded visual signals. The assault was postponed for forty-eight hours. Three patrols, however, ventured out to check that the enemy's wire had been cut. This time it had: so effectively that one patrol passed through unawares and another actually climbed into Regina Trench before fleeing under a hail of bombs.

On Saturday morning, 21 October, Tolkien was ensconced once more with his equipment and runners in a dugout where Hessian Trench came closest to the enemy line, which lay a furlong downhill, out of sight beyond a bulge of ground. The rain clouds had blown away under a strong, icy wind. The mercury had fallen to its lowest since the Big Push began, and a sharp frost had paralysed that other enemy, the mud. Tolkien and the others in headquarters were given a hot meal, as were the men squatting and standing along three miles of frozen trench: the Fusiliers, the three battalions to their right, and the five to their left. All was as quiet as the front line could ever be, though way off to the west fighting could be heard around the Schwaben Redoubt.

Six minutes after midday the heavy guns and howitzers launched the cannonade. The first two companies of Fusiliers climbed out into the noise and smoke, followed quickly by the second wave: 'A' Company with their picks and shovels strapped to their backs, flanked by the battalion bombers. Tolkien's signallers went last, with the third wave, accompanied by men hauling machine guns and heavy trench mortars. Abruptly, the crowded, narrow trench was almost empty, and the Fusiliers were vanishing over the whale's back of No Man's Land towards the curtain of shells falling before Regina Trench. Evers, the padre, followed with the stretcher bearers. After a minute and a half the artillery barrage crept further away to fall directly on Regina Trench opposite Tolkien's headquarters.

Another two and a half minutes, and explosions abruptly shook Hessian itself: the big German guns had woken up. By now the trench was filled with men of the Royal Irish Rifles, who had moved forward from their support position. Flares went up on the far side of No Man's Land, but not the red flares the Fusiliers had taken to signal their positions. The minutes ticked by. Over to the left an enemy machine gun chattered.

Then figures came tumbling in over the parapet. They wore enemy field grey, but they were desperate, defeated men. At 12.20 p.m., Tolkien told brigade headquarters that Hessian Trench had begun to receive its first German prisoners.

The demoralized men of the 73rd and 74th Landwehr had been taken by surprise when the Fusiliers reached Regina Trench. Many had not got up from the 'funk-holes' gouged into the chalky walls in which they slept, and they had been caught still wrapped in groundsheets against the piercing cold. The distress flares had gone up, but most of the Germans had surrendered and were sent back across No Man's Land, through their own retaliatory bombardment. Now the Royal Irish were marching the prisoners at gunpoint out of Hessian Trench, towards the divisional cage.

Directly opposite battalion headquarters a tiny group of defenders held out for a while but then joined the mass surrender. Over to the right, bursts of rifle fire and grenade explosions indicated a more stubborn pocket of resistance. Signallers flashed across a request for more grenades to be sent over and the Royal Irish started carrying them across. Finally, the fifteen or so ragged survivors of this last German stand were also back in Hessian Trench. The other half had been killed by the Fusiliers: bombed or bayoneted, or machine-gunned from their own parapet.

News filtered back from the battle fitfully. One of Tolkien's runners who brought messages through the German bombardment was later decorated for bravery. The signaller hauling the battalion's pigeon basket across No Man's Land was hit, though another man rescued the basket and released a pigeon from Regina Trench with news of victory for divisional headquarters. The Fusiliers set up their red flags there and at 1.12 p.m. Tolkien sent a message to brigade headquarters that they had won the objective and joined up with the Loyal North Lancashires to their left. At 1.55 p.m. he reported that they had linked up with the unit to their right, too. Through the afternoon the other battalions won through, and Tolkien's division alone took more than seven hundred prisoners. Regina Trench was littered with the bodies of those who had not surrendered.

In No Man's Land lay fallen Fusiliers, most of them hit by their own artillery as they tried to keep close to the 'creeping barrage'; Captain Metcalfe and the other company leader in the first wave had both been wounded before reaching the enemy line. Forty-one Lancashire Fusiliers were dead or missing. Evers, the padre, tended to many of the 117 wounded. 'Some had the will to live and others hadn't,' he said. 'I remember going up to one with whom I could find nothing very serious and telling him that I would return shortly with a stretcher party, to find when I had done so that he had passed out. Others that really were badly knocked about retained their courage and were carried back to safety.' Evers finally walked back into Hessian Trench the next day, covered in blood and astonished to be greeted by a cheering battalion. He had been out all the bitterly cold night under shellfire. Later he wrote, 'There is a war picture depicting a shadowy Christ alongside an RAMC officer helping in a wounded man – well, I saw no such vision, but I was nonetheless conscious of His presence during those hours.'

The Fusiliers were relieved on Sunday, slowly and fearfully, as darkness fell and shells crumped around them. The officers from battalion headquarters rode out on horseback. On the way down to Ovillers Post they encountered several of the fabled tanks, crawling noisily up to the line. 'The horses were thoroughly frightened,' said a wounded officer riding with them. 'Neither horses nor riders had ever seen, or heard, any tanks before.'

For Second Lieutenant Tolkien, the 11th Lancashire Fusiliers, and the 25th Division, the Battle of the Somme was over; but comfort, ease, and safety seemed far away. They were being switched from the Fifth Army, which had commanded them on the Somme, to the Second Army, long associated with Ypres, a name of ill omen. Monday 23 October 1916 dawned misty and damp outside Tolkien's tent in the camp between Albert and Bouzincourt: wet weather just in time for a series of parades. The 74th Brigade was inspected by its brigadier-general at Albert, then taken by bus ten miles west for inspection by the divisional major-general. At least there was a hut to sleep in that night. On Tuesday came a final route march, thirteen miles along liquid roads from Vadencourt to Beauval, where Tolkien had attended Mass on the way to Franqueville back in September. Since leaving Étaples in June, he had packed his kit and moved forty-five times. Now, for the first time in nearly a month, he slept not under canvas or in a hut or a hole, but under a proper roof, in Beauval's Rue d'Épinelte.

On Wednesday 25 October Tolkien felt weak and unwell, but he did not report sick until after the Fusiliers had been inspected and thanked by General Gough of the Fifth Army and by Field-Marshal Haig, the British commander-in-chief. On Friday, a cold and showery day, he went to the medical officer with a temperature of 103.

He had trench fever, a gift of the inescapable lice that had bred in the seams of his clothes and fed on him, passing a bacterium, *Rickettsia quintana*, into his bloodstream. That could have happened anything from two weeks to a month ago. British soldiers typically blamed lice on the German trenches they had to occupy, perhaps with more justice than prejudice: soldiers close to defeat, after all, are likely to prove less fastidious than the incoming victors. Evers recounts a scene from the Somme that may feature Tolkien, unnamed, in the role of the signals officer: 'On one occasion I spent the night with the Brigade Machine Gun Officer and the Signals Officer in one of the captured German dug-outs . . . We dossed down for the night in the hopes of getting some sleep, but it was not to be. We no sooner lay down than hordes of lice got up. So we went round to the Medical Officer, who was also in the dug-out with his equipment, and he gave us some ointment which he assured us would keep the little brutes away. We anointed ourselves all over with the stuff and again lay down in great hopes, but it was not to be, because instead of discouraging them it seemed to act like a kind of *hors d'oeuvre* and the little beggars went at their feast with renewed vigour.'

The medical corps of 1916, for all their heroic work, were not much more use against trench fever itself, which they labelled 'pyrexia of unknown origin'. The symptoms – a sudden loss of strength and balance, often accompanied by a rash, headaches, and severe pain in the legs and back – were left to run their course through rest. In some few cases the persistent fever might lead to heart failure; but for Tolkien, *Rickettsia quintana* proved a life-saver.

The army was notoriously suspicious about any attempt to 'cry off sick', but there was no question about Tolkien's condition. He left the 11th Lancashire Fusiliers exactly four months after he joined them, on Saturday 28 October 1916, and was transferred to an officers' hospital a short distance from Beauval, at Gézaincourt. On Sunday he was taken on the ambulance train from Candas to Le Touquet, and a bed at the Duchess of Westmorland Hospital. That night the 11th Lancashire Fusiliers also left Candas by rail, Flanders-bound. Since his arrival the battalion had lost nearly six hundred men: four hundred and fifty of them wounded, sixty dead, and seventy-four missing. Only the drafts it had received during the same period had enabled the unit to continue. But Tolkien had survived whole in body, and for the time being he was safe.

PART THREE

The Lonely Isle

ELEVEN

Castles in the air

The fever persisted. Tolkien wrote to Lieutenant-Colonel Bird, his commanding officer, explaining his whereabouts, but All Hallows went by and after nine days in hospital at Le Touquet he was sent by train to Le Havre. There, on 8 November 1916, he boarded the soldier's joy, 'the Blighty boat'. A packet ship in peacetime, the steam liner *Asturias* was now brilliantly lit up and painted white, with green stripes and red crosses, to tell enemy submarines that she was a hospital ship and not a military target. She was large and comfortable, with cosy beds; and during the ten-hour crossing the next day there were sea-water baths to be had. Most homeward-bound soldiers were walking wounded, happy to have a minor but honourable 'Blighty' wound. The worst-hit survivors of battle never got further than the tented 'moribund ward' of the casualty clearing station in the field. Some, especially now that winter was here, were simply ill, like Tolkien; but others suffered from something worse than feverish delirium: they trembled or twitched uncontrollably and had an otherworldly look.

England glimmered into view: the Lonely Isle, 'sea-girdled and alone'. The *Asturias* steamed into Southampton and the same day a train took Tolkien back to the city of his childhood. That night, Thursday 9 November, he was in a bed at the Birmingham University Hospital. Soon he was reunited with Edith, five months after the parting that had seemed 'like a death'.

The First Southern General Hospital (as it was officially known) had been set up in September 1914 in the grand arched halls and corridors of the university at Edgbaston and was continually being expanded under pressure of war casualties, who were cared for by the Medical Corps with the assistance of Red Cross and St John Ambulance volunteers. Tolkien was not the only old TCBSite invalided home to Birmingham, for T. K. Barnsley was back too. Buried alive by a trench mortar at Beaumont-Hamel in August, Tea-Cake had been packed off to England with a split eardrum and suffering from shell shock. Rob Gilson's sister, Molly, dressed wounds here for the army surgeon, Major Leonard Gamgee. A man of some repute, and an Old Edwardian, he was a relative of the famous Sampson Gamgee who had invented, and given his name to, surgical *gamgee-tissue*, mentioned by Tolkien as the source of Sam Gamgee's surname in *The Lord of the Rings*.

Tolkien would not be here for long, if his commanding officer had his way. Captain Munday, the 11th Lancashire Fusilier's new adjutant (Kempson having been shot through the shoulder in the attack on Regina Trench) sent a note for Tolkien to hand to the military authorities as soon as he was discharged from hospital. The battalion was short of officers, his signallers were under a non-commissioned officer, and he was needed badly, it said, adding: 'Lt-Col Bird wishes me to state that he values the services of Lt Tolkien very highly.' The CO was going to be very disappointed; but not so Tolkien's friends. 'Stay a long time in England,' exhorted G. B. Smith when he heard. 'Do you know I was horribly afraid you had been settled for good? I am beyond measure delighted . . .' If Wiseman shared those fears he did not voice them, but he was equally merry when Smith passed on the news. 'If you had offered me 500 guesses,' he declared, 'I would never had thought of your being in giddy old Brum, as you once called it. I wish I could get off for one day only, and would go straight there and see you.' Tolkien, he noted, had sent him no poetry since their argument about its 'freakishness' back in March. Tolkien duly despatched some of his verses and, thanks perhaps to Wiseman's prompting, during November he revised the long semi-autobiographical poem he had written in the midst of that argument, 'The Wanderer's Allegiance',

The Great Twin Brethren: Wiseman and Tolkien stand shoulder to shoulder in the middle of the back row among the King Edward's School First XV team for 1909–10. (The annotations are Tolkien's.)

Measures' house, with Tolkien to the left of Mr Measures, Wiseman seated far right and Gilson in half-profile far left.

Right: Tolkien's drawing of *Gipsy Green*, a house to the west of Cannock Chase where the family stayed in 1918. It lent the name Fladweth Amrod to Tolkien's mythology

Below: *Caerthilian Cove and Lion Rock*, a sketch from Tolkien's Cornish summer holiday, drawn a week after Britain entered the war

Smith in Aristophanes' *The Frogs*

King Edward's School

GIPSY GREEN

The TCBS at war: clockwise from left, Christopher Wiseman in naval uniform, Rob Gilson of the Cambridgeshire Battalion, J.R.R. Tolkien of the Lancashire Fusiliers and G.B. Smith of the 3rd Salford Pals

Desolation: British soldiers sit in the chalky remains of a German trench running from the Roman road up to Ovillers, where Tolkien saw battle in July 1916

German prisoners are brought in from Thiepval, September 1916

‘The universal weariness of all this war’: Exhausted troops in a captured enemy trench at Ovillers, July 1916

‘A few acres of mud’: the flooded valley of the Ancre in October

Tolkien in the 1930s, when a wide audience finally glimpsed his mythology

renaming the sequence 'The Town of Dreams and the City of Present Sorrow'.

On Saturday 2 December 1916 Tolkien was called before a military medical board. His temperature had been back to normal for a week, but he was still pale and weak and beset by persistent aches and pains in his legs. The board predicted that he would be fit for action in six weeks. In fact Tolkien was considering a transfer to the Royal Engineers, which ought to be safer than a combat unit. The idea perhaps had something to do with his father's sister Mabel and her husband Tom Mitton, whose home in Moseley Tolkien was using as a correspondence address and whose son, Thomas Ewart Mitton, was a signaller in the Royal Engineers. Christopher Wiseman had suggested that Tolkien appeal to Tea-Cake's father, Sir John Barnsley, to let him into his brigade. Nothing came of the idea; but in the meantime he was unfit for service, and the board told him to go home.

In his absence Edith had traced his movements on the map on her wall. Until now, any knock at her door could have brought a dreaded War Office telegram. His return to Great Haywood was thus an emotionally charged moment, which Tolkien marked with a six-stanza ballad, 'The Grey Bridge of Tavrobel'. *Tavrobel* ('wood-home') is the Gnomish equivalent of Haywood ('enclosed wood'), but on this occasion any mythological considerations seem secondary to the personal ones.* The scene is set with 'two rivers running fleetly' – the Trent and the Sow – and a reference to the old packhorse bridge that spans them at Great Haywood. Further parallels with Tolkien's situation do not need spelling out as the ballad moves into a dialogue of love and longing:

---

* Among the earliest instances of Gnomish are three heraldic devices of the towns of *Tol Erethrin* (Tol Eressëa): *Taurobel* (a variant of Tavrobel), *Cortirion* (Kortirion, or Warwick), and *Celbaros*, which depicts a fountain and intertwined rings appropriate to Cheltenham, the spa town where Tolkien asked Edith Bratt to marry him. *Ranon* and *Ecthelin* (suggesting the Gnomish for 'fountain') stand for 'Ronald' and 'Edith'.

'O! tell me, little damozelle,
  Why smile you in the gloaming
On the old grey bridge of Tavrobel
  As the grey folk come a-homing?'

'I smile because you come to me
  O'er the grey bridge in the gloaming:
I have waited, waited, wearily
  To see you come a-homing.

In Tavrobel things go but ill,
  And my little garden withers
In Tavrobel beneath the hill,
  While you're beyond the rivers.'

'Ay, long and long I have been away
  O'er sea and land and river
Dreaming always of the day
  Of my returning hither.'

With a final stanza that laments lost 'days of sunlight', 'The Grey Bridge of Tavrobel' is slight yet haunting. By contrast, Tolkien's last batch of poems was unreservedly declared 'magnificent' by Christopher Wiseman, who promised that if Tolkien were to publish he could arrange for a decent notice in the *Manchester Guardian*. 'I am convinced,' he declared from the *Superb*, 'that if you do come out in print you will startle our generation as no one has as yet . . . Really it is presumptuous in me to say anything about the poems themselves, but I am afraid they will kill the dear old XIXth Century altogether . . . Where you are going to lead us is a mystery . . .' Wiseman now felt that G. B. Smith was lagging behind and was still fundamentally a Victorian writer. Surely, he added, the TCBS was 'one of the most extraordinary associations ever', what with its two antithetical poets and himself, more likely to become a finance minister.

* * *

Wiseman was concerned about Smith, and not just about his current poetic output, which he felt was 'rather below his usual standard'. He had asked Tolkien to write 'and tell me all about him'; but Tolkien had not seen Smith since August, and letters had become more and more brief. With the conversion of the 3rd Salford Pals to a 'pioneer' battalion of navvies, they had taken part in one attack but largely just laid roads and dug trenches. Such a unit had no use for intelligence work, so Smith had shouldered the dull duties of billeting officer. Every time the battalion moved he would go on ahead to arrange accommodation and then meet the troops as they marched up behind. Small wonder that he had complained 'sheer vacancy' was destroying him. At the end of October 1916, as Tolkien lay in hospital in Le Touquet, Smith had become adjutant, responsible for all the manpower requirements of the Pals. He announced the fact with a humorist's false modesty ('For such I am, eheu, eheu'), but in practice being adjutant was unexciting, and in a pioneer battalion it meant little more than churning out routine marching orders. 'Fur undercoats will be neatly rolled and strapped on top of packs,' he would write. 'Strict march discipline must be observed and on no account must men be allowed to straggle. . . Battalion Order No. 252 para 3, re carrying of loose articles or parcels on the line of march, will also be strictly complied with.'

All this was contrary to Smith's guiding spirit. By nature he was undisciplined and passionately skittish. He had once written despairingly: 'My career in the Army has not been a success, because I *cannot* set myself or realise the Army ideals in business matters. What is *clean*? What is *just*? What is *severe*? I know not, nor ever shall, although I have tried very hard, from a sense of duty.' Now he joked bitterly, 'The Corps Commander is in the yard . . . and your humble servant sits in his Adjutant's rabbit hole and simply shivers. I am so much afraid he will rush in and ask me why I haven't complied with his XYX/S7/U^5/3F of yesterday's date or something.' The schoolboy who had found the 'engaging rascal' Robin Hood 'one of the most living characters in all literature', and the 'wild and whole-hearted admirer' of Tolkien's mythology, were imprisoned behind an army desk.

Smith's training in the language of military orders and reports had enabled him to describe with detachment in his official intelligence report for 1 July the slaughter of the men with whom he had lived and worked for eighteen months: 'Owing to hostile MG fire the advance was made by short rushes. Casualties were heavy.' So far as poetry communicates feeling, this was the reverse of poetry. The sheer horror of war, of course, also conspired to de-sensitize, as Smith knew when he wrote, of his generation,

> Who battled have with bloody hands
> Through evil times in barren lands,
> To whom the voice of guns
> Speaks and no longer stuns . . .

All this, combined with the sheer grind of winter life on the Somme, amply explains any decline in Smith's writing. But war seemed endless; and if he felt sorry for himself, it is hard not to join him in sympathy. In one of his late pieces he addressed the spirits of Rob Gilson and other dead friends:

> Shapes in the mist, ye see me lonely,
> Lonely and sad in the dim firelight:
> How far now to the last of all battles?
> (Listen, the guns are loud tonight!)

At least the Salford Pals, stationed for the past two months just behind the front line, had lost no men in all that time. He had entertained his widowed mother with letters about his riding experiences, and the news of his friend's safe return home seemed to have cheered Smith immensely. Unfortunately, his promotion to adjutant had delayed his next opportunity to get away, but on 16 November he wrote to Tolkien: 'I hope I shall be able to come to Great Haywood, for my leave is assuredly on the wing.'

* * *

When the Battle of the Somme finally petered out in late November 1916, G. B. Smith was stationed with the Salford Pals at the non-descript village of Souastre, nine miles north of Bouzincourt where he had last seen Tolkien. The pioneers spent the short, freezing days in bursts of rain, sleet, and snow. On the morning of Wednesday 29 November, Smith was overseeing the usual repairing and drainage work on one of the roads leading out of the village, but he had organized a football match for the men that afternoon and was looking forward to playing. He was walking along the road when the air was split by the shriek of shells. A German howitzer had fired somewhere to the east, four miles or more away. Two fragments from a bursting shell struck Smith in the right arm and buttock.

He walked to the dressing station and, while waiting for an ambulance, he smoked a cigarette and wrote a letter to his mother telling her not to worry: his wounds were slight and soon he would be back at the base, Étaples. At the casualty clearing station he was in the care of nurses whom he knew and liked.

After two days, however, he developed gas gangrene. Bacteria from the soil had infected his thigh wound, killing off his tissues and swelling them with gas. Surgeons operated to stem the advance. 'After that he quickly sank,' his mother Ruth told Tolkien. 'He dictated a letter to me saying I am doing famously and shall be in England soon after Christmas. He thought so, never realising the danger he was in . . .'

Geoffrey Bache Smith died at half past three in the morning on 3 December 1916, at Warlincourt. His commanding officer told Mrs Smith that those who had survived the terrible first days of the Somme thought they might live to see the end of the war.

Smith wrote his most fully achieved poem, 'The Burial of Sophocles' (begun before the war and rewritten in the trenches after being lost *en route* to France) as a riposte to the axiom that those whom the gods love die young. In it he had envisaged the perfection of a completed life:

O seven times happy he is that dies
  After the splendid harvest-tide,
When strong barns shield from winter skies
  The grain that's rightly stored inside:
There death shall scatter no more tears
Than o'er the falling of the years.

Aye, happy seven times is he
  Who enters not the silent doors
Before his time, but tenderly
  Death beckons unto him, because
There's rest within for weary feet
Now all the journey is complete.

Christopher Wiseman broke the news to Tolkien. 'My dear JR,' he wrote. 'I have just received news from home about GBS, who has succumbed to injuries received from shells bursting on Dec. 3rd. I can't say very much about it now. I humbly pray Almighty God I may be accounted worthy of him. Chris.' In reply to a letter of condolence, Ruth Smith asked Tolkien to send copies of any poems of Geoffrey's he might have, so they could be published. 'You can imagine what is this loss to me,' she said. After the death of her husband, Geoffrey had become her chief support and strength, and he had relied equally on her. 'He had never left home until going to Oxford and we built many castles in the air of the life we would have together after the War.'

Tolkien had been gathering himself for a spring. Probably while still in hospital, he made a new list of Qenya words drawn from his lexicon, calling it 'The Poetic and Mythologic Words of Eldarissa' (another name for the language). Halfway through, he interrupted it with a chart of denizens of Faërie, in which every Qenya word is translated not only into English, but also into a second invented language, Gnomish or Goldogrin. In accordance with historical linguistics, his academic speciality, Tolkien had derived Qenya fictively from an older ancestral language via a series of regular sound shifts and word-forming affixes. He created Gnomish, Qenya's sibling, by filtering the same originating language, Primitive Eldarin, through different sound shifts, sometimes also applying different morphological elements. This, principally, is how German and English have both grown out of the language spoken in common by the Germanic peoples in the first centuries A.D. Tolkien, however, followed his heart, not his head, by finding the inspiration for his two invented tongues in a pair of real-world languages that are utterly unrelated. Just as Qenya reflected Tolkien's passion for Finnish, so Goldogrin reflected his love of Welsh. Qenya liked trailing vowels, but Gnomish forgot them. Qenya favoured the 'hard', voiceless stops *k*, *t*, and *p*, but Gnomish allowed their 'softer' voiced counterparts *g*, *d*, and *b* to flourish. (The names of the Finnish and Welsh national myths, *Kalevala* and *Mabinogion*, illustrate these characteristics well.*) Aesthetically, Goldogrin sounds as if it has been worn smooth by change and experience, as befits a tongue spoken in exile among the fading woods of our mortal world, in contrast to Qenya, spoken in stately, immutable Kôr. It seems apt that Qenya, the language of lore, had been devised when Tolkien was an undergraduate and a soldier in training, whereas Gnomish, the language of adventure, tragedy, and war, should emerge after the Somme.

The distinction between the two served Tolkien for the rest of his creative life, though he constantly altered both languages and their histories. He ultimately took Gnomish off the Gnomes and gave it to the Grey-elves of the 'Silmarillion', renaming it *Sindarin*. The Gnomes, or Noldor as they were called by that

---

* Indeed, under certain conditions, where a Qenya word had a voiceless sound, the related Goldogrin word would have its voiced equivalent instead; so *Taniqetil*, the mountain of Valinor, was called by the Gnomes *Danigwethl*, and 'lamentation' or the weeping willow not *siqilissë* but *sigwithiel*. There were, of course, many more phonological differences between the two languages. *Sigwithiel* also shows a morphological difference, being built from the same root as *siqilissë*, SIQI, using a quite distinct affix.

time, were then allowed to borrow it. But that was far in the future.

In the meantime, below the fairies and the ogres on his chart, Tolkien wrote *Eärendl*, the name of the sky-mariner who had presaged his mythology back in September 1914. Since then, Eärendel had remained a solitary figure, more of a symbol than an individual, but now Tolkien finally gave him a dynasty. Eärendel was to be half man but half Gnome (or *Noldo*): the son of a human father, *Tuor*, and a faëry mother, *Idril*. Idril's father was 'king of the Free-noldor', *Turgon*, who ruled over *Gondolin*, the City of Seven Names. In hospital and on leave after returning from the Battle of the Somme, Tolkien wrote his tale, 'The Fall of Gondolin', a major imaginative turning point.

The long periods of marching, or watching and waiting in the trenches, and then convalescing in bed, had allowed Tolkien's ideas to ferment. Finally free to write again, he did so with tremendous fluency. The established matter of sky myths and Valinor and the Lonely Isle were set aside for the time being, as 'The Fall of Gondolin' came out of his head 'almost fully formed'. An explosion of creative power, it established the moral parameters of Tolkien's world, enshrining aspects of good and evil in faëry races and demiurgic beings who are locked in perpetual conflict.

Compared with later writings – even those composed immediately after the First World War – 'The Fall of Gondolin' shows very little of that detailed 'historical' context that is one of Tolkien's mature hallmarks. Very few lands or peoples are named. The spotlight falls strongly on the city of Gondolin itself, and especially its constituent kindreds; but there are only occasional glimpses of the momentous history of the *Noldoli*, or Gnomes, and of how this branch of Elf-kind came to establish their city. He already saw 'The Fall of Gondolin' (or 'Tuor and the Exiles of Gondolin', as he initially called it) as part of a much larger narrative in which the history of the Gnomes would be told in full. But for now that history emerged only piecemeal.

A terrible oppression has befallen the Gnomes. Most have been enslaved and are kept in 'the Hells of Iron' by the tyrannical Melko, who infests the north with his goblins and spies. Those who are not physically kept prisoner are penned in mountain-ringed Aryador and in mental shackles. The free Gnomes have fled to the hidden refuge of Gondolin.

It is in Aryador that the tale begins, already marked as a land of primitive mortals ignorant of the fairy 'shadow-folk' in their midst. But the hero, Tuor, is different from the outset. He shows signs of poetic inspiration, singing rough but powerful songs on his bear-sinew harp; yet he leaves as soon as an audience gathers. Tuor escapes Aryador by way of a river tunnel, then pursues the stream to the sea. A distinct air of the Finnish *Kalevala*, with its forest-dwelling lakeside harpers and hunters, now gives way to a mode of romance used by William Morris in books such as *The Well at the World's End*, in which callow youths achieve moral stature traversing an imaginary topography. Yet already Tolkien's landscapes make Morris's seem slapdash and vague. It is hard not to become immersed in the sensory world Tuor explores, sharing his wonder as he approaches the unrumoured sea:

> He wandered till he came to the black cliffs by the sea and saw the ocean and its waves for the first time, and at that hour the sun sank beyond the rim of Earth far out to sea, and he stood on the cliff-top with outspread arms, and his heart was filled with a longing very great indeed. Now some say that he was the first of Men to reach the Sea and look upon it and know the desire it brings . . .

In fact Tuor has been unwittingly drawn to the sea by Ulmo, demiurge of the deep, for reasons that remain unspoken: to enrich his spirit yet purge his desire for solitude, perhaps, or to ensure that he returns there at the end of the tale when he has a son, the mariner-to-be Eärendel.

For now, however, once the sea has made its mark, Ulmo silently prompts Tuor to move inland; but in the Land of

Willows disaster almost strikes. Tuor succumbs to the delight of naming the butterflies, moths, bees, and beetles, and he works on his songs. The temptation to linger acquires its own voice: 'Now there dwelt in these dark places a spirit of whispers, and it whispered to Tuor at dusk and he was loth to depart.' But hints of war appear in the descriptions of peace, where 'beneath the willows the green swords of the flaglilies were drawn, and sedges stood, and reeds in embattled array'.

It is tempting to see parallels with Tolkien's own life during 1914 and 1915. (In the abortive 1951 recasting of 'The Fall of Gondolin', Tuor is twenty-three when he sets out, Tolkien's age when he began both his mythology and his military service.) Tuor is a singer seeking wonders, a coiner of words, and a loner, as Tolkien was a poet with a Romantic bent, an inventor of languages, and elusive even to his closest friends. As duty found Tolkien amid the 'Oxford "sleepies"', so it finds Tuor among the sluggish waters.

Ulmo, perceiving that the 'spirit of whispers' may thwart his plan, now reveals himself in his majesty, telling Tuor he must bear a secret message to the free Gnomes of Gondolin. Several thrall-Noldoli clandestinely guide him until fear of Melko and his spies drives all but one away. With the help of the faithful Voronwë, however, Tuor finds the secret Way of Escape into Gondolin, a faëry land like a 'dream of the gods'.

The city of Gondolin, built on a flat-topped hill with towers, marble walls, and seedlings of the Two Trees, was modelled on immutable Kôr on the rocks of Eldamar. It is, however, a flawed copy. A place of learning, living memory, and alertness, like Oxford in 'The Wanderer's Allegiance', it is in danger of becoming a 'town of dreams' like Warwick. Ulmo's message is that Gondolin must arm itself and strike against Melko on behalf of the thrall-Noldoli, and before the tyrant overwhelms the world. King Turgon refuses to risk his city on the advice of one of the Valar, who 'hide their land and weave about it inaccessible magic, that no tidings of evil come ever to their ears'. The weary

Tuor falls back into a contented repose among the Gnomes, who brush off Ulmo's warning with declarations that Gondolin will 'stand as long as Taniquetil or the Mountains of Valinor'. 'The Wanderer's Allegiance' had said as much about Oxford, asserting that 'No tide of evil can thy glory drown'; but Tolkien's first mythological story highlights the perilous complacency in such claims.

If the first half of 'The Fall of Gondolin' appears to echo Tolkien's creative development and slow acceptance of duty in the first year of the war, the second half surely reverberates to his collision with war itself. The vivid extremes of the Somme, its terrors and sorrows, its heroism and high hopes, its abomination and ruin, seem to have thrown his vision of things into mountainous relief. A bright light illuminated the world and raised awful shadows. In this tale, Tolkien's mythology becomes, for the first time, what it would remain: a mythology of the conflict between good and evil. The idea that the conflict must be perpetual arose directly from a long-held scepticism about the blandly optimistic prognoses prevailing during the Great War, as Tolkien recalled in an interview nearly half a century later: 'That, I suppose, was an actual conscious reaction from the War – from the stuff I was brought up on in the "War to end wars" – that kind of stuff, which I didn't believe in at the time and I believe in less now.'

In 'The Fall of Gondolin', too, his fairies shed the diminutive stature they had assumed in Shakespearean and Victorian traditions. The shift may have had something to do with Wiseman's cautionary words in March about Tolkien's love of 'little, delicate, beautiful creatures', or it may have been in answer to a creative need: now the Elves would have to play a part in war on a grand scale. Though still 'small and slender and lithe' the Noldoli are the same order of size as humans, solid and physical, capable of dealing wounds and receiving them. This reversion to a more ancient view of elves also allowed Tolkien to draw upon the old motif of the faëry bride, with the intermarriage of human Tuor with Idril of Gondolin, and so bring Eärendel into the story as their child.

A story ensues of spies and counsels of war like a fairy-tale relation of John Buchan's 1915 thriller *The Thirty-Nine Steps*, set in the uneasy pre-war years. But the jealous Gnome Meglin, betrayer of Gondolin, seems to come from old romance by way of battlefield reality: captured by the enemy, he reveals Gondolin's weaknesses in exchange for his life. Tuor takes a chief part in the defence of the city when Melko's monsters come up over the mountain fence, and he leads its refugees in flight to the sea.

'The Fall of Gondolin' is one of Tolkien's most sustained accounts of battle. But Gondolin under attack is not the Somme, despite its corpse-choked waters and smoke-filled claustrophobia. Least of all does the tale dress up the English as Gnomes and the Germans as Goblins. Prior to the Somme, Tolkien had written the Germans into his Qenya lexicon as *kalimbardi*, associated with *kalimbo*, 'a savage, uncivilized man, barbarian. – giant, monster, troll'. These words now appeared in the more recent 'Poetic and Mythologic Words' simply as 'goblins', 'goblin, monster'.* In England, news of the destruction of Louvain, or submarine attacks on merchant vessels, made it easy to see the Germans as barbaric, or even monstrous. Cary Gilson had written to Tolkien from Marston Green after Rob's death: 'That you are going to win – and restore righteousness and mercy to their place in the counsels of mankind I am certain: and it is a glorious privilege whether one dies or lives.' Even in the midst of the Somme, Tolkien wrote that the war was 'for all the evil of our own side in the large view good against evil'. Yet on the battlefield he had faced an enemy with all the hallmarks of humanity. Meanwhile, the Allies also used poison gas and unofficially sanctioned the killing of captives. Tolkien later insisted there was no parallel between the Goblins he had

* The Gnomish equivalent *Calumoth* in the 'Poetic and Mythologic Words' was shortlived, but *Glamhoth*, 'folk of dreadful hate' in 'The Fall of Gondolin', is surely its phonaesthetic heir; and so the influence of the barbaric *kalimbardi* can be traced all the way to the name of Gandalf's sword *Glamdring*, 'Foehammer'.

invented and the Germans he had fought, declaring, 'I've never had those sort of feelings about the Germans. I'm very anti that kind of thing.'

'The Fall of Gondolin' is not war propaganda, but myth and moral drama. Like Robert Louis Stevenson in 'Dr Jekyll and Mr Hyde', Tolkien took the confused moral landscape of the real world and attempted to clarify it into polarities of good and evil; but he applied the principle on an epic scale. He explained his approach much later in a letter to his son Christopher. 'I think the orcs as real a creation as anything in "realistic" fiction,' he wrote, 'only in real life they are on both sides, of course. For "romance" has grown out of "allegory", and its wars are still derived from the "inner war" of allegory in which good is on one side and various modes of badness on the other. In real (exterior) life men are on both sides: which means a motley alliance of orcs, beasts, demons, plain naturally honest men, and angels.' So it might be said that the Goblins embody 'all the evil of our own side' in the real war, as well as all the evil on the German side. They wreck and pillage, and they kill prisoners. The Gnomes of Gondolin, meanwhile, embody virtues on which no nation had a monopoly. They represent (as he wrote of his Elves in general) 'beauty and grace of life and artefact'.

The battalions of Gondolin rally behind the dynastic standards of the Pillar, the Tower of Snow, the Tree, the Golden Flower, the Harp, the Mole, the Swallow, and the White Wing, each with its own heraldic livery: 'they of the Heavenly Arch being a folk of uncounted wealth were arrayed in a glory of colours, and their arms were set with jewels that flamed in the light . . .' Their folk-names recall the Wolfings, the Hartings, the Elkings, and the Beamings of William Morris's *The House of the Wolfings*: Gothic tribes whose names reflect an intimate bond with the land they defend from the acquisitive Romans. Morris turned the classical view upside down, so that his forest-dwelling Goths uphold civilized values while imperial Rome represents barbarism. Tolkien's moral compass has a similar orientation. The Noldoli see nature as a thing of intrinsic value, not simply as a commodity. Like all of Tolkien's Elves, they also embody the older faëry tradition in which they are the spiritual representatives of the natural world, as angels are of heaven. They defend nature herself against a covetous power whose aim is to possess, exploit, and despoil.

Tolkien had listed several monstrous creatures in the 'Poetic and Mythologic Words of Eldarissa' and its ethnological chart: *tauler*, *tyulqin*, and *sarqin*, names which in Qenya indicate tree-like stature or an appetite for flesh. All these new races of monsters proved transitory, bar two: the Balrogs and the Orcs. Orcs were bred in 'the subterranean heats and slime' by Melko: 'Their hearts were of granite and their bodies deformed; foul their faces which smiled not, but their laugh that of the clash of metal . . .' The name had been taken from the Old English *orc*, 'demon', but only because it was phonetically suitable. The role of demon properly belongs to Balrogs, whose Goldogrin name means 'cruel demon' or 'demon of anguish'. These are Melko's flame-wielding shock troops and battlefield captains, the cohorts of Evil.

Orcs and Balrogs, however, are not enough to achieve the destruction of Gondolin. 'From the greatness of his wealth of metals and his powers of fire' Melko constructs a host of 'beasts like snakes and dragons of irresistible might that should overcreep the Encircling Hills and lap that plain and its fair city in flame and death'. The work of 'smiths and sorcerers', these forms (in three varieties) violate the boundary between mythical monster and machine, between magic and technology. The bronze dragons in the assault move ponderously and open breaches in the city walls. Fiery versions are thwarted by the smooth, steep incline of Gondolin's hill. But a third variety, the iron dragons, carry Orcs within and move on 'iron so cunningly linked that they might flow . . . around and above all obstacles before them'; they break down the city gates 'by reason of the exceeding heaviness of their bodies' and, under bombardment, 'their hollow bellies clanged . . . yet it availed not for they might not be broken, and the fires rolled off them'.

The more they differ from the dragons of mythology, however, the more these monsters resemble the tanks of the Somme. One wartime diarist noted with amusement how the newspapers compared these new armoured vehicles with 'the icthyosaurus, jabberwocks, mastodons, Leviathans, boojums, snarks, and other antediluvian and mythical monsters'. Max Ernst, who was in the German field artillery in 1916, enshrined such comparisons on canvas in his iconic surrealist painting *Celebes* (1921), an armour-plated, elephantine menace with blank, bestial eyes. *The Times* trumpeted a German report of this British invention: 'The monster approached slowly, hobbling, moving from side to side, rocking and pitching, but it came nearer. Nothing obstructed it: a supernatural force seemed to drive it onwards. Someone in the trenches cried, "The devil comes," and that word ran down the line like lightning. Suddenly tongues of fire licked out of the armoured shine of the iron caterpillar . . . the English waves of infantry surged up behind the devil's chariot.' *The Times*'s own correspondent, Philip Gibbs, wrote later that the advance of tanks on the Somme was 'like fairy-tales of war by H. G. Wells'.

Indeed, there is a whiff of science fiction about the army attacking Gondolin, a host that has 'only at that time been seen and shall not again be till the Great End'. In 1916, Tolkien was anticipating the dictum of Arthur C. Clarke that 'Any sufficiently advanced technology is indistinguishable from magic.' From a modern perspective, this enemy host appears technological, if futuristic; the 'hearts and spirits of blazing fire' of its brazen dragons remind us of the internal combustion engine. But to the Noldoli the host seems the product of sorcery. 'The Fall of Gondolin', in Tolkien's grand unfolding design, is a story told by an Elf; and the combustion engine, seen through enchanted eyes, could appear as nothing other than a metal heart filled with flame.

Melko, the tyrant making war on Gondolin, is the Devil himself. But he is not sequestered in a Miltonic Pandemonium across the abyss of Chaos. The road to his hell runs northwards and downwards, as in Norse myth. A byname, *Yelur*, links him to Qenya *Yelin*, 'winter', seen in notes from late 1915 for 'Kortirion among the Trees' that speak of the 'wintry spell of Yelin' and 'the icy blue-tipped sp[ears] of winter marching up beh[ind]'.* Melko himself did not apparently exist in Tolkien's mythology before the Somme, but this poetic metaphor of a warlord bent on destroying light and life prefigured him, and he shares the same wintry functions.

Tolkien's use of his sources was always daring. Unlike the Satan of Christian tradition, Melko is jailer to living beings – the thrall-Noldoli who slave for him in his Hells of Iron. But by making the Gnomes' sojourn there a matter of compulsion, Tolkien was also rewriting traditions about underworlds ruled by faëry races such as the Irish Tuatha Dé Danann so that they seem to foreshadow Christian eschatology. It is the harrowing of this Elvish hell that Ulmo, through the agency of Tuor, hopes to achieve.

Captives who somehow leave the Hells of Iron are afflicted by 'a binding terror' so that even when they are far from Melko's domain 'he seemed ever nigh them . . . and their hearts quaked and they fled not even when they could'. Meglin, released by Melko after betraying Gondolin's secrets, resumes his public life in Gondolin as if nothing has happened, but he will no longer work and seeks to 'drown his fear and disquiet' in false gaiety. He, too, is now under Melko's 'spell of bottomless dread'.

Melko (who is better known by his later names *Melkor* and *Morgoth*) represents the tyranny of the machine over life and nature, exploiting the earth and its people in the construction of a vast armoury. With a brutal inevitability, the Gnomes, with their medieval technology, lose the contest. Tolkien's myth underlines the almost insuperable efficacy of the machine against mere skill of hand and eye. Yet it recognizes that the machine would not exist without the inventor and the craftsman. Melko

* In the finished 'Kortirion among the Trees' this became 'Winter, and his blue-tipped spears / Marching unconquerable upon the sun / Of bright All-Hallows'.

does not know how to achieve the destruction of the Gnomes' city: chillingly, it is Meglin of Gondolin who hatches the plan for the creeping beast-machines that will surmount its defences. The Gnomes are driven by 'unconquerable eagerness after knowledge'. Melko has little use for their eagerness, but he depends on their knowledge, and so he has the thrall-Noldoli dig his ore and work his metals, leaving them stooped with their labours. In the Hells of Iron, the higher arts and sciences are subsumed or crushed in the service of mechanical industry – endlessly repetitious and motivated by nothing but the desire for more power.

As a literary creation, Melko is more than a winter-symbol or an abstraction of destructiveness and greed. He appeared in 1916 with remarkable timing. With his dreams of world domination, his spies, his vast armies, his industrial slaves, and his 'spell of bottomless dread', he anticipated the totalitarianism that lay just around the corner. Within a year, the Russian Revolution had established the first totalitarian dictatorship, its aim being to crush the individual will in the service of the economy and Bolshevik power. Lenin became a template for Hitler, Stalin, Mao, and the other political monsters of the twentieth century. But all that the totalitarian dictators did was to take to a logical extreme the dehumanization already seen in heavy industry, and to exploit the break with the past that the Great War had introduced. In its capacity to warn about such extremes, fantastic fiction has the edge over what is called realism. 'Realism' has a knee-jerk tendency to avoid extremes as implausible, but 'fantasy' actively embraces them. It magnifies and clarifies the human condition. It can even keep pace with the calamitous imaginings of would-be dictators. Doubtless Tolkien had no intention of making political predictions, but his work nevertheless foreshadowed things to come. A spiritual kinship exists between the unhappy Meglin and Winston Smith, downing his Victory gin under the eyes of Big Brother.

TWELVE

Tol Withernon and Fladweth Amrod

'You ought to start the epic,' Christopher Wiseman told Tolkien in the chill January of 1917. 'When you do, however,' he added, 'mind you get on your high horse, not your high horse on you.' It seems likely that Tolkien was already firmly in charge of the reins in 'The Fall of Gondolin', and in another, shorter piece, 'The Cottage of Lost Play', which would introduce the whole cycle of tales now planned. For this introductory section, Tolkien devised a new mariner figure to be a seeker of wonders; unlike Eärendel, however, he was not to be a wonder in himself.

The new arrival belonged not to myth, but to the post-mythological twilight, that period on the margins of known history that so haunted Tolkien. The mariner's role was to hear, and to pass on to posterity, the stories told about Faërie by the fairies. Even from the vantage-point of 'The Cottage of Lost Play', though, Gondolin and the other 'Lost Tales' would be ancient history; and the mariner would act as a mediator half-way between these unfathomably remote events and the modern day. The structure owes much to Chaucer's *Canterbury Tales* – although a more immediate precursor was William Morris's *The Earthly Paradise*, in which Norse seafarers swap stories with the sequestered descendants of ancient Greeks whom they encounter on a remote island.

In all ways Tolkien's mariner fits his fictional era, emerging (according to background notes) from the western coast of Germanic Europe and sailing to the Lonely Isle, the island of Britain. He is the father of Hengest and Horsa, the historical warlords who led the Anglo-Saxon invasion. Into the design Tolkien also wove parallels with his own life. The mariner's original name is *Ottor*, which is simply the Old English equivalent of *Otter*. That seems to have been Tolkien's name for himself in Animalic, an invented language he had shared with his Incledon cousins in childhood. Ottor is also called by his own people *Wǽfre*, 'restless, wandering'. He has suffered a profound spiritual longing since being orphaned in boyhood and his past has been blighted by a terrible war. In the Lonely Isle he will marry an elfmaid and their younger son, Heorrenda, will have his capital at Great Haywood, while Hengest and Horsa will be associated with Warwick and Oxford. Crucially, through Ottor the English will learn 'the true tradition of the fairies'. The name given to Ottor in the Lonely Isle is *Eriol*, 'One who dreams alone'. Without intruding any detail that would jar with his imaginative portrayal of an ancient world, Tolkien left his own signature on the canvas.

Arriving one peaceful evening at a town at the heart of the Lonely Isle, Eriol finds the Cottage of Lost Play – *Mar Vanwa Tyaliéva* in Qenya – a home from home that offers peace, rest, and food for the imagination. A man who has surfeited on experience, now he will adventure no more but will simply listen to the history of the Elves and Gnomes.

The cottage threshold leads back into childhood, both for Eriol and for the reader, and 'all who enter must be very small indeed, or of their own good wish become as very little folk'. The wayfarer steps inside, and to his amazement finds himself in a spacious house, where the courteous elven hosts, Lindo and Vairë, make him their guest. It is a place of joy, comfort, and ceremony, where daily rituals centre around feasting and story-telling.

> At that same moment a great gong sounded far off in the house with a sweet noise, and a sound followed as of the laughter of many voices mingled with a great pattering of feet. Then Vairë said to Eriol, seeing his face filled with a happy wonderment: 'That is the voice of Tombo, the Gong of the Children, which stands outside the Hall of Play Regained, and it rings once to

summon them to this hall at the times for eating and drinking, and three times to summon them to the Room of the Log Fire for the telling of tales' . . .

The 'Cottage of Lost Play' comes with liberal doses of 'magic' and a population of jolly miniatures who might have trooped out of a Victorian nursery book. Their high spirits are unleavened by either the amoral laughter of the inhabitants of Neverland in *Peter Pan* or the earthy scepticism that Tolkien later gave to the hobbits. That 'the walls shake with mirth' when a tale is to be told seems strange, as humour is hardly the dominant characteristic of the 'Lost Tales'. The note of gaiety also chimes uneasily with the deeper themes of exile and loss in Eriol's past and in the strange history of the cottage.

The magical house is situated in Kortirion, and 'The Cottage of Lost Play' returns to the idea of the two versions of Faërie that had been developed in the Qenya lexicon and 'Kortirion among the Trees'. The Elves here in the Lonely Isle are exiles, and Kortirion, their capital, is just an echo of Kôr, the city in Valinor across the western ocean that they left long ago after 'hearing the lament of the world'. The cottage Eriol finds in Kortirion is built in remembrance of a more ancient house in Valinor, next to the silver sea and not far from Kôr. 'This was the Cottage of the Children, or of the Play of Sleep,' explains Vairë, 'and not of Lost Play, as has wrongly been said in song among Men – for no play was lost then, and here alas only and now is the Cottage of Lost Play.'*

The two cottages, in Valinor and Kortirion, encompass between them a whole complex of relations between dream, reality, and story. Once upon a time, 'the children of the fathers

* This is a sly reference to Tolkien's own April 1915 poem 'You and Me and the Cottage of Lost Play', which indeed depicts the original cottage. Tolkien planned to weave his earlier poetry into his prose 'Book of Lost Tales', and the story of Eriol's arrival in the Lonely Isle also contains references to the song he made about Kortirion ('Kortirion among the Trees') and the Sleeper in the Tower of Pearl from 'The Happy Mariners'.

of the fathers of men' could reach the Cottage of the Play of Sleep by travelling the Path of Dreams, which ran (like the rainbow-bridge Bifrost in Norse myth) from mortal to immortal lands. There they would play at bows and arrows or climb on the roof, like the Lost Boys who follow Peter Pan in J. M. Barrie's Neverland. Children who became friends there in their dream-play might later meet in waking life, as lovers or close comrades.

Dream visits to the old cottage had their perils, Eriol hears. Dreamers who strayed beyond the garden into Kôr itself, and saw Valinor, the home of the gods, suffered a complete estrangement from their own people, becoming silent and 'wild' and filled with yearning. It is in the nature of Faërie to enchant beyond mortal limits. On the other hand, some of the straying dreamers returned to mortal lands with heads filled not with madness, but with wonder. 'Of the misty aftermemories of these,' Eriol is told, 'of their broken tales and snatches of song, came many strange legends that delighted Men for long, and still do, it may be; for of such were the poets of the Great Lands.' Tolkien had been inspired and tantalized by the mythologies and folk traditions of the ancient world, and especially by the fragmentary remnants of Germanic legend he had found scattered through *Beowulf*, Cynewulf's *Crist*, and elsewhere. Now he was devising a fiction in which these fragments represented the last vestiges of visions seen in Valinor itself.

Times change. When the Elves left Kôr, the Path of Dreams was closed, so that the Cottage of the Play of Sleep now stands desolate on the shores of Valinor. Lindo and Vairë, exiled in the Lonely Isle, established the Cottage of Lost Play as a place where 'old tales, old songs, and elfin music' might still be celebrated. But it is also the home of fairy-tales, and from here come the fairies who visit 'lonely children and whisper to them at dusk in early bed by night-light and candle-flame, or comfort those that weep' (an urgent need, it might be noted, not only in Tolkien's own childhood, but also in the Great War's world of orphans). So the age of myth and the Cottage of the Play of Sleep cedes place to the age of fairy-story and the Cottage of Lost Play.

However, the truer vision of the old myth-makers may yet return. Eriol is given a glimpse of a radiant future when the roads to Valinor 'shall be thronged with the sons and daughters of Men' and the Cottage of the Play of Sleep will once more be filled with life. The scales, presumably, will fall from mortal eyes, and the earthly paradise be opened to them. This is expected to follow 'the Faring Forth and the Rekindling of the Magic Sun', to which the exiles of Kortirion raise their cups. Sadly, Tolkien never reached the point of describing these momentous events in any detail before his eschatological ideas changed completely, and he left only a hint of the universal consolation to come.

Readers of *The Lord of the Rings* may find two elements in 'The Cottage of Lost Play' familiar. In Mar Vanwa Tyaliéva itself there is more than a hint of elven Rivendell, with its Hall of Fire where tales are told and songs sung; and the queen of the Lonely Isle in 'The Book of Lost Tales', Meril-i-Turinqi, has something of Galadriel about her. She lives among her maidens in a ceremonial circle of trees in Kortirion, like Galadriel in her city of trees in Lothlórien. Meril is a descendant of Inwë, the elven-king over the sea, as Galadriel is of Ingwë, his counterpart in later stages of the mythology. Both elf-queens are repositories of ancient knowledge, but each also is the source of a supernaturally enduring vitality: Meril through the marvellous drink *limpë* that she dispenses, Galadriel through the power to arrest decay in her realm. It is symptomatic of both the fluidity and the stability of Tolkien's mythopoeic conceptions that, while names evolved and the interrelationships of individuals and peoples changed almost beyond recognition through years of writing, rewriting, and recasting, these embodiments of quintessential elvishness – the house of lore and the queen of trees – recurred.*

* * *

* In 'The Book of Lost Tales' Meril herself took the place that had been occupied in early Qenya lexicon entries by Erinti, the Vala of love, music, beauty, and purity, who likewise lived in a circle of elms guarded by fairies in Kortirion. Erinti, as previously noted, was partly a representation of Edith Tolkien, who therefore has a curious link with Galadriel.

'The Cottage of Lost Play', complete by early February 1917, makes plain that Tolkien already had in mind the idea that Eriol would hear the Lost Tales in Kortirion. In one note, the tales were to be written down by Heorrenda of Hægwudu (Great Haywood), Eriol's son by the elf-maid Naimi, in a 'Golden Book': the Qenya and Gnomish lexicons give translations for this title. But it was also to be known as *i·band a·gwentin laithra*, the 'Book of Lost Tales'.

The title recalls R. W. Chambers' reference to 'the lost *Tale of Wade*', in a chapter of his study of the Old English poem *Widsith* that focuses on the old sea-legends of the ancient Germanic tribes of the north-western European coastlands (and which also deals with Éarendel). Chambers' book reads like a message to Tolkien. He rages against the Romans for disdaining the illiterate Germans and failing to record their songs and tales, and laments the fact that, despite King Alfred's love for the old lays, the Anglo-Saxons wrote too few of them down. 'So this world of high-spirited, chivalrous song has passed away,' says Chambers. 'It is our duty then to gather up reverently such fragments of the old Teutonic epic as fortune has preserved in our English tongue, and to learn from them all we can of that collection of stories of which these fragments are the earliest vernacular record.' But Tolkien may have had the idea of 'lost tales' at the back of his mind even longer. Lord Macaulay, in the book that provided Tolkien with the model for his 'Battle of the Eastern Field', explains himself in similar terms: his *Lays of Ancient Rome* were attempts to recreate what the national poems of early Rome would have been like before their local character was swallowed up by the culture of Greece. In passing, he notes that oblivion has taken the ancient Germanic and English songs too.

When Tolkien summed up his youthful ambitions in a letter to Milton Waldman of Collins, the publisher, written *c.*1951, he put England at their heart: 'Do not laugh! But once upon a time (my crest has long since fallen) I had a mind to make a body of more or less connected legend, ranging from the large and cosmogonic, to the level of romantic fairy-story – the larger founded on the lesser in contact with the earth, the lesser drawing splendour from the vast backcloths – which I could dedicate simply to: to England; to my country.' But in creating this mythology for England, the younger Tolkien was responding to a particular sense of nationalism that had much in common both with Macaulay's love of early Rome, a self-contained cultural unity, and with Chambers' hatred of late Rome, an acquisitive empire. He was celebrating the linguistic and cultural roots of 'Englishness', not vaunting (or even mourning) the British Empire. His opposition to imperialism was deep-seated, and extended not only to support for Home Rule in Ireland but also, not long after the war, to a horror at the increasingly popular idea that English itself, the object of his love and his labour, would become the universal lingua franca thanks to America's entry on the world stage at the end of the Great War – 'as an ambition', he wrote, 'the most idiotic and suicidal that a language could entertain':

> Literature shrivels in a universal language, and an uprooted language rots before it dies. And it should be possible to lift the eyes above the cant of the 'language of Shakespeare' . . . sufficiently to realize the magnitude of the loss to humanity that the world-dominance of any one language now spoken would entail: no language has ever possessed but a small fraction of the varied excellences of human speech, and each language represents a different vision of life . . .

No manifesto fired Tolkien's mythology; instead, a particular 'vision of life' that was bound up with physical rather than political geography. He told Waldman: 'It should possess the tone and quality that I desired, somewhat cool and clear, be redolent of our "air" (the clime and soil of the North West, meaning Britain and the hither parts of Europe: not Italy or the Aegean, still less the East) . . .' If anything, by harking back to the common origins of the English and German languages and traditions, and by focusing on decline and fall, the mythology ran counter to wartime jingoism.

* * *

Prior to the Somme, Tolkien had spent much time playing with words and symbols and reflective lyricism. But something had happened to his ambition to become a poet, born out of the Council of London in December 1914. With the Lost Tales he turned to narrative prose, the mode for which he would chiefly be remembered. 'The Fall of Gondolin' could certainly have been written as narrative verse – the form of *Beowulf* and the *Kalevala*, of his mythological work in the 1920s, and of sections of his 1914 *Story of Kullervo*. Reasons why he now set verse aside can only be guessed at. Perhaps it had something to do with the fact that Sidgwick & Jackson had rejected his volume of poems, *The Trumpets of Faërie*. Perhaps he was suffering from some kind of poetic block: he admitted to Wiseman in August 1917 that so far that year he had only written one poem. On the other hand, he may simply have felt that prose was the pragmatic choice, free of the technical difficulties of rhythm and rhyme. He knew, after all, that as soon as he was fit he would be called back to fight.

His leave of absence ended on 12 January 1917, and, to be available for duty, Tolkien went to stay in Monument Road, Edgbaston, and in Wake Green Road, Moseley. But he had been unwell again. Hearing this, Wiseman declared himself 'unreservedly glad' and told him, 'Malinger to your utmost. I rely on Mrs T . . .' In fact, Tolkien had no need to sham illness. By the time he faced a second medical board at the Birmingham University Hospital on 23 January, the fever had returned twice, though the attacks were relatively minor. It was not unusual for trench fever to recur months, even years, after the first infection. Following his return from the Somme, Tolkien was caught between two potentially lethal forces: the War Office and illness. For now, the latter had the upper hand; he was still pale and weak and could eat little, and an ache lingered in his knees and elbows. The military doctors sent him back to Edith for another month.

The interlude at Great Haywood came to its final end on Thursday 22 February 1917. Tolkien returned to Monument Road and then to Abbotsford, Moseley. On 27 February a medical board saw Tolkien at Lichfield Military Hospital and found that his health had improved little. Pending his return to service overseas, he had been earmarked for the 3rd Lancashire Fusiliers, which guarded the Yorkshire coast and the mouth of the River Humber against invasion. Accordingly, he was now sent to a convalescent hospital for officers in Harrogate, on the edge of the Yorkshire Dales, and far from home.

There was, of course, one major compensation for the upheaval, as Edith reminded him: 'Every day in bed means another day in England.' Every day also brought him closer to health. At the end of his month at Furness Auxiliary Hospital, though his joints were still causing him pain, he was found fit for light duty.

First Tolkien was granted three weeks' leave, at 95 Valley Drive, where Edith and her cousin Jennie Grove had taken lodgings early in March. In the middle of April, Wiseman finally obtained shore leave and invited himself rambunctiously to the Tolkiens': 'I am going to burst into your literary solitudes, with the permission of Mrs Tolkien, and with or without yours,' he declared. 'So here's to the Council of Harrogate.' He was overjoyed to find his friend still in England and likely to stay there for some while to come. 'Meanwhile let all the pushes go merrily on in France and finish before you get out again,' he wrote.

Despite his predilection for humour, there is no reason to think that Wiseman had been joking when he urged Tolkien to malinger. Of the TCBS, only the Great Twin Brethren were left, and he had every reason to fear that Tolkien might join Rob Gilson and G. B. Smith in the corner of some foreign field.

'As you said,' Wiseman had written early in the year, 'it is you and I now, Greenfield Crescent and Gothic, the old and original. The whole thing is so ineffably mysterious. To have seen two of God's giants pass before our eyes, to have lived and laughed with them, to have learnt of them, to have found them something like ourselves, and to see them go back again into the mist whence they came out.'

True to these sentiments, Wiseman had suggested that he and Tolkien, as the two surviving TCBSites, should take an interest in Smith's creative legacy, his poetry, and in Ruth Smith's efforts to have it published. She had now lost her other son, Roger, a subaltern attached to the Royal Welch Fusiliers on the Tigris front in Mesopotamia (modern-day Iraq), who had been killed in action at Basra in January. 'I cannot believe the terrible thing that has befallen me,' their mother wrote to John Ronald. 'To lose two such fine sons is indeed crushing.' Her sole consolation was the thought that Roger never knew his brother was dead. Wiseman summed up the tragedy to Tolkien: 'I suppose very few people have given more than Mrs Smith; it is unspeakably sad. I ought to write to her, but can't find words to do so with.'

By the time Tolkien and Wiseman met in Harrogate on 18 April 1917, the German forces had fallen back from the Somme; though not in defeat. It was a strategic withdrawal that straightened and shortened their line, making it easier to defend. But it made a mockery of months of bitter battle and appalling loss of life. All that Britain and its allies gained was 'a few acres of mud', as Wiseman said. Such events made the struggle to salvage emotional, moral, and spiritual meaning ever more acute. This was the year the French army mutinied and the Russian army collapsed completely.

Life in England was a shadow of its pre-war self; 'the starvation-year', Tolkien called 1917. At the end of January, Germany had resumed unrestricted naval warfare, which had been held in abeyance through much of 1916. Now U-boats laid siege to Britain, attacking not only military vessels but also merchant vessels and hospital ships. The *Asturias*, which had borne Tolkien in fever back from France in November, was torpedoed without warning and sunk off the south coast of England on 20 March; it had offloaded its cargo of invalids but forty-one crew and staff died. In April, a quarter of the ships leaving British ports fell victim to mines or submarines. The U-boat campaign also brought America into the war against Germany, but it would be a long time before US troops arrived in Europe in decisive numbers. In the midst of England's increasing austerity, and after nearly six months of almost continuous leave from the army, Tolkien was plunged back into military life. He was still very run down, and not yet fit to return to the 11th Lancashire Fusiliers. Instead he was despatched to the Humber Garrison, on the north-east coast.

Tolkien arrived there on Thursday 19 April 1917, immediately after 'the Council of Harrogate' and just before the Battle of Arras. He may have been posted initially to Hornsea, where the 3rd Lancashire Fusiliers had an outpost and musketry school; at any rate it was in this seaside town that Edith and Jennie Grove took lodgings. But if Tolkien was ever sent there, he did not stay for long. The battalion had its headquarters at Thirtle Bridge, fifteen miles south, on the peninsula of Holderness, a low land of hollows and hummocks and shallow ridges. Holderness was critically placed, stretched like a guardian sea-lion between the North Sea and the mouth of the Humber, which had provided an inroad for the ships of the early Anglo-Saxon settlers. Centuries on, Edward II began defensive works at Hull, and later Henry VIII extended the defences to the coast. With the advent of the First World War, fortresses had been built in the midst of the broad, muddy estuary, and the banks were dotted with watch-posts, signals stations, and batteries. Thirtle Bridge Camp itself had been established on farmland where the road from coastal Withernsea ran across an old drainage ditch on the way to the village of Roos, a mile further inland.

Life here was notoriously dull. The railway was nearly three miles from Thirtle Bridge, at Withernsea, and the visiting wives of officers had to be ferried from the station to the camp by pony and trap. As one subaltern put it, 'Here some sixty officers and nearly fifteen hundred men passed laborious days of work and leisure. Which of the two was calculated to bore one more, would be hard to say.' More than half of the officers were unfit, like Tolkien, and among them at various times were several from the 11th Lancashire Fusiliers. Fawcett-Barry, the former commander of 'A' Company, was adjutant at Thirtle Bridge for a while, and Lieutenant-Colonel Bird, Tolkien's commanding officer on the Somme, now organized battalion sports, plays, and concerts here. Tolkien's friend Huxtable, still recovering from being buried alive in the trenches, was stationed at nearby Tunstall Hall, but was sent back to France in September.

In a 1917 photograph with Edith at the seaside, Tolkien is noticeably thin, and his baggy officer's breeches look too big. Twelve days after his posting, a medical board at Hull found him fit for general home front duties; but the doctors said he still needed 'hardening'. From the time Tolkien joined the 3rd Lancashire Fusiliers until the end of the war, it sent close on seven hundred officers overseas, including those who had been invalided home. He had to get fighting fit again through the old slog of physical training. How else he was occupied is unclear, but the battalion's new recruits needed signals training, and there were patrols to be carried out along the low seaward cliffs: a dangerous job on stormy nights because no lights must be shown. Zeppelins made incursions over the coast, and from Thirtle Bridge their bombs could be seen exploding in and around Hull. Searchlights showed them up like silver cigars, high in the sky.

The Holderness landscape, though bleak, bordered the sea, which haunted so much of what Tolkien wrote. Its cliffs provide a precarious defence against the depredations of the hungry waves. Land disappears at Withernsea and southwards faster than almost anywhere in the world – nearly six feet a year. The North Sea has devoured swathes of shoreline here, gnawing its way westwards through the shales and clays since before the Anglo-Saxons came. More than thirty towns have been swallowed up since the twelfth century, and from time to time the sea casts ashore bones from graves it has robbed. The Humber and the North Sea have worked other remarkable changes on topography. A lowland to the south is called Sunk Island, though in fact it originally rose as a sandbank out of the estuary waters in the reign of Charles II before joining the mainland. The long, protruding sand spit of Spurn Point, continually remodelled by the elements, swings very slowly east and west like a geological pendulum.

The clearest evidence that the shifting Holderness landscape entered into Tolkien's imaginary world is contained, characteristically, in a fragment of an invented language. G. B. Smith had left him some books of Welsh, including the four branches of the *Mabinogi*, and at this time Tolkien was jotting down words and etymologies for his own Welsh-influenced tongue, Gnomish or Goldogrin. He decided that his new lexicon could be an artefact created by Eriol, and he wrote the mariner's name on the cover under the title *i·Lam na·Ngoldathon*. But below he added in Gnomish the dateline 'Tol Withernon (and many places besides), 1917'. The date indicates that here, on one level, *Eriol* is Tolkien's *nom de plume*, while *Tol Withernon*, which occurs nowhere else, evokes Withernsea, the nearest town to Thirtle Bridge. He might have meant it as Eriol's landfall: to Holderness, in the dim origins of English history, came the Germanic seafarers across the North Sea from Angeln.

The origin of *Withern-* in *Withernsea* is debatable, and it is unclear whether Tolkien intended his Goldogrin equivalent to be meaningful. But Gnomish *tol* means 'island', suggesting that he thought the ending of *Withernsea* was Old Norse *ey* or Old English *ēg*, *īeg*, all with that meaning. On the face of it, this would be a strange interpretation, for Withernsea is part of mainland Britain. However, near the town's edge is a reedy flat that used to be a lake until the thirteenth century; and local tradition held that the North Sea once flowed in here, running in a winding channel to the Humber itself and cutting off the southern half of the Holderness peninsula from the mainland.* In *Tol Withernon* we perhaps glimpse a matching conception of an island on the eastern edge of the larger Tol Eressëa.

The transformative power of the sea was to play a key role in Middle-earth, a world repeatedly refashioned by its waters in the wars between the Valar and Morgoth and in the destruction of Númenor, Tolkien's 1930s version of Atlantis. But in 1917, the gale-battered coast of Holderness made an appropriate setting

---

* Generally the second element in *Withernsea* is derived from *sǣ*, meaning 'mere', with reference to the old lake there.

for a further complete reworking of 'Sea Chant of an Elder Day', the storm poem Tolkien had last worked on two and a half years earlier. The 1917 version, written while he was living in a lonely house near Roos, provides a glimpse of an early Tolkienian cosmogony remarkable for its violence:

> in those eldest of the days
> When the world reeled in the tumult as the Great Gods tore the Earth
> In the darkness, in the tempest of the cycles ere our birth.

The lines seem of a piece with the era, when world-shaking human conflicts and the harsh cycles of nature might have looked like two aspects of a single truth. War was unrelenting, and in Russia, where the Tsar had abdicated, revolutionaries were calling on workers of the world to rise up. But this conception of nature created from conflict also mirrors the rending and rebuilding of Holderness. In the 1917 version of the sea poem, it manifests itself in the actions of the capricious sea-spirit Ossë, who assails coasts, wrecks ships, and sends

> the embattled tempest roaring up behind the tide
> When the trumpet of the first winds sounded, and the grey sea sang and cried
> As a new white wrath woke in him, and his armies rose to war
> And swept in billowed cavalry towards the walled and moveless shore.

Mindful of the ambivalent nature of the sea, Tolkien had assigned to it not one but two tutelary spirits. The greater of the two is not Ossë, despite his furious strength, but Ulmo (Gnomish *Ylmir*) 'the upholder', who understands the hearts of Elves and Men and whose music haunts its hearers. Accordingly, he now renamed the poem 'The Horns of Ulmo', tying it for the first time to his infant mythology. Additional lines identified the song as Tuor's account of how he heard the music of Ulmo in the Vale of Willows.

In the twilight by the river on a hollow thing of shell
He made immortal music, till my heart beneath his spell
Was broken in the twilight, and the meadows faded dim
To great grey waters heaving round the rocks where sea-birds
swim.

Even when Tuor emerges from the spell, a salt mist redolent of Holderness lies over the Oxford-like Vale of Willows.

Only the reeds were rustling, but a mist lay on the streams
Like a sea-roke drawn far inland, like a shred of salt sea-dreams.
'Twas in the Land of Willows that I heard th'unfathomed breath
Of the Horns of Ylmir calling – and shall hear them till my death.

* * *

For a while during the spring of 1917, Tolkien was put in charge of an outpost of the Humber Garrison near Thirtle Bridge at Roos (in a house next to the post office, according to local tradition) and Edith was able to live with him.

'In those days her hair was raven, her skin clear, her eyes brighter than you have seen them, and she could sing – and *dance*,' he wrote to their son Christopher after her death in 1971. When duty permitted, they would stroll in a nearby wood, which Roos tradition identifies as Dents Garth, at the south end of the village, beside the parish church of All Saints. Here, at the feet of the ash, oak, sycamore, and beech trees, tall flowers with white umbels burst into bloom from mid-April until the end of May. The flowers, *Anthriscus sylvestris*, are what books might call cow parsley, wild chervil, or Queen Anne's lace, among many other names; but Tolkien referred to all such white-flowered umbellifers (and not just the highly poisonous *Conium maculatum*) by the usual rural name of *hemlock*.* Among these cloudy white heads,

* Christopher Tolkien notes that his father 'regarded the restriction of a vernacular name to this or that species within a large group of plants not easily distinguishable to the eye as the pedantry of popularizing botanists – who ought to content themselves with the Linnean names'.

Edith danced and sang. The scene fixed itself in Tolkien's mind. It could have come from fairy-tale, a vision of sylvan loveliness glimpsed by a wanderer returned from war. When he next had the leisure to compose at length, Tolkien put the scene at the heart of just such a tale.

But in the meantime, on Friday 1 June 1917, RAMC officers at Hull found him fit for general service. The timing could hardly have been worse. Three days later, the 3rd Lancashire Fusiliers sent more than a hundred men off to various fronts. On 7 June, the 11th Lancashire Fusiliers (who had not seen frontline duty since their arrival in Flanders in October) took part in a huge British attack on Messines Ridge, south of Ypres: an entirely triumphant reprise of the strategy at the start of the Somme, preceded by three weeks' artillery bombardment and the explosion of nineteen huge mines. Bowyer, the quartermaster, was the only officer killed in Tolkien's old battalion.

Tolkien, however, was told to continue with the Humber Garrison. He already had responsibilities with the 3rd Lancashire Fusiliers and there was a strong likelihood that he might soon be made signals officer at Thirtle Bridge. In July he sat the exam; but he failed. Possibly his health was to blame. On 1 August he joined Huxtable and others at the regiment's annual Minden Day dinner; but a fortnight later he succumbed to fever again and was admitted to hospital once more.

Brooklands Officers' Hospital, in Cottingham Road on the north side of Hull, was overseen by a woman glorying in the name of Mrs Strickland Constable. As Tolkien lay there, German aeroplanes flew in over the coast and Zeppelins carried out a bombing raid on the city. In Russia, the provisional government that had ousted the Tsar was running into crisis. In Flanders, 'Third Ypres' was under way: the murderous quagmire of Passchendaele. The 11th Lancashire Fusiliers had marched up to the line under intense shelling that killed Captain Edwards of Tolkien's old 'A' Company, still just twenty years old.

Tolkien's temperature ran high for the first six weeks and he was kept at Brooklands for a further three weeks. The journey from Hornsea was arduous for Edith, who had conceived during her husband's winter convalescence at Great Haywood and was now more than six months pregnant. His latest relapse brought matters to a crisis, and she abandoned her increasingly miserable lodgings in the seaside town, returning with Jennie Grove to Cheltenham. She had lived there for the three years prior to their engagement in 1913 and wanted to have the baby there. Christopher Wiseman wrote in an attempt to console Tolkien, but found words inadequate. 'It is all the more distressing now that I cannot help you even vicariously as I could before,' he said, 'and though we are the TCBS we have each got to see the other shouldering his load by himself without being able to lend a finger to steady him.' Failing (characteristically) to post the letter at the start of September, Wiseman learned five weeks later that Edith was still in Cheltenham and John Ronald still in hospital. 'I am very anxious for news of you, and also of your missis,' he wrote. But he added, 'So the Army do not contain quite so many fools as I supposed. I expected them to send you out before now, and I am delighted they haven't.'

Tolkien sent Wiseman the one poem he had written that year, 'Companions of the Rose'. As yet unpublished, this is an elegiac piece about G. B. Smith and Rob Gilson; its title refers to the fact that both belonged to regiments that had fought at Minden, commemorated by the wearing of the white rose on 1 August. Wiseman, who approved of the poem, consoled him: 'There is of course no legislation that touches the Muse, and she has not been entirely idle because you have spent a good time on the mythology.'

Indeed, when he was well enough Tolkien found the hospital a haven of congenial company (which included a regimental friend), and conducive to writing. Here, he wrote 'The Tale of Tinúviel', the love story at the heart of the 'Lost Tales' that had been inspired by that moment of fleeting beauty earlier in 1917 when he had gone walking with Edith in a wood at Roos. The second tale to be written down, it moved far from the vast war that had taken centre-stage in 'The Fall of Gondolin'. The threat posed by Melko remained in the background, and the stage was given over to a personal romance. Around this time Tolkien also began to prepare the ground for a darker counterpart to this story, the 'Tale of Turambar'. This was a direct descendant of his attempt, in the first months of the Great War, to retell the section of the Finnish *Kalevala* that deals with Kullervo, who kills himself after unwittingly seducing his sister.*

The large and complex mythological background to these tales was still evolving slowly, mostly by a process of accretion and alteration in name-lists and lexicons as Tolkien followed his linguistic muse. By the time he arrived at Brooklands, he had probably begun to enlarge the pantheon of 'gods' or Valar beyond the tiny handful he had named before the Somme. They were headed by *Manwë* and *Varda* and also included *Aulë* the smith, *Lòrien Olofantur* of dreams and *Mandos Vefantur* of death, the goddesses *Yavanna* and *Vana*, and possibly the hunter *Oromë*, in addition to the sea-deities *Ulmo* and *Ossë*. As for the Elves, Tolkien had probably decided by now that they first came into being beside *Koivië·nēni*, the 'waters of awakening'. He knew that the Two Trees of Valinor, painted back in May 1915, were both to be destroyed by Melko and *Gloomweaver*, clearly the Spider of Night who had appeared in an early outline of Eärendel's voyage. He also knew that the fortunes of the Gnomes in the war against Melko would pivot around the terrible battle of *Nînin Udathriol*, 'unnumbered tears'. Most would become thralls to Melko, and those who remained free would be largely destroyed in the Fall of Gondolin, leaving a remnant led by Eärendel. In the end the Vala Noldorin would lead a host of Elves from Kôr across the sea in a quest to liberate the captive Gnomes, but Orcs would overwhelm them in the Land of Willows. Noldorin, surviving the attack, would fight Melko at the *Pools of Twilight* with *Tulkas*, another Vala. But these are shreds of story, and it is impossible to guess what else Tolkien was revolving in his head before the full narratives took shape in the Lost Tales he wrote immediately after the war.

* * *

---

* Tolkien erased the original tales and wrote new versions over them in ink soon after the war. They are discussed in the Epilogue below, together with the rest of 'The Book of Lost Tales' composed at that time.

Tolkien was discharged from Brooklands on 16 October, still delicate and troubled by pain in his shins and arms. A month later, on Friday 16 November 1917, Edith gave birth at the Royal Nursing Home in Cheltenham. It was an ordeal that left her in a critical condition. But her husband could not be there. On the day his son, John Francis Reuel, was born, Tolkien stood before yet another medical board in Hull. His fever had recurred slightly but now he was judged fit to carry on full duties at Thirtle Bridge.

England was under siege, and Tolkien was standing guard at the sea-wall, chronically unwell. The Bolsheviks under Lenin had seized power in Russia and called an armistice, allowing Germany to begin moving vast numbers of troops from the Eastern Front to the Western. 'The end of the war seemed as far-off as it does now,' Tolkien told his second son, Michael, in the darkness of 1941. He could get no leave to go to Cheltenham until almost a week later, just after the great but short-lived British tank advance at Cambrai. By then Edith was recovering, and Father Francis came down from Birmingham to baptize John. From Scapa Flow, Christopher Wiseman sent the kind of wish that is only made during a war. 'When your kiddie comes to take his place with the rest of us who have spent their lives fighting God's enemies, perhaps he will find I can teach him to use his sword,' he wrote. In the meantime, he added, 'I insist on the appointment of uncle, or some such position symbolic of incurable bachelorhood and benevolence essential to the proper inculcation of some TCBS rites and doctrines.'

Tolkien sold the last of his patrimonial shares in the South African mines to pay for Edith's stay in the nursing home, but there was no pay rise when he was promoted to lieutenant soon afterwards. He returned to Holderness, and Edith now took rooms for herself and the baby in Roos itself.

His own health remained a problem and a mild fever took hold twice more, consigning him to bed for five days. But before the year was over, Tolkien had been transferred away from Roos and Thirtle Bridge to another coastal defence unit in Holderness, where his duties would be less demanding and he could receive on-going medical care.

The Royal Defence Corps had been set up in 1916 to make use of men too old to fight. A short-lived forerunner to the famous Home Guard of the Second World War, it also drew in soldiers such as Tolkien who were of fighting age but not fighting-fit. A unit for the old or unwell, it was a symptom of the damage war had dealt to Britain's population. Tolkien was sent to Easington, a tiny farming hamlet of three hundred people huddled near the tip of the peninsula, where the 9th Battalion of the Royal Defence Corps spent desolate days watching the sea. It was considerably more bleak here than at Thirtle Bridge ten miles to the north. Cliffs rose nearly ninety feet out of the North Sea, the air was salty, and the land treeless. A century before, soldiers had watched for Napoleon's ships from Dimlington, a tiny neighbouring settlement founded by the Angles; but Dimlington had since fallen into the sea. Close by, the cliffs dwindled and the land tapered into a long low tail stretching out into the mouth of the Humber: Spurn Point. A military railway ran past to the gun battery on the tip of the spit of land, built to replace the old road that the sea had also claimed.

The sea-tang enters again into 'The Song of Eriol', not so much a new poem as a reconfiguration of the old opening of 'The Wanderer's Allegiance', which had apparently dealt with Tolkien's 'father's sires' in Saxony. Christopher Wiseman had made some stringent criticisms of the 'apparent lack of connection' between parts of the poem. Now Tolkien pared the first part away from the longer sections dealing with Warwick, Town of Dreams, and Oxford, City of Present Sorrow, and reassigned the German ancestors to Eriol's bloodline. So his ever-hungry mythology took a bite out of one of his rare pieces of autobiographical poetry.

Nevertheless, like the period in which it was devised, Eriol's emergent back-history is dominated by an armed struggle spanning Europe, or the Great Lands, as Tolkien now called the continent. Just as it had in 'The Wanderer's Allegiance', the scene shifts from the 'sunlit goodliness' of the rural ancestral idyll to a time of devastating conflict.

Wars of great kings and clash of armouries,
Whose swords no man could tell, whose spears
Were numerous as a wheatfield's ears,
Rolled over all the Great Lands; and the Seas

Were loud with navies; their devouring fires
Behind the armies burned both fields and towns;
And sacked and crumbled or to flaming pyres
Were cities made, where treasuries and crowns,

Kings and their folk, their wives and tender maids
Were all consumed . . .

Despite the very twentieth-century scale of these armies and the scarred landscapes (not to mention the anachronistic reference to naval warfare), the singer's vantage-point is medieval. This is manifestly the Dark Ages, when the Germanic peoples who were thrust ever westward in waves of migrations and invasions set up their new homes in lands still marked by the ruinous stone-works of the fallen Roman civilization.

Now silent are those courts,
Ruined the towers, whose old shape slowly fades,
And no feet pass beneath their broken ports.

The sentiment echoes that of the Old English poem *The Wanderer*, in which 'ealda enta geweorc idlu stodon', the old work of giants stood desolate. Like the Anglo-Saxon Wanderer, too, Eriol has been bereaved by an apocalyptic war. Orphaned and made captive, he heard somehow the distant call of the great sea and escaped through 'wasted valleys and dead lands' to the western shores, arriving eventually in the Lonely Isle.

But that was long ago
And now the dark bays and unknown waves I know,
The twilight capes, the misty archipelago,
And all the perilous sounds and salt wastes 'tween this isle
Of magic and the coasts I knew awhile.

The inhospitable, fogbound tip of Holderness seems to make its presence felt here at the end of Eriol's wanderings, while the sea, ever ambivalent, loses some of its lustre for him, much as it did for Tuor.

Tolkien found 1918 an ordeal. As the new year came in and he turned twenty-six, he was feeling much stronger, but then the pace of recovery slowed down. Exercise still left him exhausted, and he looked weak. Two months later he was struck down by a bout of 'flu which confined him to his bed for five days, though this was before the terrible Spanish influenza epidemic that left millions dead across Europe in the latter half of the year.

But in March, medical officers at the Humber Garrison put an end to his treatment. The Royal Defence Corps was being wound down, and on Tuesday 19 March Tolkien was sent back for further 'hardening' with the 3rd Lancashire Fusiliers at Thirtle Bridge. He was reunited with Edith, and on 10 April he was found to be fighting fit again. Then, to Edith's despair, he was posted back to Cannock Chase in Staffordshire, and the 13th Lancashire Fusiliers.

The War Office needed every man it could get. The Germans had launched their long-expected Spring Offensive on 21 March, using all the vast manpower that had been freed from the Eastern Front when the Bolsheviks pulled Russia out of the war. For Germany this was a last gamble before Americans could arrive in their millions. For a while it seemed a wildly successful throw of the dice.

Having withdrawn from the Somme in 1917, the Germans now swept over the British line. Tolkien's comrades-in-arms in the 11th Lancashire Fusiliers were among those pushed back with great loss by the relentless tide, finding themselves on 26 March – after a sixteen-mile retreat – defending the old Somme front line where it had stood at the very beginning of the great 1916 battle. And this was only the first of five grand assaults by Germany.

Whatever the War Office had in mind for Tolkien, he was stationed initially at Penkridge Camp, an outlying section of Rugeley Camp on a ridge east of the Sher Brook, where he had stayed for a while during training for France. The barrenness of the heath was here relieved by a plantation of trees, and in the spring the Chase was more bearable than it had been when he had first arrived in late 1915. Later he was moved to Brocton Camp on the other side of the brook.

The return to Staffordshire ushered in a relatively happy interlude. Edith, baby John, and Jennie Grove found lodgings at a pleasant, rambling house called Gipsy Green, in Teddesley Hay, a manorial estate at the western foot of the Chase, and Tolkien was able to stay with them. He took out his sketchbooks again after a long break and drew the house, together with a tableau of scenes of family life. In his Gnomish lexicon, where he was outlining ideas for further 'Lost Tales' during 1918, Gipsy Green followed Warwick, Great Haywood, Oxford, and Withernsea into the topography of the Lonely Isle, becoming *Fladweth Amrod* or Nomad's Green, 'a place in *Tol Erethrin* where *Eriol* sojourned a while, nigh to *Tavrobel*'. In the summer, his shared labours with Christopher Wiseman over G. B. Smith's verse came to fruition when it was published by Erskine Macdonald as a small volume entitled *A Spring Harvest*.

But the Gipsy Green idyll, such as it was, ended on 29 June, when Tolkien succumbed to gastritis at Brocton Camp. He was sent back to Brooklands in Hull; and as soon as he had recovered he might be posted to nearby Thirtle Bridge. Edith teased him, 'I should think you ought never to feel tired again, for the amount of *Bed* you have had since you came back from France nearly two years ago is enormous.' Edith herself was still far from well, and she refused to move again. With Jennie she had lived in twenty-two different sets of lodgings in the two years since leaving Warwick in the spring of 1915 and had found it a 'miserable wandering homeless sort of life'. Nor was it over: Tolkien himself looked back on the period from John's birth until 1925 as 'a long nomadic series of arrivals at houses or lodgings that proved horrible – or worse: in some cases finding none at all'. But Edith's exasperated decision now to stay at Gipsy Green was well timed: her husband spent the remainder of the war in hospital.

The gastritis that struck him down in 1918 may have saved his life, just as trench fever had saved it before. The cruel pushes on the Western Front had taken their toll. Men were becoming scarce and, despite the arrival of the Americans, the war was far from won. On Friday 26 July Tolkien received orders to embark for Boulogne the next day in order to join his battalion in France. Almost as soon as it was issued, the embarkation order was cancelled. The War Office pen-pusher responsible had failed to take note not only that Lieutenant Tolkien was laid up in hospital, but also that his service battalion had effectively ceased to exist.

Straight after their pursuit by the Germans across the old Somme battlefield, the 11th Lancashire Fusiliers had once more been moved to Ypres, in time to be on the receiving end of the second great German offensive of 1918, on 9 April. Despite heavy losses, they were sent unsuccessfully against Mount Kemmel on 25 April (a day after the Germans had destroyed the defending unit, G. B. Smith's old battalion, the 3rd Salford Pals). Then they had been moved far afield to unfamiliar territory in the French sector of the line, on the River Aisne, where on 27 May they bore the brunt of one of the fiercest bombardments of the war, and the Germans' third 1918 offensive. After two days of fighting and falling back, they turned at bay to cover the retreat of the rest of the 74th Brigade. Nothing was heard from them again. All that was left of the battalion Tolkien had fought in were sixteen men who had stayed in reserve (led by Major Rodney Beswick, who had been with him at Regina Trench). The 11th Lancashire Fusiliers were officially disbanded in August.

At Brooklands, Tolkien managed to pursue his mythological work, further developing Qenya and Goldogrin. He brushed up on his Spanish and Italian and – just as the Western Allies effectively joined the White Russians' war against the Bolsheviks

– he began to study Russian. But military duties of any sort were beyond Tolkien. Meals were followed by pain and stomach upsets. He lost two stone and regaining it proved to be a slow struggle. The Humber Garrison medical board decided he was out of danger and now needed little more than rest; but the War Office had ended the practice of sending officers home to convalesce, having decided that they made no efforts to get well.

He was saved from action for one last, crucial period. Germany's astonishing 1918 offensives had failed to decide the war in the Kaiser's favour. Now the tide had visibly turned as the Americans arrived in ever increasing force and Spanish influenza laid waste the half-starved German troops. The Somme, and more, had been swiftly regained by an armada of tanks. The Great War was hastening to an end.

Now Tolkien's obstinate ill health at last registered with the War Office, or rather its manpower needs were finally easing. Despite a barrage of red tape, the bonds of service were cut with surprising speed. At the start of October, Tolkien was allowed to ask Lloyd George's new Ministry of Labour if he could be employed outside the military. He was no longer attached to the 3rd Lancashire Fusiliers.

On 11 October he was released from Brooklands and sent across the north of England to Blackpool, and the Savoy Convalescent Hospital.

He was well enough now to enjoy a formal Italian meal there with several officers, including two *carabinieri*, on Sunday 13 October, and the next day a medical board found him unfit for any military duty for six months – but fit for a desk job. He was discharged from the hospital there and then.

The Great War ended on 11 November, with scenes of jubilation on the streets of Britain and 'unwonted silence' in No Man's Land. Tolkien, who would remain a soldier of the British Army until he was demobilized, asked after Armistice Day to be stationed at Oxford 'for the purposes of completing his education'. Like many who find themselves once more masters of their own fate after a long remission, he had returned immediately to where he had last been a free man. His ambition before enlistment had been to begin an academic career, and nothing (certainly not his unpublished, unfinished, and painstaking mythology) had changed his mind. He cast about for work but found nothing, until his undergraduate tutor in Old Norse, William Craigie, one of the editors of the *Oxford English Dictionary*, offered to find him employment as an assistant lexicographer. From the viewpoint of the dictionary's editors, Tolkien would be an asset, but from the perspective of a jobless soldier facing a future that had never seemed less certain, this was a big break (and one he remembered with gratitude in his valedictory address forty-one years later at the end of his tenure as Merton Professor of English Language and Literature). An Old Edwardian in Oxford reported back to the school *Chronicle* some time later: 'We rejoice to have Tolkien still among us – rumours of a dictionary beside which all previous dictionaries shall be as vocabularies reach us, and we go on our way shivering.'

By Christmas, Tolkien had found rooms at 50 St John Street, up the road from the 'Johnner', the digs he had shared with Colin Cullis, and he moved in with Edith, John, and Jennie Grove. Students were flooding back from the armed forces, although they would not return to their pre-war numbers for a while and as yet, in the words of one historian, 'were acutely aware of stepping into the shoes of dead men'. Soon Tolkien was earning extra pennies by giving tuition, chiefly to women students, and re-reading Chaucer and *Sir Gawain and the Green Knight*. At Exeter College, Tolkien's old friend T. W. Earp had (in the words of Robert Graves) 'set himself the task of keeping the Oxford tradition alive through the dead years', preserving the minute-books of many undergraduateless societies, which were now re-formed. The Essay Club became the first public audience for Tolkien's mythology when he read 'The Fall of Gondolin'.

In the real world it was 'the enemy' that had fallen: the empires of Germany, Austro-Hungary, and Ottoman Turkey. But the old world had gone too, leaving the new one with a legacy of uncertainty, cruelty, and suffering. Millions had died, and very few were untouched by bereavement. Many of the young men who had stood beside Tolkien in those black-and-white photographs of rugby teams or dining clubs at King Edward's School and Exeter College were gone.* From Tolkien's school, 243 died; from his college, 141. From Oxford University as a whole, nearly one in five servicemen was killed, considerably more than the national average because so many had been junior officers.

Even Colin Cullis did not long survive the war in which he had been judged physically unfit to serve: pneumonia, brought on by the influenza epidemic, claimed his life just after Tolkien was demobbed. From King Edward's, Tolkien's cousin Thomas Ewart Mitton, five years his junior and a fellow poet, had been killed in an accident while serving as a signaller at Ypres. Of the broad Birmingham TCBS, Ralph Payton had died on the Somme in 1916 and the wise-cracking 'Tea-Cake' Barnsley, having recovered from shell shock, had been killed in action with the Coldstream Guards near Ypres in 1917. Rob Gilson was gone. The loss of so many friends remained, in the words of Tolkien's children, 'a lifelong sadness'. It was for G. B. Smith that Tolkien mourned most deeply; the two had understood each other's social background and maternal upbringing; they had shared a school, a university, a regiment, and a bloody page of history; they had been akin in their reverence for poetry and the imagination, and had spurred each other into creative flight.

The war also weakened the bond between the Great Twin Brethren. Back in 1916, as Tolkien lay in the Birmingham University Hospital, Christopher Wiseman had looked forward to days of peace when he might go to Oxford and study law at Christ Church. He and Tolkien might share digs, he declared; 'perhaps in the ever-famous "Johnner"'. After Smith's death, and that of

---

* Four of the King Edward's casualties had sat in front of Tolkien and Wiseman in the 1910 portrait of the school rugby XV reproduced in this volume: H. L. Higgins and H. Patterson, severely wounded in France, and John Drummond Crichton and George Frederick Cottrell, killed by shells at Cambrai and Ypres.

his own mother in August 1917, Wiseman had been abject, writing, 'We must contrive to stick together somehow. I can't bear to be cut off from the seventh heaven I lived in my younger days.'

But while Tolkien was at Easington they had had another 'grand old quarrel' of the sort that used to invigorate their walks to school up Harborne Road and Broad Street. Typically, it started from a small observation and became a battle royal between rationalism and mysticism. Tolkien found the most mundane human misunderstandings depressing, and blamed a 'clash of backgrounds' arising from what he called 'the decay of faith, the break up of that huge atmosphere or background of faith which was common to Europe in the Middle Ages'. Wiseman was scornful: 'That huge atmosphere of magic; that ghastly atmosphere of superstition: that it is that has gone.' This was a religious dispute, with Tolkien speaking for the pre-schismatic Roman Catholic world, Wiseman for the Protestant Reformation and its legacy.

Wiseman had argued that the true modern clash was between *foregrounds*, with individuals too busy about their own lives to fully understand each other. 'That,' he said, 'was the whole glory of the TCBS, that in spite of the clash of our foregrounds, which was very great, we had discovered the essential similarity of our backgrounds. The TCBS arose partly as a protest against the assumption of artificial foregrounds.' Though he had used the past tense when writing of the group, he was emphatic: 'I am still a TCBSite. I love you, and pray for you and yours.'

The bond had suffered much wear and tear. Through much of 1918 the two lost track of each other's movements, but in December Wiseman wrote to say that he was going to Cambridge to teach junior officers. 'So the TCBS will again be represented at both 'Varsities, and perhaps may assemble from time to time,' he said. He expressed 'parental anxiety' for Tolkien and Edith and baby John, but the TCBSian future, once colossal and world-bestriding, now looked merely life-sized.

* * *

On 15 July 1919 Tolkien made his way on a travel warrant to the village of Fovant on Salisbury Plain, a few miles south of G. B. Smith's old training camp at Codford St Mary, to be demobbed. He was handed a ration book and for the next six months he received a small disability pension because of persistent health problems. The next day, almost exactly four years after he received his commission, he was released from service.

Epilogue. 'A new light'

Once, Christopher Wiseman had allowed faith to take the place of mere hope and imagined that the TCBS would be saved for better things than war. Neither Rob Gilson nor G. B. Smith had achieved their ambitions in life, and the bond they had all forged now seemed fruitless. As Wiseman had said in a letter to Tolkien after Smith's death, 'What is not done, is left undone; and love that is voided becomes strangely like a mockery.'

Yet there remained another way to see their hopes fulfilled. Wiseman himself had once said that he, Smith, and Gilson wrote Tolkien's poems. Smith had put it more tactfully: 'We believe in your work, we others, and recognise with pleasure our own finger in it.' Facing death, he had drawn consolation from the fact that Tolkien would survive, and there would 'still be left a member of the great TCBS to voice what I dreamed and what we all agreed upon'. Smith had wanted them to leave the world a better place than when they found it, to 're-establish sanity, cleanliness, and the love of real and true beauty' through art embodying TCBSian principles. Beyond such broad outlines, what Smith dreamed is unguessable – as Wiseman lamented, he 'never lived to write the "tales"' he planned – but it may be surmised that he envisaged Tolkien, rather than Wiseman or Gilson, voicing the dream.

Gilson's artistic talent had been in recording beauty or truth, rather than originating it. Otherwise his strength lay in personal relations. Ironically, his most widely circulated work was an anonymous platoon drill for coordinated trench-digging, which appeared in a wartime military manual aimed at school training corps – a significant contribution to the war effort, but surely not part of the TCBSian dream.

Wiseman insisted that his own ambitions had outlived Smith and Gilson, declaring, 'I can still ask for the weight of glory we cared so light-heartedly to crave for in the old days, promising to pay the last farthing I have for it.' But although he wrote a little music now and then, he never really found a medium in which he could match Tolkien or Smith. He did not become a finance minister, as he had threatened in a letter to Tolkien in 1916, but was drawn instead into the headmastership of a Methodist public school, Queen's College in Taunton, Somerset, taking it on in 1926 as a duty rather than a pleasure. Here, he passed on the TCBSian virtues on a smaller scale, nurturing in his pupils a love of music, personally learning the oboe and clarinet to help raise a woodwind section for the school orchestra he formed, and teaching the violin to a whole class *en masse*.

As to fulfilling the TCBSian dream of kindling 'a new light' in the world at large, only Tolkien was left, as Smith had foreseen. Now he had a duty to his old friend, and to whatever divinity lay in his own survival, to pursue the mythology he had started to map out.

Straight after the war Tolkien set about the task of completing 'The Book of Lost Tales' in earnest, starting out with a grand myth of world-making, 'The Music of the Ainur'. The influence of the TCBS may be seen here, if anywhere. Back before the Somme, Wiseman had declared that the Elves only seemed alive to Tolkien because he was still creating them, and that the same principle held for all art and science. 'The completed work is vanity, the process of the working is everlasting . . . The "conquests" vanish when they are made; they are only vital in the making,' he had said – adding in a characteristic musical analogy, 'the fugue is nothing on the page; it is only vital as it works its way out . . .' As if he had Wiseman's words in mind, Tolkien now depicted the creation of the world as an on-going act, and music as the primal creative form. Song is also the medium for supernatural power in the *Kalevala*; while Tolkien had already equated the music of Ulmo with the very sound of the sea. But 'The Music of the Ainur' portrays the whole universe as a choral work conceived by the Heavenly Father, Ilúvatar, and sung by the angelic host of the Ainur, who elaborate upon his themes. At the end, Ilúvatar reveals that their music has shaped the world and its history, while he has given it substance and essence.

> Now when they reached the midmost void they beheld a sight of surpassing beauty and wonder where before had been emptiness; but Ilúvatar said: 'Behold your choiring and your music! . . . Each one herein will find contained within the design that is mine the adornments and embellishments that he himself devised . . . One thing only have I added, the fire that giveth Life and Reality' – and behold, the Secret Fire burnt at the heart of the world.

The early lexicon of Qenya may shed some light on the last statement, explaining that *Sā*, 'fire, especially in temples, etc.', is also 'A mystic name identified with the Holy Ghost'. Ilúvatar's further solo contribution is the creation of Elves and Men, together with their distinguishing talent – language.

Elevated subject and style should not obscure the tale's pertinence to the terrible times Tolkien had known. It is nothing less than an attempt to justify God's creation of an imperfect world filled with suffering, loss, and grief. The primal rebel Melko covets Ilúvatar's creativity where the Satan of Milton's *Paradise Lost* coveted God's authority, a distinction reflecting Tolkien's aestheticist anti-industrialism and Milton's puritan anti-monarchism. Melko enters the void to search for the Secret Fire, yet having failed to find it he nevertheless introduces his own discordant music, brash but marked by 'unity and a system of its own'. But in this collaborative Genesis, he distorts Creation itself, as Ilúvatar reveals: 'Through him has pain and misery been made in the clash of overwhelming musics; and with confusion of sound have cruelty, and ravening, and darkness, loathly mire and all putrescence of thought or thing, foul mists and violent flame, cold without mercy, been born, and death without hope.' These ills (universal, though strikingly evocative of the Somme) do not arise exclusively from Melko's repetitive music; rather, they spring from its 'clash' with Ilúvatar's themes.

In Tolkien's view, creative decadence and spiritual schism were inextricably linked. During the TCBS crisis of 1914, he had told Wiseman: 'It is the tragedy of modern life that no one knows upon what the universe is built to the mind of the man next to him in the tram: it is this that makes it so tiring, so distracting; that produces its bewilderment, lack of beauty and design; its ugliness; its atmosphere antagonistic to supreme excellence.' In 1917 he had again bemoaned the decay in 'beauty in all men's works and fabrications for more than two centuries', and located its cause and symptom in the 'clash of backgrounds' that had opened up since the Middle Ages.

'The Music of the Ainur' portrayed such schism on a universal scale, but moved beyond complaint to reach a consolatory view. Ilúvatar insists that the cosmogonic discords will ultimately make 'the theme more worth hearing, Life more worth the living, and the World so much the more wonderful and marvellous'. As if to shed some light on this rather bald assertion, he cites the beauty of ice and snow, produced from water (Ulmo's work) by intemperate cold (Melko's). So much for natural wonders and marvels; but how do the discords improve the experience of life for the individual facing 'cold without mercy . . . and death without hope'? This is left as a riddle for the ensuing stories of good and evil to unravel.

In the tales that follow, angels eager to continue the work of creation descend into the new-coined world to be its guardians. Here they are known as the Valar, frequently called gods. Eriol, indeed, has never heard of a Creator or Heavenly Father, but he knows about the Anglo-Saxon gods *Wóden* (Odin) and *Þunor* (Thor), whom the Elves identify as Manwë, chief of the Valar, and Tulkas, their champion.

Tolkien's pantheon is quirky and assymetric. There are no simple dualisms among the Valar: no god of happiness to counterbalance mournful Fui, for example, and no shepherd or sower to contrast with the hunter Oromë. The brotherhood of Mandos and Lórien, the gods of death and dreams, implies a visionary connection with the spirit world. Others of the Valar are not only actors in the drama but also elemental forces of nature: Manwë's breath is the breeze, and Melko's very presence in his native north breeds glaciers and icebergs.

The battle god Makar and his sister Méassë are anomalous. Their court hosts a perpetual battle in which Méassë urges Makar's warriors to blows or revives them with wine, her arms 'reddened to the elbow dabbling in that welter'. The scenario incorporates a powerful motif from Norse myth: Valhalla, the hall to which Odin's shieldmaidens, the Valkyries, bring warriors slain in battle to fight every day under Odin's eye. But the presence of Makar and Méassë and their brutalist iron hall in Valinor suggests an ambivalent view of war as a necessary evil. Notably, it is not Makar but Tulkas, a sporting champion 'who loveth games and twanging of bows and boxing, wrestling, running, and leaping', who deals blows for the Valar against Melko.* Méassë and her brother play only a minor role in the Lost Tales, and later vanished from the mythology.

The Valar of the Lost Tales have many of the imperfections of the Gods of Asgard or Olympus. Clashing temperaments meet in unruly council under Manwë, disagreeing especially over their duty towards Elves and Men. First among equals rather than absolute monarch, Manwë makes several poor decisions, misreads others' motives, and stands aside when more impatient gods defy him. The Valar may be hot-headed, devious, and violent under provocation. But in general they err on the side of caution, shutting themselves away from the troubled world.

Melko precedes the Valar into the world, not as an outcast from heaven like Satan, but as a petitioner pledging to moderate the violence and intemperate extremes his music has brought about. His ensuing conflict with the Valar makes a whole history

---

* Tulkas, with his laughter, yellow hair, and sporting prowess, may catch aspects of Christopher Wiseman, as Erinti does of Edith, Noldorin of Tolkien, and Amillo of his brother Hilary.

out of the biblical declaration, 'Let there be light'.* The first era is the age of the Gods, when they live in the midst of the flat earth lit by Lamps at north and south. In the second era, they withdraw to a sanctuary in the west, Valinor, illuminated by Two Trees of silver and gold, but they set stars in the perpetual night east of Valinor for the advent of the Elves, Ilúvatar's first-born children. But after Elvenhome has been established in bright Valinor, Melko destroys the Trees, as he destroyed the Lamps. In the third era, light is restored to the whole world by the Sun and Moon, the last fruit and flower of the Trees, and humans enter the drama. Elves fade from general view in the fourth era, which begins when Melko impairs the Sun's original magic. So it is that the Elves whom mortal Eriol meets in the Cottage of Lost Play look forward to a 'Rekindling of the Magic Sun'.

In this mythology of light, primeval darkness is embodied in the spider-form of Gloomweaver or Wirilómë, who helps Melko destroy the Trees. Her provenance is a mystery even to the Valar. 'Mayhap she was bred of mists and darkness on the confines of the Shadowy Seas, in that utter dark that came between the overthrow of the Lamps and the kindling of the Trees,' comments the story-teller Lindo, 'but more like she has always been'. By contrast, primeval light is a liquid that flows around the young world but is gradually used up in the creation of the earthly and celestial lights, leaving only the intangible radiation we know. It is tempting to connect these primordial principles with the ancient void and the Secret Fire of creation. Darkness such as Wirilómë represents is unholy, 'a denial of all light', rather than its mere absence. But already it is possible to see abundant consolations for Melko's discords and destructiveness: without them, neither Trees nor Sun and Moon would have been created.

Such paradoxes also run through the history of the Elves (also called fairies or *Eldar*, 'beings from outside'). Their fall from unity into division, beginning on the long journey from the

* Tolkien did not number the four epochs of this history of light, and they should not to be confused with the later, well-known division of Middle-earth's history into the First, Second, Third, and Fourth Ages.

place of their first awakening to Valinor, is responsible for the diverse flowering of Faërie across the world. The first group to reach their destination, the *Teleri*, devote themselves to the arts of music and poetry; the second, the Gnomes (*Noldoli*), to science; together these two clans establish the town of Kôr. Through the diaspora of the third tribe, the world's wild places become populated by fairies who have more to do with nature than culture. Those who strayed from the route are accounted the Lost Elves, the elusive Shadow-folk who haunt the 1915 poem 'A Song of Aryador'. Only a portion of the third kindred at last reach Valinor and settle near Kôr on the Bay of Faërie as the Shoreland-pipers (*Solosimpi*).

They play a key role in a further thread of the legendarium, the hallowed prehistory of England. The British archipelago appears early on as a single unbroken island, serving as a vast ship on which the sea-god Ossë ferries the Valar to Valinor after the cataclysm of the Lamps. Later Ulmo, god of the deep, harnesses the primeval whale Uin to tow the fairies to Valinor, kindred by kindred. Catching the gleam of the Two Trees on two such voyages, the island flourishes into the very crown of nature. But proprietorial Ossë halts the third crossing westward, when the Solosimpi are on board. The ensuing tug-of-war between the rival water divinities exemplifies the occasional light-heartedness and frequent exuberance of the Lost Tales:

> Vainly doth Ulmo trumpet and Uin with the flukes of his unmeasured tail lash the seas to wrath, for thither Ossë now brings every kind of deep sea creature that buildeth itself a house and dwelling of stony shell; and these he planted about the base of the island: corals there were of every kind and barnacles and sponges like stone . . . the isle has grown fast in the most lonely waters of the world.

When Eriol makes landfall to hear the Lost Tales, the Lonely Isle has yet to make the final voyage to its current location just off the European coast.

In leaving their place of origin, the Waters of Awakening, for a better life in the earthly paradise of Elvenhome, the Eldar follow the same progression as the Valar, who left heaven for their first paradise in the midst of the world. This curious repeated pattern, quite distinct from the Judaeo-Christian myth of Eden, seems less surprising in the context of Tolkien's own wandering existence, particularly his childhood idyll, after leaving South Africa, in the English West Midlands – a home 'perhaps more poignant to me because I wasn't born in it'. This is not to say that the mythology was 'about' his own life; but that, like any artist, he instilled his creation with his values. For the Valar and the Elves, home is a blessing discovered, not inherited. Furthermore, no paradise may be taken for granted. Tolkien's sense of home was fraught: his own rural idyll had soon been left behind for industrial Birmingham; he had lost both his parents; and since 1911 he had remained in no single place for more than a few months. In his mythology, Melko destroys both the divine and the faëry paradises.

The Elves find the serpent already loose in the garden. By the time they arrive in Valinor, Melko has been imprisoned and then released there as a penitent. Faithful only to his own original spirit, he exercises his malevolence again through envy of others' creations – this time, that of the Eldar, whose art emulates the divine artistry behind the green world. In Tolkien's poem 'Kortirion among the Trees', the fairies sing a 'woven song of stars and gleaming leaves'; and in 'The Fall of Gondolin' the heraldry of the elven battalions is a celebration of nature. The Gnomes of Kôr are the creators of the world's gems, by a distinctively faëry science involving the infusion of stones with the multiform essences of light. Lusting for the products of this profligate genius, Melko pillages their treasury, destroys the Trees, and brings the vengeful Gnomes in hot pursuit to the Great Lands, where the rest of the Lost Tales take place.

But the Gnomes have fallen from creativity into possessiveness and have been suborned by Melko into rebellion against the Valar, who now shut Valinor against them so that the only way back for the exiles is the Road of Death. The story so far is

Tolkien's *Paradise Lost*, an account of the fall in heaven and the fall on earth it precipitates. The sequence embodies his early ambition (as expressed many years later to Milton Waldman) to depict 'the large and cosmogonic' upon 'the vast backcloths' of his mythology for England.

At the opposite end of the scale, 'the level of romantic fairy-story . . . in contact with the earth', lies 'The Tale of Tinúviel', set in the Great Lands some time after the Valar have restored light to the wide world by creating the Sun and Moon. 'Tinúviel', drafted in the summer of 1917 and inspired by a walk in the Roos 'hemlocks' with Edith, features a love story, woodland fairies, and comedy in the kitchen of the Prince of Cats. But for all its light-heartedness, this Lost Tale most closely approaches the range of mood in *The Lord of the Rings*, ultimately acquiring the gravity of myth. The dialogue of low and high was something Tolkien had long valued; his comments in 1914 about the mystic poet Francis Thompson fit his own work perfectly: 'One must begin with the elfin and delicate and progress to the profound: listen first to the violin and the flute, and then learn to hearken to the organ of being's harmony.'

Depicting the realm of Artanor, a wood where fairies hunt and revel but the intruder is bewildered or enchanted, Tolkien challenges the Shakespearean view of elves and fairies as frivolous, diminutive mischief-makers. First he restores the dignity of the fairy queen, whimsically maligned in *Romeo and Juliet* as Mab, the midwife of delusionary dreams whose carriage is

> Drawn with a team of little atomies
> Athwart men's noses as they lie asleep;
> Her waggon-spokes made of long spinners' legs,
> The cover of the wings of grasshoppers,
> The traces of the smallest spider's web . . .

Such is the imagery that led Tolkien to pronounce 'a murrain on Will Shakespeare and his damned cobwebs' for debasing

Faërie. His own fairy queen, Gwendeling, is less ornamental and more substantial, a figure of mystery with a retinue of nightingales and a divine power of dream:

> Her skin was white and pale, but her eyes shone and seemed deep, and she was clad in filmy garments most lovely yet of black, jet-spangled and girt with silver. If ever she sang, or if she danced, dreams and slumbers passed over your head and made it heavy. Indeed she was a sprite that escaped from Lórien's gardens . . .

Gwendeling, one of the primeval spirits who accompanied the Valar into the world, is queen of fairies through marriage to Tinwelint, original leader of the third elven tribe. Their daughter Tinúviel inherits not only Gwendeling's beauty and trappings, but also – in this most thaumaturgic of Tolkien's tales – her powers of enchantment.

But this is also a love story in which love, transfixing and transfiguring the wanderer Beren when he sees Tinúviel dance among the hemlocks, seems a kind of magic. Its first enemy is not a demonic power but prejudice and mockery. Tinwelint regards the Gnomish Beren with suspicion because of his people's thraldom to Melko.* When Beren asks for his daughter's hand in marriage, he sets a seemingly impossible test: Beren must bring him one of the three Silmarils, peerless masterpieces of the Gnomes' gem-making craft, now set in Melko's iron crown. Tinwelint thinks this is impossible, and simply means no; but Beren takes the challenge at face value, pausing only to comment that the king holds his daughter cheap. His quest for the Silmaril is also a quest to overturn belittling irony and re-establish true worth.

Tolkien's attempt to 'reconstruct' the lost tales behind surviving fragments – to restore the fairy queen's dignity, for example

---

* Evidence suggests that in the 1917 version, Beren was a mortal man (as he is subsequently in the 'Silmarillion'), rendering the background of distrust even more acute.

– is an allied endeavour. For the confinement of Tinúviel in a fantastic tree-house, and Beren's concurrent servitude under Tevildo, Prince of Cats, he excavated two familiar stories. He made a coherent, if mystical, narrative out of one of the surreal moments in 'Rapunzel', a story he knew from a childhood favourite, Andrew Lang's *Red Fairy Book*. Whereas Rapunzel hauls visitors up to her treetop prison with her impossibly long hair, Tinúviel uses hers (vastly propagated by magic) to escape: Rapunzel is a thoroughly passive victim, Tinúviel anything but. Meanwhile Tevildo's name (Gnomish *Tifil*, *Tiberth* – all related to Elvish words for 'hate') evokes *Tybalt/Tibert*, a cat name popular from the tom-cat in the medieval *Reynard the Fox*. Such beast fables left Tolkien dissatisfied; the beast was only 'a mask upon a human face, a device of the satirist or the preacher', he later said. He imagined therefore that the surviving incarnations of Tibert/Tybalt – down to *Romeo and Juliet*'s strutting street-fighter, who has shed his animal mask altogether – were only the shadows of a now-forgotten monster, Tevildo:

> His eyes were long and very narrow and slanted, and gleamed both red and green, but his great grey whiskers were as stout and as sharp as needles. His purr was like the roll of drums and his growl like thunder, but when he yelled in wrath it turned the blood cold, and indeed small beasts and birds were frozen as to stone, or dropped lifeless often at the very sound.

It is a pity that later, as the exuberant Lost Tales gave way to the austere 'Silmarillion', there was no longer any place for this astonishing grotesque, vain, capricious, and cruel; but at least his role as Beren's captor passed to no less a figure than Sauron the Necromancer. Meanwhile, Tevildo and the other animals in this tale, the faithful talking hound Huan and Karkaras, 'the greatest wolf the world has ever seen', are bold, blunt creations with magic in their blood; such human characteristics as they possess serve to reveal the beast within.

But the cat-and-dog story is only the test before the real crisis. Arriving in Melko's stronghold, Angband, a shadowy immensity above an industrial slave-pit, we reach the crux of Tolkien's narrative: the moment when the small but resolute confronts the demonic embodiment of tyranny and destruction. Tolkien came to regard the tale of Beren and Tinúviel as 'the first example of the motive (to become dominant in Hobbits) that the great policies of world history, "the wheels of the world", are often turned not by the Lords and Governors, even gods, but by the seemingly unknown and weak'. Such a worldview is inherent in the fairy-tale (and Christian) idea of the happy ending in which the dispossessed are restored to joy; but perhaps Tolkien was also struck by the way it had been borne out in the Great War, when ordinary people stepped out of ordinary lives to carry the fate of nations.

The lovers' clandestine entry into Angband, under the dark cloak of slumber that Tinúviel has woven from her own hair, provides an intriguing parallel with the assault upon the Two Trees by Melko and Gloomweaver under the cover of the Spider's suffocating webs. It is as if the quest for the Silmaril, in which the light of the Trees is preserved, were in its small way an exorcism of the older nightmare. But the enemy cannot be engaged on his own terms. Confronting Melko, Tinúviel's weapon is aesthetic: her spellbinding dance, to which she adds a dream-song that brings the sound of the nightingale into the heart of darkness.

The scene epitomizes a narrative moment that Tolkien saw in life, and in fairy-tales, but rarely in other literary forms. He coined a word for it in his essay 'On Fairy-stories': *eucatastrophe*, from the Greek *eu* 'good' and *katastrophe*, 'sudden turn', and saw it as a glimpse of the glad tidings (*evangelium*) of eternal life.

> The consolation of fairy-stories, the joy of the happy ending: or more correctly of the good catastrophe, the sudden joyous 'turn' (for there is no true end to any fairy-tale): this joy, which is one of the things which fairy-stories can produce supremely well, is . . . a sudden and miraculous grace: never to be counted on to recur. It does not deny the existence of *dyscatastrophe*, of sorrow and failure: the possibility of these is necessary to the joy of deliverance; it denies (in the face of much evidence, if you will) universal final

> defeat and in so far is *evangelium*, giving a fleeting glimpse of Joy, Joy beyond the walls of the world, poignant as grief.

Tinúviel's attendant bird, the nightingale, is a fitting emblem of eucatastrophe, pouring out its fluting song when all is dark. Its symbolic significance may be measured in the words of men on the Western Front. Rob Gilson, hearing a nightingale in the early hours one May morning from his trench dugout, thought it 'wonderful that shells and bullets shouldn't have banished them, when they are always so shy of everything human', while Siegfried Sassoon wrote that 'the perfect performance of a nightingale . . . seemed miraculous after the desolation of the trenches'.

The glimpse of joy from the depths of hell is nothing if not fleeting, and during the flight from Angband the wolf Karkaras bites off the hand in which Beren holds the recovered Silmaril. Victory, you might say, has been snatched by the jaws of defeat, and Beren must return to Artanor a visibly reduced figure. Yet far from accepting that the joke is on him, Beren repays King Tinwelint's earlier mockery with a richer jest by declaring, 'I have a Silmaril in my hand even now,' before revealing his maimed arm. It is a lesson in true value: instead of the bride-price, Beren delivers proof of immeasurable courage and love. Conceived when thousands of men were returning from the battlefront permanently disabled, this seems a brave and timely illustration of Ilúvatar's promise of consolation for the discords in Creation. Through endurance, Beren has achieved a moral victory against which material acquisitions are nothing.

Love conquers all – even, in the end, death. For its final impassioned paean to love, 'The Tale of Tinúviel' enters the plane of myth. As the Silmaril is regained in a wolf-hunt, Beren is fatally injured; soon grief-stricken Tinúviel follows him down the Road of Death. But at her plea, Mandos releases the lovers from the halls of the dead, and they return to earthly life. Yet even this resurrection may not be the ultimate release, but only its prelude, as we shall see.

* * *

Túrin Turambar's story is the unhappy counterpart to Beren's, telling of hopes betrayed, fruitless heroism and love gone awry.

Tolkien was not alone among latter-day writers in characterizing the individual's fate as the work of a malicious demiurgic power. Thomas Hardy pictured Tess Durbeyfield as a victim of an Olympian 'President of the Immortals', while the First World War poet Wilfred Owen, in 'Soldier's Dream', imagined merciful Jesus spiking all the guns but God fixing them again. In contrast, though, Tolkien's faith in God and the mythological method may be gauged by his personification of cruel destiny in satanic Melko rather than in Manwë or Ilúvatar; and by Melko's status as an actor in the drama rather than a metaphor. Túrin falls victim to the demiurge's curse on his father, Úrin, a soldier taken captive but defiant to Angband after battle.

In its scale, centrality, and tragedy, the Battle of Unnumbered Tears (though never directly recounted in the Lost Tales) inevitably bears comparison with the Somme – though it spans days at most and produces an outright victory for the enemy rather than a Pyrrhic victory for the allies. Nearly half of these countless, hopeful battalions of Gnomes and Men are killed. Tolkien provides an arresting and concentrated emblem for the terrible carnage in the Hill of Death, 'the greatest cairn in the world', into which the Gnomes' corpses are gathered. Survivors, many of them driven to vagabondage, do not speak of the battle. Of the fates of fathers and husbands, families hear nothing.

Yet the Battle of Unnumbered Tears is much more than a military disaster. An epochal stage in a war that Tolkien saw as everlasting, it ushers in the enslavement of individual art and craft by impersonal industry and cold avarice: the thraldom of the Gnomes in Melko's mines, and their demoralization under the Spell of Bottomless Dread. Imagination thrives now only in scattered faëry refuges, such as Gondolin and Artanor, a 'bulwark . . . against the arrogance of the Vala of Iron'. The majority of Men, meanwhile, having proved faithless in battle, are cut off from Elves and the inspiration that they represent.

Úrin's people, who stood firm, are corralled by Melko in shadowy Aryador, whence his wife Mavwin, with an infant daughter to look after, sends young Túrin to fosterage in Artanor. This separation is only 'the first of the sorrows that befell him', the tale notes, beginning a tally. Four times Túrin travels from a new home (Aryador, Artanor, the hidden Gnomish kingdom of the Rodothlim, and a village of human wood-rangers) into peril (near-starvation in the forest as a child, capture by orcs as a grown man, capture by the dragon Glorund, the dragon's return). In successive phases he draws nearer to happiness and heroic stature, but is then plunged into yet deeper anguish.

Savage irony is at work here. It is not simply that good times are replaced by bad: happiness and heroism are the very causes of sorrow and failure; their promise turns out to be not hollow, but false. By tremendous daring and 'the luck of the Valar', Túrin's dearest friend, the elven archer Beleg, rescues him from orc captors; but in the dark, Túrin mistakes him for an assailant and kills him. In the final pages he finds a beautiful stranger wandering distraught in the woods, her memory a blank; but every step towards joyous union with Níniel 'daughter of tears' (as he names her) is a step towards tragedy: she is his long-lost sister.

This final, most fiendish irony is set up by Melko's servant, Glorund. A creature apart from the mechanistic dragons of 'The Fall of Gondolin', he belongs to the same species as Fafnir in the Icelandic *Volsunga Saga* and Smaug in *The Hobbit*: carnal monsters who 'love lies and lust after gold and precious things with a great fierceness of desire, albeit they may not use nor enjoy them', in the words of the Lost Tale. His trail is desolation:

> The land had become all barren and was blasted for a great distance about the ancient caverns of the Rodothlim, and the trees were crushed to the earth or snapped. Towards the hills a black heath stretched and the lands were scored with the great slots that that loathly worm made in his creeping.

Glorund's particular genius, then, is to undermine beauty and truth, either by destroying them or by rendering them morally worthless. His despoliation of treasuries, his desecration of nature, and his delight in irony are of a piece.

The contrast with 'The Tale of Tinúviel' could not be greater. Beren could overturn mockery, but it vitiates Túrin's every achievement. The elven lovers escaped all prisons, but Úrin only leaves Angband at Melko's will, after years of extraordinary psychological torture. Tinúviel could hide in her enchanted cloak and Beren could shift his shape; but Túrin can only change his name. You can almost hear the laughter of Glorund when, on the eve of his unwitting incest, Túrin celebrates his foresight in taking the pseudonym *Turambar*, 'Conqueror of Fate': 'for lo! I have overcome the doom of evil that was woven about my feet.' There is a hint that, if he had told Níniel his real name, her memory would have returned, thwarting calamity.

But a darkness falls between families, friends, and lovers (surely reflecting something of Tolkien's own wartime experience). Tolkien underlines the point with a mythographer's flourish, in a scene in which Níniel and Mavwin meet Glorund's eye: 'a swoon came upon their minds, and them seemed that they groped in endless tunnels of darkness, and there they found not one another ever again, and calling only vain echoes answered and there was no glimmer of light.'

The narrative divides to follow first Túrin then, in a long flashback, his mother and sister, as the siblings move towards their collision. Thus the reader exchanges ignorance for infinitely more uncomfortable knowledge. We can taste the impotent misery of Úrin, whose torture is to watch from a place of vision in Angband as the curse slowly destroys his family. In an acutely distressing scene prior to the reunion of the fatal siblings, Túrin is similarly immobilized by Glorund while orcs take away the elven woman who might have been his own Tinúviel:

> In that sad band stood Failivrin in horror, and she stretched out her arms towards Túrin, but Túrin was held by the spell of the drake, for that beast had a foul magic in his glance, as have many others of his kind, and he turned the sinews of Túrin as it were to stone, for his eye held Túrin's eye so that his will died, and he could not stir of his own purpose, yet might he hear and see ... Even now did the Orcs begin to drive away that host of

> thralls, and his heart broke at the sight, yet he moved not; and the pale face of Failivrin faded afar, and her voice was borne to him crying: 'O Túrin Mormakil, where is thy heart; O my beloved, wherefore dost thou forsake me?'

Knowledge does not bring power. Instead, when the isolating darkness in this tale lifts, the revelation can lacerate. For Turambar and Níniel at the end, the truth is unendurable.

'The Tale of Turambar' would not be a success if the hero were simply a puppet in Melko's maleficent hands. The god's curse appears to work not only through external circumstance, the 'bad luck' that haunts the family, but also through Túrin's stubborn misjudgements and occasionally murderous impulses. Whereas Beren survives his emotional and physical injuries with innate resilience, Túrin endures his traumas through sheer obduracy, never losing their imprint. He first becomes a warrior to 'ease his sorrow and the rage of his heart, that remembered always how Úrin and his folk had gone down in battle against Melko'; and later he invokes the memory of the Battle of Unnumbered Tears to persuade the Rodothlim to cast aside their secrecy, courting disaster. The curse is often indistinguishable, then, from what might be called psychological damage.

Tolkien's declared aim was to create myths and fairy-tales, but there are haunting notes here from a more contemporary repertoire. One is naturalism. The desolation of Túrin's world is often brought home through modest but eloquent tableaux: his cries as a seven-year-old taken from his mother; the swallows mustering under her roof when he returns years later to find her gone; his wine-soaked hand after murder at the feast. The other is ambiguity. Túrin's victory over Glorund might be read as a final victory over his fate, yet it brings the curse to its full fruition by withdrawing the veil from Níniel's memory. His dogged struggle through serial tragedy is courageous, but it causes terrible suffering. Likewise Úrin's defiant words to Melko, 'At least none shall pity him for this, that he had a craven for father.'

'The Tale of Turambar' is not so much fairy-story as human-story, told by a mortal occupant of the Cottage of Lost Play and immersed in what Tolkien later termed dyscatastrophe. Its only major flaw is the upturn at the very end, where the spirits of Túrin and Níniel pass through purgatorial flame and join the ranks of the Valar. Too similar to the climax of 'The Tale of Tinúviel', and contrary to the dark spirit of 'Turambar', it seems a clumsy way of depicting the consolatory Joy that Tolkien elsewhere reserved for those who have passed, not merely beyond life, but beyond the created world altogether.

Tolkien, still developing the story of Túrin many years later, wrote in 1951 that it 'might be said (by people who like that sort of thing, though it is not very useful) to be derived from elements in Sigurd the Volsung, Oedipus, and the Finnish Kullervo'. Yet this is a judgement about criticism, not a denial of influence; and by the time he made the comment he had indeed moved far from the concept of unearthing lost tales. Through the narrator of 'The Tale of Turambar' he acknowledges his debt, while declaring the fictional premise of the whole 'Book of Lost Tales':

> In these days many such stories do Men tell still, and more have they told in the past especially in those kingdoms of the North that once I knew. Maybe the deeds of other of their warriors have become mingled therein, and many matters beside that are not in the most ancient tale – but now I will tell to you the true and lamentable tale . . .

To Tolkien the philologist, deriving a single story from these overlapping but disparate narratives must have seemed no more strange than reconstructing an unrecorded Indo-European root from related words in various languages. Yet this is neither plagiarism nor, in fact, reconstruction at all, but a highly individual imaginative enterprise. Figures such as Beleg, the fugitive slave Flinding, and bright-eyed Failivrin enter 'The Tale of Turambar' unforeshadowed by Tolkien's sources; the background and web of motives is all his own; and in stitching disparate elements together with many more of his own invention he brings the plot to a pitch of suspense and horror he rarely bettered. Most importantly, perhaps, Tolkien amplified the aspects of these myths and traditions that spoke most eloquently to his own era, replete with tragedy and irony.

Undoubtedly Tolkien meant the sequel to Túrin's story, 'The Tale of the Nauglafring', to be the 'lost tale' behind the garbled references in Norse myth to the mysterious Brísingamen, a necklace forged by dwarves, worn by the love-goddess Freyja, and stolen by the trickster Loki. Possibly it was this scheme that originally gave rise to the Silmarils, their fabulous radiance (relating *Brísingamen* to Old Norse *brísingr*, 'fire'), their theft by Melko, and their association with half-divine Tinúviel. However that may be, the curse of Glorund's hoard now brings Artanor to ruin as Tinwelint orders the gold to be made into a necklace for the Silmaril that Beren cut from Melko's crown.

The elf-king's dealings and double-dealings with the dwarven smiths form one of the least satisfying elements in the Lost Tales. Self-interested greed could have sharpened Tinwelint's wits, but instead it appears to stupefy him. The only real artistic flaw, however, is that the Dwarves, misshapen in body and soul, come close to caricature. The narrative briefly regains potency as Tinwelint appears resplendent in the Necklace of the Dwarves:

> Behold now Tinwelint the king rode forth a-hunting, and more glorious was his array than ever aforetime, and the helm of gold was above his flowing locks, and with gold were the trappings of his steed adorned; and the sunlight amid the trees fell upon his face, and it seemed to those that beheld it like to the glorious face of the sun at morning . . .

The procession of paratactic clauses, fusing annalistic distance with breathless excitement, became a hallmark of Tolkien's writing. So did what follows: a daring shift from the main event to another scene, cranking up the tension and foreboding before the denouement. We learn of Tinwelint's fate only when his stricken queen is presented with his head still 'crowned and helmed in gold'. His glorious ride to the hunt turns out to have been the swansong of Faërie in the Great Lands.

The muted tone of the rest of the tale suggests the ebb of enchantment. Artanor falls not with a bang, but a whimper. Not even Beren and Tinúviel are allowed to escape the decline as they reappear to reclaim the Silmaril. In their second span of life the resurrected lovers are now mortal, and the Necklace hastens Tinúviel's death; Beren ends in lonely wandering. Deprived even of the honour of a tragic ending, their exit reflects what Tom Shippey has called (with reference to the fate of Frodo in *The Lord of the Rings*) an 'unrecognized touch of hardness' in Tolkien.

But now, probably in 1919 or 1920, he was contemplating a huge narrative enterprise, certainly mournful but nevertheless shot through with splendour and enchantment. He had arrived at the longest-planned story of all, to which the 'Nauglafring' was merely the prologue. If the scheme had been realized, Christopher Tolkien calculates, 'the whole *Tale of Eärendel* would have been somewhere near half the length of all the tales that were in fact written'. Beyond the arrival of Tinúviel's granddaughter Elwing at the shoreland refuge of Tuor and the exiles of Gondolin, virtually nothing of the remainder of 'The Book of Lost Tales' passed beyond notes and outlines. The tale would have recounted Eärendel's many hazardous sailings west and his final voyage into the starry skies, transfigured by suffering: a considerably more solemn figure than the blithe fugitive whom Tolkien had envisioned in his poem of September 1914. Meanwhile, the Elves of Kôr would march out into the Great Lands to cast Melko down from the pinnacle of his triumph.

After Eärendel's tale, two further sections were planned before the book would be finished. For his account of how the rebel archangel is finally stripped of his powers, Tolkien would have waded into 'that very primitive undergrowth' of folklore he had praised in the *Kalevala*. Melko was to escape his bonds and stir strife among the Elves, mostly now gathered in the Lonely Isle; but he was to be chased up a gigantic pinetree at Tavrobel (Great Haywood) into the sky, becoming a creature of envy 'gnawing his fingers and gazing in anger on the world'. With his marring of the Sun's primal magic and the inexorable rise of the human race, the Lost Tales told to Eriol were to reach an end, as the chronological narrative caught up with the Germanic wanderer's own day.

In a coda involving Eriol (or his son Heorrenda, according to some projections) the faëry island was to be hauled to its latter-day location off the Great Lands of Europe, but then broken asunder into Ireland and Britain in another tussle of the sea gods. The island Elves would march to the aid of their diminishing mainland kin in a war against Melko's servants: the great Faring Forth. Despite hopes of a new golden age, with the rekindling of the 'Magic Sun' or even the Two Trees, it seems that human treachery was to bring about the outright defeat of the Elves, and Men were to begin the invasion of Britain.

The final crisis may be glimpsed in a powerful 'Epilogue' that Tolkien dashed down on paper, purporting to be the words of Eriol before he sealed his Book of Lost Tales at Tavrobel:

> And now is the end of the fair times come very nigh, and behold, all the beauty that yet was on earth – fragments of the unimagined loveliness of Valinor whence came the folk of the Elves long long ago – now goeth it all up in smoke.

Eriol, writing with the immediacy of a diarist, has fled in the face of a terrible battle between Men on the High Heath nearby – surely Cannock Chase with the Sher Brook (Old English *scír*, 'bright') running down towards Great Haywood:

> Behold, I stole by the evening from the ruined heath, and my way fled winding down the valley of the Brook of Glass, but the setting of the Sun was blackened with the reek of fires, and the waters of the stream were fouled with the war of men and grime of strife . . .
>
> And now sorrow . . . has come upon the Elves, empty is Tavrobel and all are fled, [?fearing] the enemy that sitteth on the ruined heath, who is not a league away; whose hands are red

> with the blood of Elves and stained with the lives of his own kin, who has made himself an ally to Melko . . .

In words that echo the last ride of Tinwelint, Eriol recalls Gilfanon, oldest of the Eldar of the Lonely Isle, in a cavalcade of light and song; and the people of Tavrobel dancing 'as clad in dreams' about the grey bridge and the rivers' meeting. But now, Eriol records, the island-Elves are fading too, or Men growing yet more blind. His last words are a prophecy of disenchantment, when most will scoff at the idea of fairies, 'lies told to the children'. Some will at least regard them fondly as metaphors of nature, 'a wraith of vanishing loveliness in the trees'. Only a few will believe, and be able to see the Elves thronging their ancient towns in Autumn, their season, 'fallen as they are upon the Autumn of their days'.

> But behold, Tavrobel shall not know its name, and all the land be changed, and even these written words of mine belike will all be lost, and so I lay down the pen, and so of the fairies cease to tell.

It may be no more than coincidence that *A Spring Harvest*, the posthumous volume of Smith's poems arranged by Tolkien and Christopher Wiseman, closes with this sestet:

> So we lay down the pen,
> So we forbear the building of the rime,
> And bid our hearts be steel for times and a time
> Till ends the strife, and then,
> When the New Age is verily begun,
> God grant that we may do the things undone.

But it seems equally likely that here, at the projected close of his Lost Tales, Tolkien meant to pay a quiet tribute to G. B. Smith, who had looked forward so eagerly to reading them.

* * *

The fading of the Elves, a phenomenon surely intended to 'explain' the Shakespearean and Victorian view of fairies, leaves the world and its fate in human hands. On the face of it, this seems a grim conclusion: man, in Eriol's closing words, is 'blind, and a fool, and destruction alone is his knowledge'. Tolkien did not get very far with his Lost Tale of how Ilúvatar's secondborn children arrived in the era of the Sun; but what little he wrote shows that Melko corrupted them early on. Losing their first home through his machinations, unlike the Valar and the Eldar they found no new Eden. 'The Tale of Turambar', meanwhile, may be taken as a distillation of Men's unhappy lot; and even after Melko is banished to the sky and deprived of his earthly powers, he is able to plant evil in the human heart.

There seems every reason to envy the Elves, graced with superhuman skill, beauty, and longevity, living on until 'the Great End' with much of the vigour of youth and, should they die from violence or grief, even being reborn as elf-children. Tolkien's Eldar could not be less like the deathless Struldbruggs of Jonathan Swift's *Gulliver's Travels*, whose life is an endless descent into fathomless depths of physical and mental decrepitude.

Yet without the agency of human beings, Ilúvatar's universal drama would not reach completion. Whereas the cosmogonic Music prescribed the fate of the Elves, and even the Ainur, humans were granted 'a free virtue' to act beyond it, so that 'everything should in shape and deed be completed, and the world fulfilled unto the last and smallest'. Without this 'free virtue', it seems, all would be complete in conception (if not execution) as soon as the Music was over; there would be nothing for us to do but follow our pre-ordained steps. (Happily, Tolkien seems not to have tried to illustrate the implication that the Elves, the Valar, and Melko lack free will, which would surely have blighted his narratives.)

Taken together with the Lost Tales, the idea of this 'free virtue' sheds light on the riddle of how Melko's discords may make 'Life more worth the living'. A parallel may be drawn with a phenomenon that Tolkien found deeply moving: the 'ennoblement of the ignoble' through hardship and fear. 'On a journey of a length sufficient to provide the untoward in any degree from discomfort to fear', he once wrote, in a transparent reference to the Great War, 'the change in companions well-known in "ordinary life" (and in oneself) is often startling.' The potential for such change or ennoblement in the face of danger lies at the heart of all his portrayals of character. It is this equation, by which individuals become far more than the sum of their parts, that takes them beyond the provisions of the Music towards a destination altogether unforeseen. So it is that in Tolkien's legendarium the weak rise up to shake the world, embodying what he called 'the secret life in creation, and the part unknowable to all wisdom but One, that resides in the intrusions of the Children of God into the Drama'.

Humans in his pre-Christian mythology cannot commune consciously with their Creator through sacraments and prayer, but glimpse him uncomprehendingly through the sublimities of nature. Tuor and Eriol are captivated by the ambivalent, alien sea because 'there liveth still in water a deeper echo of the Music of the Ainur than in any substance else that is in the world, and at this latest day many of the Sons of Men will hearken unsatedly to the voice of the Sea and long for they know not what'. What they long for, unconsciously, is eternal life in heaven. It is a yearning for home: the souls of Men will outlive the world in which their bodies die.

One of Tolkien's most radical imaginative leaps was to put this tenet of his faith in perspective by placing his human figures in a picture dominated by – indeed, painted by – a sibling race with a destiny apart. To Swift, the human desire for immortality was a folly to be satirized without mercy through the Struldbruggs. Tolkien took a more sympathetic view: to him, immortality was indeed in our nature, and the human folly lay only in mistakenly coveting mere corporeal permanence. From the earliest writings onwards, he left the question of what will happen to the Elves after the End a profound enigma. Their own opinion seems to be that they will expire with the world, and they have little hope of bliss in Ilúvatar's heaven. Death, Tolkien later wrote, was the 'Gift of Ilúvatar' to Men, releasing them into an eternal life that is more than mere longevity. The resurrection of Beren and Tinúviel, therefore, may be sadly brief compared to the earthly span they might have enjoyed as Elves, but implicitly their second death will give them what no other Elves can have: a future 'beyond the walls of the world'. In Tolkien's view, that is the ultimate release.

The spring, summer, and ages-long autumn of the Elves may be regarded as a consummation of the intrinsic potential in creation, but a consummation as limited and flawed as the finite world itself. Except for what they have learned of elvish art and grace, Men remain the benighted travellers we first encountered in 'A Song of Aryador' of 1915. Meanwhile, the imperfect gods under God are bound to founder in their care of the world. So one of the narrators of the Lost Tales declares that the Valar ought to have gone to war against Melko straight after the destruction of the Two Trees, adding suggestively: 'and who knows if the salvation of the world and the freeing of Men and Elves shall ever come from them again? Some there are who whisper that it is not so, and hope dwelleth only in a far land of Men, but how so that may be I do not know.' The implication must surely be that the failure of God's angelic representatives would ultimately pave the way for God's direct intervention as Christ.

The Lost Tales emerged at a steady pace. Etymological work among the *Oxford English Dictionary* slips in the Old Ashmolean took up little more than half the day, and although Tolkien also began taking private pupils in Old English he did not make enough money from this to give up the dictionary work until the spring of 1920. The family moved out of St John Street in late summer of 1919, and Tolkien remained sufficiently unwell to take a small army pension; but, compared to the years before and after, this was a settled interlude of uninterrupted creativity.

However, Tolkien never wrote the Lost Tales describing the birth of Men, the Battle of Unnumbered Tears, the voyage of

Eärendel, the expulsion of Melko, the Faring Forth, or the Battle of the High Heath. The full expression of these events had to wait until he had found a different form for the mythology, and in some points was never achieved. By the early 1920s, problems had come into focus that needed solutions, and his concepts had shifted – not least at the linguistic foundations of his mythology. He continued to refine his invented languages, making time-consuming changes to their internal histories and their phonological and morphological foundations (so, for example, the tongue of the Gnomes now commonly formed plurals by vowel mutation rather than by adding a suffix, as English does in rare instances such as *foot/feet**). He revised, rewrote, and rearranged the Lost Tales he had already written. Eriol became Ælfwine, a mariner from Anglo-Saxon England as late as the eleventh century. Tolkien now conceived Elvish Tol Eressëa as an entirely distinct island to the west. He also set to work retelling the story of Turambar as a long narrative poem.

There were further practical barriers to completing 'The Book of Lost Tales'. In 1920 Tolkien had finally launched the academic career that the war had delayed, taking a position at Leeds University, where he energetically revivified the English language syllabus. At the same time he compiled, with long and meticulous labour, *A Middle English Vocabulary* to accompany an anthology edited by Kenneth Sisam, his former tutor at Oxford. When that was published in 1922 he was working on a new edition of the alliterative Middle English poem *Sir Gawain and the Green Knight* with a Leeds colleague, E. V. Gordon. In 1924 Tolkien was made a professor at Leeds, but the following year he won the Rawlinson Bosworth Professorship of Anglo-Saxon at Oxford. By then he was also the father of three young children.

Tolkien's bigger difficulty, however, was a niggling perfectionism. He was well aware of it and, much later, he wrote a story,

* The vowel change actually (as in English) shows the impact of a suffix that has been lost, so Gnomish *orn*, 'tree', from a primitive *ornĕ*, pluralizes as *yrn*, showing the influence of the old plural suffix *–i* in primitive *ornei*.

'Leaf by Niggle', in which the problem is borne by a painter doomed never to complete his enormous picture of a tree. In years to come the legendarium grew into a vast complex of interwoven histories, sagas, and genealogies, of phonologies, grammars, and vocabularies, and of philological and philosophical disquisitions. Left to his own devices it seems quite likely that Tolkien would never have finished a single book in his life. What he needed were publishers' deadlines and a keen audience.

Back in November 1917, his old schoolmaster R. W. Reynolds had expressed himself 'much interested in the book of tales you are at work on', urging Tolkien to send it to him as soon as it was 'in a state to travel'. But in 1922 Reynolds and his novelist wife, Dorothea Deakin, moved for health reasons to Capri in the Bay of Naples, and by the time he got back in touch, following her death in 1925, Tolkien had long left the tales incomplete. Instead he sent several poems out to Capri, including two works in progress: his alliterative lay about Túrin and a rhymed *geste* about Beren and Lúthien Tinúviel (as she was now called). Reynolds had little or nothing good to say about the first, and thought the second promising but prolix. He was being true to form. 'Kortirion among the Trees' – the poem G. B. Smith had carried around the trenches of Thiepval Wood 'like a treasure' – had seemed to Reynolds merely 'charming', but not gripping. Before the 1914 Council of London, Tolkien had told Wiseman he thought Reynolds was to blame for Smith's excess of aestheticism over moral character. Wiseman had commented since then that Smith's poetry was beyond Reynolds' grasp. If that was so, he could scarcely have engaged with Tolkien's.

Tolkien did no further work on the Túrin poem, though he pursued the *geste* for several more years. Yet the intervention of Reynolds had a radical effect on Tolkien's central mythological project. To furnish his old teacher with the background information necessary for an understanding of the two narrative lays, Tolkien summed up 'The Book of Lost Tales' in a 'sketch' of the mythology. So many of his ideas, linguistic inventions, and stylistic preferences had changed that the Lost Tales as originally written now seemed to him inadequate. To take a key example, the Silmarils, their maker Fëanor, and his seven oath-driven sons had assumed a central role in terms of narrative and theme that was barely portended in the Lost Tales. The précis turned into a replacement. By and large, the tales he had laboriously written out in exercise books from late 1916 onwards were filed away for ever. When he next worked on the mythology as a whole – or the 'Silmarillion', as he came to call it – he consulted not the Lost Tales, but the sketch.

The effect of this decision was to remove at a stroke the ebullience, earthiness, and humour of the original mythology. It is a great shame that Tolkien compressed these stories, when given more time and less perfectionism he might have expanded each one to produce something commensurate with a William Morris romance; he was certainly Morris's superior in imaginative and descriptive powers. But in the versions that followed, culminating in *The Silmarillion*, posthumously published in 1977, the physical and psychological detail of the narrative poems was largely excluded as well. The Valar became increasingly civic and humane, but perhaps less interesting. The frame-story, with its elm-grown city, its curious elven cottage, and its dreaming mariner, all but vanished. The long English prehistory between the voyage of Eärendel and the Faring Forth was abandoned. The 'Silmarillion' in all its versions retreats from fairy-story, and the 'contact with the earth' that Tolkien had thought so important fades away, while the epic heroes tend to merge into the 'vast backcloths'.

Both Wiseman and Reynolds had warned Tolkien of such problems during the war. Reynolds had said 'Kortirion among the Trees' was 'lacking in experience of life'. Somehow ignoring the brute fact of the Somme, Wiseman felt in 1917 that Tolkien had still not been through enough to write at his best, and that therefore he should indeed start with epic, 'the only form of serious verse available for a poet who has not yet experienced life', as he put it. His reasoning was false: 'In an epic you make no pretence of dealing with life; so experience of it is unnecessary,' he said. But his prophecy was spot on: 'You can't go on writing epics all your life; but until you can do something else, you simply must write epics.' What kept Tolkien ploughing his lonely furrow, however, was not inexperience but reverence for epic as a literary mode. He did not give other forms much serious thought. As Wayne G. Hammond has observed, it was writing children's stories that 'gave him opportunities (or excuses) to experiment with other modes of story-telling than the formal prose or poetry he used in writing his mythology'.

After the death of G. B. Smith, Tolkien had no 'wild and whole-hearted admirer'. At times Wiseman found Tolkien's work astonishing and unprecedented, and they shared some interests – Arthurian legend, for example. But the two were often at odds. Relishing a good argument, they frequently offended each other. Such problems, quickly resolved at school, festered between letters exchanged at long intervals. The forthright Wiseman did not conceal his basic lack of sympathy with the Lost Tales, though there is no evidence that he ever read them. In 1917, he had told Tolkien that he could not compete with Alexander Pope or Matthew Arnold and that the project must be a mere prelude to more worthwhile things. It might produce an epic, or a great poem, or a mythology, Wiseman had conceded; but, he urged, 'I want you to get this stage over and go on to something else.'

Wiseman and Tolkien saw a little of one another, on and off, but when one became a headmaster and the other an Oxford professor they started to feel they had little in common. The deaths of Smith and Gilson perhaps also cast a shadow over their thoughts of each other. There was no rift; John Ronald spoke fondly of Christopher ever afterwards, and named his third son after him. Yet they drifted apart, and Tolkien lost a stern but useful critic. The direct influence of the TCBS ended forever.

C. S. Lewis stepped into the breach they had left. The two met in 1926 and Lewis, an English don and medievalist from Magdalen College, Oxford, joined the Coalbiters, a group founded by Tolkien to read the Icelandic myths and sagas. Later

Tolkien became a regular in the Inklings, the literary clique that revolved around Lewis from the 1930s. By that time they had recognized in each other a common love of 'Northernness', and Lewis had become a closer friend to Tolkien than anyone since the heyday of the TCBS. Indeed, Lewis rolled into one forceful personality their several roles: the generous social gifts of Rob Gilson, the critical insight of Christopher Wiseman, and, most importantly, the passionate imaginative sympathies of G. B. Smith. Just like Tolkien, Lewis had written reams of unpublished material, and still wanted to be a great poet, but regarded the majority of contemporary writers with impatience. 'Only from him did I ever get the idea that my "stuff" could be more than a private hobby,' Tolkien wrote. Clearly, he had left far behind the heady days when his three old schoolfriends had urged him to publish before he was sent in to battle.

By the time Lewis read 'The Lay of Leithian', the long Tinúviel poem, Tolkien had another enthusiastic audience: his family. Edith's early involvement in his writing (she made fair copies of 'The Cottage of Lost Play' in February 1917 and 'The Fall of Gondolin' around 1919) had not lasted. But Tolkien had started writing stories for their children as early as 1920, when he first sent John a letter purporting to be from Father Christmas. That year Edith had a second son, Michael, and in 1924 a third, Christopher. In 1929 a daughter, Priscilla, was born. It was for their entertainment that he wrote 'The Hobbit', showing it to an enthusiastic Lewis in 1933.

'The Hobbit' became absorbed into the margins of Tolkien's mythology, a process that began, characteristically, with the problem of naming a half-elf whom Bilbo was to meet early in his adventure. He plucked the name *Elrond* from 'The Silmarillion', where it belonged to none other than the son of Eärendel the star-mariner. Quickly the two Elronds became one, and even Gondolin appeared as part of a barely glimpsed but atmospheric ancient history.

News of this unique and stirring children's story reached the publishers George Allen & Unwin in 1936, and *The Hobbit* appeared the following September to enthusiastic reviews. With prospects bright, Allen & Unwin quickly asked for a sequel, and in December 1937 Tolkien began writing the first chapter of 'a new story about Hobbits'. So began the long gestation of Tolkien's masterpiece, a tale which (as he later wrote), 'grew in the telling, until it became a history of the Great War of the Ring and included many glimpses of the yet more ancient history that preceded it'.

The two remaining representatives of 1914's inspirational Council of London met up again at last, late in life, when both were living in retirement on the South Coast: Tolkien, the author of *The Hobbit* and *The Lord of the Rings*, hiding from fame in Bournemouth, and Wiseman, retired headmaster and energetic chairman of the village association in nearby Milford-on-Sea.

In November 1971 Edith died, leaving her husband bereft. On her tombstone in north Oxford he had the name *Lúthien* inscribed, 'which says for me more than a multitude of words: she was (and knew she was) my Lúthien,' he wrote. 'But the story has gone crooked, and I am left, and *I* cannot plead before the inexorable Mandos.'

Three months after her death, Tolkien moved back to Oxford to live in rooms provided by Merton College, still hoping somehow to finish the mythological work he had begun with such high ambition in the months after the Battle of the Somme. In the meantime, though, he had paid a visit to Wiseman – also now a recent widower, following the death of Christine, the woman who in 1946 had finally cured his 'incurable bachelorhood'. But Wiseman had just remarried, and his second wife Patricia and her daughter Susan walked in the garden with Tolkien. He seemed, they thought, very much a hobbit in his green waistcoat, delighted by the flowers and fascinated by the insects, about which he spoke knowledgeably. But as for the two surviving members of the Immortal Four: they did not speak to each other very much, or once mention their recent bereavements, and Wiseman at least (though he played his own part in this conspiracy of silence) was privately hurt.

Yet the bond, if strained, was certainly not broken. When Tolkien next wrote, from Oxford in May 1973, he thanked Wiseman for drawing him from his 'lair' and signed himself, 'Your most devoted friend', adding after his own initials the letters 'TCBS'. Near the end of August, Tolkien was back in Bournemouth, staying with friends, and made a reservation to stay at his retirement haunt, the Hotel Miramar, for a few days from 4 September. He explained in a note to his daughter Priscilla, 'I wish v. much to visit various people here,' he said, 'also Chris Wiseman at Milford . . .' But two days after the letter, he was taken to hospital suffering from an acute bleeding gastric ulcer. J. R. R. Tolkien died at the age of eighty-one, on 2 September 1973. He was buried next to Edith, with the name *Beren* beneath his own.

Postscript

Postscript. 'One who dreams alone'

A pale, drawn man sits in a convalescent bed of a wartime hospital. He takes up a school exercise book and writes on its cover, with a calligraphic flourish: 'Tuor and the Exiles of Gondolin'. Then he pauses, lets out a long sigh between the teeth clenched around his pipe, and mutters, 'No, that won't do anymore.' He crosses out the title and writes (without the flourish): 'A Subaltern on the Somme'.

That is not what happened, of course. Tolkien produced a mythology, not a trench memoir. Middle-earth contradicts the prevalent view of literary history, that the Great War finished off the epic and heroic traditions in any serious form. This postscript will argue that despite its unorthodoxy – and quite contrary to its undeserved reputation as escapism – Tolkien's writing reflects the impact of the war; furthermore, that his maverick voice expresses aspects of the war experience neglected by his contemporaries. This is not to say that his mythology was a response to the poetry and prose of his contemporaries, but that they represent widely divergent responses to the same traumatic epoch.

Literature hit a crisis point in 1916, in the assessment of critic Samuel Hynes: 'a "dead spot" at the centre of the war' when 'creative energies seemed to sink to a low point' among British writers. G. B. Smith and his poetry were both languishing on the Somme; 'sheer vacancy is destroying me', he said. A very different writer, Ford Madox Ford, was in a similar rut at Ypres, asking himself 'why I can write nothing – why I cannot even think anything that to myself seems worth thinking'.

Tolkien's poetry does seem to have come close to drying up in the wake of the Somme, with just one piece ('Companions of the

Rose') written in the first eight months of 1917. But he had hardly been idle, as Wiseman pointed out. Whatever malaise was afflicting other writers, his creative energies were at a peak when he began 'The Book of Lost Tales' in the winter of 1916–17.

Out of the 'dead spot', two new and enormously influential literary movements emerged: firstly, a style of war writing that has attained 'classic' status; secondly, modernism. But the impact of these on Tolkien was negligible.

In the modernist experimentation that took off in the post-war years – largely a reflection of the shock, moral chaos, and bewildering scale of the war – he played no part. The era of *The Waste Land* and *Ulysses* was in his view 'an age when almost all auctorial manhandling of English is permitted (especially if disruptive) in the name of art or "personal expression"'.

Nor did he participate in the kind of literature now seen as the epitome of the trenches. Out of the diversity of writing produced by soldiers, what is remembered is an amalgam of bitter protest and gritty close-ups, uncompromisingly direct in its depiction of trench life and death. Spearheading this style, Robert Graves, his friend Siegfried Sassoon, and Sassoon's brilliant protégé Wilfred Owen take pride of place in anthologies of 'Great War writing'. A handful of Owen's poems have become the measure of all other portrayals of the First World War – even of war in general.

In pursuit of directness, Graves and his followers threw away the rulebook used by newspapers, recruitment literature, and mainstream poetry, which filtered the war through a style inherited from previous conflicts. Owen's most famous poem, 'Anthem for Doomed Youth', highlights the mismatch between the sacramental imagery of the inherited language and the reality of his war:

> What passing-bells for these who die as cattle?
> Only the monstrous anger of the guns.

The old style traced its way back to Arthurian romance by way of Shakespeare, the Romantics, and High Victorian medievalism.

It had action, heroism, and epic sweep; it purported to show the big picture and employed the 'high diction' of valour. Paul Fussell, in his influential book *The Great War and Modern Memory*, provides a lexicon of this language, in which 'A horse is a *steed*, or *charger*; the enemy is *the foe*, or *the host*; danger is *peril*', and so forth. He regards high diction as a form of censorship. Historian Jay Winter rages at the armchair militarists of 1914–18: 'Those too old to fight had created an imaginary war, filled with medieval knights, noble warriors, and sacred moments of sacrifice. Such writing . . . was worse than banal; it was obscene.'

By the yardstick of Owen's poetry, the Somme would seem to have had no effect on Tolkien's writing at all. Problematically, he wrote about an imaginary war that looks rather like the kind of thing Winter derides and is packed with high diction.

It has earned him the opprobrium of reviewers who cannot see his prose style without suspecting him of jingoism: a general taint has attached itself to this sort of language thanks to the First World War. Tolkien's style has made some of his admirers uncomfortable too. In an essay that raises some interesting points about how the Somme may have influenced Middle-earth, Hugh Brogan asks bluntly 'how it was that Tolkien, a man whose life was language, could have gone through the Great War, with all its rants and lies, and still come out committed to a "feudal" literary style'. Brogan concludes that in refusing to conform to the new rules established by Robert Graves and the arch-modernist Ezra Pound, Tolkien was engaged in 'an act of deliberate defiance of modern history'.

There are good reasons for Tolkien's apparent stubbornness. Samuel Hynes has noted that the war ushered in a censorious campaign against German intellectual and artistic influences. By chance, this affected every area of secular culture and learning that Tolkien espoused. Even five years after the armistice, he complained that '"philology" itself, conceived as a purely German invention, is in some quarters treated as though it were one of the things that the late war was fought to end . . . a thing whose absence does credit to an Englishman'. Alongside this assault on such rationalist traditions came an attack on Romanticism, in which Germany had also been Britain's teacher, and which played a major part in Tolkien's creative thought.

In fact, he had swum against the tide even before the war, when his fascination with the ancient North ran counter to the classicism of King Edward's School. He would not or could not now turn his back on philology, matters Germanic, or Romanticism. During the Great War, with an audience of six at most – the TCBS, Edith, Wade-Gery of the Salford Pals, and R. W. Reynolds of King Edward's School – he was under little pressure to change; but in any case, as C. S. Lewis once said, 'No one ever influenced Tolkien. You might as well try to influence a bandersnatch.'

Despite his taste for romance and high diction, however, Tolkien did not find the war adventurous, dashing, or sacred. He summed up trench life as 'animal horror'. Even in 1910, when he spoofed Lord Macaulay's *Lays of Ancient Rome* in 'The Battle of the Eastern Field', he knew the old language of war could be used for false heroics. Having been through the training camps and the trenches, he was acutely aware of its shortcomings, declaring, 'The utter stupid waste of war, not only material but moral and spiritual, is so staggering to those who have to endure it. And always was (despite the poets), and always will be (despite the propagandists) . . .'

But even if Tolkien had been more like Pound or Graves in outlook, he would have been unable to join their literary movements when he was finding his voice as a writer. Modernism, such as it had been before the war, had been silenced as decadent, while scarcely a scrap of what we now see as classic Great War poetry had been published by the end of 1916. As for the other paths then available to a young writer, none appealed to Tolkien's imagination as much as the romances and epic adventures of writers such as William Morris and Rider Haggard – both labelled by Fussell as 'tutors' in high diction to the war propagandists.

Yet Tolkien's greater passion was for the genuinely medieval, from *Beowulf* to *Sir Gawain and the Green Knight*. As he said after the publication of *The Lord of the Rings* (in a reply, never sent, to a friendly but critical letter from Brogan), 'not being especially well read in modern English, and far more familiar with works in the ancient and "middle" idioms, my own ear is to some extent affected; so that though I could easily recollect how a modern would put this and that, what comes easiest to mind or pen is not quite that'. Tolkien remained committed to an archaic air because it was the one he breathed.

The abuse of high diction in battlefield journalism or recruitment pamphlets does not devalue the medievalism that Tolkien pursued – any more than the kicking of footballs as a morale-booster during the Somme assault renders the game itself obscene or obsolete. He rebelled against what he called 'the extraordinary 20th C. delusion that its usages *per se* and simply as "contemporary" – irrespective of whether they are terser, more vivid (or even nobler!) – have some peculiar validity, above those of all other times, so that not to use them (even when quite unsuitable in tone) is a solecism, a gaffe, a thing at which one's friends shudder or feel hot in the collar'. In 'The Book of Lost Tales' and elsewhere, he adopted a style that suited his mythological and legendary content. It was a choice as conscious and serious as the opposite but complementary decision made by Graves, Sassoon, and Owen.

Its justification lies in the history of Tolkien's register – in its cultural, moral, and poetic weight. Pointing out that the *Beowulf* poet's style had been archaic by the standards of his Anglo-Saxon audience, he said:

> This sort of thing – the building up of a poetic language out of words and forms archaic and dialectal or used in special senses – may be regretted or disliked. There is nonetheless a case for it: the development of a form of language familiar in meaning and yet freed from trivial associations, and filled with the memory of good and evil, is an achievement, and its possessors are richer than those who have no such tradition.

Tolkien's stylistic values reverse Ezra Pound's famous modernist exhortation to 'Make it new!' To Tolkien, language accumulated qualities that could not be replaced and ought not to be lightly discarded. In a century when revolutionaries dismissed the whole concept of good and evil as a delusion of the weak or deviant, this became a substantial issue, and already during the Great War it was an urgent one. For Tolkien's mythology, 'the memory of good and evil' is the keynote.

Just when the old ways of telling were being misused by the military propagandists and rejected by the trench writers, Tolkien envisioned 'The Book of Lost Tales', a sequence of stories salvaged from the wreck of history. That he saw the value in traditions that most others rejected is one of his gifts to posterity: truth should never be the property of one literary mode, any more than it should be the monopoly of one authoritarian voice.

Tolkien was not immune to epochal change, however. He did not simply preserve the traditions the war threatened, but reinvigorated them for his own era. His most distinctive success was with fairy-story. Robert Graves pictured the simultaneous arrival of maturity and war as the obliteration of Faërie:

> Wisdom made a breach and battered
> Babylon to bits: she scattered
> To the hedges and ditches
> All our nursery gnomes and witches.
> Lob and Puck, poor frantic elves,
> Drag their treasures from the shelves.

This was more than metaphor. Faërie came close to vanishing altogether during the First World War, thanks to this associative confusion of the pre-war era, childhood, and fairy-tales. Yet Tolkien did not regard fairies as childish, and he was not writing nursery-tales, but an epic history of the world through faëry eyes. In her galloping survey of fairy traditions, *Troublesome Things*, Diane Purkiss says that 'The Western Front made the fairy aesthetic seem both desperately necessary and hopelessly anachronistic.' Tolkien's account of the tragic decline of the

Elves acknowledges that their time is over but urges the desperate necessity of holding on to the values they represented. Far from being a sign that the war had no impact on Tolkien, his commitment to Faërie was a consequence of it. 'A real taste for fairy-stories was wakened by philology on the threshold of manhood,' he wrote later, 'and quickened to full life by war.'

Tolkien's use of Faërie and its diction has brought accusations of escapism. Indeed, Hugh Brogan argues that the 'Lost Tales' and what followed them were 'therapy for a mind wounded in war, and before that by deep sorrow in childhood and young manhood' – in other words, that Middle-earth was just a kind of fantastic laudanum for its author. Many commentators clearly believe, by extension, that it is nothing but a general opiate for millions of readers.

No one has defended Tolkien more eloquently against this charge of 'escapism' than Tolkien himself, who pointed out in 'On Fairy-stories' that in real life escape is 'very practical, and may even be heroic', but that literary critics tend to confound 'the Escape of the Prisoner with the Flight of the Deserter', often wilfully.

> Just so a Party-spokesman might have labelled departure from the misery of the Führer's or any other Reich and even criticism of it as treachery. In the same way these critics . . . so to bring into contempt their opponents, stick their label of scorn not only on to Desertion, but on to real Escape, and what are often its companions, Disgust, Anger, Condemnation, and Revolt.

Speaking in 1939, six years into Hitler's murderous chancellorship, Tolkien was not mincing his words. Though he was himself a master of naturalism, especially in his depictions of landscape, he was acutely aware that in his lifetime realism had combined with modernism in an overbearing, intolerant, and denunciatory orthodoxy, a monolith dominating the academic and cultural establishments. Its advocates liked to think of this as progress, as if it were the only approach vindicated by the forward march of time. In fact, the new orthodoxy had grown contingently, like totalitarianism, in the often violent scramble for new certainties that followed the First World War. A Romantic and an individualist, Tolkien had opposed these orthodoxies for just as long, as his invention of Eärendel the escapee (1914) and Melko the tyrant (1916) testify. He was not purveying imaginary opiates: disgust, anger, and condemnation were perennial factors in his 'escape' into fairy-tale, myth, and ancientry.

For Tolkien, the distant past was a frame of reference, a daily currency. So, too, for Robert Graves; but Graves liked to cash in ancient for modern, 'translating' Anglo-Saxon poetry into trench imagery, with 'Beowulf lying wrapped in a blanket among his platoon of drunken thanes in the Gothland billet; Judith going for a promenade to Holofernes's staff tent; and Brunaburgh with its bayonet-and-cosh fight'. Tolkien's tendency was the opposite; he might see the German *Flammenwerfer* and think of Greek fire, exchanging new coin for old. A glance at some of the parallels between his creations and his immediate circumstances suggests that such double vision helped him construct his myth of a fictional ancient past; so that in war-emptied Oxford he devised the deserted elven capital Kôr, in troop-crowded Whittington Heath the migrant encampments of Aryador, and after the Somme the 'dragon' attack on Gondolin.

In a similar way, the pitmen and labourers of the 11th Lancashire Fusiliers may perhaps be discerned in one of the Gnome-kindreds in 'The Fall of Gondolin', the Hammer of Wrath. These smiths or craftsmen, many of them escapees from Melko's slave-mines, form the last-named battalion but the first to meet the enemy onslaught: 'Very numerous was that battalion, nor had any amongst them a faint heart, and they won the greatest glory of all those fair houses in that struggle against doom; yet were they ill-fated, and none ever fared away from that field . . .' The enemy draws them out and surrounds them; but they die taking many of their foes with them.

It is difficult to imagine that Tolkien devised this scenario without thinking about the Somme. Units virtually obliterated in the Big Push of 1 July 1916 included Rob Gilson's Cambridgeshires and G. B. Smith's Salford Pals. His own battalion suffered appalling losses a week later (while Tolkien was with divisional signals at Bouzincourt), when 'C' Company was wiped out.

The company had made a daring 1,200-yard night advance up the hill east of La Boisselle, but daybreak showed they had gone twice as far as planned. In a German trench that was only half-dug, they were bombarded by the enemy and their own side: 'The problem was to know where our chaps were,' said one British artilleryman. But it was afternoon before Captain John Metcalfe, still barely twenty, abandoned his position with the six men who remained unscathed; only he and a sergeant reached safety.

Tolkien's view of the incident is not known. His academic studies criticize both Beowulf and the Anglo-Saxon duke Beorhtnoth for recklessly endangering others in a sportsmanlike pursuit of honour and glory. But the Hammer of Wrath's over-extended advance was the first of several such heroic tragedies in his legendarium: Fëanor in the 'Silmarillion' and Théoden in *The Lord of the Rings* also pay with their lives for charging too deeply into enemy territory. The questions of courage, honour, leadership, and responsibility exercised both Tolkien's heart and his mind, possibly in different directions.

Whether or not the Hammer of Wrath recalls 'C' Company, it is clear that other writers might have turned this Somme incident into a blast of vitriol at Metcalfe or the makers of trench maps. But personal reticence made Tolkien temperamentally incapable of writing protest verse like Sassoon's or Owen's. Recalling his own tribulations as a soldier, in 1944 he sent his son Christopher, then with the RAF in South Africa, the Latin advice *Aequam serva mentem, comprime linguam*: 'Keep a calm mind, restrain the tongue.' He once described himself to W. H. Auden as a writer 'whose instinct is to cloak such self-knowledge as he has, and such criticisms of life as he knows it, under mythical and legendary dress'.

Although Tolkien had a rare genius for this 'cloaking', as he called it, he was far from alone in his desire to apply the patterns of myth and legend to the experience of real life. Although the stereotypical picture of the Western Front does not include soldiers reading the *Mabinogion* with its Welsh Arthuriana, as G. B. Smith did, or William Morris's *The Earthly Paradise*, which Tolkien carried, in fact quest literature was profoundly popular. Books such as Morris's *The Well at the World's End* and John Bunyan's *The Pilgrim's Progress* provided a key without which this life of tribulation and death seemed incomprehensible, as Paul Fussell admits: 'The experiences of a man going up to the line to his destiny cannot help seeming to him like those of a hero of medieval romance if his imagination has been steeped in actual literary romances . . .'

Christopher Wiseman, declaring in 1917 that experience of life was unnecessary in writing epics since they 'make no pretence of dealing with life', was thoroughly mistaken. Had Tolkien felt no need to express his shock at the outbreak of war, his heightened awareness of mortality, and his horror at mechanized warfare, it is possible that he would not have pursued fantasy at all. But his own metaphor of the concealing cloak is misleading. The distillation of experience into myth could reveal the prevailing elements in a moral morass such as the Great War, show the big picture where trench writers like Robert Graves tended to home in on the detail. Tolkien is not the first mythographer to produce a grave and pertinent epic in time of war and revolution. However else they differ from him, in this John Milton and William Blake are his forebears. When the world changes, and reality assumes an unfamiliar face, the epic and fantastic imagination may thrive.

At the opposite pole from heroic romance, the fairy-tale aspects of Tolkien's world could paradoxically provide a mirror for the world at war. In her lucid study, *A Question of Time*, Verlyn Flieger considers Tolkien's haunting 1930s poem, 'Looney', and its better known 1960s incarnation, 'The Sea-bell', which recount a bewildering lone odyssey to Faërie and the return of the traveller to mortal lands, where he finds himself estranged from his kind. Flieger notes that, whereas fairy-stories and war would seem to be opposites,

> Beneath the surface, however, [Tolkien's] words suggest a deep but unmanifest connection between these apparently unlike things . . . Both are set beyond the reach of ordinary human experience. Both are equally indifferent to the needs of ordinary humanity. Both can change those who return so that they become 'pinned in a kind of ghostly deathlessness', not just unable to say where they have been but unable to communicate to those who have not been there what they have seen or experienced. Perhaps worst of all, both war and Faërie can change out of all recognition the wanderer's perception of the world to which he returns, so that never again can it be what it once was.

Strikingly, Tolkien wrote his first account of a mortal's arrival in Faërie, 'The Cottage of Lost Play', just after his return to England from the Somme with trench fever. Eriol's first impressions of the Lonely Isle are much happier than those in 'Looney' and 'The Sea-bell', but he glimpses Faërie's indifference to humanity. Tolkien's outlines show that the mariner would eventually become alienated from his kind; and in the last pages of 'The Book of Lost Tales', Eriol expresses his fear that his message to human posterity – the tales he has recorded – will be lost.

Viewed in the context of 1916–17, the arrival of Eriol, 'One who dreams alone', in the Lonely Isle, 'the Land of Release', has the air of a soldier's anticipatory dream of a homecoming in which everything will turn out alright again. But he is escaping the current of his own time and entering the timelessness of Faërie. Similarly, for the soldier, time seemed to have moved on incalculably in the trenches but fallen behind in England. The Lonely Isle, then, may be seen as a symbolic version of the England that had slipped away. *Nostalgia*, a word that had hitherto always meant homesickness, began to appear in its now prevalent sense – regretful or wistful yearning for the past – straight after the Great War. To Tolkien's generation, nostalgia was a constant companion: they were looking over their shoulders, like the survivors of Gondolin, at an old home that seemed now to embody everything beautiful and doomed. Tolkien's myth expresses the desire for such apparently timeless beauty, but constantly recognizes that it is indeed doomed: for all its apparent imperviousness, in the long run the Lonely Isle, like Gondolin, must succumb to implacable change.

The war memoirist Charles Douie looked back on *Peter Pan* as a kind of prophecy. 'Did no feeling of apprehension darken the mind of any mother in that audience which first heard, "My sons shall die like English gentlemen"; did no foreboding enter into the exultation with which those sons first heard youth's defiance of death – "To die would be an awfully big adventure"?'

It was Peter's perpetual youth that came closest to the mark during the Great War, when so many young men would never grow old; and Tolkien's Elves, forever in the prime of adulthood, hit the bullseye. As Tom Shippey notes, 'There is no difficulty in seeing why Tolkien, from 1916 on, was preoccupied with the theme of death . . . The theme of escape from death might then naturally seem attractive.' Much more robust than the airy miniatures of Victorian and Shakespearean fancy, the Eldar could shoulder the burden of these weightier themes. Their ancient roots in Germanic and Celtic myth, furthermore, made them apt symbols of timelessness in a twentieth-century epic about loss.

Neither Milton nor Blake saw battle itself. That Tolkien did may explain the central or climactic role of battles in his stories. The tank-like 'dragons' in the assault on Gondolin strongly imply that this is the case. So does the strategic importance of timing in many of Tolkien's fictional clashes. The failure of units to coordinate their attacks, a disastrous feature of the Battle of Unnumbered Tears as developed in the 'Silmarillion', parallels a fatal problem in the Somme offensive. The last-minute intervention of a fresh force to save the day, a staple of military engagements in Middle-earth, may seem less realistic and more 'escapist', but this was the part his own battalion played in the taking of Ovillers and the rescue of the Warwickshires, when he was present as a signaller.

Tolkien's even-handed depiction of war as both terrible and stirring is well matched by a comment from Charles Carrington (one of the beleaguered Warwickshires), who writes that, for the soldier in the midst of mortal danger, 'There was an arguing realism, a cynical side to one's nature that raised practical objections and suggested dangers, and against it there strove a romantic ardour for the battle that was almost joyful.' Túrin, 'sick and weary' after the fray, illustrates the frequent sequel to such ardour – the resurgence of reality. But high diction, which sets Tolkien so far apart from the classic trench writers, expresses perfectly a psychological truth of war they tend to neglect. In all its enormity and strangeness, combat could induce what Carrington calls the 'exaltation of battle . . . an elevated state of mind which a doctor might have defined as neurosis'; he says he was 'uplifted in spirit'.

A similar observation in Frederic Manning's acute Somme novel, *The Middle Parts of Fortune*, points to a more profound parallel between the view on the battlefield and Tolkien's creative vision. Manning relates the exaltation of combat to the soldiers' conviction that they were fighting in a just cause, a 'moral impetus' that 'carried them forward on a wave of emotional excitement, transfiguring all the circumstances of their life so that these could only be expressed in the terms of heroic tragedy, of some superhuman or even divine conflict with the powers of evil . . .' Tolkien's legendarium assumed the dimensions of a conflict between good and evil immediately after the Somme. Might that be partly the result of a desire to express this singular experience, so far beyond the scope of conventional literary expression?

Whatever the answer, Tolkien's moral vision is utterly different in application from the soldier's and the propagandist's. With the possible exception of the Hammer of Wrath, noted above, Orcs and Elves do not equate to the Germans and the British; on the contrary, they distil the cruelty and the courage he saw on both sides in war, as well as more general qualities of barbarism and civilization. It was not the Kaiser that Tolkien demonized in Melko, but the tyranny of the machine over the individual, an international evil going back far earlier than 1914 but exercised with merciless abandon on the Western Front.

As Tom Shippey has pointed out, Tolkien is in good company among later writers who turned away from realism because, as combat veterans, they had seen 'something irrevocably evil'. George Orwell (the Spanish Civil War), Kurt Vonnegut and William Golding (the Second World War) fall into this category. Crucially, Shippey argues, Tolkien and these others adopted various forms of fantasy because they felt that the conventional explanations for the evil they had seen 'were hopelessly inadequate, out of date, at best irrelevant, at worst part of the evil itself'. For example, realist fictions hold that there is no absolute evil, only relative degrees of social maladjustment; but in *Lord of the Flies* Golding suggests that something intrinsically evil lurks inside us all, waiting to get out. Trench realism embraces detail and flinches from universal statements, but 'The Book of Lost Tales' mythologizes the evil that Tolkien saw in materialism. To put the last point another way, writers such as Graves, Sassoon, and Owen saw the Great War as the disease, but Tolkien saw it as merely the symptom.

During Tolkien's own war, the conventional British view as expressed in propaganda was that evil certainly existed, and it was German. Trench poets such as Wilfred Owen felt that the real enemy was the blind self-interest of national governments determined to gain territory whatever the human cost. But both groups shared a taste for polemic. Owen's poem about a gassed soldier leaves an indelible impression, and was meant to:

> If in some smothering dreams, you too could pace
> Behind the wagon that we flung him in,
> And watch the white eyes writhing in his face . . .
> My friend, you would not tell with such high zest
> To children ardent for some desperate glory,
> The old Lie: Dulce et decorum est
> Pro patria mori.

The personal address, 'my friend', is only the salute before the bayonet-thrust. You, it says, are passing on lies to your children, and so they may one day suffer torments such as this I saw. The voice of the trench writer has primacy, as a guarantor of eyewitness reliability but also as a badge of unimpeachable moral authority.

Tolkien eschewed polemical rhetoric, part of the evil of tyranny and orthodoxy that he opposed. In his work, a multitude of characters speak in diverse voices, but the author stays well out of sight. While trench writers such as Owen challenged the propagandists and censors for the monopoly on truth, Tolkien moved away from the idea of a monopoly altogether, telling his Lost Tales through multiple narrators (rather as Ilúvatar in 'The Music of the Ainur' allows his seraphic choirs to elaborate his themes). The idea survived into the 'Silmarillion', a collation of disparate historical accounts, and *The Hobbit* and *The Lord of the Rings*, which purport to have been edited from the writings of their protagonists.

But the evil that Tolkien's mythology most squarely opposes, disenchantment, is burned into the fabric of classic Great War literature.

By editing G. B. Smith's *A Spring Harvest*, Tolkien contributed to a spate of fallen soldiers' poetry, most of which is now forgotten. The little that is still remembered, including Owen's poetry, was not cemented into the cultural memory until several more years had passed, when trench survivors broke their traumatized silence. A flurry of memoirs and novels appeared between 1926 and 1934, including Sassoon's *Memoirs of an Infantry Officer*, Graves's *Good-bye to All That*, and the start of Henry Williamson's *Chronicle of Ancient Sunlight* sequence. Now, in the words of Samuel Hynes, 'the Myth of the War was defined and fixed in the version that retains authority': the disenchanted version.

This 'myth' implies that the war consisted almost entirely of passive suffering. In his poetry, Sassoon neglects to mention his solo killing sprees in the German lines; in his prose he downplays the daring involved. In Wilfred Owen's verse, men trudge through mud, or move a dying comrade into the sun, or simply wait to be attacked. He declared his subject to be pity, not heroes or deeds. In other words, action and heroism were omitted for a more effective protest against the war.

The revisionist approach of the late 1920s, which Owen had heralded, underlined the bitter irony of lives squandered for 'a few acres of mud', as Christopher Wiseman had put it. The snapshot narratives in the literature of disenchantment typically pivot on ironic incidents in which action is proved futile and courage a waste. Paul Fussell identifies classic trench writing with the 'ironic' mode of narrative that Northrop Frye (in *The Anatomy of Criticism*) defined as characterizing the latter phase of a typical cycle of literary history. The earliest fictions (myth, romance, epic, and tragedy) portrayed heroes who enjoyed greater power of action than their audience; but in the quintessentially modern ironic mode the protagonist has less power of action than ourselves, and is caught in a 'scene of bondage, frustration, or absurdity'.

These days it tends to be forgotten that many veterans resented the way their story was being told from 1926 onwards. 'Book after book related a succession of disasters and discomforts with no intermission and no gleam of achievement,' wrote Carrington. 'Every battle a defeat, every officer a nincompoop, every soldier a coward.' The wounded pride of a disgruntled officer, perhaps; but Carrington's own memoir is hardly a rose-tinted affair.

The disenchanted view has left us a skewed picture of an important and complex historical event; a problem only exacerbated by a cultural and academic tendency to canonize the best and forget the rest. Coming after the desperate cheer of frontline letters home, the newspaper and government propaganda and the stilted elegies of the war era, the former soldier Charles Douie thought that the new approach restored balance; but he added:

> The authors of this poetry and prose of horror have overstated the case in quite as great a degree as we understated it during the war. The sight of blood has gone to their heads. They can see nothing else . . . Are the prose and poetry of this age to be charged with disillusion and despair?

The disenchanted view of the war stripped meaning from what many soldiers saw as the defining experience of their lives.

'The Book of Lost Tales', composed between 1916 and *c.*1920, is the same vintage as Charles Carrington's *A Subaltern's War*, largely written in 1919–20. Carrington's later words about his memoir apply equally to Tolkien's mythology. 'It is thus anterior to the pacifist reaction of the nineteen-thirties and is untainted by the influence of the later writers who invented the powerful image of "disenchantment" or "disillusion",' Carrington wrote. 'I go back to an earlier stage in the history of ideas.'

The metaphorical uses of *disenchanted* and *disillusioned* have so overtaken the literal that it is easy to forget what they once meant. To say you are 'disenchanted' with the government or a love affair or a career, for example, is to say that you no longer value them. Wilfred Owen was disenchanted with a whole set of archaic values, declaring that his poetry was not about 'deeds, or lands, or anything about glory, honour, might, majesty, dominion, or power, except War'. But Robert Graves's image of the end of innocence – wisdom scattering the nursery fairies – indicates the literal meaning of *disenchantment*. The Great War had broken a kind of spell.

Tolkien stands against disenchantment in both its literal and metaphorical senses; indeed, they cannot strictly be separated in his work. The disenchanted view, metaphorically speaking, is that failure renders effort meaningless. In contrast, Tolkien's protagonists are heroes not because of their successes, which are often limited, but because of their courage and tenacity in trying. By implication, worth cannot be measured by results alone, but is intrinsic. His stories depict the struggle to uphold inherited, instinctive, or inspirational values – matters of intrinsic and immeasurable worth – against the forces of chaos and destruction. But Tolkien's world is literally enchanted, too. Not only does it contain talking swords, moving islands, and spells of sleep, but even its most 'normal' objects and inhabitants possess a spiritual value that has nothing to do with any practical usefulness: no one has argued more energetically than Tolkien that a tree is more than a source of wood. Furthermore, according to 'The Music of the Ainur', the world is a spell in progress, a work of *enchantment* – etymologically, a magic that is sung.

Tolkien's story of Túrin Turambar may appear to come close to the 'disenchanted' mode of literature. The ironies of inescapable circumstance either deprive Túrin of victory or they cheat him of its fruits. However, Tolkien parts company with his contemporaries in his depiction of the individual's response to circumstance. Túrin's dogged struggle against fate sets the seal on the heroic status he achieves in combat. Fate may laugh at his efforts, but he refuses to be humbled.

Irony is sometimes accounted an absolute virtue in literature, as if depicting reversals of fortune were evidence of a wise detachment from life, or saying the opposite of what is meant demonstrated a wry wit and paid a compliment to the reader's cleverness. Tolkien recognized that ironic circumstance exists and must be portrayed, but it is clear that he did not account irony a virtue. He had stood with Christopher Wiseman when the latter complained, in late 1914, that the TCBS had become dominated by a waggish and sarcastic element 'who sneer at everything and lose their temper at nothing'. His characterization of the dragon Glorund as the ironist who engineers Túrin's destruction illustrates his own disapproval of those who delight in mockery.

Tolkien's other narratives may stand further from 'disenchanted' literature, yet they still frequently involve the ironic downturn characteristic of classic trench writing: the disaster or discovery that undermines all achievements and threatens to snuff out hope. That downturn, however, is not the pivotal moment that matters most in Middle-earth. Tolkien propels his plots beyond it and so reaches the emotional crux that truly interested him: 'eucatastrophe', the sudden turn for the better when hope rises unforeseeably from the ashes. He makes despair or 'disenchantment' the prelude to a redemptive restoration of meaning.

From Tuor onwards he recorded how individuals are transfigured by extraordinary circumstances. His characters set out, more often than not, from a point something like Frye's 'ironic' mode, in bondage, frustration, or absurdity, but they break free of those conditions, and so become heroes. They achieve greater power of action than ourselves, and so reach the condition of characters in the older modes identified by Northrop Frye in his cyclical view of literary history: myth, romance, and epic. So Tolkien dramatized the joy of victory against all odds in Beren and Tinúviel, whose courage and tenacity overcome not only Melko but also the mockery Beren has suffered in the court of Tinúviel's father. This liberation from the chains of circumstance makes his stories especially vital in an age of disenchantment.

Heroism does happen, as Tolkien vouched with characteristic reticence in his landmark 1936 paper on *Beowulf*: 'Even to-day . . . you may find men not ignorant of tragic legend and history, who have heard of heroes and indeed seen them . . .' Courage had not changed since the days of 'the old heroes . . . dying with their backs to the wall', he said. The metaphor is commonplace, but loaded with meaning in contexts ancient and modern, public and perhaps personal. It recalls how, in the Old English poem *The Wanderer*, the lord's retainers '*eal gecrong / wlonc bi wealle*' – 'all perished, proud beside the wall'. Tolkien might have remembered that Christopher Wiseman had used the same metaphor in his letter calling the TCBS to order after Rob Gilson's death: 'Now we stand with our backs to the wall, and yet we haver and question as to whether we had better not all put our backs against separate walls.' For Tolkien's inter-war audience, however, it would surely have evoked Field-Marshal Haig's inspirational order during the German Spring Offensive of 1918: 'With our backs to the wall, and believing in the justice of our cause, each one of us must fight on to the end.' Through his narratives of hard-won and partial victory, Tolkien suggests that we should go on, whether we can or not.

Like Milton, he also tries to justify the ways of God to Men. Following the introduction of discord into the Music of the Ainur, Ilúvatar asserts that 'even shall those beings, who must now dwell among his evil and endure through Melko misery and sorrow, terror and wickedness, declare in the end that it redoundeth only to my great glory, and doth but make the theme more worth the hearing, Life more worth the living, and the World so much the more wonderful and marvellous'. In a more sceptical era, it is easy to scoff at this as a kind of faith that is blind to the reality of suffering; but Tolkien was not blind, and in the years immediately prior to writing those words he had witnessed suffering on an industrial scale. Others who lived through the shocks and turmoils of his times sought for similar consolatory explanations of God's mysterious ways. Concluding his soldiering memoir, *The Weary Road*, Charles Douie wrote: 'Perhaps some day later generations may begin to see our war in a truer perspective, and may discern it as an inevitable step in the tragic process by which consciousness has informed the will of man, by which in time all things will be fashioned fair.' Tolkien was not writing about later generations, but about the end of the world. F. L. Lucas, the classicist–soldier whose enlistment had precipitated Rob Gilson's, wrote that the purpose of tragic drama was 'to portray life that its tears become a joy forever'. In Tolkien's myth, our immortal souls will be able to contemplate the drama in which we have taken part as a finished work of art. They will also join the Ainur in a second, greater Music, when Ilúvatar's themes will 'be played aright; for then Ainur and Men will know his mind and heart as well as may be, and all his intent'.

Close to two decades separate the composition of 'The Book of Lost Tales' from the publication of *The Hobbit*; closer to four divide it from the appearance of *The Lord of the Rings*. The 'Silmarillion' continued to evolve until Tolkien's death, involving major developments at every level of detail from cosmology to nomenclature. Though a full examination of the question would be out of place here, I would argue that most of what has been said in this postscript holds true for all this later work.

By the time *The Hobbit* appeared, Tolkien had long abandoned the identification of the Lonely Isle with Britain, and the story of a Germanic or Anglo-Saxon mariner hearing the 'true tradition' of the Elves had dwindled to the occasional 'editorial' aside in the 'Silmarillion'. The myth was no longer, in any geographical or cultural respect, about the genesis of England. But the loosening of these links – together with the new scope for naturalistic portraiture that accompanied his move away from epic modes – meant paradoxically that Tolkien could now write about 'Englishness' in a more meaningful way than in drawing linear connections through vast aeons. He could model hobbits directly on English people as he had known them in and around his cherished childhood home of Sarehole near Birmingham, borrowing aspects of custom, society, character, and speech. Hobbits, he said, constitute a community that is 'more or less a Warwickshire village of about the period of the Diamond Jubilee'. He admitted, 'I take my models like anyone else – from such "life" as I know.' A figure standing uncertainly at the doorway into adventure, Bilbo Baggins is an engaging mixture of timidity and temerity, but he learns and grows with astonishing speed, until he can look death calmly in the eye. Bilbo is simply much more like us, Tolkien's readers, than Beren or Tinúviel or Túrin could be. Meanwhile, the tincture of Englishness and the aura of 1897 draw this story closer to the First World War – the end of the era that hobbits evoke – than the Lost Tales that were actually written during and immediately after it.

It would be misleading to suggest that *The Hobbit* is Tolkien's wartime experience in disguise; yet it is easy to see how some of his memories must have invigorated this tale of an ennobling rite of passage past the fearful jaws of death. The middle-class hero is thrown in with proud but stolid companions who have been forced to sink 'as low as blacksmith-work or even coalmining'. The goblins they meet recall those of 'The Fall of Gondolin', though in *The Hobbit* – because he made no bones about addressing a twentieth-century audience – Tolkien was much more explicit about the kind of evil they represent: 'It is not unlikely that they invented some of the machines that have since troubled the world, especially the ingenious devices for killing large numbers of people at once, for wheels and engines and explosions always delighted them . . . but in those days . . . they had not advanced (as it is called) so far.' The company approaches the end of its quest across the desolation created by Smaug, a dragon of Glorund's ilk: a once green land with now 'neither bush nor tree, and only broken and blackened stumps to speak of ones long vanished'. Scenes of sudden, violent ruin ensue (Tom Shippey sees elements of First World War attitudes in Bard the Bowman's defence of Laketown); we visit the camps of the sick and wounded and listen to wranglings over matters of command and strategy. And all culminates in a battle involving those old enemies, the Elves and the Orcs. Horror and mourning, two attitudes to battlefield death, appear side by side, the Orcs lying 'piled in heaps till Dale was dark and hideous with their corpses', but among them 'many a fair elf that should have lived yet long ages merrily in the wood'.

In 1916, from a trench in Thiepval Wood, G. B. Smith had written Tolkien a letter he thought might be his last. 'May God bless you, my dear John Ronald, and may you say the things I have tried to say long after I am not there to say them, if such be my lot.' The 24-year-old Tolkien had believed just as strongly in the dream shared by the TCBS, and felt that they 'had been granted some spark of fire . . . that was destined to kindle a new light, or, what is the same thing, rekindle an old light in the world . . .' At 48, however, Tolkien felt that the Great War had come down like winter on his creative powers in their first bloom. 'I was pitched into it all, just when I was full of stuff to write, and of things to learn; and never picked it all up again,' he said in October 1940.

What he would have written had he not been 'pitched into it all' is difficult to imagine. The war imposed urgency and gravity, took him through terror, sorrow, and unexpected joy, and reinvented the real world in a strange, extreme form. Without the war, it is arguable whether his fictions would have focused on a conflict between good and evil; or if they had, whether good and evil would have taken a similar shape. The same may be said for his thoughts on death and immortality, dyscatastrophe and eucatastrophe, enchantment and irony, the significance of fairy-story, the importance of ordinary people in events of historic magnitude, and, crucially, the relationship between language and mythology. If we were lucky enough now to survey a twentieth century in which there had been no Great War, we might know of a minor craftsman in the tradition of William Morris called J. R. R. Tolkien; or we might know him only as a brilliant academic. Middle-earth, I suspect, looks so engagingly familiar to us, and speaks to us so eloquently, because it was born with the modern world and marked by the same terrible birth pangs.

Tolkien's retrospective view in 1940 seems clouded. He was struggling to push on with his sequel to *The Hobbit* after a year's hiatus under the pall of a new global conflict, but he had little sense of what the book would become.

But *The Lord of the Rings*, the masterpiece that was published a decade and a half later, stands as the fruition of the TCBSian dream, a light drawn from ancient sources to illuminate a darkening world. Some of its success may be attributed to a sense of depth and detail unparalleled in an imagined world: the result of a long germination that began not in December 1937, when the first sentence of this new story was written, but in 1914, with 'The Voyage of Éarendel the Evening Star'; *The Lord of the Rings* was a part of the same tree that the Great War spurred into growth. But a good measure of its strength, surely, derives from its roots in Tolkien's war. When it was published, baffled critics tried their hardest to interpret it as an allegory of the struggle against Nazi Germany; but Tolkien responded:

> One has indeed personally to come under the shadow of war to feel fully its oppression; but as the years go by it seems now often forgotten that to be caught in youth by 1914 was no less hideous an experience than to be involved in 1939 and the following years. By 1918 all but one of my close friends were dead.

If you really must look for a meaningful biographical or historical influence, he would appear to be saying, 1914–18 is where you ought to start.

Tolkien intentionally contributed very little to such evidence as exists; his statements on the influence or otherwise of the First World War on *The Lord of the Rings* are few and wary. While no longer prone to assign himself any kind of walk-on role in his stories, as he had half-done with Eriol in 'The Book of Lost Tales', he nevertheless conceded that out of the entire dramatis personae, 'As far as any character is "like me" it is Faramir – except that I lack what all my characters possess (let the psychoanalysts note!) *Courage*.' Faramir, of course, is an officer but also a scholar, with a reverence for the old histories and sacred values that helps him through a bitter war. Tolkien asserted a less specific but much more concrete connection between the Great War and *The Lord of the Rings* by declaring, 'My "Sam Gamgee" is indeed a reflexion of the English soldier, of the privates and batmen I knew in the 1914 war, and recognised as so far superior to myself.' Finally, he said that the Somme battlefield had re-emerged in the desolate approaches to Mordor:

> Personally I do not think that either war . . . had any influence upon either the plot or the manner of its unfolding. Perhaps in landscape. The Dead Marshes and the approaches to the Morannon owe something to Northern France after the Battle of the Somme. They owe more to William Morris and his Huns and Romans, as in *The House of the Wolfings* or *The Roots of the Mountains*.

Though couched within a sweeping denial of influence, the admission has stuck. A survey of 'British fiction writers of the First World War' by Hugh Cecil focuses on such authors as Richard Aldington, Wilfrid Ewart, and Oliver Onions, but by way of introducing the Western Front it turns first to Tolkien's description of the Dead Marshes, a scene of morbid desolation that has become, in effect, a shorthand symbol for the trenches.

C. S. Lewis leaned strongly towards the view that the war of their generation had cast its shadow on his friend's story. Lewis had also served on the Western Front, discovering camaraderie in the midst of horror, suffering trench fever and then sustaining a 'Blighty' wound at the Battle of Arras. Reviewing *The Lord of the Rings* in 1955, he wrote about one of the book's 'general excellences', its surprising realism:

> This war has the very quality of the war my generation knew. It is all here: the endless, unintelligible movement, the sinister quiet of the front when 'everything is now ready', the flying civilians, the lively, vivid friendships, the background of something like despair and the merry foreground, and such heavensent windfalls as a *cache* of tobacco 'salvaged' from a ruin. The author has told us elsewhere that his taste for fairy-tale was wakened into maturity by active service; that, no doubt, is why we can say of his war scenes (quoting Gimli the Dwarf), 'There is good rock here. This country has tough bones.'

More might be added to Lewis's list: the atmosphere of pre-war tension and watchfulness, Frodo Baggins's restless impatience with his parochial countrymen in the Shire, the world's dizzying plunge into peril and mass mobilizations; tenacious courage revealed in the ordinary people of town and farm, with camaraderie and love as their chief motivations; the striking absence of women from much of the action; the machine-dominated mind of Saruman. Tom Shippey notes that the failure of the Shire to fête Frodo Baggins on his return reflects in Tolkien 'the disillusionment of the returned veteran'.

Lewis failed to mention the equally surprising pertinence of superficially *un*realistic elements in *The Lord of the Rings*. Here are a few that suggest the influence of 1914–18: the sweeping surveillance of the Eye of Sauron, the moments when reality shifts into dream during those long marches, or into nightmare in the midst of battle, the battlefield dominated by lumbering elephantine behemoths and previously unseen airborne killers, the Black Breath of despair that brings down even the bravest; the revenge of the trees for their wanton destruction. The popularity of William Morris's quest stories on the Western Front has been noted. Tolkien completed the circle by drawing on his experiences of the Great War for a series of 'medieval' romances, beginning with 'The Fall of Gondolin' and, it may be judged, most fully achieved in *The Lord of the Rings.*

The book recounts the piteous predicament of the soldier down in the battlefield mud, but it also tackles the themes that Wilfred Owen ruled off-limits: deeds, lands, glory, honour, might, majesty, dominion, power. It examines how the individual's experience of war relates to those grand old abstractions; for example, it puts glory, honour, majesty, as well as courage, under such stress that they often fracture, but are not utterly destroyed. Mindful, no doubt, of the schism of war literature into propaganda and protest, Lewis called *The Lord of the Rings* 'a recall from facile optimism and wailing pessimism alike' that presides at 'the cool middle point between illusion and disillusionment'.

The last word may go to Siegfried Sassoon, a quintessential Great War writer. In *The Lord of the Rings* the embattled city of Minas Tirith is saved by the intervention of a host of the dead out of ancient legends: people who deserted their allies three thousand years before, and have come at last to redeem their oath and to fight. It is an astonishing, fantastic scenario, and morally striking: ghosts joining the war against evil. Yet how similar this is to a visionary moment in *Memoirs of an Infantry Officer*, where Sassoon recalls the shock of witnessing the return of his men to rest after eleven days in the Somme trenches:

> I had seen something that night which overawed me. It was all in the day's work – an exhausted Division returning from the Somme Offensive – but for me it was as though I had watched an army of ghosts. It was as though I had seen the War as it might be envisioned by the mind of some epic poet a hundred years hence.

Tolkien, more famous for prose than poetry, was already at work on his mythology in 1916; but otherwise we may justly regard him as the epic writer Sassoon imagined.

Notes

Abbreviations and short titles used in notes

See bibliography for full details of books and papers. Where no author is given (except in the cases of *Artist*, *Biography*, and *Family Album*), the author is JRRT.

Artist	Wayne Hammond and Christina Scull, *J. R. R. Tolkien: Artist and Illustrator*
Biography	Humphrey Carpenter, *J. R. R. Tolkien: A Biography*
CLW	Christopher Luke Wiseman
CWGC	Commonwealth War Graves Commission
EK	Estelle King
EMB, EMT	Edith Mary Bratt, later Edith Mary Tolkien
Family Album	John and Priscilla Tolkien, *The Tolkien Family Album*
GBS	Geoffrey Bache Smith
JRRT	John Ronald Reuel Tolkien
Letters	*Letters of J. R. R. Tolkien: A Selection*
LF	The Lancashire Fusiliers
LT1	*The Book of Lost Tales, Part One*
LT2	*The Book of Lost Tales, Part Two*
KES	King Edward's School
KESC	*King Edward's School Chronicle*
MCG	Mrs Marianne Cary Gilson ('Donna')
Monsters	Tolkien, *The Monsters and the Critics*
OEG	*Old Edwardians Gazette*
RCG	Robert Cary Gilson
RQG	Robert Quilter Gilson
RWR	Richard William Reynolds

Correspondence dates in square brackets are those established by the author, sometimes tentatively, where a date is not given or is clearly in error.

Prologue

p.3 Rugby match: RQG to MCG, 30 November 1913; 'a beaten pack', match details: undated report, *KESC*, March 1914, 11–12.

p.4 JRRT ill: *KESC*, March 1914, 9.
CLW's health and sport: *KESC*, December 1912, 86.
CLW's musicianship (and his settings for 'Sing we the King' and 'Trull'): Lightwood, *The Music of the Methodist Hymn Book*, 94–5, 398.

p.5 JRRT and CLW: CLW memoir, *OEG*. Their disputes: CLW to JRRT, 15 November 1914. Great Twin Brotherhood and Trought: ibid.; JRRT to CLW, 16 November 1914.
Librarianship: CLW to JRRT, 27 April 1911.
Literary papers: *KESC*, March 1911, 19–20; April 1912, 28; July 1910, 79; December 1910, 92.
'almost the last word': CLW to JRRT, 27 October 1915.

p.6 Campaign against cynics: CLW to JRRT, 10 November 1914, 27 October 1915, 1 March 1916.
Light-hearted TCBS: CLW to JRRT, 5 June 1913, 10 November 1914.
1911, 'the sweltering town populations . . .': Ensor, 442.

p.7 *KESC* does not list T. K. Barnsley among the TCBS, probably because it only lists prefects.
Barnsley and GBS agree to play: RQG to MCG, 30 November 1913; TKB's expressions: ibid., 17 and 22 February 1914.

p.8 ''Twas a good road . . .': unsigned *KESC* Editorial, July 1911, 53.
Four dead: the fourth was JRRT's full-back, George Morley Smith.

pp.8–9 War dead: J. M. Winter, 1986, 92–9.

ONE *Before*

pp.11–12 Life up to 1910: *Biography*, 9–49.
'If your first Christmas tree . . .': 1964 interview with Denis Gueroult, BBC Sound Archives.

pp.12–13 Drawing: Priestman, 9, 12, 19; *Letters*, 377.

p.13 Handwriting: *Biography*, 18, 21, 57; Priestman, 8–10; *Artist*, 201; *Letters*, 377.

'I was brought up . . .': *Letters*, 172.
Reading: 'On Fairy-stories', *Monsters*, 134–5; *Letters*, 311; read '*too* much . . .': Mabel Tolkien, *Biography*, 28.
Poetry: *Biography*, 47–8; *Letters*, 213.

pp.13–14 JRRT on Francis Thompson: Stapeldon Society minutes, 4 March 1914.

p.14 'Wood-sunshine': excerpted in *Biography*, 47.
TCBS and Pre-Raphaelites: CLW to GBS, 30 August 1916.
'It seemed rather as if words . . .': *Biography*, 22.
'The fluidity . . .': 'English and Welsh', *Monsters*, 191.

pp.14–16 Languages: 'English and Welsh', *Monsters*, 191–2; *Letters*, 213–14, 357.

p.15 Chambers' *Etymological Dictionary*: Bodleian Tolkien E16/8.

p.16 School record: KES class lists.
'quite a great authority . . .': RQG to MCG, 22 May 1914; RQG to EK, 10 March 1916.
'the highest epic genius . . .': *KESC*, March 1911, 19–20.

p.17 'Reading Homer . . .': CLW memoir, *OEG*.
Language invention and friendship: CLW to JRRT, 10 November 1914, and Mrs Patricia Wiseman in conversation with the author.
'It's not uncommon . . .': interview excerpted in Sibley, *Audio Portrait*.
'serve the needs . . .': 'A Secret Vice', *Monsters*, 201.
Gautisk: *Parma Eldalamberon* 12, iv, x–xi; advice from Arden R. Smith.
Sobriquets (footnote): RQG to JRRT 4 October 1911 and 21 March 1913.

p.18 *The Peace*: *KESC*, October 1911, 72; *Biography*, 49; the Greek Plays: William H. Tait in *OEG*, June 1972, 17; *The Clouds*: *KESC*, October 1912, 66. GBS as the Ass: KES photograph of *The Frogs* [July 1913].
'As a boy . . .' (C. V. L. Lycett); TCBS not aloof: *Letters*, 429.
Nicknames: CLW to JRRT, 27 April and 17 August 1911, 19 March and 20 November 1912; CLW memoir, *OEG*.

p.19 Classical tags (footnote): *KESC*, March 1909, March 1910, March 1911.

'My dear Gabriel', etc.: CLW to JRRT, 27 April 1911. 'gracing our ancestral hearth', etc.: RQG to JRRT, 10 June 1913.
'a daft slang . . .': J. B. Priestley, *The Edwardians*, 82.

p.20 Macaulay's 'The Battle of Lake Regillus': Yates, '"The Battle of the Eastern Field": A Commentary', *Mallorn* 13, 3–5.
'The Battle of the Eastern Field': *KESC*, March 1911, 22–7; 'Sekhet, the lion-headed': Haggard, *She*, 281.

p.21 'Our country is now supreme . . .': *KESC*, February 1909, 9.
'hooliganism and uproar'; foreign policy: Stapledon Society minutes, 1 December and 7 November 1913.
'Court of Arbiters' debate: *KESC*, February 1911, 5.

p.22 Debate demanding war: *KESC*, October 1911, 79.
KES anthem, by Alfred Hayes (1857–1936): Trott, *No Place for Fop or Idler*, 1; *The Annotated Hobbit*, 344.

p.23 A good shot: Priscilla and Michael Tolkien, quoted in an unsigned report, *Amon Hen* 13, October 1974, 9.
OTC presented to the King: *KESC*, November 1910, 69, 73.
'kindled an immovable smile': unsigned editorial, *KESC*, June 1911, 33.
Footnote on *Adfuit omen*: T. A. Shippey to the author.
Coronation trip: *KESC*, July 1911, 59–60; *Letters*, 391 (which says the party was twelve-strong).

pp.23–4 Aldershot camp: *KESC*, November 1910, 69.

p.24 Tidworth Pennings camp: William H. Tait in *OEG*, June 1972, 17.

pp.24–5 King Edward's Horse: James, *The History of King Edward's Horse*, 1–53; *The Stapeldon Magazine*, December 1911, 117–18; JRRT service record.
JRRT and horses: Priscilla and Michael Tolkien, quoted in *Amon Hen* 13, 9. (The unsigned report says erroneously that Tolkien began his war service in King Edward's Horse.)

p.25 'In fact we have done nothing . . .': unsigned 'Oxford Letter', *KESC*, December 1911, 100.
'predominant vice . . .': CLW to JRRT, 27 April 1911; 'Very lazy': Lorise Topliffe, 'Tolkien as an Undergraduate', *Exeter College Association Register*, 32.

'a winger . . .': *The Stapeldon Magazine*, December 1911, 110–11.
'immensely attracted . . .': *Letters*, 214. The popular edition that JRRT read was W. F. Kirby's.
Kalevala overdue: RQG to JRRT, 4 October 1911.

p.26 Eliot's *Finnish Grammar* was the first written in the English language. JRRT borrowed it from 25 November to 5 December 1911, 25 October to 5 December 1912, and 14 November 1914 to 16 January 1915 (Exeter College library register).
'It was like discovering . . .': *Letters*, 214.
Kullervo: begun 1912 to 1913, according to *Letters*, 214–15, but ibid. 7 shows that Tolkien was still working on it in October 1914.
'hurrying and febrile . . .': Priestley, *The Edwardians*, 218.
Brooke and Housman: Parker, *The Old Lie*, 94.

p.27 Emily Annie Gilson's death: *KESC*, June 1907, 36. Thomas Smith, commercial clerk: *Corpus Christi Biographical Register 1880–1974*.
'The passing of certain . . .', etc.: RQG to JRRT, 4 October 1911. 'the old shrine': CLW to JRRT, 19 March 1912.
Mock strike; 'induce the Library . . .': *KESC*, October 1911, 70, 73.
The Rivals: *KESC*, March 1912, 14; *Biography*, 57–8.

p.28 Trought's death; 'Poor old Vincent . . .': CLW to JRRT, 21 and 22 January 1912.
Trought's character; 'some of his verses . . .', etc.: *KESC*, March 1912, 4.

p.29 'Ishnesses': *Artist*, 34–40. Those named here were produced between December 1911 and summer 1913.

pp.29–30 Farnell: Farnell, *An Oxonian Looks Back*; *Letters*, 7. His *magnum opus* was *The Cults of the Greek States* (1896–1909).

p.30 'People couldn't make out . . .': interview excerpted in Sibley, *Audio Portrait*.
Joseph Wright: *Letters*, 397. Wright's *Comparative Grammar of the Greek Language* was published in January 1912.
RCG had expected a First from JRRT: RQG to JRRT, 27 April 1913.

Farnell and German culture: Farnell, *An Oxonian Looks Back*, 57.

Switch in courses: *Letters*, 397, 406.

p.31 *The Rivals* revival: *KESC*, October 1912, 67–9. Old Boys' debate: *KESC*, February 1913, 7–8. JRRT in Birmingham, Christmas 1912: *Biography*, 59.

Oxford Old Edwardians: JRRT to EMB, 2 February 1913, in *Family Album*, 35; *KESC*, December 1911, 101.

RQG with Scopes in France: RQG to MCG, 7 and 13 April 1913.

College clubs: *Biography*, 54–5, 69, and photograph facing p. 83.

Cards on mantelpiece: *KESC*, December 1912, 85.

Draws cards: Priestman, *Life and Legend*, 26.

Role in Stapeldon Society: Stapeldon Society minutes. Colin Cullis was secretary under JRRT's presidency.

p.32 'I envy you Smith . . .': CLW to JRRT, 20 November 1912.

GBS on King Arthur: *KESC*, February 1913, 5–6.

'We have managed to relieve . . .': RQG to JRRT, 2 November 1913.

'I am very anxious to breathe . . .': CLW to JRRT, 12 December 1913. CLW presumably refers to JRRT's planned visit to Cambridge with GBS on 4 December (RQG to MCG, 30 November 1913).

Rugby match: undated report, *KESC*, March 1914, 11–12.

'We had such a splendid week-end . . .': RQG to MCG, 17 February 1914. Scopes, like GBS, was studying history at Corpus Christi.

p.33 'The only fear . . .': CLW to JRRT, 20 December 1913, written during a visit from GBS. 'Convention bids me . . .': RQG to JRRT, 4 January 1914, written when RQG had just received a summons from GBS to a TCBS meeting. There is no evidence for the view (*Biography*, 68) that JRRT wrote directly to RQG and CLW with news of his engagement.

JRRT's fear of being cut off from TCBS: GBS to JRRT, 9 February 1916.

p.34 'hoard the hill-haunter . . .': JRRT's undergraduate translation from the Latin *Gesta Danorum*, by the twelfth-century Danish chronicler Saxo Grammaticus; Bodleian Tolkien A21/5.

Speculations on Germanic legend: Bodleian Tolkien A21/9.

JRRT on Norse sagas: *The Stapeldon Magazine*, June 1913, 276.

p.35 Skeat Prize: *The Monsters and the Critics*, 192; *Biography*, 69.

J. Morris Jones's *Welsh Grammar* was published in 1913.

p.36 'the images drawn . . .'; 'One must begin with the elfin . . .': Essay Club minutes.

'international affairs . . .': *The Stapeldon Magazine*, June 1914, 93.

p.37 Prince Lichnowsky: Farnell, *An Oxonian Looks Back*, 327–8.

Sexcentenary dinner: *The Stapeldon Magazine*, June 1914, 44–5.

Chequers Club 'Binge': Priestman, *Life and Legend*, 25–6.

'All our festivities . . .': L. R. Farnell, 'Sexcentenary Celebration of the College', in *The Stapeldon Magazine*, December 1914, 109.

TWO *A young man with too much imagination*

p.38 'A real taste . . .': 'On Fairy-stories', *Monsters*, 135.

'I sense amongst all your pains . . .': *Letters*, 78.

p.39 Language experiments around the outbreak of war: JRRT headed one 1914 college notebook (Bodleian Tolkien A21/10) 'Toleka, Oksuortia', a rendering of his name and university in what looks like a nascent form of his 1915 invention, Qenya. Christopher Gilson has pointed out to the author that if *-eka* translates *-kien* (cognate with English 'keen'), the name *Toleka* may reflect the emergence of the Qenya root EKE (*Parma Eldalamberon* 12, 35, with derivatives referring to sharp objects such as swords and thorns), perhaps inspired by Old English *ecg*, 'edge', and Old High German *ekka*. If Tolkien was on the path towards Qenya now, its true codification, however, did not take place until 1915.

'But yet a pride is ours . . .': GBS, 'Anglia Valida in Senectute', *A Spring Harvest*, 50.

p.40 Cornish drawings: *Artist*, 24–5.
'The light got very "eerie"', etc.: *Biography*, 70–1.

pp.40–1 Birmingham recruitment: Carter, *Birmingham Pals*, 35–42.
'Patriotism insists . . .': *Birmingham Daily Post*, 28 August 1914, quoted in ibid. 36.

p.41 T. K. Barnsley, RQG, and the Old Edwardian recruits: RQG to EK, 4 October 1914.
Hilary Tolkien enlists: *Family Album*, 39; *Biography*, 72; Heath, *Service Record of King Edward's School*, 143.
'In those days chaps joined up . . .': *Letters*, 53.

p.42 Saxon paternal ancestry: *Letters*, 218; cf. *Biography*, 18–19.
Germanic tribes: Bodleian Tolkien A21/10.
'that noble northern spirit . . .': *Letters*, 55–6.
Wright and the wounded Germans: E. M. Wright, *The Life of Joseph Wright*, ii. 459.
'I have been accustomed . . .': *Letters*, 37.
'As the long prosperous years . . .': Jenkyns, *The Victorians and Ancient Greece*, 24.

p.43 'full of old lays . . .': 'The Homecoming of Beorhtnoth', *Poems and Stories*, 79.
'though as a whole . . .': *KESC*, March 1911, 19–20.
'man at war . . .': 'Beowulf: The Monsters and the Critics', *Monsters*, 18.
'a young man . . .': *Letters*, 53.
'I have nothing to say against Tolkien . . .': C. H. Jessop to Stephen Gateley, *Family Album*, 34.
'He did not join the Army . . .': RQG to EK, 10 March 1916.

p.44 'a lamentable bore', etc.: JRRT to Paul Bibire, 30 June 1969, in Hostetter, introduction to 'The Rivers and Beacon-hills of Gondor', *Vinyar Tengwar* 42, 6–7.
'*Eala Earendel* . . .': Grein/Wülcker, *Bibliothek der angelsächsischen Poesie*, 5. During this crucial period (19 June to 14 October 1914) Tolkien also borrowed Earle's *The Deeds of Beowulf* and Morris's *Old English Miscellany*; Exeter College library register.
'I felt a curious thrill . . .': 'The Notion Club Papers', *Sauron Defeated*, 236; see also 285, notes 35 and 36, and *Letters*, 385.

p.45 'The Voyage of Éarendel the Evening Star': *LT2*, 267–9; date clarified by Douglas A. Anderson.
'over the cup . . .', etc.: JRRT's undergraduate translation from *Beowulf*, line 1208, Bodleian Tolkien A21/9; 'magnificent expression', he remarked.
Éarendel and OE *ēar*: Hostetter, 'Over Middle-earth Sent Unto Men', *Mythlore* 65, 5–10. See also Hostetter and Smith, 'A Mythology for England', *Proceedings of the JRR Tolkien Centenary Conference*, 282.

p.48 'We are of course very mad . . .': RQG to MCG, 7 October 1914.
JRRT at the Oratory: *Letters*, 7.
Birmingham battalions: Carter, *Birmingham Pals*, 45–7, 63–4.
Despair: *Biography*, 30.
'the collapse of all my world': *Letters*, 393.
'It is awful . . .': *Biography*, 72.

pp.48–9 Wartime Oxford: Winter, 'Oxford and the First World War', 3–18. Exeter College: *The Stapeldon Magazine*, December 1914, 103–5.

p.49 'the Johnner': CLW to JRRT, 8 December 1916.
Undergraduate activities: Stapeldon Society minutes, 20 October 1914 (letters of support, 'lowering clouds . . .'); 27 October (sub-rector, the Superman); 3 November (spelling reform, 'no doubt . . . economising . . .'); 17 November 1914 (stringent economy).

pp.49–50 The Yser: Strachan, *The First World War*, i. 276. Orange Free State: ibid. 553.

p.50 Exonians and the university OTC: *The Stapeldon Magazine*, December 1914, 120.
'We had a drill . . .': *Letters*, 7.
Milton and Dante: RQG to MCG, 22 June 1913.
Rifles taken away: RQG to MCG, 5 November 1914.
'Oxford "sleepies"', etc.: *Biography*, 73.
Kalevala: *Letters*, 7, and *Biography*, 73.

p.51 Defence of nationalism: Stapeldon Society minutes, 17 November 1914.
'I don't defend "Deutschland über alles" . . .': JRRT to CLW, 16 November 1914.

Inherited linguistic aptitude: *Letters*, 213.

'I am indeed . . .': *Letters*, 218.

p.52 'in a speech attempting . . .' etc.: *KESC*, December 1910, 95.

'The mythological ballads . . .': *Biography*, 59. JRRT on 'The Finnish National Epic': Sundial Society minutes.

Essay Club meeting: *Letters*, 7–8.

p.53 GBS on 'Éarendel'; 'I don't know . . .': *Biography*, 75.

'Earendel's boat . . .': *LT2*, 261–3. The only invented names (*Kôr*, *Solosimpë*, *Eldamar*) were additions; apart from these the plot outline certainly predates JRRT's first onomastic experiments of 1915.

THREE *The Council of London*

p.54 GBS visits Cambridge; 'Tolkien was to come too . . .', etc.: RQG to MCG, 1 November 1914.

pp.54–5 Humorous styles of Barrowclough, CLW, and GBS: *KESC*, June 1912, 39–40. 'a gift for rapping out . . .': RQG to MCG, 1 November 1914. 'I played Rugger yesterday . . .': GBS to JRRT, 16 November 1916.

pp.55–6 Rift in TCBS: CLW to JRRT, 10 November ('I should only go there . . .', etc.), 15 November ('I tell you, when I had finished . . .', etc.), and 16 November 1914 ('TCBS über alles'); JRRT to CLW, 16 November 1914 ('alien spirit', etc.).

p.56 RQG enlists; fears missing 'Council': RQG to MCG, 6 and 10 December 1914. CLW delays enlisting: CLW to Dr Peter Liddle.

RCG urges delay: RQG to EK, 4 October 1914.

p.57 F. L. Lucas; 'He is not at all the sort . . .', etc.: RQG to MCG, 9 November 1914.

GBS undisciplined: GBS to JRRT, 12 January 1916.

'much more like a fish . . .': RQG to MCG, 6 December 1914.

GBS enlists: GBS service record; Heath, *Service Record of King Edward's School*, 133.

'Ave Atque Vale' later appeared in Smith, *A Spring Harvest*, 53–4.

p.58 Cherry Hinton: RQG to MCG, 10 December 1914.

Wiseman hilarity: RQG to MCG, 26 April 1914.

pp.58–9 Council of London: RQG to JRRT, 1 March 1915 ('absolutely undistracted . . .', 'I never spent . . .'); *Letters*, 10 ('the inspiration that . . .', 'the hope and ambitions . . .'); *Biography*, 73. CLW memoir, *OEG*, says erroneously that the last TCBS meeting was 'The Council of London . . . in the summer of 1914 in our house in Routh Road'. (They met again in Lichfield later in 1915.)
TCBS and 'allowable distance apart': JRRT to CLW, 16 November 1914.

p.59 *Kullervo*: *Letters*, 214–15.
A poet: *Biography*, 73.
'I sat on the ruined margin . . .': March 1915 version ('Sea Chant of an Elder Day'), *Artist*, 45–6, 66. Later, JRRT recalled writing versions of this poem as early as 1910; *The Shaping of Middle-earth*, 214–15.

p.60 'That Council . . .': *Letters*, 10.
The Land of Pohja: *Artist*, 44–5.
Skeat's *Complete Works of Geoffrey Chaucer* and Eliot's *Finnish Grammar* (14 November 1914 to 16 January 1915): Exeter College library register.
Studied Finnish for sake of Qenya: *Letters*, 214.
Birth of Qenya: *Parma Eldalamberon* 12, iii–v.
'an entirely different mythological world': 'A Secret Vice', *Monsters*, 218; *Letters*, 345.

p.61 *liri-* and cognates (footnote): *Parma Eldalamberon* 12, 54.

pp.61–3 Qenya sound-shift 'laws': ibid. 3–28; vocabulary: ibid., 29–106.

p.63 'I have quite lost now . . .': RQG to MCG, 13 February 1915.
Hardships of training: ibid., December 1914 to March 1915.
'My whole endurance . . .', etc.; JRRT urged to visit Cambridge: RQG to JRRT, 1 March 1915; CLW to JRRT, 2 March 1915.
Ultimatum: RQG, CLW, and GBS to JRRT, 6 March 1915.
'When we sent . . .': CLW to JRRT, 11 March 1915.

pp.63–4 Confidence on English course: *Biography*, 63.

p.64 Vacation work: 'Middle English Texts', Bodleian Tolkien A21/6.
JRRT borrowed vol. ii of Skeat's *Chaucer* and Morris's *Old English Miscellany*, a set text; Exeter College library register.

'Sea Chant of an Elder Day': *The Shaping of Middle-earth*, 214.

JRRT's poems circulate: GBS to JRRT [27 March 1915]; RQG to JRRT, 31 March 1915; CLW to JRRT, 15 April 1915.

GBS and 'The Voyage of Éarendel': *Biography*, 75. Eärendel 'fragments': GBS to JRRT [27 March 1915].

Georgian Poetry: GBS to JRRT [14 May, 25 June, 9 July 1915]. 'good authors'; JRRT's poems 'amazingly good': GBS to JRRT [22 March 1915]. GBS urges simplicity: ibid. [27 March 1915]. Conservative perplexity at JRRT's Romanticism: ibid., 9 February 1916.

Wade-Gery: Barlow, *Salford Brigade*, 75, 79.

pp.64–5 Wade-Gery on JRRT's poetry: GBS to JRRT [25 March 1915].

p.65 'Lo! young we are . . .': *Biography*, 74.

pp.65–6 'Why the Man in the Moon came down too soon': *A Northern Venture*, 17–20 (a close variant in *LT1* 204–6 is later; Hammond with Anderson, *Bibliography*, 247, 283). Favoured by GBS and Wade-Gery: GBS to JRRT [22 and 25 March 1915].

'The man in the moon . . .' (trad.): Iona and Peter Opie, *The Oxford Dictionary of Nursery Rhymes*, 346.

p.67 'Glastonbury': *A Spring Harvest*, 13–23. 'the most TCBSian mosaic . . .'; sent to JRRT: GBS to JRRT [14 March]; [25 March 1915].

Abortive Oxford meeting: CLW to JRRT, 31 March and 5, 13, and 15 April 1915; GBS to JRRT, 13 April 1915.

GBS's transfer: ibid., and GBS to JRRT [19 or 26 April 1915] ('think often of the TCBS . . .'); Army List May 1915. It probably took place on 10 May 1915, the start of the second of his two army payroll periods (GBS service record).

'You can be sure . . .', etc.: GBS to JRRT [19 or 26 April 1915].

p.68 'other literary Oxford lights', etc.: RQG to Mrs Cary Gilson, 12 September 1915.

Origin of 3rd Salford Pals: Latter, *Lancashire Fusiliers*, 99.

pp.68–9 Lancashire Fusiliers up to the landing of the 1st Battalion at Gallipoli: Barlow, *Salford Brigade*, pp. 15–19.

p.70 'I can't think where . . .', etc.: CLW to JRRT, 25 April 1915.

FOUR *The shores of Faërie*

p.71 'Will shall be the sterner . . .': 'The Homecoming of Beorhtnoth Beorhthelm's Son', in *Poems and Stories*, 79.

p.72 Rupert Brooke: GBS to JRRT, 10 July 1915.

pp.72–3 'You and Me and the Cottage of Lost Play': references are to the earliest form, *LT1*, 27–30.

p.73 'Indescribable but . . .': *Biography*, 47.

pp.73–4 'Goblin Feet': Cole and Earp (eds.), *Oxford Poetry 1915*, 120–1; excerpted in *Biography*, 74–5.

pp.74–5 'Tinfang Warble': version published in a Catholic journal in Oxford referred to by JRRT as '*I.U.M.*' (presumably the *Inter-university Magazine*, the journal of the Federation of University Catholic Societies), 1927, and *LT1*, 108 (Hammond with Anderson, *Bibliography*, 344). The earliest, unpublished form was shorter (Douglas A. Anderson to the author).

p.75 'little one', etc.: *Biography*, 67.
'I wish the unhappy . . .': *LT1*, 32.
Fading of the Elves: *LT1*, 32, 235; *LT2*, 142, 159, 281; *Morgoth's Ring*, 219, 342.

p.76 'mistook elves for gnomes . . .': CLW to JRRT, 15 April 1915.
'a strange race . . .': MacDonald, *The Princess and the Goblin*, 3.
gnome: *Letters*, 318, 449; *The Peoples of Middle-earth*, 76–7; *Parma Eldalamberon* 12, 67.
'a little precious': RWR to JRRT, 2 August 1915. 'rather spoiled': ibid., 19 September 1915.

p.77 'a sort of talisman': Charlotte Gear and Lionel Lambourne in Martineau (ed.), *Victorian Fairy Painting*, 153.
'the war called up . . .': Purkiss, *Troublesome Things*, 279–80. The play she cites is *Britain's Defenders, or Peggy's peep into fairyland, a fairy play*, Samuel French, 1917, 6.
'There was a fantastic "scheme" . . .': RQG to MCG, 4 March 1915.
'I should as soon . . .': MacDonald, 'The Fantastic Imagination', *The Complete Fairy Tales*, 5.

Recovery, escape and consolation: 'On Fairy-stories', *Monsters*, 145–54.

p.78 Philanthropist: Frank Pick, commercial manager of London Underground (Hutchinson, *London Transport Posters*, 21, and plate 16).

'Unhappily a great many . . .': Jellicoe, foreword to Pearce, *The Navy Book of Fairy Tales*.

pp.78–9 'Kôr: In a City Lost and Dead': *LT1*, 136.

'Henty, Haggard . . .': *KESC*, October 1911, 73; *The Lost Explorers*: ibid., July 1912, 17.

p.79 'I know not how . . .': Haggard, *She*, 262–3.

p.80 'Kôr' and *Tanaqui*: *Artist*, 47.

Qenya lexicon: *Parma Eldalamberon* 12, 35, 42, 48.

pp.80–1 Eärendel's Atlantic voyagings: *LT2*, 261. The added phrases accord with the early lexicon entries mentioned already, and must date from the same time.

p.81 Qenya lexicon date: Christopher Gilson, 'Chronology', *Parma Eldalamberon* 12, x–xvii, argues that composition began no earlier than spring 1915. A few points may be added that suggest it began no later than April. First, the long loan of Eliot's *Finnish Grammar* coincides with the creative breakthrough that followed the December 1914 'Council of London'. Second, the poem 'Kôr' accords perfectly with the lexicon at the very points where it differs from Haggard. Third, the lexicon was undoubtedly in existence by early July, yet JRRT is less likely to have found time to work on it in May and June than between December 1915 and April.

The Shores of Faëry (painting): *Artist*, 47–8. The poem of the same title that accompanies the painting was probably added in July (Douglas A. Anderson to the author).

Shakespeare: *Biography*, 27–8; *Letters*, 88; Shippey, *Author of the Century*, 192–5.

p.82 Book loans: Exeter College library register.

'Don't worry about Schools . . .': GBS to JRRT [5 June].

Welsh grammar: ibid. [14 May].

English finalists: *The Times*, 3 July 1915, 6.

Stainforth certain to take JRRT: GBS to JRRT [10 June 1915].

'matters Martian', etc.: GBS to JRRT [19 June 1915].
GBS promoted (on 16 June): *The Times*, 16 July 1915, 15.
'Do not be afraid . . .': GBS to JRRT [28 June 1915]. To Brough Hall Camp: ibid. [19 June 1915].

pp.82–3 RQG to Lindrick Camp: RQG to MCG, 19 and 22 June 1915.

p.83 'bolted': *Letters*, 53.
Enlistment: JRRT service record.
Schools results: *The Times*, 3 July 1915, 6. 'one of the highest distinctions', etc.: GBS to JRRT [4 July].
With EMB in Warwick: GBS to JRRT [4 July] 1915.

pp.83–4 'The Shores of Faëry' (poem): version from the 'Book of Ishness', *Artist*, 48–9. Variants appear in *Biography*, 76–7, and (alongside evidence for composition date) *LT2*, 271–2. 'First poem . . .': *LT2*, 271; start of a 'Lay of Eärendel': *Biography*, 76. Perhaps 'The Shores of Faëry' was meant to introduce the already existing 'Eärendel fragments'.

p.85 Fusion of language and mythology: by contrast, September 1914's 'The Voyage of Éarendel the Evening Star' featured aspects of a Tolkienian cosmology but none of the nomenclature that would accompany them later; the name *Éarendel* was Old English, not Qenya.
'It was just as . . .', etc.: *Letters*, 231.
'thought and experience . . .': ibid., 144; see also 345.
Wartime rumours: Fussell, *The Great War and Modern Memory*, 116–24.

pp.85–6 'Angels of Mons': ibid., 115–16; Gilbert, *First World War*, 58. Machen's 'The Bowmen' appeared in the London *Evening News* on 29 September 1914.

p.86 Wartime language: Strachan, *The First World War*, i. 142.
Neverland and Valinor: on a copy of 'The Shores of Faëry' JRRT wrote much later 'Valinor [?thought of about] 1910' (*LT2*, 271). This was the year he saw *Peter Pan*; but it seems perhaps too early for the conception of Valinor.

pp.86–7 *Guingelot*: JRRT stated the influence of this name in a note from 1968 or later (*The Peoples of Middle-earth*, 371). Cf. *The Lays of Beleriand*, 143–4. 'Concerning Wade . . .': Thomas Speght, in Skeat's *Complete Works of Chaucer*, v. 356–7 (borrowed by JRRT from Exeter College library over Christmas 1914).

'timbered a boat . . .', etc.: Grimm, *Teutonic Mythology*, i. 376–8; cf. Chambers, *Widsith*, 95–100, on Wade. For JRRT's use of Germanic sources, see especially Shippey, *The Road to Middle-earth*.

p.87 'and the meaning . . .', etc.: CLW to JRRT, 11 July 1915. Naval recruitment advertisement: CLW to Dr Peter Liddle.

p.88 'You have been posted . . .': Col. W. Elliot to JRRT, 9 July 1915 (Bodleian Tolkien).

'I am simply bowled over . . .': GBS to JRRT [13 July 1915]. Safer in 13th LF: ibid. [18 July 1915].

To Bedford; allowance: Col. W. Elliot to JRRT (Bodleian Tolkien). 'All else seems to me . . .', etc.: GBS to JRRT [19 June 1915].

FIVE *Benighted wanderers*

p.89 Report to Col. Tobin: Col. W. Elliot to JRRT (Bodleian Tolkien). At Bedford: *Biography*, 77. Comfortable: RWR to JRRT, 2 August 1915.

'philosophick': GBS to JRRT [22 July 1915]. Chances of transfer; '*tact, tact, tact*', etc.: ibid. [23 July 1915].

pp.89–91 'The Happy Mariners': *The Stapeldon Magazine*, June 1920 (with 'Earendel' where I provide 'Eärendel'). The 1915 form is unpublished. A 1940 revision appears in *LT2*, 273–6.

p.91 Waking of the Sleeper in the Tower of Pearl: *LT1*, 15.

pp.91–2 'Lost Tales' cosmology and 'the song of the Sleeper': 'The Hiding of Valinor', in *LT1*, 215–16.

p.92 '"The Happy Mariners" was apparently . . .': *LT2*, 274.

pp.92–3 Submissions to *Oxford Poetry*: GBS to JRRT [23 July 1915]. GBS first proposed to submit verse in May (ibid. [14 May 1915]). In the event it included one poem apiece by JRRT and GBS, and three by Wade-Gery.

p.93 RWR: *KESC*, December 1921, 24; December 1922, 79–80; obituary, *OEG*, 1948.

Response to JRRT's verse: RWR to JRRT, 19 July. Advice on publishing a collection: ibid., 2 August 1915.

p.94 Lichfield units (9th Lincolnshires, 13th and 14th Sherwood Foresters, 14th Manchesters); 50 officers: monthly Army returns.

View of high-ranking officers; 'Gentlemen are non-existent . . .': *Biography*, 77–8. Contrary to Carpenter's assertion, this does not mean JRRT disliked the majority of other officers, the subalterns with whom he spent most of his time.

'All the hot days . . .': *Letters*, 8.

'What makes it so . . .', 'toad under the harrow', Fr Reade: *Letters*, 78. 'war multiplies . . .', 'men and things': ibid. 73. 'a deep sympathy . . .': ibid. 54.

p.95 'It isn't the tough stuff . . .': *Letters*, 46.

Icelandic: *Biography*, 78. RQG's designs: RQG to MCG. 'early work', etc.: *Letters*, 231.

pp.95–6 'A Song of Aryador': *LT1*, 138–9.

Impact of Mercian language and culture on JRRT: see Shippey, *Author of the Century*, 90–7, and *The Road to Middle-earth*, 111–16. For Tamworth as the capital of the Middle Kingdom in *Farmer Giles of Ham*, see ibid. 89.

p.96 *Aryador*: *Parma Eldalamberon* 12, 32 (with thanks to Patrick Wynne).

Aryan: Mallory, *In Search of the Indo-Europeans*, 126.

p.97 Gothic source of *miruvōrë*: JRRT note in *Parma Eldalamberon* 12, xi.

pp.97–8 'Iumbo, or ye Kinde of ye Oliphaunt': one of two poems comprising 'Adventures in Unnatural History and Medieval Metres, being The Freaks of Fisiologus', *The Stapeldon Magazine*, vii. 40 (June 1927), 125.

p.98 The Irminsûl: *Teutonic Mythology*, i. 115–19; 'works of the giants': 'Philology: General Works', in Lee and Boas (eds.), *The Year's Work in English Studies 1923*, 21. *pelekus*, *parasu*: Mallory, *In Search of the Indo-Europeans*, 122 (with thanks to Bill Welden).

ond: *Letters*, 410. See Carl F. Hostetter and Patrick Wynne, *Vinyar Tengwar* 30, 8–25.

pp.98–9 'A Song of Aryador': *LTI*, 138–9.

p.100 'I am really angry with myself . . .': RQG to JRRT, 13 September 1915. RQG received poems: ibid., 31 March 1915. Sent them on: CLW to JRRT, 15 April 1915.
RQG declares love for EK: RQG to MCG, 18 April, 10 June, and 17 October 1915. Her father's warning: Wilson King to RCG, 30 November 1915.
'a compartmented life': JRRT to CLW, 16 November 1914.

p.101 'of course includes your missis': CLW to JRRT, 4 February 1916.
Silence from RQG: GBS to JRRT [14 May, 28 June and 18 July 1915]. His summer and influenza: RQG to MCG. News of *Oxford Poetry*: MCG to RQG, 12 September. 'I confess that I have often . . .', etc.: RQG to JRRT, 13 September 1915.
Second sheaf of poems; 'At times like this . . .': RQG to JRRT, 17 September 1915.

pp.101–2 Council of Lichfield: ibid., 21, 23, and 24 September 1915. 'that delightful . . .': GBS to JRRT, 6 October 1915.

p.102 GBS and RQG on Salisbury Plain, 'The rain stopped . . .': RQG to MCG, 5 October 1915. 'Songs on the Downs': GBS, *A Spring Harvest*, 48. 'The steps I have taken . . .': GBS to JRRT, 6 October.

p.103 They visit Bath; 'Gibbonian periods': RQG to MCG, 17 October 1915. 'I feel that we shall . . .': GBS to JRRT, 6 October.
They urge JRRT to publish: RQG to JRRT, 5 October 1915; GBS to JRRT, 9 October 1915.
Cannock Chase camps: Whitehouse and Whitehouse, *A Town for Four Winters*. 3rd Reserve Infantry Brigade Officers' Company: RQG to JRRT, 19 October and 21 November 1915.

p.104 'These grey days . . .': *Biography*, 78. 'The usual kind of morning . . .': JRRT to EMB, 26 November 1915, in *Letters*, 8. JRRT unhappy and EMB unwell: CLW to JRRT, 27 October 1915; RQG to JRRT, 21 November 1915.

pp.104–6 TCBS in London without JRRT: GBS to JRRT, 24 October 1915 ('to drive from life . . .', 'It struck me last night . . .'); RQG to JRRT, 31 October 1915 ('I never before felt . . .', 'I suddenly saw . . .'); CLW to JRRT, 27 October 1915 ('I laughed a little . . .', 'bit of fun', 'war babies', 'woman was just . . .', 'You and GBS . . .', 'The TCBS stays . . .'). At school, CLW and JRRT had played rugby for Measures' house against Richards' house.

p.106 'sons of culture', etc.: GBS, 'To the Cultured', *A Spring Harvest*, 60. 'I have never read anything . . .': GBS to JRRT, 24 October 1915.

p.107 'the fairies came . . .': *Parma Eldalamberon* 12, 35.

pp.107–10 'Kortirion among the Trees': quotations are from the earliest published version, only slightly changed from the original MSS; *LT1*, 32–6.

p.108 'Ah! like gold . . .': *The Lord of the Rings*, 368.

p.109 'England in June attire . . .' etc.: Graves, 'To Robert Nichols', *Fairies and Fusiliers*.

p.110 Week of frost: RQG to MCG, 17 and 21 November 1915. 'Kortirion' textual history: *Letters*, 8; RQG to JRRT, 21 and 26 November 1915; RQG to Estelle King, 2 December. Stray workings: RQG to JRRT, 19 October. Tolkien recalled writing 'Kortirion' between 21 and 28 November in Warwick; yet he was back in camp by 25 November; *LT1*, 32.

pp.110–11 'I am now 21 . . .': GBS to JRRT, 19 October 1915. Units departing Salisbury Plain: RQG to MCG, 17 November 1915; Carter, *Birmingham Pals*, 90–1. GBS's movements, 'It is impossible . . .': RQG to JRRT, 21 November 1915.

p.111 Barrowclough: MCG to RQG, 12 September 1915; RW Reynolds to JRRT, 19 September 1915. T. K. Barnsley: Ross, *The Coldstream Guards*, i. 434; RQG to MCG, 27 August, 31 October 1915.
'We are now so pledged . . .': GBS to JRRT, 24 October 1915. 19th LF embark for France: Barlow, *Salford Brigade*, 73; Latter, *Lancashire Fusiliers*, 99. Stedman, *Salford Pals*, 64. 'to the peril . . .': GBS to JRRT, 2 December 1915.

pp.112–13 'Habbanan beneath the Stars': *LT1*, 91–2.

p.112 '*perilmë metto* . . .': *Parma Eldalamberon* 12, 73.

p.113 'I had always . . .': 'The Ethics of Elfland', in Auden (ed.), *G. K. Chesterton: a selection*, 187.

SIX *Too long in slumber*

p.114 Codes and alphabets: *Biography*, 40; Priestman, *Life and Legend*, 13, 17, 18.
Milne: Thwaite, *A. A. Milne*, 167.
To Brocton Camp: monthly Army returns. Envelope codework: RQG to JRRT, 26 December 1915; CLW to JRRT, 30 December 1915.

pp.114–15 Equipment training: *Biography*, 78; JRRT provisional instructor's certificate (Bodleian Tolkien).

p.115 Egypt rumour, 'Imagine the general rejoicing . . .', etc.: RQG to JRRT, 26 December 1915.
'Donna': the name RQG and his sister Molly gave to Marianne Dunstall when she married their father in 1909; RQG to MCG, 10 August 1909.
RQG and EK: RQG to MCG, 17 October and 8 November 1915; MCG to EK, 26 December 1915.
'Kortirion': RQG to EK, 2 December 1915.
'What a wonderful year! . . .': ibid., New Year 1915–16.

pp.115–16 CLW to the *Superb*: CLW to Dr Peter Liddle. 'Then I plunge . . .': CLW to JRRT, 30 December 1915. Cruiser *Natal* sinks: Gilbert, *First World War*, 222. Torpedo nets: Phil Russell to the author.

p.116 RQG embarks; 'I wish I could describe . . .': RQG to EK, 8 January 1916. Italy: ibid., 19 February 1916. New Testament and *Odyssey*: RQG to MCG, 7 January 1916.
Oxford Poetry 1915: Hammond with Anderson, *Bibliography*, 279–80. 'The idols have fallen . . .': *The Oxford Magazine*, 10 December 1915, 127–8.

p.117 'The truth is . . .': GBS to JRRT, 22 December 1915. 'terrible fellow', etc.: ibid., 12 January 1916. 2nd Manchesters: Platt papers.

pp.117–18 'It is a strange and dreary . . .': RQG to EK, 4 February 1916. 'the real business of life': RQG to MCG, 7 April 1912. RQG's absurd vision: Lt. P. V. Emrys-Evans to RCG, 13 July 1916. (Emrys-Evans, 11th Suffolks, was later a member of parliament and under-secretary in the British Dominions Office.)

pp.118–19 'a good friend of mine . . .', etc.: GBS to JRRT, 3 February 1916. (The 'three other heroes' include Tolkien again, in addition to Gilson and Wiseman.)

19th LF in Thiepval Wood trenches, 2–6 February 1916: war diary; Platt papers. Patrols: Winter, *Death's Men*, 87–8.

2nd Lt. A. C. Dixon: CWGC.

p.119 *The Trumpets of Faërie*: Priestman, *Life and Legend*, 30; GBS to JRRT, 9 February 1916 ('I remember how . . .'). JRRT must despatch 'Kortirion': ibid., 22 February 1916.

'too many precious stones': RQG to JRRT, 26 December 1915.

'I am immensely braced . . .': CLW to JRRT, 4 February 1916.

p.120 'there was more form . . .': RWR to JRRT, 10 March 1916.

pp.121–2 Quarrel over JRRT's 'freakish' earlier poetry: CLW to JRRT, 1 March ('Old days, Harborne Road . . .', etc.) and 14 March 1916 ('I say they are not . . .', etc.).

'the Eldar . . .': JRRT, quoted in ibid.

p.122 'lacking in the strings . . .', etc.: RQG to EK, 14 January 1916.

p.123 'Legend': GBS, *A Spring Harvest*, 22.

p.124 *blimp*: JRRT, 'Philology: General Works', in Lee and Boas (eds.), *The Year's Work in English Studies 1923*, 52. '*Bosch*': GBS to JRRT, 12 January 1916. 'I fully intended . . .': RQG to MCG, 12 April 1916.

p.125 'in a dirty wet marquee . . .': 'A Secret Vice', *Monsters*, 199. 'I have been reading up . . .': JRRT to EMT, 2 March 1916 (*Letters*, 8).

November quatrain ('Narqelion'): Douglas A. Anderson to the author. The second version appears in *Mythlore* 56, 48, with an analysis by Paul Nolan Hyde, and in *Vinyar Tengwar* 40, 8, with an analysis by Christopher Gilson.

pp.125–7 State of the mythology: this reconstruction is based primarily on the Qenya lexicon, along with the available poetry of 1915, and notes on Eärendel's Atlantic wanderings and 'The Shores of Faëry' (*LT2*, 261–2; internal evidence suggests other outlines in *LT2*, 253ff., were written later). JRRT is unlikely to have risked taking the lexicon on active service, and its state *circa* March 1916 may be broadly surmised by excluding all entries lacking in 'The Poetic and

Mythologic Words of Eldarissa', a list copied from it probably soon after he returned to England (*Parma Eldalamberon* 12, xvii–xxi). Some details appearing only in that list are assumed to postdate the initial lexicon phase, and omitted here. The reconstruction takes no account of unpublished poems, notes or outlines, and covers a period (beginning in early 1915) in which conceptions were probably very fluid.

p.128 Personal significance of *Erinti*, etc.: Gilson, '*Narqelion* and the Early Lexicons', *Vinyar Tengwar* 40, 9.
Vocabulary for wartime: this selection takes no account of chronology of composition (in contrast to the reconstructed 'state of the mythology' above). Only *enya*, *kasiën*, *makil* and *Kalimban*, etc., seem likely to have predated the Somme.
'the "Germanic" ideal': *Letters*, 55.

p.129 'bleed to death': Gilbert, *First World War*, 221.
'intolerable', etc.: *Letters*, 53.

pp.129–30 Marriage: *Biography*, 78. 'My goodness . . .': GBS to JRRT, 9 February 1916. 'on the contrary . . .': CLW to JRRT, 1 March 1916. 'The imminence . . .': RQG to MCG, 9 March 1916. 'I rejoice . . .': RQG to JRRT, 9 March 1916.

p.130 'always had something . . .': RQG to EK, 10 March 1916.
Degree ceremony: How, *Register of Exeter College*.

pp.130–3 'The Wanderer's Allegiance': quotations are from the November 1916 revision, 'The Town of Dreams and the City of Present Sorrow', *LT2*, 295–6.

p.130 Paternal ancestors in Germania: CLW saw only the revised poem, more than a year later; it is apparent that JRRT did not explain it all to him and, as CLW suspected ('Perhaps I know too much or too little . . .'), some of his suppositions may be wrong. CLW to JRRT, 4 March 1917.

p.134 Marriage service: Priscilla Tolkien in *Angerthas in English* 3, 5.
Honeymoon: *Biography*, 80. *The Trumpets of Faërie*: Priestman, *Life and Legend*, 30.
Farnley Park: CLW to JRRT, 14 March 1916. Test results: JRRT provisional instructor's certificate (Bodleian Tolkien);

Encyclopaedia Britannica, 11th edition. Leave: JRRT to Capt. C. A. McAllard, 8 May 1916 (Bodleian Tolkien).
Mrs Kendrick: GBS to JRRT, 26 May 1916.

pp.134–5 Nuptial blessing: Priscilla Tolkien in *Angerthas in English* 3, p. 5.

p.135 'Now spring has come . . .': GBS, 'April 1916', *A Spring Harvest*, 65. 'I wish another council . . .': GBS to JRRT, 12 January 1916. *Odyssey*: ibid., 4 March 1916. April Fool's: ibid., 6 April 1916.

pp.135–6 GBS at Great Haywood: GBS to JRRT, 23, 24, and 26 May 1916. 'Nothing could be more . . .': ibid. [1 June 1916].

p.136 'There be still some . . .': GBS, 'April 1916', *A Spring Harvest*, 65.
School exams, 'The real days . . .': CLW to JRRT, 14 March 1916. 'oasis': cited in RQG to JRRT, 22 June 1916.
'The most magnificent . . .': GBS to JRRT [23 July 1915].

p.137 'world-shaking power': cited in CLW to JRRT, 16 November 1914.
'travail underground': RQG to JRRT, 9 March 1916. 'I have faith . . .': ibid., 21 November 1915. 'Providence insists . . .': GBS to JRRT [13 July 1915].
'Really you three . . .': CLW to JRRT, 4 February 1916.
'republic': GBS to JRRT, 12 January 1916.
Embarkation orders: 13th LF adjutant to JRRT, 2 June 1916 (Bodleian Tolkien).

p.138 Plough and Harrow: *Family Album*, 39. Departure: *Biography*, 80. 'Junior officers . . .': Cater, *The Daily Telegraph*, 29 November 2001, 23.

SEVEN *Larkspur and Canterbury-bells*

From JRRT's arrival on the Somme until the end of Chapter 10, unless otherwise stated:
JRRT's movements are derived from his diary.
11th LF activities are drawn from the battalion's war diary, supplemented by those of the 74th Brigade HQ; 13th Cheshires, 9th Loyal North Lancashires, and 2nd Royal Irish Rifles; the 25th Division and its signal company. Military histories consulted

include principally *The Lancashire Fusiliers' Annual 1917*, 213–34; Latter, *Lancashire Fusiliers*; Kincaid-Smith, *The 25th Division in France and Flanders*, 10–22.

Great War soldiers' experience: especially Winter, *Death's Men*, and for the Battle of the Somme itself Keegan, *The Face of Battle*.

Topography and weather: various sources, notably Gliddon, *When the Barrage Lifts*.

p.141 Scapa Flow: CLW to Dr Peter Liddle; CLW to JRRT, 4 February 1916. 'The Snotty . . .': ibid., 4 March [1917].

p.142 Jutland: CLW to Dr Peter Liddle ('No one below decks . . .'); Arthur J. Marder, *From the Dreadnought to Scapa Flow*, iii. 100; *The Battle of Jutland: Official Despatches*, 123–5, 365–7.

p.143 Train journey: JRRT diary; 13th LF adjutant to JRRT, 2 June 1916 (Bodleian Tolkien).

Channel crossing: JRRT diary; 'The Lonely Isle', *Leeds University Verse 1914–1924*, 57. Gunship escorts were routine. RQG sketches: RQG to EK, 6 June 1916. Hoy: CLW to Dr Peter Liddle.

pp.143–4 Calais to Étaples: JRRT diary; *Biography*, 80.

p.144 Lt. W. H. Reynolds: Latter, *Lancashire Fusiliers*, 124. 'Habbanan': *LT1*, 91. Details of a 25th Division officer's life at Étaples come from the diary of Capt. Lionel Ferguson of the 13th Cheshires (hereafter 'Ferguson diary'), who was there at virtually the same time as JRRT. (Contrary to *Biography*, 81, JRRT did not meet up with his battalion proper until he reached the Somme hinterland.)

pp.144–5 'The Lonely Isle': *Leeds University Verse 1914–1924*, 57. Dedication: *LT1*, 25.

p.145 'I do pray for you . . .': GBS to JRRT, 9 June 1916.

p.146 Spies; a 'show': Ferguson diary. Trench working party: RQG to RCG, 25 June 1916. 'war was not now . . .': RQG on sportsmanship, *KESC*, March 1910, 5. 'the war at last . . .': RQG to EK, 17 June 1916. 'I have never felt . . .': RQG to JRRT, 22 June 1916. Amiens cathedral: ibid., 7 May 1916. GBS tantalizingly near: RQG to EK, 6 and 8 May 1916. Fear for

RQG's sanity: CLW to JRRT, 1 March 1916; perhaps simply thinking of RQG's sensitive nature. 'I feel now as if . . .': RQG to EK, 13 June 1916.

p.147 'When it comes down to . . .': ibid., 9 June 1916.
Peace rumour; 'I often think of the extraordinary . . .': RQG to RCG, 25 June 1916. Artillery barrage: Middlebrook, *The First Day on the Somme*, 87–8.

pp.147–8 Étaples to Rubempré: JRRT diary; *Biography*, 81. The 11th LF did not travel with JRRT to Rubempré, though a draft of troops may have: the battalion received 248 new men in June.

p.148 Rubempré: *Biography*, 81; Ferguson diary; Platt papers.

pp.148–9 Provenance of 25th Division soldiers: Latter, *Lancashire Fusiliers*, 93–4 and vol. ii. 146; Ferguson diary. Loos tradition: Evers memoir.

p.149 Platoon command: available evidence does not reveal whether Tolkien ever ran a platoon, a routine responsibility of many subalterns.
Officer numbers: 25th Division administrative staff war diary. JRRT in 'A' Company: mess accounts and other items (Bodleian Tolkien). No officers from 13th LF: *Army Book* officer lists, 1915–16. 'were in many cases . . .': *Biography*, 81. 'the most improper job . . .': *Letters*, 64.

p.150 Rubempré to Warloy-Baillon: 11th LF war diary.
'My dear John Ronald . . .': GBS to JRRT, 25 June 1916.
'Larkspur and Canterbury-bells . . .': RQG to EK, 25 June 1916. Bécourt château (footnote): Murphy, *History of the Suffolk Regiment*, 154.

p.151 'One of the few . . .': RQG to RCG, 25 June 1916.
'It is no use harrowing . . .': quoted in Lt. P. V. Emrys-Evans to RCG, 13 July 1916.

EIGHT *A bitter winnowing*

p.152 During the barrage: Middlebrook, *The First Day on the Somme*, 115–20. Cavalry: Peacock, 'A Rendezvous with Death', 317–18, 325. 'drum-fire': Ferguson diary. 'as if Wotan . . .': Lewis, *Saggitarius Rising*, 103.

11th Suffolks on eve of battle: Murphy, *The History of the Suffolk Regiment*, 154; *The First Day on the Somme*, 113.

pp.152–3 Walkover; rum: Senescall memoir.

p.153 RQG before battle: Pte. A. Bradnam to RCG, 14 July 1916 and undated [July 1916].

pp.153–5 11th Suffolks, 1 July: war diaries of the battalion, 101st Brigade and 34th Division; Peacock, 'A Rendezvous with Death'. Stedman, *Somme: La Boisselle*, 54–7; Murphy, *The History of the Suffolk Regiment*; Senescall memoir.

p.154 'dear, stupid, agricultural platoon': RQG to Estelle King, 9 April 1915.

p.155 'I am astonished . . .': RQG to MCG, undated, 1916. (Cf. Keegan, *The Face of Battle*, 234–6.)

'just like corn . . .': Jimmy Walton, 11th Suffolks, in Peacock, 'A Rendezvous with Death', 344.

'the most absolute barrier . . .': RQG to EK, 5 February 1916.

Order not to assist wounded: 11th Suffolks war diary.

pp.155–6 RQG's death: Capt. C. L. Morgan to RCG, 12 July 1916 ('perfectly calmly . . .'); Pte. A. Bradnam to MCG, 14 July 1916; Major P. F. Morton to RCG, 12 July 1916; Lt. P. V. Emrys-Evans to RCG, 13 July; a wounded company commander (perhaps Major Morton himself) quoted in Murphy, *The History of the Suffolk Regiment*; Cpl. Ashley Hicks, statement to Red Cross, 8 August 1916. There is a measure of agreement between these accounts.

p.156 RQG dead in trench: Pte. G. Gordon to RCG, 20 July 1916. Other accounts say RQG was the first to be wounded as the 11th Suffolks went over the top (Pte. W. Prentice, statement to the Red Cross, 17 August 1916); that he was hit by gunfire as he cut the enemy wire (MCG to Rachel King, 10 July 1916). As late as the fourth week in July, Cpl. H. Spalding reported seeing him alive in England (RQG service record).

Gilson household: MCG to RQG, 26 June 1916. He probably never received this letter.

'I hope I may never . . .': RQG to EK, 6 May 1916. 'in a big affair . . .': Lt. P. V. Emrys-Evans to RCG, 13 July 1916. 'It was the final . . .': 2nd Lt. A. R. Wright (later Sir Andrew Wright, governor of Cyprus) to RCG, 18 July 1916.

Only Wright unhurt: Lt. P. V. Emrys-Evans to RCG, 13 July 1916.

p.157 Mass: JRRT diary. Padre averse to Catholics: Evers memoir. Chaplain in Royal Irish Rifles: Ferguson diary.

pp.157–8 Scenes and rumours at Warloy-Baillon and Bouzincourt, 1–4 July: Ferguson diary. Burials: *Biography*, 82.

p.158 'German captive-balloons . . .': JRRT, 'Philology: General Works', in Boas and Herford (eds.), *The Year's Work in English Studies 1924*, 51.

34th Division losses: Peacock, 'A Rendezvous with Death', 329.

JRRT at Bouzincourt: *Biography*, 82. 'the fiery trial': GBS to JRRT, 9 June 1916; 'You must expect . . .': ibid., 25 June 1916. 'ordeal': RQG to JRRT, 22 June 1916.

74th Brigade movements, 5 July: 11th LF war diary; *Lancashire Fusiliers' Annual 1917*, 214. All four companies of the 11th LF left Bouzincourt (contrary to *Biography*, 83); as a matter of routine, some men remained behind.

pp.159–60 19th Lancashire Fusiliers, from June to 4 July: war diary, including GBS's intelligence reports; Stedman, *Salford Pals*, 93–6, 106–12; Latter, *Lancashire Fusiliers*, 134–6; Barlow, *Salford Brigade*, 74–5.

p.159 Intelligence officer: 19th LF war diary. (GBS's predecessor had lost a hand while instructing a class in bombing; Latter, *Lancashire Fusiliers*, 120.)

GBS's location in wood: in his new role he would certainly have been with the commanding officer, Lt.-Col. J. M. A. Graham, who was here; Stedman, *Salford Pals*, 116.

p.161 GBS at Bouzincourt: perhaps arranging accommodation for his battalion, under the *ad hoc* personnel arrangements surrounding the battle. He was later official billeting officer (19th LF war diary).

Signal office shelled: 25th Division signal company war diary. 19th LF reorganize: *Salford Pals*, 113. Bouzincourt reunion: JRRT diary; *Biography*, 83.

pp.161–2 La Boisselle and Ovillers, 7–10 July: 11th LF war diary; *Lancashire Fusiliers' Annual 1917*, 215–19. The dead: Ferguson diary.

p.162 Traffic figures: from a 21–22 July census at Fricourt; Taylor, *English History 1914–1945*, 60.
'That road was like . . .': Carrington, *A Subaltern's War*, 36–7. In eighty pages he describes a journey from Bouzincourt to battle at Ovillers on the same dates and almost exactly the same route as JRRT.

pp.162–4 To La Boisselle, 14 July: 11th LF war diary; *Lancashire Fusiliers' Annual 1917*, 220; Carrington, *A Subaltern's War*, 36–43; Brenan, *A Life of One's Own*, 205–7; Evers memoir; Gliddon, *When the Barrage Lifts*.

p.163 'Something in the make . . .': Masefield, *The Old Front Line*.
'like a volcano . . .': *The Times*, July 1916, 9.

pp.164–6 11th LF supports the 7th Brigade, 14–15 July: war diaries of 11th LF, 25th Division HQ, 74th and 7th Brigade HQs, and 8th Loyal North Lancashires and 10th Cheshires (the 7th Brigade battalions that fought alongside Tolkien's); Latter, *Lancashire Fusiliers*, 151; *Lancashire Fusiliers' Annual 1917*, 220–1.

p.164 First aid: Keegan, *The Face of Battle*, 266.

pp.164–5 La Boisselle and beyond, 14 July: Ferguson diary; Carrington, *A Subaltern's War*, 39, 43–4 ('a new country . . .'), 56 (the ambulance and the dead), 89.

p.165 JRRT at Ovillers: *Biography*, 84, asserts that JRRT's role was confined to signalling. In fact, in the face of high officer casualties, any subaltern faced possibly being put in charge of a platoon.

pp.165–6 Signals: Solano (ed.), *Signalling*, 11; 'Summary of training circulars (advisory)' issued to JRRT (Bodleian Tolkien).

pp.166–8 11th LF in the 74th Brigade attack on Ovillers, 15–17 July: war diaries of the battalion and brigade, the 25th Division HQ and signal company, 13th Cheshires, 144th Brigade, 1/4th Gloucesters and 1/7th Worcesters, and the 143rd Brigade and 1/5th Royal Warwickshires; Kincaid-Smith, *The 25th Division in France*, 14; Latter, *Lancashire Fusiliers*, 151–2; *Lancashire*

Fusiliers' Annual 1917, 221–2; ; Miles, *Military Operations*, 101; Stedman, *Somme: La Boisselle*, 95.

p.166 'a treacherous, chaotic region . . .': Brenan, *A Life of One's Own*, 207 (on travelling to Ovillers via La Boisselle *c.*20–23 July).

p.167 Bodies and faces: Courtauld, *Daily Telegraph*, 10 November 1998 (interview with Norman Edwards of the 1/6th Gloucesters, who visited Ovillers on 20 July).
'The flies were buzzing . . .': Carrington, *A Subaltern's War*, 106–7.
No enemy shelling: 25th Division signal company diary. Sleep in dugout: JRRT diary. 'Ours compared . . .': Evers memoir. 'A' Company order: Bodleian Tolkien.

pp.167–8 1/5th Royal Warwickshires stranded: Carrington, *A Subaltern's War*, 87–8, and *Soldier from the Wars Returning*, 135; Brown, *Imperial War Museum Book of the Somme*, 138–9.

p.168 'I am quite well': GBS to JRRT, 12 July 1916. 'I am safe but . . .': ibid., 15 July 1916.

NINE *'Something has gone crack'*

p.169 Somme offensive widely expected: Brown, *The Imperial War Museum Book of the Somme*, 260.
Field postcard: RQG to RCG, 30 June 1916. 'never sends anything . . .', etc.: RCG to RQG, 6 July 1916. Gilsons await news: MCG to Rachel King, 11 July 1916.

pp.169–70 Obituary: *The Times*, 11 July 1916, 8. Gilsons' grief; 'greatest friend': MCG to Rachel King, 11 July 1916.

p.170 'was loved by all those . . .': Capt. A. Seddon to RCG, 3 July 1916. 'loved by all the men . . .': Pte. A. Bradnam to MCG, 14 July 1914. 'I am almost glad . . .': Major P. F. Morton to RCG, 12 July 1916. 'everything to me . . .': 2nd Lt. A. R. Wright to RCG, 18 July 1916.

pp.170–1 Bouzincourt to Beauval, 17–19 July: JRRT diary, including mess accounts listing sums owed to him by the officers against payments made to Harrison, Arden, and Kershaw. Which batman was assigned to JRRT is not known. Officer details: service records of Lt. W. F. Waite and Capt. W. I. Edwards; Fawcett-Barry papers.

p.171 JRRT and batmen: *Biography*, 81. Letter from Pte. T. Gaskin's mother: Bodleian Tolkien (reproduced in Priestman, *Life and Legend*, 35).
Acting lieutenant: *The Lancashire Fusiliers' Annual 1917*, 222. *Ad hoc* promotions (not reflected in official papers) accompanying a more responsible job were the norm because of the high casualty rate. (C. E. Munday, 8 November 1916, addresses JRRT as Lieutenant; but a handwritten order from Lt.-Col. L. G. Bird, 7 August 1916, refers to him as Second Lieutenant; Bodleian Tolkien.)

pp.171–2 Signal officer's staff and duties: 25th Division signal company diary; Solano (ed.), *Signalling*, 11–12. Signals under scrutiny: 'Communications in the 25th Division'.

p.172 Attack order found at Ovillers: Macdonald, *The Somme*, 169–70. Capt. J. C. P. E. Metcalfe: service record; Hayter (ed.), *Charlton and Newbottle*; the Reverend Roger Bellamy to the author; *Quarterly Army List*.

pp.172–3 Auchonvillers, 24–30 July: on the front line between Praed Street and Broadway. War diaries of 11th LF, 74th Brigade and 25th Division signal company; *The Lancashire Fusiliers' Annual 1917*, 222–3.

p.173 Mailly-Maillet, 30 July–5 August: ibid., 223; 11th LF war diary. Order to JRRT: from Lt.-Col. L. G. Bird, 7 August 1916 (Bodleian Tolkien).
Sucrerie trenches, 5–10 August: referred to by JRRT as 'our second bout of trenches', *Letters* 9; they were between Egg Street and Flag Avenue, and the communication (access) trench was called Cheer'oh ('goodbye') Avenue. 11th LF war diary; *Lancashire Fusiliers' Annual 1917*, 223–4.
Bus-lès-Artois, 10–15 July: JRRT diary; 11th LF war diary; *The Lancashire Fusiliers' Annual 1917*, 224. Nights in wood: *Letters*, 9.

pp.173–4 Poem: GBS to JRRT, 25 July 1916, identifies it only as 'your thing about England'.

p.174 Brief letter from CLW: not extant because JRRT returned it to GBS. An empty envelope from GBS, postmarked 4 August 1916, implies that it was sent with no accompanying note.

'such a life . . .': GBS to JRRT, 11 August 1916.
'No filter of sentiment . . .': quoted in ibid.
'Save that poetic fire': GBS, *A Spring Harvest*, 72. The poem appears above in full.

p.175 'Blighters': Sassoon, *The War Poems*, 68.
'To the Cultured': GBS, *A Spring Harvest*, 72.
'the entirety . . .': quoted in GBS to JRRT, 19 August 1916.
'the great work': CLW to JRRT, 4 February 1916. 'doubting Thomas': GBS to JRRT, 19 August 1916.

p.176 'the universal weariness . . .', etc.: JRRT to GBS, 12–13 August 1916 (*Letters*, 10).
Lt. J. Bowyer (footnote): *The Lancashire Fusiliers' Annual 1917*, 313.

p.177 'and I can't help thinking . . .', 'He will come out . . .': CLW to JRRT, 1 March 1916.
'we shall not see it . . .': RQG to JRRT, 31 October 1915.
'the death of one . . .': GBS to JRRT, 3 February 1916.
19th LF at Ovillers, 12–14 July: Latter, *Lancashire Fusiliers*, 150; war diary. 'They were lost . . .': GBS intelligence report, ibid.
GBS's duties: 'Instructions for and duties of Brigade and Battalion Intelligence Officers' (appendix to 1 July operation orders), 19th LF war diary.
Corpses: 'Many German dead in trench 8b43 to 8c56', said a report (25th Division war diary) on 14 July, before the 19th LF vacated it. They had seized half of this 640-yard stretch of trench; 19th LF war diary.
'I am truly afraid . . .': GBS to JRRT, 25 July 1916.

p.178 19th LF, 15 July–13 August: war diary. Conversion: Mitchinson, *Pioneer Battalions in the Great War*, 65.
'Tonight I cannot sleep . . .': GBS to JRRT, 15 August 1916.
Search for JRRT: ibid., 19 August 1916.

pp.178–9 Signal officers' course: 'Communications in the 25th Division'; 25th Division signal company war diary.

p.179 'I want you to regard . . .', etc.: GBS to JRRT, 19 August 1916.
Reunion: *Biography*, 85, asserts that they met at Acheux, where JRRT diary notes he slept every night from 15 to 23

August. But GBS, 19 August 1916, indicates no plan to travel to Acheux that day. It seems as likely that JRRT, hearing his friend had inquired after him, made his way to Hédauville.

pp.179–80 Debate over TCBS: JRRT to GBS, 12–13 August 1916, published almost in full in *Letters*, 9–10 ('holiness and nobility', etc.); GBS to JRRT, 19 August 1916 ('Who knows whether Rob . . .', etc.)

p.180 End of the TCBSian dream: possibly JRRT concluded that the TCBS was finished not because of RQG's death itself, but because of the reactions of the surviving members to it: perhaps he felt CLW and GBS had lost sight of the TCBSian ideal of 'greatness' (the potential to 'kindle a new light . . . in the world'), by confounding it with an heroic ideal of 'greatness' (death in battle in a good cause). But it is impossible to be sure in the absence of CLW's letter, to which JRRT's and GBS's respond.

p.181 End to doubt: GBS to JRRT, 19 August 1916. GBS's recent writings: ibid., 25 July 1916.

'a sacrifice of blood outpoured', etc.: 'For RQG', GBS, *A Spring Harvest*, 69. 'Let us tell quiet stories of kind eyes', ibid. 71. 'The Last Meeting', 'Memories' and 'Sun and shadow and winds of spring', ibid. 58, 63, and 70, may also refer to RQG.

p.182 Birmingham battalions (footnote): Carter, *Birmingham Pals*, 103.

W. H. Payton: RQG to EK, 6 June 1916.

pp.182–3 R. S. Payton's death; 'Heaven grant . . .': RCG to JRRT, 15 August 1916. With 14th Warwickshires on Somme: Carter, *Birmingham Pals*, 69, 173, 176–86.

p.183 Debating society: *KESC*, March 1912, 15–16. Character: ibid., June 1912, 41. 'the Barrovian-par-excellence': CLW to JRRT, 19 March 1912.

Speech Day: *KESC*, October 1916, 60.

pp.183–5 'frequent meetings with JR', 'At first nebulous . . .', etc.: CLW to GBS, 30 August 1916.

p.185 'On the constitution . . .': GBS to JRRT, 16 September 1916. Bouzincourt meal, 22 August: JRRT diary; *Biography*, 85.

The Earthly Paradise: Wade-Gery gave JRRT vol. v in Bouzincourt, date unknown; Douglas A. Anderson to the author.

TEN *In a hole in the ground*

p.186 'That's all spoof,' etc.: Norman, *Sunday Times Magazine*, 15 January 1967.

Dugout: JRRT diary. 'Kortirion' revisions: Douglas A. Anderson to the author.

'Some people talk . . .': RQG to EK, 3 March 1916. GBS's reading in France: ibid., 5 April 1916.

'The Burial of Sophocles': GBS to JRRT, 2 December 1915. GBS sends home JRRT piece: ibid., 25 July 1916.

'ghastly gallows-trees': Blunden, *Undertones of War*, 134.

p.187 'The wood was never . . .': Douie, *The Weary Road*, 141–2.

'I think a lot . . .': *Letters*, 231.

'down in dugouts . . .', 'It did not make . . .': *Letters*, 78.

'The Old British Line . . .': Blunden, *Undertones of War*, 25–6.

In GBS's footsteps: 19th LF war diaries; Platt papers. 'like a treasure': GBS to JRRT, 12 January.

pp.187–8 Thiepval Wood, 24–7 August: 11th LF war diary.

p.188 End of course: 25th Division signals company diary. Military situation, 24 August: Stedman, *Thiepval*, 84; Cuttell, *148 Days on the Somme*, 196.

'always long . . .': RQG to EK, 6 March 1916. 'the joy of getting out . . .': ibid., 26 February 1916.

Bouzincourt, 27–8 August: 11th LF diary; JRRT diary.

pp.188–9 Trench duty, 28–30 August: the 11th LF were in a series of small trenches south-west of Pole Trench; 11th LF war diary; 25th Division signal company war diary; 'Communications in the 25th Division'; *Lancashire Fusiliers' Annual 1917*, 224–5; Cuttell, *148 Days on the Somme*, 130.

p.188 'I feel that if I survive . . .': RQG to EK, 3 March 1916.

'an appalling bit of line . . .'; 'extraordinary cheeriness': Evers memoir.

p.189 French language and cooking: *Letters*, 288–9. Wine: ibid. 314, 405.

France trip, 1913; 'the vulgarity . . .': *Biography*, 22, 67–8.
'Gallophobia': *Biography*, 129.
JRRT's French: d'Ardenne, 'The Man and the Scholar', in Salu and Farrell (eds.), *J. R. R. Tolkien, Scholar and Storyteller*, 35.
'I can see clearly . . .': *Letters*, 111.
Westward, 6–12 September: 11th LF war diary.

p.190 'endless marching . . .', etc.: *Family Album*, 40.
Franqueville, 12–25 September: 11th LF war diary; *The Lancashire Fusiliers' Annual 1917*, 225; Kincaid-Smith, *The 25th Division in France and Flanders*, 18.
New signallers for each battalion: 25th Divisional signal company war diary.
2nd Lt. L. R. Huxtable: service record; 11th LF war diary. To 13th LF: *The Times*, 28 July 1915; 'L. R. Huxtable. 13th Lancs Fusrs. F & G Lines' appears in Tolkien's hand on an envelope attached to GBS to JRRT, 23, 24, and 26 May 1916.
Signal course: Potts papers. JRRT's understudy: 'Communications in the 25th Division' states that one officer per battalion was trained at Franqueville as battalion signal officer.
Disagreement with superior; 'I am intensely sorry . . .': GBS to JRRT, 16 September 1916. J. C. P. E. Metcalfe in command: service record.
'Hux'; shares tent: JRRT diary. In 'A' Company: Fawcett-Barry papers.
'the first War . . .', etc.: *Letters*, 111.

p.191 Military situation: Cuttell, *148 Days on the Somme*, 199–200.

pp.191–3 Thiepval Wood, 27–29 September: ibid., 202; war diaries of the 11th LF, 74th Brigade, brigade signal officer, and 25th Division signal company; JRRT diary; Latter, *Lancashire Fusiliers*, 163–5; *The Lancashire Fusiliers' Annual 1917*, 225–8; Kincaid-Smith, *The 25th Division in France and Flanders*, 18.

p.192 Captive officer: *Biography*, 84–5.
'If guards insufficient . . .': 'Summary of training circulars (advisory)', issued to JRRT on 26 September 1916 (Bodleian Tolkien).

Captain shot: Roger Ganly; *Lancashire Fusiliers' Annual 1916*, 235–6.

R. Mellor's 'Ode to a Fullerphone' (footnote): in *Jimmy*, journal of the Royal Corps of Signals in the Middle East (with thanks to Louis Meulstee's *Wireless for the Warrior* website).

p.193 2nd Lt. Stanley Rowson's disappearance: Pte. Connor, in Rowson's service record ('I was blown . . .'); Fawcett-Barry papers.

'Dear Sir . . .': Mrs M. Sumner to the commanding officer of 'B' Company, 26 September 1916 (Bodleian Tolkien). The letter must have been passed to JRRT because he was battalion signal officer.

Englebelmer and Bouzincourt, 30 September–6 October: JRRT diary; 11th LF war diary.

pp.193–5 Ferme de Mouquet, Zollern Redoubt, and Ovillers Post, 7–18 October: JRRT diary; war diaries of the 11th LF, 74th Brigade, and 25th Division HQ and signal company; 'Communications in the 25th Division'; *The Lancashire Fusiliers' Annual 1917*, 228–9; Latter, *Lancashire Fusiliers*, 170–1; and Cuttell, *148 Days on the Somme*, 202–4.

p.194 Ferme de Mouquet map: 19th LF war diary.

Huxtable wounded: service record; JRRT diary.

p.195 Unit designations: '25th Division Code Letter Calls', 11 October 1916 (Bodleian Tolkien). They are marked in crayon on a map incorporating intelligence for the attack on Regina Trench (Bodleian Tolkien; reproduced in *Life and Legend*, 32); 'WF' denotes JRRT's battalion HQ in Hessian Trench, near the junction with Lancashire Trench. (The German position due north of battalion HQ is now occupied by Regina Trench Cemetery.) The 11th LF line of advance is bounded by vertical lines in purple crayon. The map appears, with westward extension, in 74th Brigade and 25th Division war diaries and was probably drawn by army cartographers, not by JRRT as stated in *Family Album*, 40. On the other hand, its red and black ink, title-lettering, and compass rose are reminiscent of his style; while the equally amateur RGQ spent much time making maps for his battalion and brigade (RQG to EK, 29 February 1916).

GBS's worst apprehensions: GBS to JRRT, 19 October 1915. *Mabinogion*; 'Raconteur . . .'; 'his discovery . . .': ibid., 10 September 1916. Lost lunacy; 'Perhaps this note . . .': ibid., 16 September 1916.

p.196 'Thoughts of leave . . .': ibid., 3 October 1916.

JRRT's leave ever imminent: *Biography*, 85. 'universal weariness': *Letters*, 10.

'There were times . . .': Douie, *The Weary Road*, 168.

'astonished that flesh . . .': Alfred Bundy, quoted in Brown, *The Imperial War Museum Book of the Somme*, 225.

pp.196–9 Hessian Trench and Regina Trench, 19–22 October: JRRT diary; war diaries of the 11th LF, 74th Brigade, and 25th Division HQ and signal company; 'Communications in the 25th Division'; *The Lancashire Fusiliers' Annual 1917*, 229–34; Latter, *Lancashire Fusiliers*, 171–3; Kincaid-Smith, *The 25th Division in France and Flanders*, 20–22; Miles, *Military Operations, France and Belgium 1916*, 463; Cuttell, *148 Days on the Somme*, 204.

pp.198–9 Padre's experience; 'Some had the will . . .', etc.: Evers memoir.

p.199 Horseback encounter with tank: Potts papers.

pp.199–200 Albert to Beauval, 22–28 October: JRRT diary; 11th LF war diary; *The Lancashire Fusiliers' Annual 1917*, 233–4.

p.200 JRRT falls ill: medical board, 2 December 1916, in JRRT service record.

Lice blamed on German trenches: Carrington, *A Subaltern's War*, 47.

'On one occasion . . .': Evers memoir. The signals officer in the captured dugout could equally be Lt. W. H. Reynolds, Tolkien's predecessor in the 11th Lancashire Fusiliers and then his superior at brigade level.

p.201 Beauval to Le Touquet, 28–29 October: JRRT diary. The Duchess of Westmorland Hospital was officially known as the No. 1 Red Cross Hospital.

Battalion losses and drafts: figures for 28 June–22 October

1916; 25th Division adjutant and administrative staff war diaries.

ELEVEN *Castles in the air*

p.205 Itinerary; fever: JRRT diary and service record.
Writes to Lt.-Col. L. G. Bird: Capt. E. Munday to JRRT, 8 November 1916 (Bodleian Tolkien).
The *Asturias*: Gibson and Prendergast, *The German Submarine War 1914–1918*, 21; Platt papers (describing a crossing on the same ship in June 1916). Impressions of a 'Blighty boat': Ferguson diary. Moribund wards: Keegan, *The Face of Battle*, 267.
'sea-girdled . . .': Tolkien, 'The Lonely Isle', *Leeds University Verse 1914–1924*, 57.
'like a death': Cater, *The Daily Telegraph*, 29 November 2001, 23.

pp.205–6 First Southern General Hospital: Brazier and Sandford, *Birmingham and the Great War*, 49, 154–8.

p.206 T. K. Barnsley: service record; CLW to JRRT, 16 November 1916. Molly Gilson: MCG to EK, 10 July 1916. Major L. Gamgee: ibid.; Hutton, *King Edward's School, Birmingham*, 164; Heath, *Service Record of King Edward's School, Birmingham*, 55.
Source of hobbit-name *Gamgee*: *Letters*, 88, 245, 348, 410.
'Lt-Col Bird wishes me . . .': Capt. E. Munday to JRRT, 8 November 1916 (Bodleian Tolkien). Lt. V. H. Kempson: *Lancashire Fusiliers' Annual 1917*, 233.
'Stay a long time . . .', etc.: GBS to JRRT, 16 November 1916. Forwarded letter to CLW: ibid., 18 November 1916. 'If you had offered me . . .': CLW to JRRT, 16 November 1916. JRRT sends poems: ibid., 8 December 1916.

pp.206–7 'The Town of Dreams and the City of Present Sorrow': *LT2*, 295–7.

p.207 Medical board: JRRT service record. Correspondence address: 22 November 1916 form, ibid. JRRT considers Royal Engineers: CLW to JRRT, 8 December 1916. T. E. Mitton: KES register; Heath, *Service Record of King Edward's School, Birmingham*, 102.

pp.207–8 'The Grey Bridge at Tavrobel': published (like 'Tinfang Warble') in the late 1920s in a journal referred to by JRRT as '*I.U.M.*' (Hammond with Anderson, *Bibliography*, 344; Douglas A. Anderson to the author.)

p.207 *Tavrobel*: *Parma Eldalamberon* 11, 69. *Haywood*: *LT2*, 328. Heraldic devices (footnote): *Parma Eldalamberon* 13, 93–6.

p.208 'magnificent', etc.: CLW to JRRT, 8 December 1916.

p.209 'rather below his usual standard', etc.: CLW to JRRT, 16 November 1916. Billeting officer; 'Fur undercoats . . .', etc.: 19th LF war diary. 'sheer vacancy': GBS to JRRT, 16 September 1916. 'for such I am . . .': ibid., 16 November 1916.

'My career in the Army . . .': GBS to JRRT, 12 January. 'The Corps Commander . . .': ibid., 18 November 1916.

'engaging rascal', etc.: RQG, report on GBS's paper 'Early English Ballads', *KESC*, December 1911, 90. 'wild and whole-hearted admirer': ibid., 3 February 1916.

p.210 Military writing: Keegan, *The Face of Battle*, 20–2. 'Owing to hostile MG fire . . .': GBS's intelligence report, 1 July 1916, 19th LF war diary.

'Who battled have with bloody hands . . .': GBS, 'We who have bowed ourselves to time', *A Spring Harvest*, 49. 'Shapes in the mist . . .': 'Memories', ibid. 63.

Riding experiences: Ruth Smith to JRRT, 13 November 1916. 'I hope I shall be able . . .': GBS to JRRT, 16 November 1916.

p.211 GBS's death: GBS service record; 19th LF war diary; Ruth Smith to JRRT, 22 December 1916 ('after that he quickly sank . . .'). Words of CO (Major J. Ambrose Smith) to Ruth Smith: ibid., 26 December 1916.

pp.211–12 'O seven times happy . . .': GBS, 'The Burial of Sophocles', *A Spring Harvest*, 77. History of poem: ibid. 7; GBS to JRRT, 2 December 1915. Riposte to axiom about those the Gods love: ibid., 9 February 1916.

p.212 'My dear JR . . .': CLW to JRRT, 16 December 1916. GBS as his mother's chief support: ibid., 18 January 1917.

Request for poems: Ruth Smith to JRRT, 22 December 1916. 'The Poetic and Mythologic Words of Eldarissa': *Parma Eldalamberon* 12, xvii–xxi, 29–106 *passim*. If JRRT left his

Qenya lexicon at home when he went to France (as seems likely in view of Smith losing 'The Burial of Sophocles'), perhaps this new word list was written in hospital in Birmingham so he could refamiliarize himself with Qenya. It adds little to the content of the lexicon (upon which he continued to work), and makes no attempt at alphabetical order.

pp.212, 214 'Early chart of names'; *Earendl*, etc.: *Parma Eldalamberon* 13, 98–9.

p.214 'almost fully formed': *Letters*, 215. JRRT recalled that 'The Fall of Gondolin' was 'written in hospital and on leave after surviving the Battle of the Somme in 1916' (*Letters* 221; cf. 366). At Le Touquet he had a high fever but by the end of the second week in November he was writing letters from the Birmingham University Hospital; his handwriting on a 22 November form (service record) was firm and assured. He also said the tale emerged 'during sick-leave at the end of 1916' (215; cf. 345). Other letters (345, 386) indicate that composition continued into 1917. Feasibly the tale was written after 'The Cottage of Lost Play' (see Chapter 12), and the hospital in question might have been in Harrogate, where he spent most of March 1917.

pp.215–23 *Aryador*, etc.: where possible, names and other readings in 'The Fall of Gondolin' are given as first written, in the text referred to by its editor, Christopher Tolkien, as 'Tuor A' (*LT2*, 202–3). But most quotations here are from the revised text, 'Tuor B' (which was written over the top of the original, largely obscuring it, and is published in *LT2*, 149–97). To give one illustrative example of the name changes involved, the shadow land of *Aryador* became by emendation to the first manuscript *Mathusdor* and then *Dor Lómin*, which was the name that endured.

p.215 'he wandered . . .': *LT2*, 151.

p.216 'Now there dwelt . . .': ibid., 153–4.

Tuor at 23: 'Of Tuor and his Coming to Gondolin', *Unfinished Tales*, 20. 'Oxford "sleepies"': *Biography*, 73. 'dream of the gods': *LT2*, 159.

'hide their land . . .': ibid., 162.

p.217 'stand as long as Taniquetil . . .': ibid. 171. 'No tide of evil . . .': *LT2*, 297.

'That, I suppose . . .': 1964 interview with Denis Gueroult, BBC Sound Archives.

'little, delicate, beautiful creatures': CLW to JRRT, 1 March 1916. 'small and slender and lithe': *LT2*, 198 (note 18).

p.218 *kalimbardi*, etc.: *Parma Eldalamberon* 12, 44. *Calum(oth)* (footnote): *Parma Eldalamberon* 13, 99. 'folk of dreadful hate': *LT2*, 160.

'That you are going to win . . .': RCG to JRRT, 14 August 1916. 'for all the evil . . .': JRRT to GBS, 12 August 1916 (*Letters*, 10; reading clarified by Douglas A. Anderson).

p.219 'I've never had those . . .': Norman, *Sunday Times Magazine*, London, 15 January 1967, 34–6.

'I think the orcs . . .': *Letters*, 82. 'beauty and grace . . .': ibid. 85.

'they of the Heavenly Arch . . .': *LT2*, 173.

p.220 'the subterranean . . .', 'Their hearts . . .': *LT2*, 159–60.

orc: *Letters*, 177–8; *Morgoth's Ring*, 124, 422; JRRT, 'Guide to the Names in The Lord of the Rings', in Lobdell (ed.), *A Tolkien Compass*, 171.

Balrog: *Parma Eldalamberon* 11, 21, 42; see also *LT1*, 240.

'From the greatness . . .', 'beasts like snakes . . .': *LT2*, 169.

'smiths and sorcerers', 'iron so cunningly linked . . .': ibid. 170. 'by reason of the exceeding . . .', 'their hollow bellies . . .': ibid. 176.

p.221 'the icthyosaurus, jabberwocks . . .': civilian Frederick Arthur Robinson, quoted in Brown, *The Imperial War Museum Book of the Somme*, 267. Ernst, *Celebes*: see Cork, *A Bitter Truth*, 170, 258–60. 'The monster approached . . .': *The Times*, 25 October 1916, citing the *Dusseldorfer Generalanzeiger*. 'like fairy-tales of war . . .': Gibbs, *Now It Can Be Told*.

pp.221–2 Road to hell: 'Gylfaginning' Chapter 49, in Snorri Sturluson, *Edda*.

p.222 'Winter, and his blue-tipped spears . . .' (footnote): *LT1*, 34.

'wintry spell of Yelin', etc.: written on the envelope of a

letter from RQG to JRRT, 19 October 1915. *Yelin, Yelur*: *Parma Eldalamberon* 12, 105–6. '*Yelur* = Melko' in the Qenya lexicon may have preceded the separate entry for *Melko*; both seem to have been added after Tolkien made the list of 'Poetic and Mythologic Words'. In Gnomish, *c.*1917, Melko was labelled 'Lord of utter heat and cold, of violence and evil', with bynames *Geluim*, 'Ice', related to *Gilim*, 'winter'; *Parma Eldalamberon* 11, 22, 38.

'a binding terror', etc.: *LT*2, 159. 'drown his fear and disquiet': ibid. 169.

p.223 'unconquerable eagerness . . .': *LT*2, 159. Thrall-Noldoli bent with their labours: ibid. 198 (note 18).

TWELVE *Tol Withernon and Fladweth Amrod*

p.224 'You ought to start . . .': CLW to JRRT, 18 January 1917. There is no knowing when Tolkien had announced his plans for an epic, but it seems likely that Wiseman was here responding to a letter (no longer extant) written prior to Smith's death, perhaps as early as November.

'The Cottage of Lost Play': name changes in or between the first, undated text and a fair copy begun by Edith Tolkien on 12 February 1917 match those in the early chart of names in 'The Poetic and Mythologic Words of Eldarissa', which clearly predated 'The Fall of Gondolin'. The elf-king's name *Ing* in 'The Cottage of Lost Play' was emended to *Inwë*, his name in 'The Fall of Gondolin'. The sun-tree of Valinor was first *Glingol*, a name given in the latter to the tree's seedling in Gondolin itself. Most interesting is the occurrence of *Manwë* as a name for an Elf (emended to *Valwë*): in 'The Fall of Gondolin' and all later mythological texts *Manwë* is the name of the chief of the Valar. (*LT*1, 13, 21–2; *Parma Eldalamberon* 12, xx; *Parma Eldalamberon* 13, 98–9.)

pp.224–5 Background of Ottor/Eriol; 'the true tradition . . .': *LT*2, 290–2. Animalic *Otter*: Wynne and Smith, 'Tolkien and Esperanto', in *Seven* 17, 32–3.

p.225 'all who enter . . .': *LT*1, 14.

pp.225–6 'At that same moment . . .'; 'the walls shake with mirth': ibid. 15.

p.226 'hearing the lament of the world': ibid. 16.

pp.226–7 'This was the Cottage . . .'; 'the children of the fathers . . .'; 'Of the misty aftermemories . . .': ibid. 19.

pp.227–8 'old tales . . .'; 'lonely children . . .'; 'shall be thronged . . .': ibid. 20.

p.228 'the Faring Forth . . .': ibid. 17.

p.229 'Golden Book': *LT2*, 290–1; *Parma Eldalamberon* 12, 72; *Parma Eldalamberon* 11, 63. *i·band a·gwentin laithra*: ibid. 11–12.

'the lost *Tale of Wade*': Chambers, *Widsith*, 98. 'So this world . . .', etc.: ibid. 3–4. Recreating early Roman poems: Macaulay, *Lays of Ancient Rome*, 405–9. Cf. Shippey, *Author of the Century*, 233–6.

'Do not laugh . . .': *Letters*, 144.

p.230 Support for Irish Home Rule: JRRT to CLW, 16 November 1914.

'as an ambition . . .': Boas and Herford (eds.), *The Year's Work in English Studies, 1925*, 59–60.

p.231 Poetic output in 1917: CLW to JRRT, 1 September 1917.

End of leave; 23 January medical board: JRRT service record.

'unreservedly glad'; 'malinger . . .': CLW to JRRT, 18 January 1917.

pp.231–2 Late February: service record. The 3rd LF commanding officer had been kept informed of JRRT's situation since 15 December 1916.

p.232 'Every day in bed . . .': *Biography*, 95. It may be noted here that where Humphrey Carpenter's account of 1917 does not seem to match JRRT's service record, I have followed the latter.

Council of Harrogate: CLW to JRRT, 14, 15 ('I am going to burst into . . .', etc.) and 17 April 1917.

'As you said, it is you and I now . . .': ibid., 4 March 1917.

pp.232–3 Surviving TCBSites and GBS's poetry: ibid., 18 January 1917.

p.233 Roger Smith's death: ibid., 4 March 1917; service record; Ruth

Smith to JRRT, 6 March 1917. Never knew of GBS's death: ibid., 22 January 1917.

'I suppose very few . . .'; 'a few acres of mud': CLW to JRRT, 4 March 1917.

'the starvation-year': *Letters*, 53. The *Asturias*: Gibson and Prendergast, *The German Submarine War 1914–1918*, 164.

Shipping losses: Taylor, *English History 1914–1945*, 84.

p.234 Hornsea: *Biography*, 95. Musketry school: *Lancashire Fusiliers' Annual 1917*, 304.

Holderness defences: Dorman, *Guardians of the Humber*, 13–65.

Wives' visits to Thirtle Bridge: Cyril Dunn to the author.

'Here some sixty . . .': Platt papers.

Officers' service fitness: weekly return of the British Army.

pp.234–5 11th LF officers: Fawcett-Barry papers; *Lancashire Fusiliers' Annual 1917*, 317–18, 340–1, 348; service records of L. R. Huxtable and J. C. P. E. Metcalfe.

p.235 1917 photograph: *Family Album*, 41. Medical board, 1 May: JRRT service record. Patrols and Zeppelins: Mills memoir. Land and sea: Van De Noort and Ellis (eds.), *Wetlands Heritage of Holderness*, 15; Miles and Richardson, *A History of Withernsea*, 11, 237.

p.236 Books of Welsh: as well as J. Gwenogvryn Evans, *Pedeir Kainc y Mabinogi*, Smith bequeathed to Tolkien J. M. Edwards, *Hanes A Chan*; Thomas Evan, *Gwaith / Twn o'r Nant*; Samuel Roberts, *Gwaith*; William Spurrell, *An English-Welsh Pronouncing Dictionary*; and M. Williams, *Essai sur la composition du Roman Gallois* (Bodleian and English Faculty library catalogues, Oxford University).

Tol Withernon and *Withernsea*: *Parma Eldalamberon* 11, 3–4, 46, 71; Smith, *The Place-names of the East Riding of Yorkshire and York*, 26–7; Ekwall, *The Concise Oxford Dictionary of English Place-names*, 502–3; Phillips, *Illustrations of the Geology of Yorkshire, Part 1*, 72. With thanks to Carl F. Hostetter and Patrick Wynne.

pp.237–8 'The Horns of Ulmo': *The Shaping of Middle-earth*, 214–17. 'the upholder': *Parma Eldalamberon* 11, 43.

p.238 Commanded outpost; lived with Edith: *Letters*, 420. Next to post office; Dents Garth: Peter Cook to the author.
JRRT, flower names and *hemlock*: Christopher Tolkien to the author.

p.239 1 June medical board: JRRT service record. Messines: Latter, *Lancashire Fusiliers*, 206–9.
Signals exam: *Biography*, 96. Minden Day: signed menu (Bodleian Tolkien).
Brooklands: Sheppard, *Kingston-Upon-Hull Before, During and After the Great War*, 114–15.
Passchendaele: Latter, *Lancashire Fusiliers*, 219–21.

p.240 Edith's return to Cheltenham: *Biography*, 96.
'It is all the more distressing . . .'; 'I am very anxious . . .': CLW to JRRT, 1 September 1917.
'Companions of the Rose': CLW to JRRT, 1 September 1917 ('There is of course no legislation . . .'); Douglas A. Anderson to the author.
'Tinúviel' textual history: *LT2*, 3; *Letters*, 345, 420. *Biography*, 97–8, implies erroneously that the inspirational walk at Roos took place in 1918, owing to a misreading of '1917' that is repeated in *Letters*, 221 (Christina Scull to the author).

pp.240–1 'Turambar' textual history: *LT2*, 69. That it was written in 1917 (*Biography*, 96) seems no more than a guess. But an early outline (*LT2*, 138–9) contains almost exclusively Qenya names, just like the 1917 pencil version of 'Tinúviel', in contrast to the extant revisions of the two tales, in which Gnomish forms replace them. The Qenya name *Foalókë* shows the 'Turambar' outline is later than 'The Poetic and Mythologic Words of Eldarissa' of late 1916 (*Parma Eldalamberon* 12, 38).

p.241 State of the mythology: JRRT wrote his first Gnomish lexicon in pencil but over-wrote it in ink, probably late in 1917, obscuring most of the original definitions and germs of story. Additions to the Qenya lexicon continued, none of them datable. Beyond what has already been said here about 'The Fall of Gondolin' and 'The Cottage of Lost Play', only the barest hints can be gleaned about the state of the mythology in 1917. The best view of the flow of creativity in 1917 and 1918 can be gained from the two lexicons; many of the mythological concepts in them are reproduced in appendices to *LT1* and *LT2*. Most published excerpts of other 'Lost Tales' notebooks appear from internal evidence to have been written after the war. The mythological concepts outlined in the list here, not exhaustive, are drawn from the 'Poetic and Mythologic Words of Eldarissa'; the first version of 'The Fall of Gondolin'; 1917's 'The Horns of Ulmo' (*The Shaping of Middle-earth*, 215–7); the early pencil layer of the Gnomish lexicon, and the earlier or contemporaneous Gnomish grammar (*Parma Eldalamberon* 11); and matching Qenya lexicon entries.

p.242 Health: 16 October and 16 November medical boards, JRRT service record.
Birth of John Tolkien: *Biography*, 96–7.
'The end of the war . . .': *Letters*, 53.
'when your kiddie . . .': CLW to JRRT, 20 December 1917.
Patrimonial shares: *Letters*, 53.
Visits Cheltenham; Edith returns: *Biography*, 97.
Lieutenant: 19 January 1918 medical board (service record).
Fever recurs; unit transfer: ibid.

p.243 Royal Defence Corps: weekly return of the British Army.
Easington: Allison (ed.), *Holderness: southern part*, 21–31.
'apparent lack of connection': CLW to JRRT, 4 March 1917.

pp.243–5 'The Song of Eriol': *LT2*, 298–300.

p.245 1918 an ordeal: CLW to JRRT, 16 December 1918. Health to April: JRRT service record. Return to 13th LF: *Biography*, 98. Spring Offensive: Latter, *Lancashire Fusiliers*, 301–3.

p.246 Penkridge Camp: *Biography*, 98. Brocton Camp: JRRT service record.
Staffordshire interlude: Priscilla Tolkien in *Angerthas in English* 3, 6–7; *Artist*, 26–8.
Fladweth Amrod: *Parma Eldalamberon* 11, 35.
A Spring Harvest: Hammond with Anderson, *Bibliography*, 280–1.
Gastritis: medical board, 4 September 1918, JRRT service record.

Edith; 'I should think you ought . . .': *Biography*, 98 (which gives an account slightly at odds with JRRT service record). 'a long nomadic series . . .': *Letters*, 430.

p.247 Embarkation orders: JRRT service record.
Fate of 11th and 19th LF: Stedman, *Salford Pals*, 160–7; Latter, *Lancashire Fusiliers*, 332–5, 344–7, 349–53.

pp.247–8 Brooklands: *Biography*, 98; medical board, 4 September 1918.

p.248 Home convalescence: Graves, *Good-bye to All That*, 261.
Blackpool: JRRT service record. Italian meal: signed menu (Bodleian Tolkien).
'unwonted silence': Douie, *The Weary Road*, 16.
'for the purposes . . .': *Biography*, 98.

p.249 *New English Dictionary*: ibid. 98–9; Gilliver, 'At the Wordface', in Reynolds and GoodKnight (eds.), *Proceedings of the J. R. R. Tolkien Centenary Conference*, 173–4. Gratitude to Craigie: 'Valedictory Address', *Monsters*, 238. 'We rejoice . . .': anonymous 'Oxford Letter', *KESC*, December 1919, 76.
50 St John Street: CLW to JRRT, 27 December 1918; *Biography*, 99–100.
'were acutely aware . . .': Winter, 'Oxford and the First World War', in Harrison (ed.), *The History of the University of Oxford*, viii. 18.
1919 reading: Exeter College library register.
'set himself the task . . .': Graves, *Good-bye to All That*, 257.
'The Fall of Gondolin': Exeter College Essay Club minutes, 10 March 1920.
1910 rugby XV: *Biography*, facing p. 82.

p.250 Numbers of war dead: Heath, *Service Record of King Edward's School*; How, *Register of Exeter College Oxford 1891–1921*; Winter, 'Oxford and the First World War', in Harrison (ed.), *The History of the University of Oxford*, viii. 19–20.
Colin Cullis: death certificate. T. E. Mitton: KES registration details; *KESC*, December 1914, 77–8, and March 1918, 86.
T. K. Barnsley: service record. GBS: *Family Album*, 41.
'perhaps in the ever-famous "Johnner"': CLW to JRRT, 8 December 1916.

p.251 'We must contrive . . .': ibid., 1 September 1917.
'grand old quarrel': ibid., 1 March 1916. 'clash of backgrounds'; 'the decay of faith . . .' (quoting JRRT); 'That huge atmosphere . . .', etc.: ibid., 20 December 1917.
Lost track of each other: ibid., 16 December 1918. 'So the TCBS will again . . .': ibid., 27 December 1918.

p.252 Demobilization: JRRT service record; protection certificate, etc. (Bodleian Tolkien). Pension: granted in T. P. Evans to JRRT, 4 September 1919 (ibid.), but backdated to 16 July.

EPILOGUE *'a new light'*

p.253 TCBS would outlive war: CLW to JRRT, 1 March 1916. 'What is not . . .': ibid., 18 January 1917.
'We believe in . . .': GBS to JRRT, 9 February 1916.
Smith's goal and method: CLW to JRRT, 27 October 1915.
're-establish sanity . . .': GBS to JRRT, 24 October 1915.
'he never lived . . .': CLW to JRRT, undated [summer 1917]. Wiseman referred to the 'tales of our trodden course' promised in 'We who have bowed ourselves to time', Smith, *A Spring Harvest*, 49.
RQG's trench-digging drill: uncredited, in William Allport Brockington, *Elements of Military Education* (1916), 300–2. Brockington promised to name its originator in any second edition. (Lt. A. S. Langley to Cary Gilson, 1 November 1916; Brockington to Langley, 28 November 1916.)

pp.253–4 'I can still ask . . .': CLW to JRRT, 18 January 1917.
Finance minister: ibid., 8 December 1916. CLW's career: CLW memoir, *OEG*; Mrs Patricia Wiseman. Music teaching: Lightwood, *The Music of the Methodist Hymn Book*, 94–5.

p.254 'a new light': *Letters*, 10.
'The Music of the Ainur': features of Qenya, together with the paucity of mythological detail in the original version (*Manwë* is named simply *Súlimo*) might suggest a date close to the composition of 'The Cottage of Lost Play', which also has *Solosimpë* as a plural (for later *Solosimpi*) and likewise was written on slips rather than in notebooks like the rest of the Lost Tales. However, JRRT said 'The Music of the Ainur'

was written in Oxford, while he was on the staff of the *OED*. He implied that it was the first tale he wrote after 'Tinúviel' and therefore that the rest of the Lost Tales came afterwards. (*Letters*, 345, *LT1*, 14, 45, 52, 60–1.)

'The completed work . . .'; 'the fugue . . .': CLW to JRRT, 14 March 1916.

pp.254–5 *Ainur*: this soon became fixed as the plural of *Ainu*, but in the original manuscript *Ainu* is both singular and plural. For clarity, the account of 'The Book of Lost Tales' in this chapter uses the later and better-known forms unless otherwise stated.

Ilúvatar, *Sā*: *Parma Eldalamberon* 12, 42, 81.

p.255 Ilúvatar's gift of language: *LT1*, 232, 236.

'unity and a system . . .': ibid., 54.

'Through him has pain . . .': ibid., 55.

p.256 'It is the tragedy . . .': JRRT to CLW, 16 November 1914.

'beauty in all . . .', etc.: JRRT, quoted in CLW to JRRT, 20 December 1917.

'the theme more worth . . .': *LT1*, 55.

The Valar and the Germanic Gods: plot outline, *LT2*, 290.

p.257 'reddened . . .': *LT1*, 78.

'who loveth games . . .': ibid., 75.

p.258 'Mayhap she . . .', 'a denial . . .': ibid., 152.

Eldar: 'a being from outside' is the gloss of the cognate *Egla* in the Gnomish lexicon; the Qenya lexicon gives no original meaning. *Parma Eldalamberon* 11, 32, and *Parma Eldalamberon* 12, 35.

p.259 'Vainly doth Ulmo . . .': *LT1*, 120.

p.260 'perhaps more poignant . . .': 1964 interview with Denis Gueroult, BBC Sound Archives.

p.261 'the large and cosmogonic', etc.: *Letters*, 144. 'One must begin with the elfin . . .': Essay Club minutes, Exeter College library.

'drawn with a team . . .': *Romeo and Juliet*, I. iv.

'a murrain . . .': *Letters*, 143; cf. also 212 (for the Ents and *Macbeth*) and 'On Fairy-stories', *Monsters*, 111–12.

p.262 'her skin was . . .': *LT2*, 8.

Beren human in 1917 'Tinúviel' (footnote): ibid., 52, 71–2, 139.

p.263 'Rapunzel': Lang, *The Red Fairy Book*, 282–5. Favourite book as a child: *Biography*, 22.

Tevildo, Tifil, Tiberth: *LT2*, 15, 45; *Parma Eldalamberon* 11, 70; *Parma Eldalamberon* 12, 90.

'a mask . . .': 'On Fairy-stories', *Monsters*, 117.

'His eyes were long . . .': *LT2*, 16.

'the greatest wolf . . .': ibid., 31.

p.264 'the first example . . .': *Letters*, 149.

'The consolation . . .': 'On Fairy-stories', *Monsters*, 153.

p.265 'wonderful that shells . . .': RQG to EK, 22 May 1916.

'Such things seemed miraculous . . .': Sassoon, *The Complete Memoirs of George Sherston*, 287–8.

'I have a Silmaril . . .': *LT2*, 37.

p.266 'Soldier's Dream': Owen, *The Collected Poems*, 84.

'the greatest cairn . . .': *LT1*, 241; the reference in these notes to the burial of the Gnomes beneath this cairn is uncertain, but would be in keeping with all later versions of the story.

'bulwark . . .': *LT2*, 73.

Battle of Unnumbered Tears: *LT1*, 240–1; *LT2*, 70.

p.267 'the luck . . .': *LT2*, 79.

'love lies . . .': ibid., 85. 'the land had become . . .': ibid., 96.

p.268 'for lo! . . .': *LT2*, 102.

'a swoon came . . .': ibid., 99.

pp.268–9 'In that sad band . . .': ibid., 85–6. *Mormakil*, 'Blacksword', is Túrin's pseudonym among the Rodothlim.

p.269 'ease his sorrow . . .': ibid., 74.

'At least none . . .': ibid., 71.

p.270 'might be said . . .': *Letters*, 150. Elsewhere (*Letters*, 214, 345) JRRT said Kullervo had been the germ of his legendarium, even if in the story of Túrin 'it is entirely changed except in the tragic ending'. The Qenya lexicon (*Parma Eldalamberon* 12, 95–6) compares *Turambar*, 'master of doom', to Old Norse *Sigurðr* (*sigr*, 'victory', *urðr*, 'fate, destiny'). JRRT studied Sophocles' *Oedipus Rex* during his final year of Classics (Exeter College Library register).

'In these days . . .': *LT2*, 70.

p.271 Necklace of the Brísings: a genealogy of *c.*1930 calls Feänor in Old English *Finbrós* and his sons *Brósingas*, a reference to the fabled necklace of the Brósings (*Beowulf*, line 1199), which has been equated with the Norse *Brísingamen*. *The Shaping of Middle-earth*, 212.
'Behold now Tinwelint . . .': *LT2*, 231.
'crowned and helmed . . .': ibid., 232.

p.272 'an unrecognised . . .': Shippey, *Author of the Century*, 155.
'the whole *Tale* . . .': *LT2*, 253.
'the very primitive undergrowth': *Biography*, 59.
'gnawing his fingers . . .': *LT2*, 282.

p.273 Cannock Chase: G. L. Elkin, cited in *The Lost Road*, 413, suggests on the contrary that the High Heath is based on Hopton Heath, a few miles north-west of Great Haywood, where a Civil War battle was fought in 1643.

pp.273–4 'And now is the end . . .', etc.: *LT2*, 287–9.

p.274 'So we lay down the pen . . .': GBS, *A Spring Harvest*, 78.

p.275 'blind, and a fool . . .': *LT2*, 288. 'a free virtue', 'everything should . . .': *LT1*, 59.

p.276 'ennoblement': *Letters*, 220. 'On a journey . . .': ibid., 240. 'the secret life . . .': ibid., 149.
'there liveth still . . .': *LT1*, 56.
'and who knows . . .': ibid., 220. Nothing similar replaced this rejected draft text, but decades later JRRT returned to the idea that his legendarium might adumbrate the Christian story more or less explicitly; see *Morgoth's Ring*, 351–2, 356.

pp.277–8 Chronology of composition: In 1964 JRRT remembered writing 'The Music of the Ainur' in Oxford, i.e., no earlier than November 1918. The Lost Tales of Valinor seem likely to have been composed after the creation myth, along with the tales of the Great Lands, including ink revisions of 'The Tale of Turambar' and 'The Tale of Tinúviel'. A copy of lines from 'The Tale of Turambar' written in Rúmilian script refers to Tinwelint as *Thingol*, the name the elven-king was to keep. It must postdate almost all of the Lost Tales, which still have *Tinwelint*, except the third, typescript version of

'The Tale of Tinúviel', which has *Thingol.* According to Humphrey Carpenter, JRRT was using this version of the ever-changing Rúmilian script in his diary around June 1919. However, six or seven months seems a very short time for such a volume of complex writing. (*LT1*, 203; *LT2*, 312; *Biography*, 100–3; *Parma Eldalamberon* 13, 20; JRRT service record.)

p.278 *orn*, etc. (footnote): 'Early Noldorin Fragments', *Parma Eldalamberon* 13, 116.

Leeds: *Biography*, 102ff.

p.279 'much interested . . .', etc.: RWR to JRRT, 19 November 1917.

Poems sent to RWR: *The Lays of Beleriand*, 3, 150.

p.280 'vast backcloths': *Letters*, 144.

'lacking in experience . . .' (RWR); 'the only form . . .', etc.: CLW to JRRT, 4 March 1917.

p.281 'gave him opportunities . . .': Wayne G. Hammond, *Canadian C. S. Lewis Journal*, Spring 2000, 62, quoted in Douglas A. Anderson (ed.), *The Annotated Hobbit*, 5.

'I want you to get . . .': CLW to JRRT, 4 March 1917.

Christopher Tolkien named after CLW: *Letters*, 395.

p.282 Lewis's ambitions: Rateliff, 'The Lost Road, The Dark Tower, and the Notion Club Papers', in Flieger and Hostetter (eds.), *Tolkien's Legendarium*, 200–1.

'Only from him . . .': *Letters*, 362.

EMT's copies: *LT1*, 13; *LT2*, 146.

Elrond: *Letters*, 346–7; Douglas A. Anderson (ed.), *The Annotated Hobbit*, 94–6.

p.283 'a new story . . .': *Letters*, 27.

'grew in the telling . . .': 'Foreword to the Second Edition', *The Lord of the Rings*, xv.

'which says for me . . .': *Letters*, 420.

'incurable bachelorhood': CLW to JRRT, 20 December 1917.

TCBS reunion: Mrs Patricia Wiseman and Mrs Susan Wood, interview with the author.

p.284 'lair', etc.: *Letters*, 429.

'I wish v. much . . .': *Letters*, 431–2.

POSTSCRIPT *'One who dreams alone'*

p.287 'dead spot': Hynes, *A War Imagined*, 101. 'Why I can write nothing . . .': ibid. 105–6.
'sheer vacancy': GBS to JRRT, 16 September 1916. GBS's poetry: CLW to JRRT, 16 November 1916.

pp.287–8 'Companions of the Rose'; Tolkien productive in 1917: CLW to JRRT, 1 September 1917; Douglas A. Anderson to the author.

p.288 'an age when . . .': *Letters*, 225.

p.289 'A horse is a . . .': Fussell, *The Great War and Modern Memory*, 22. A form of censorship: ibid. 174–5.
'Those too old . . .': Winter, *Sites of Memory, Sites of Mourning*, 204.
'how it was that Tolkien . . .', etc.: Brogan, 'Tolkien's Great War', in Avery and Briggs (eds.), *Children and their Books*, 356.

pp.289–90 Anti-Germanism and the breach with the past: Hynes, *A War Imagined*, 78.
'philology itself . . .': Tolkien, 'Philology: General Works', in Lee and Boas (eds.), *The Year's Work in English Studies, 1923*, 37.
Romanticism tainted: Hynes, *A War Imagined*, 78.

p.290 'No one ever influenced . . .': W. H. Lewis (ed.), *Letters of C. S. Lewis*, 287.
'animal horror': *Letters*, 72. 'The utter stupid waste . . .': ibid. 75.
'tutors' in high diction: Fussell, *The Great War and Modern Memory*, 21.

p.291 'not being especially . . .': *Letters*, 225. 'the extraordinary . . .': ibid., 225–6.
'This sort of thing . . .': 'On Translating Beowulf', *Monsters*, 55.

p.292 'Wisdom made . . .': Graves, 'Babylon', *Fairies and Fusiliers*.
'The Western Front made . . .': Purkiss, *Troublesome Things*, 291.

p.293 'A real taste . . .': 'On Fairy-stories', *Monsters*, 135.
'therapy for a mind . . .', etc.: Brogan, 'Tolkien's Great War', in Avery and Briggs (eds.), *Children and their Books*, 358.

Tolkien on 'escapism': 'On Fairy-stories', *Monsters*, 148–50.

p.294 'Beowulf lying . . .': Graves, *Good-bye to All That*, 304. *Flammenwerfer*: *Letters*, 133. 'Very numerous . . .': *LT2*, 174.

p.295 'C' Company disaster: *The Lancashire Fusiliers Annual 1917*, 215–20; Latter, *Lancashire Fusiliers*, 148; 11th LF war diary. 'The problem was . . .': C. H. David of the 25th Division's Royal Field Artillery brigade, whose guns were covering this network of trenches at around this time (Imperial War Museum).

Beowulf, Beorhtnoth: 'The Homecoming of Beorhtnoth, Beorhthelm's Son', *Poems and Stories*, 103.

'*Aequam serva* . . .': *Letters*, 73.

'whose instinct is . . .': ibid., 211.

p.296 The *Mabinogion*: GBS to JRRT, 10 September 1916. *The Earthly Paradise*: Douglas A. Anderson to the author. Morris, Bunyan, etc.: Fussell, *The Great War and Modern Memory*, 138–9, 135.

'make no pretence . . .': CLW to JRRT, 4 March 1917.

p.297 'Beneath the surface . . .': Flieger, *A Question of Time*, 224. The phrase 'pinned in a kind of ghostly deathlessness' comes from Tolkien's discussion of J. M. Barrie's *Mary Rose* in unpublished drafts of 'On Fairy-stories', quoted more fully on p. 53 of Flieger's book.

p.297 Eriol's experience of Faërie: *LT1*, 47; *LT2*, 284, 287–9.

p.298 'Did no feeling . . .': Douie, *The Weary Road*, 222.

'There is no difficulty . . .': Shippey, *Author of the Century*, 248.

p.299 'There was an arguing . . .', etc.: Carrington, *A Subaltern's War*, 35.

'sick and weary': *LT2*, 90. 'moral impetus . . .', etc.: Manning, *The Middle Parts of Fortune*, 39.

p.300 'something irrevocably evil', etc.: Shippey, *Author of the Century*, xxx.

'If in some smothering . . .': 'Dulce et decorum est', Owen, *The Collected Poems*, p. 55.

p.301 'the Myth of the War . . .': Hynes, *A War Imagined*, 424.

p.302 'a few acres of mud': CLW to JRRT, 4 March 1917.

Frye's modes and the war: Fussell, *The Great War and Modern Memory*, 311–12.
'Book after book . . .': Carrington, *Soldier from the Wars Returning*, 293.

p.303 'the authors of this poetry . . .': Douie, *The Weary Road*, 7, 9.
'It is thus anterior . . .': Carrington, *Soldier from the Wars Returning*, 14. *A Subaltern's War* was not published until 1929.
'deeds, or lands . . .': C. Day Lewis (ed.), *The Collected Poems of Wilfred Owen*, 31.

p.304 'who sneer . . .': CLW to JRRT, 10 November 1914.

p.305 'Even to-day . . .', etc.: 'Beowulf: The Monsters and the Critics', *Monsters*, 16, 17.
'Now we stand . . .': CLW to GBS, 30 August 1916.
'With our backs . . .': 'To all ranks of the British Army in France and Flanders', Douglas Haig, 11 April 1918. I have echoed Vera Brittain – a voluntary nurse tending the wounded at Étaples at the time of the Spring Offensive – who noted the later tarnishing of Haig's reputation but said, 'I can think of him only as the author of that Special Order, for after I read it I knew that I should go on, whether I could or not.' (*Testament of Youth*, 420.)

p.306 'even shall those . . .': *LT1*, 54–5.
'Perhaps some day . . .': Douie, *The Weary Road*, 226.
'to portray life . . .': Lucas, *Tragedy: Serious drama in relation to Aristotle's Poetics*, 79.

p.307 'more or less a Warwickshire village . . .': *Letters*, 230. 'I take my models . . .': ibid. 235.

pp.307–8 'as low as blacksmith-work . . .': *The Hobbit*, 56. 'It is not unlikely . . .': ibid. 109. 'neither bush . . .': ibid. 257. 'piled in heaps . . .': ibid. 344.

p.308 Laketown: Shippey, *Author of the Century*, 40.
'May God bless you . . .': GBS to JRRT, 3 February 1916. 'had been granted . . .': JRRT to GBS, 12–13 August 1916.
'I was pitched . . .': *Letters*, 46.

p.310 'One has indeed personally . . .': Foreword to the second edition, *The Lord of the Rings*, xvii.

'As far as any character . . .': *Letters*, 232 (footnote).
'My "Sam Gamgee" . . .': *Biography*, 81.
'Personally I do not . . .': *Letters*, 303.

p.311 Survey of fiction writers: Cecil, *The Flower of Battle*, 1.
'This war has the very . . .': Lewis, 'The Dethronement of Power', *Time & Tide* 36 (22 October 1955); reprinted in Isaacs and Zimbardo, *Tolkien and the Critics*, 14.
'the disillusionment . . .': Shippey, *Author of the Century*, 156.

p.312 'a recall from facile . . .': Lewis, 'Tolkien's *The Lord of the Rings*', *Essay Collection: Literature, philosophy and short stories*, 116.

p.313 'I had seen something . . .': Sassoon, *The Complete Memoirs of George Sherston*, 362.

Bibliography

A: Private papers

Letters from JRRT to Geoffrey Bache Smith and Christopher Luke Wiseman; letters to JRRT from Robert Cary Gilson, Robert Quilter Gilson, R. W. Reynolds, G. B. Smith, Ruth Smith, and C. L. Wiseman (Bodleian Tolkien family papers 2/1 and 2/2).

JRRT's personal military papers, including his cursory 'Diary of Brief Time in France and of Last Seven Times I Saw GBS' [JRRT diary] (Bodleian Tolkien family papers 2/6).

Other papers belonging to JRRT, including college notebooks and books from his library (Bodleian Tolkien; shelfmarks given in source notes).

All of the above are courtesy of the Tolkien Estate and the Bodleian Library.

Letters from R. Q. Gilson to R. C. Gilson, Marianne Cary Gilson ('Donna') and Estelle King; other Gilson correspondence (all courtesy of Julia Margretts and Frances Harper).

Letter from C. L. Wiseman to Dr Peter Liddle, 22 July 1977, recalling his naval service; memoir of W. J. Senescall, 11th Suffolks [Senescall memoir] (courtesy of the Liddle Collection, Brotherton Library, University of Leeds).

Letters and notebooks of Lt. C. L. Platt, 19th Lancashire Fusiliers [Platt papers]; diary of Capt. Lionel Ferguson, 13th Cheshires [Ferguson diary]; the Revd M. S. Evers, 'The Memoirs of Mervyn' [Evers memoir]; papers of Capt. P. F. J. Fawcett-Barry [Fawcett-Barry papers]; narrative and notebook by 2nd Lt. G. A. Potts [Potts papers]; memoir '1914 to 1919' by F. Mills [Mills memoir]; narrative from the notes of Col. C. H. David, 111th Brigade, Royal Field Artillery [David narrative] (all courtesy of the Imperial War Museum).

B: Works by JRR Tolkien

References in square brackets are to the abbreviations and short titles used in the source notes. Place of publication is London, unless otherwise stated.

The Book of Lost Tales, Part One, ed. Christopher Tolkien (George Allen & Unwin, 1983) [*LT1*].

The Book of Lost Tales, Part Two, ed. Christopher Tolkien (George Allen & Unwin, 1984) [*LT2*].

'Early Noldorin Fragments': see *Parma Eldalamberon* 13, under Periodicals.

'Guide to the Names in *The Lord of the Rings*', in Jared Lobdell (ed.), *A Tolkien Compass* (Open Court, 1975).

The Hobbit: references are to *The Annotated Hobbit*, annotated by Douglas A. Anderson (New York: Houghton Mifflin, 2002).

'The Homecoming of Beorhtnoth Beorhthelm's Son', in *Essays and Studies* vi (John Murray, 1953). References are to the Tolkien anthology *Poems and Stories* (HarperCollins, 1992).

'I·Lam na·Ngoldathon: The Grammar and Lexicon of the Gnomish Tongue': see *Parma Eldalamberon* 11, under Periodicals.

The Lays of Beleriand, ed. Christopher Tolkien (George Allen & Unwin, 1985).

Letters of J. R. R. Tolkien: A Selection, ed. Humphrey Carpenter with Christopher Tolkien (George Allen & Unwin, 1981) [*Letters*].

The Lord of the Rings (HarperCollins, 1995): a standard one-volume edition.

The Monsters and the Critics and Other Essays, ed. Christopher Tolkien (George Allen & Unwin, 1983) [*Monsters*].

Morgoth's Ring, ed. Christopher Tolkien (HarperCollins, 1993).

The Peoples of Middle-earth, ed. Christopher Tolkien (HarperCollins, 1996).

'Philology: General Works', annual survey in Lee and Boas (eds.), *The Year's Work in English Studies, 1923*; Boas and Herford (eds.), *The Year's Work in English Studies, 1924*.

'The Poetic and Mythologic Words of Eldarissa': see *Parma Eldalamberon* 12, under Periodicals.

'Qenyaqetsa: The Qenya Phonology and Lexicon': see *Parma Eldalamberon* 12, under Periodicals.

Sauron Defeated, ed. Christopher Tolkien (HarperCollins, 1992).

The Shaping of Middle-earth: The Quenta, the Ambarkanta, and the Annals together with the earliest 'Silmarillion' and the first Map, ed. Christopher Tolkien (George Allen & Unwin, 1986).

Unfinished Tales, ed. Christopher Tolkien (George Allen & Unwin, 1980).

C: Books and articles by others

Allison, K. J. (ed.), *A History of the County of York, East Riding, vol. v. Holderness: southern part* (Oxford: Oxford University Press, 1984).

Auden, W. H. (ed.), *G. K. Chesterton: A selection from his non-fictional prose* (Faber & Faber, 1970).

Barlow, Sir C. A. Montague, *The Lancashire Fusiliers, The Roll of Honour of the Salford Brigade* (Sherratt and Hughes, 1919) [Barlow, *Salford Brigade*].

The Battle of Jutland: Official Despatches (HMSO, 1920).

Blunden, Edmund, *Undertones of War* (Cobden-Sanderson, 1928). References are to the Penguin edition, 1982.

Boas, F. S., and Herford, C. H. (eds.), *The Year's Work in English Studies*, vol. v: 1924 (Oxford: Oxford University Press, 1925).

— *The Year's Work in English Studies*, vol. vi: 1925 (Oxford: Oxford University Press 1927).

Brazier, Reginald H., and Sandford, Ernest, *Birmingham and the Great War* (Birmingham: Cornish Brothers, 1921).

Brenan, Gerald, *A Life of One's Own: Childhood and youth* (Cambridge: Cambridge University Press, 1962).

Brittain, Vera, *Testament of Youth* (Victor Gollancz, 1933). References are to the Virago edition, 1978.

Brockington, W. A., *Elements of Military Education* (Longmans, Green, 1916).

Brogan, Hugh, 'Tolkien's Great War', in Gillian Avery and Julia Briggs (eds.), *Children and their Books: A celebration of the works of Iona and Peter Opie* (Oxford: Clarendon Press, 1989).

Brown, Malcolm, *The Imperial War Museum Book of the Somme* (Pan, 1997).

Carpenter, Humphrey, *J. R. R. Tolkien: A biography* (George Allen & Unwin, 1977) [*Biography*].

Carrington, Charles (pseudonymously as 'Charles Edmonds'), *A Subaltern's War* (Peter Davies, 1929).

— *Soldier from the Wars Returning* (Hutchinson, 1965).

Carter, Terry, *Birmingham Pals: 14th, 15th & 16th (Service) Battalions of the Royal Warwickshire Regiment* (Barnsley: Pen & Sword Books, 1997).

Cater, Bill, 'We talked of love, death and fairy tales', *The Daily Telegraph* (29 November 2001), 23.

Cecil, Hugh, *The Flower of Battle* (Secker & Warburg, 1995).

Chambers, R. W., *Widsith: A study in Old English heroic legend* (Cambridge: Cambridge University Press, 1912).

Cole, G. D. H., and Earp, T. W. (eds.), *Oxford Poetry 1915* (Oxford: Blackwell, 1915).

Cork, Richard, *A Bitter Truth: Avant-garde art and the Great War* (New Haven and London: Yale University Press, 1994).

Courtauld, Simon, 'In Remembrance: and the memories of a living hero', *The Daily Telegraph* (10 November 1998), 9.

Cuttell, Barry, *148 Days on the Somme* (Peterborough: GMS Enterprises, 2000).

d'Ardenne, S. R. T. O., 'The Man and the Scholar', in *J. R. R. Tolkien, Scholar and Storyteller: Essays in memoriam*, ed. Mary Salu and Robert T. Farrell (Ithaca and London: Cornell University Press, 1979).

Dorman, J. E., *Guardians of the Humber: The Humber defences 1856–1956* (Hull: Humberside Leisure Services, 1990).

Douie, Charles, *The Weary Road: Recollections of a subaltern of infantry* (John Murray, 1929).

Earle, John, *The Deeds of Beowulf: An English epic of the eighth century done into modern prose* (Oxford: Clarendon Press, 1892).

Ekwall, Eilert, *The Concise Oxford Dictionary of English Place-names* (Oxford: Oxford University Press, 1936).

Eliot, C. N. E., *A Finnish Grammar* (Oxford: Oxford University Press, 1890).

English School Association, Leeds, *A Northern Venture: Verses by members of the Leeds University English School Association* (Leeds: The Swan Press, 1923).

— *Leeds University Verse 1914–24* (Leeds: The Swan Press, 1924).

Ensor, Sir Robert, *England 1870–1914* (Oxford: Clarendon Press, 1936).

Farnell, Lewis R., *An Oxonian Looks Back* (Martin Hopkinson, 1934).

Ferguson, Niall, *The Pity of War* (Penguin, 1999).

Flieger, Verlyn, *A Question of Time: Tolkien's road to Faërie* (Ohio: Kent State University Press, 1997).

Fussell, Paul, *The Great War and Modern Memory* (Oxford: Oxford University Press, 1975).

Gibbs, Philip, *Now It Can Be Told* (New York: Harper, 1920).

Gibson, R. H., and Prendergast, Maurice, *The German Submarine War 1914–1918* (Constable, 1931).

Gilbert, Martin, *The First World War* (HarperCollins, 1995).

Gilliver, Peter M., 'At the Wordface', *Proceedings of the J. R. R. Tolkien Centenary Conference*, ed. Patricia Reynolds and Glen GoodKnight (Milton Keynes and Altadena: The Tolkien Society and the Mythopoeic Press, 1995).

Gilson, Christopher, '"Narqelion" and the Early Lexicons: Some Notes on the First Elvish Poem', *Vinyar Tengwar* 40 (Crofton, 1999).

Gliddon, Gerald, *When the Barrage Lifts* (Leo Cooper, 1990).

Graves, Robert, *Fairies and Fusiliers* (William Heinemann, 1917).

— *Good-bye to All That* (Jonathan Cape, 1929). References are to the Penguin edition, 1960.

Grein, C. W. M., 2nd edition of R. P. Wülcker, *Bibliothek der angelsächsischen Poesie* (Kassel/Leipzig: Georg H. Wigand, 1881–3).

Grimm, Jacob, *Teutonic Mythology*, tr. J. S. Stallybrass (George Bell & Sons, 1883).

Haggard, Henry Rider, *She: A history of adventure* (Longmans, Green, 1887). References are to the Penguin Classics edition, 2001.

Hammond, Wayne G., and Scull, Christina, *J. R. R. Tolkien: Artist and illustrator* (HarperCollins, 1995) [*Artist*].

Hammond, Wayne G., with Anderson, Douglas A., *J. R. R. Tolkien: A descriptive bibliography* (New Castle, Delaware: Oak Knoll Books, 1993).

Hayter, P. D. G. (ed.), *Charlton and Newbottle: A history of two villages* (Charlton and Newbottle History Society, 2000).

Heath, Charles H., *Service Record of King Edward's School, Birmingham* (Birmingham: Cornish Brothers Ltd, 1920; with additions and corrections, 1931).

The Historical Register of the University of Cambridge, Supplement, 1911–20 (Cambridge: Cambridge University Press, 1922).

Hostetter, Carl F., and Smith, Arden R., 'A Mythology for England', *Proceedings of the J. R. R. Tolkien Centenary Conference*, ed. Patricia Reynolds and Glen GoodKnight (Milton Keynes and Altadena: The Tolkien Society and the Mythopoeic Press, 1995).

Hostetter, Carl F., 'Over Middle-earth Sent Unto Men: On the Philological Origins of Tolkien's Eärendel Myth', *Mythlore* 65 (Spring 1991).

— introduction to Tolkien's 'The Rivers and Beacon-hills of Gondor', *Vinyar Tengwar* 42 (Crofton 2001).

How, A. B., *Register of Exeter College Oxford 1891–1921* (Oxford: Blackwell, 1928).

Hutchinson, Harold F., *London Transport Posters* (London Transport Board, 1963).

Hutton, T. W., *King Edward's School, Birmingham, 1552–1952* (Oxford: Blackwell, 1952).

Hyde, Paul Nolan, 'Narqelion: A Single, Falling Leaf at Sun-fading', *Mythlore* 56 (Altadena, 1988).

Hynes, Samuel, *A War Imagined: The First World War and English culture* (The Bodley Head, 1990).

James, Lt.-Col. Lionel, DSO, *The History of King Edward's Horse (The King's Oversea Dominions Regiment)* (Sifton, Praed and Co., 1921).

Jenkyns, Richard, *The Victorians and Ancient Greece* (Oxford: Blackwell, 1980).

Keegan, John, *The Face of Battle* (Pimlico, 1991).

Kincaid-Smith, Lt.-Col. M., *The 25th Division in France and Flanders* (Harrison & Sons, 1918).

Kirby, William Forsell (ed.), *Kalevala* (Everyman, 1907).

Lang, Andrew (ed.), *The Red Fairy Book* (Longmans, 1890). References are to the Dover edition (New York, 1966).

Latter, Major-General J. C., *The History of the Lancashire Fusiliers, 1914–1918*, 2 vols. (Aldershot: Gale & Polden, 1949) [Latter, *Lancashire Fusiliers*; all references are to vol. i unless otherwise stated].

Lee, Sir Sidney, and Boas, F. S. (eds.), *The Year's Work in English Studies, vol. iv: 1923* (Oxford: Oxford University Press, 1924).

Lewis, Cecil, *Sagittarius Rising* (Peter Davies, 1936).

Lewis, C. S., 'The Dethronement of Power', *Time & Tide* 36 (22 October 1955); reprinted in Isaacs and Zimbardo, *Tolkien and the Critics* (Indiana: University of Notre Dame Press, 1968).

— 'Tolkien's *The Lord of the Rings*', in C. S. Lewis, *Essay Collection: Literature, philosophy and short stories* (HarperCollins, 2002).

Lewis, W. H., *Letters of C. S. Lewis* (Geoffrey Bles, 1966).

Lightwood, James T., *The Music of the Methodist Hymn Book* (Epworth, 1955).

Lucas, F. L., *Tragedy: Serious drama in relation to Aristotle's Poetics* (Hogarth Press, 1927).

Macaulay, Lord, *Lays of Ancient Rome* (Longman, Brown, Green & Longmans, 1842). References are to *Lays of Ancient Rome and Miscellaneous Essays and Poems* (Dent, 1910).

Macdonald, Alexander, *The Lost Explorers* (Blackie & Son, 1907).

MacDonald, George, *The Complete Fairy Tales* (Penguin, 1999).

— *The Princess and the Goblin* (Strahan, 1872).

Macdonald, Lyn, *The Somme* (Michael Joseph, 1983).

Machen, Arthur, 'The Bowmen', London *Evening News* (29 September 1914).

Mallory, J. P., *In Search of the Indo-Europeans: Language, Archaeology and Myth* (Thames & Hudson, 1991).

Manning, Frederic, *The Middle Parts of Fortune* (Piazza Press, 1929). References are to the Penguin edition, 1990.

Marder, Arthur J., *From the Dreadnought to Scapa Flow, vol. iii. Jutland and After: May 1916–December 1916* (Oxford: Oxford University Press, 1966).

Marsh, Edward (ed.), *Georgian Poetry* (Poetry Bookshop, 1913).

Martineau, Jane (ed.), *Victorian Fairy Painting* (Royal Academy of Art and Merrell Holberton, 1997).

Masefield, John, *The Old Front Line; or, the beginning of the battle of the Somme* (William Heinemann, 1917).

Middlebrook, Martin, *The First Day on the Somme* (Penguin, 1984).

Miles, G. T. J., and Richardson, William, *A History of Withernsea* (Hull: A. Brown & Sons, 1911).

Miles, Wilfrid, *Military Operations, France and Belgium, 1916. 2nd July to the end of the battles of the Somme, vol. i* (Macmillan, 1938). (Part of the *History of the Great War based on Official Documents.*)

Mitchinson, K. W., *Pioneer Battalions in the Great War* (Leo Cooper, 1997).

Morris Jones, J., *A Welsh Grammar, Historical and Comparative* (Oxford: Clarendon Press, 1913).

Morris, Richard, *An Old English Miscellany* (Early English Text Society, 1872).

Murphy, C. C. R., *History of the Suffolk Regiment* (Hutchinson, 1928).

Norman, Philip, 'The Hobbit Man', *Sunday Times Magazine* (15 January 1967), 34–6.

Owen, Wilfred, *The Collected Poems of Wilfred Owen*, ed. C. Day Lewis (Chatto & Windus, 1963).

Parker, Peter, *The Old Lie: The Great War and the public-school ethos* (Constable, 1987).

Peacock, Dr A. J., 'A Rendezvous with Death', *Gun Fire* 5 (York: Western Front Association, 1986).

Pearce, Hilda, *The Navy Book of Fairy Tales* (J. J. Bennett, 1916).

Phillips, J., *Illustrations of the Geology of Yorkshire. Part i: The Yorkshire coast* (John Murray, 1875).

Priestley, J. B., *The Edwardians* (Heinemann, 1970). References are to the Penguin edition, 2000.

Priestman, Judith, *J. R. R. Tolkien: Life and Legend* (Oxford: Bodleian Library, 1992).

Purkiss, Diane, *Troublesome Things* (Penguin, 2001).

Rateliff, John D., 'The Lost Road, The Dark Tower, and the Notion Club Papers: Tolkien and Lewis's Time Travel Triad', in Verlyn Flieger and Carl F. Hostetter (eds.), *Tolkien's Legendarium: Essays on* 'The History of Middle-earth' (Westport, Connecticut: Greenwood Press, 2000).

Ross, Sir John, *The Coldstream Guards, 1914–1918* (Oxford: Oxford University Press, 1928).

Sassoon, Siegfried, *The Complete Memoirs of George Sherston* (Faber & Faber, 1937). References are to the 1972 Faber edition.

— *The War Poems*, ed. Rupert Hart-Davis (Faber & Faber, 1983).

Sheppard, Thomas, *Kingston-Upon-Hull Before, During and After the Great War* (London and Hull: A. Brown & Sons, 1919).

Shippey, Tom, *J. R. R. Tolkien: Author of the Century* (HarperCollins, 2000).

— *The Road to Middle-earth* (HarperCollins, 1992).

— 'Tolkien and the West Midlands: The Roots of Romance' in *Lembas Extra 1995* (Leiden: Tolkien Genootschap *Unquendor*, 1995).

Simkins, Peter, *Kitchener's Army: The raising of the new armies, 1914–16* (Manchester: Manchester University Press, 1988).

Skeat, Walter W. (ed.), *The Complete Works of Geoffrey Chaucer*, 5 vols. (Oxford: Clarendon Press, Oxford 1894).

Smith, A. H., *The Place-names of the East Riding of Yorkshire and York* (Cambridge: Cambridge University Press, 1937).

Smith, G. B., *A Spring Harvest*, ed. (uncredited) by J. R. R. Tolkien and Christopher Wiseman (Erskine Macdonald, 1918).

Smyth, Major B., *The Lancashire Fusiliers' Annual 1916* and *1917* (Dublin: Sackville Press, 1917 and 1918).

Solano, E. J. (ed.), *Signalling: Morse, Semaphore, Station Work, Despatch Riding, Telephone Cables, Map Reading*, 4th edition (John Murray, December 1915).

Stedman, Michael, *Salford Pals: 15th, 16th, 19th and 20th Battalions Lancashire Fusiliers* (Barnsley: Pen & Sword Books, 1993).

— *Somme: La Boisselle, Ovillers/Contalmaison* (Leo Cooper, 1997).

— *Somme: Thiepval* (Leo Cooper, 1995).

Strachan, Huw, *The First World War. Volume i: To Arms* (Oxford: Oxford University Press, 2001).

Taylor, A. J. P., *English History 1914–1945* (Oxford: Clarendon Press, 1965).

Thwaite, Ann, *A. A. Milne: His life* (Faber & Faber, 1990).

Tolkien, John and Priscilla, *The Tolkien Family Album* (HarperCollins, 1992) [*Family Album*].

Tolkien, Priscilla, 'J. R. R. Tolkien and Edith Tolkien's Stay in Staffordshire 1916, 1917 and 1918', *Angerthas in English* 3 (Bergen: Arthedain [The Tolkien Society of Norway], 1997).

Topliffe, Lorise, 'Tolkien as an Undergraduate', *Exeter College Association Register* (Oxford 1992).

Trott, Anthony, *No Place for Fop or Idler: The story of King Edward's School, Birmingham* (James & James, 1992).

Van De Noort, Robert, and Ellis, Stephen (eds.), *Wetlands Heritage of Holderness: An archaeological survey* (Kingston-upon-Hull: University of Hull, 1995).

Whitehouse, C. J. and G. P., *A Town for Four Winters: An original study of military camps on Cannock Chase during the Great War, 1914–19* (published by the authors, 1983).

Winter, Denis, *Death's Men: Soldiers of the Great War* (Penguin, 1979).

Winter, Jay, *Sites of Memory, Sites of Mourning* (Cambridge: Cambridge University Press, 1996).

Winter, J. M., *The Great War and the British People* (Macmillan, 1986).

— 'Oxford and the First World War' in Brian Harrison (ed.), *The History of the University of Oxford. Volume viii: The Twentieth Century* (Oxford: Clarendon Press, 1994).

Wiseman, Christopher Luke, eponymous memoir, *Old Edwardians Gazette* (April 1988), 22, 24.

Wright, Elizabeth Mary, *The Life of Joseph Wright* (Oxford: Oxford University Press, 1932).

Wynne, Patrick, and Smith, Arden R., 'Tolkien and Esperanto', in Barbara Reynolds (ed.), *Seven: An Anglo-American Literary Review*, 17 (Wheaton, Illinois, 2000).

Yates, Jessica, '"The Battle of the Eastern Field": A Commentary', *Mallorn* 13 (The Tolkien Society, 1979).

D: Periodicals

Amon Hen: bulletin of the Tolkien Society of Great Britain. No. 13 includes an unsigned 'Oxonmoot '74 Report' describing a conversation with Priscilla and Michael Tolkien.

Gun Fire: journal of First World War history, ed. Dr A. J. Peacock (York).

King Edward's School Chronicle [*KESC*].

Mallorn: journal of the Tolkien Society of Great Britain.

Old Edwardians Gazette [*OEG*].

The Oxford Magazine.

Parma Eldalamberon, ed. Christopher Gilson, Carl F. Hostetter, Patrick Wynne, and Arden R. Smith. No. 11 (Walnut Creek, California, 1995) contains Tolkien's 'I·Lam na·Ngoldathon: The Grammar and Lexicon of the Gnomish Tongue'; no. 12 (Cupertino, California, 1998) contains his 'Qenyaqetsa: The Qenya Phonology and Lexicon' and 'The Poetic and Mythologic Words of Eldarissa'; no. 13 (Cupertino, 2001) contains a series of 'Early Noldorin Fragments', as well as Tolkien's notes on 'The Alphabet of Rúmil' (ed. Arden R. Smith), in which he wrote his diary from early 1919.

The Stapeldon Magazine: journal of Exeter College, Oxford.

Vinyar Tengwar: journal of the Elvish Linguistic Fellowship, ed. Carl F. Hostetter (Crofton, Maryland).

E: Service records, war diaries and other official papers

Public Record Office reference follows in parentheses. In addition to the day-to-day summaries of events, war diaries contain invaluable official records, including orders, intelligence, and communications.

J. R. R. Tolkien's service record (WO 339/34423).

G. B. Smith's service record (WO 339/28936).

R. Q. Gilson's service record (WO 339/29720).

Service records of T. K. Barnsley (WO 339/12939) and R. S. Payton (WO 339/16911), formerly of the TCBS; Roger Smith (WO 339/42691); and various 11th Lancashire Fusiliers officers.

War diaries of the 11th Lancashire Fusiliers, 13th Cheshires, 9th Loyal North Lancashires and 2nd Royal Irish Rifles (WO 95/2246–7); 74th Brigade HQ (2245); 25th Division HQ (2222–4), adjutant and administrative staff (2228), and signal company (2238). Also those of the 7th Brigade (2241), 8th Loyal North Lancashires and 10th Cheshires (2243); 144th Brigade (2757), 1/4th Gloucesters (2758) and 1/7th Worcesters (2759); 143rd Brigade (2754) and 1/5th Warwickshires (2755).

'Communications in the 25th Division from 1st July to 23rd October 1916' (part of WO 95/2222).
19th Lancashire Fusiliers war diary (WO 95/2785).
War diaries of the 11th Suffolks (WO 95/2458), 101st Brigade (WO 95/2455), and 34th Division (WO 95/2432).
Weekly return of the British Army (WO 114/33–5).
Monthly Army returns (WO 73/100, WO 73/102).
Quarterly Army Lists, 1915–16 (WO 66).
Commonwealth War Graves Commission [CWGC].

F: Miscellaneous

Essay Club minutes (courtesy of Exeter College, Oxford).
Exeter College library register (courtesy of Exeter College, Oxford).
Sibley, Brian, *J. R. R. Tolkien: An audio portrait* (BBC Worldwide, 2001).
Stapeldon Society minutes (courtesy of Exeter College, Oxford).
Sundial Society minutes (courtesy of Corpus Christi College, Oxford).

Index

Diacritics have been standardized; for example, macrons have been replaced by acute accents. Items from Tolkien's early mythology are briefly defined (rather than translated) in parentheses. For abbreviations, see p. 315.